Tragic Posture
and
Tragic Vision

Tragic Posture
and
Tragic Vision

Against the Modern
Failure of Nerve

Louis A. Ruprecht, Jr.

CONTINUUM • NEW YORK

1994

The Continuum Publishing Company
370 Lexington Avenue, New York, NY 10017

Printed in the United States of America

Library of Congress Cataloging-in-Publication Data

Ruprecht, Louis A.
Tragic posture and tragic vision : against the modern failure of
   nerve / by Louis A. Ruprecht, Jr.
      p.   cm.
   Includes bibliographical references and index.
   ISBN 0-8264-0686-6 (alk. paper)
   Tragic, The—Religious aspects—Christianity.
2. Postmodernism—Religious aspects—Christianity.   3. Pessimism—
Moral and ethical aspects.   4. Optimism—Moral and ethical aspects.
BR115.T73R87   1994
901–dc20   94-21314
                                                          CIP

πολλὰ τὰ δεινὰ κοὐδὲν ἀν-
θρώπου δεινότερον πέλει·

—Sophocles, *Antigone,* 332–333

Attic tragedy, particularly that of Aeschylus and Sophocles, is the true continuation of the epic. Reflections upon justice highlight it without ever intervening; force appears there in all of its cold harshness, always accompanied by fatal effects from which neither he who exercises it nor he who suffers it can be exempt. The humiliation of the soul under constraint is not disguised, nor wrapped in pity which comes too cheaply, nor presented with scorn. More than one being bruised by the degradation of suffering is offered up here for our admiration. The Gospel is the last marvelous expression of the Greek genius as the *Iliad* is the first; the spirit of Greece shows itself there...in the human misery which it exposes — and that in a divine being who is at the same time quite human. The stories of the Passion show that a divine spirit, bound to the flesh, is altered by suffering, trembles before agony and death, feels itself, in the depths of its distress, to be separated from men and God. This feeling for human misery lends that accent of simplicity which is the hallmark of the Greek genius, and which makes Attic tragedy and the *Iliad* what they are....

[F]or the feeling of human misery is a precondition of justice, and of love. He who ignores the extent to which variable Fortune and necessity constrain every human soul by their dependence is not able to regard as similar, nor to love as he loves himself, those whom Fortune separates from him by an abyss. The diversity of constraints which weigh upon humanity bring to birth the illusion that there exists a separate species, incommunicable to us. Only one who understands the empire of force and knows how not to respect it is capable of love and justice.

The relations of the human soul to fate; in what measure each soul creates its own proper destiny; that in the soul which a pitiless Necessity transforms and that which is able to remain intact through the power of virtue and of grace — these things are all matters in which the lie is simple, and seductive....In particular, nothing is so rare as a fair portrayal of suffering; almost always the overriding tendency is to pretend that misfortune is the natural vocation of the sufferer, or else that a soul may bear suffering without its leaving a mark. The Greeks possessed the spiritual fortitude which forbade self-deception. It allowed them to achieve in every matter the highest degree of lucidity, purity, simplicity. But the spirit which is transmitted from the *Iliad* to the Gospel by way of the philosophers and the tragic poets hardly passed beyond the limits of Greek civilization, and since Greece was destroyed, nothing remains but pale reflections.

—SIMONE WEIL

Contents

❦

Introduction

Tragic Posture and Tragic Vision

I

We are living in a great age of crisis. The news is full of it. The movies are full of it. Our scholarly books, popular and not-so-popular, seem all to agree in this diagnosis. Doubtless it is fun, in a peculiar way, to be the one who has successfully predicted a disaster, the one who composes the jeremiad and presides over the death of one's own world. It is satisfying, somehow, to be able to say, in the face of others' (and even one's own) despair, "I told you so." Yet, increasingly these days, there is something petty rather than prophetic in all the talk. The specious account of modernity's collapse has been so overworn as a literary trope as to lose all real meaning. And it makes for rather thin reading.

I am much interested in this characteristically "modern" sense of crisis. I notice especially the presence of a great many "after-words" in the self-portrait we moderns paint: the notion that we live *after* something else — an earlier time, perhaps, which possessed a harmony and coherence that our own times so sorely lack. I am particularly struck by the presence of *Greece* — as contrast, as alternative, as ideal — in these modernist self-portraits. Greece endures as a sort of symbolic road not taken, a clear beacon speaking to the nobly serene and quietly grand possibility of recovering precisely the things our own world so sorely misses. Greece provides in some cases an alternative vision that could serve, just possibly, as the road to (modern) self-recovery. She is the *pre*modern alternative to our modern, and now even postmodern, discontents.

This book will provide a systematic calling into question of that discontent. Its single, perhaps complete, purpose is to pause over two words, 'modern' and 'tragic,' to hold them up for a closer and more careful look. I mean to ask if we have perhaps made far too much of the former, far too little of the latter. I think that we have. This book attempts to take the first step in a much larger intellectual project, by relating the two words. It is one of the central tenets of this book that one cannot make too much of the concept of "tragedy." I am calling the modernist pose of cultural discontent "the tragic posture," arguing that it relies on a distorting notion of what the word originally meant to the Greeks. *Tragōidia* is a Greek word, as the theater is a Greek invention; they both present us with an essential contemporary challenge. Their tragic vision calls our modern posture systematically into question. Over against those who read the Greek *polis* as some sort of more holistic social order, I present the thesis here that Greece's richest legacy is to be found in her tragic and erotic literature, not in moral or political philosophy. Plato's *Symposium* and *Phaedrus,* rather than the *Republic* or the *Laws.*

As should be clear, the intellectual terrain is vast, but the breadth of this book will be a problem only if its dominant themes are not clearly marked. That is a task for beginning. The themes of this book represent, I hope, invitations to gaze with different eyes upon our world — in a manner that seems more authentically "tragic" to me. I will not take the time to argue for these assertions at this point; the book as a whole is intended to do that. For now, I mean only to identify what they are. Four themes, or assumptions, that have consistently emerged in the antimodern portraits I have been reading are as follows:

1. There is a subtle and pervasive pessimism that lies at the heart of most cultures that today call themselves "modern."

The study of how such a term as 'modern' has devolved from a real vote of cultural confidence to a contemporary term of philosophical abuse is itself a fascinating topic in the history of knowledge. With astonishing suddenness, many thinkers are no longer content to be "modern" — want, in fact, either to be "postmodern" or else to revert to some sort of idyllic "premodernity." This pessimism expresses itself in many ways — from the existential (loosely so-called) view that seems to entail the belief that "authentic" existence needs to be a little bit unhappy, to the much more commonplace, and therefore all the more significant, prejudice of scholars who look down their noses at anyone, or anything, "optimistic." 'Optimistic' and 'naive' have become very nearly synonymous in modernist discourse.

There is a parable in the academy today — what I would like to call the parable of Humpty-Dumpty[1] — whose moral is all too simple. We live in a broken world. It cannot, and will not, be put together again — if not by all the king's horses and men, then still less so by the likes of us. To undertake these sorts of repairs — exercises in futility, really —

---

1. For a classic statement of this, see Richard L. Rubenstein, *After Auschwitz: Radical Theology and Contemporary Judaism* (Indianapolis: Bobbs-Merrill, 1966) 243–245.

is indicative of a fundamental misunderstanding of the modern situation
and the nature of the problems that confront us. It is time and past time
to stop trying to shore up foundations that are no longer architecturally
sound. The situation may always have been bleak, precarious, but we
used to cover over this truth with happier stories — the subtle artifice
of narrative, or, less kindly, of the lie. We no longer have the luxury of
mythology, or faith, and cannot hide from the bitter truths modernity
has still to teach us.

There is a century of sociology that lies back of this pessimism.[2] It
tells a story of our decline and fall — a decline and fall *into* modernity —
from a world that once made sense, into a world that makes sense no
longer. There is a profound nostalgia here, a deep sense that we are living at the end of something. The crisis takes many forms: the breakdown
of traditional societies and the structures of common belief; the disinte-
gration of moral language into a morass of emotive individualism; the
sudden and shocking impossibility of religious belief; the nightmare of
technology that now seems entirely out of our hands, seems almost to
have assumed the status of a Fate.

Of all these various construals, the one concerning technology seems
most warranted. I am like many of us today — profoundly ambivalent
and unsettled by the scope and the rapidity of technological progress.
We worry about the *soullessness* of the world of the machine. We worry
about the spiritual implications of gene mapping, and splicing, and the
like — even where we are not, by and large, able to say specifically what
worries us so. Now, whether technology — which is both a blessing
and a curse, at once — makes the modern world some sort of a spiritual apocalypse is another matter entirely. But that is precisely what the
tragic posture requires: *an apocalypse*. It tells a story in the most seductive of genres available: the rise and fall. It presumes that we once had
in abundance what we are now no longer able to have, and presumably
never will have again.

---

2. For now, Anthony Giddens is a fitting representative for the sociological tradition
I have in mind, a tradition that moves from Marx, through Weber and Durkheim,
and on to Foucault. As such, sociology is an academic tradition that was born in the
latter nineteenth century as a response to, and a reflection upon, the emergence of
the "modern" world. That is sociology's inescapable double-bind, the source of both
its promise and its problems. It has asserted, assumed really, the existence of the very
"differences," the very "modernity," it means to interrogate. Giddens is explicit about
this: "*The* task of 'sociology,' as I would formulate the role of that discipline at any rate,
is to seek to analyze the nature of the novel world which in the late twentieth century,
we now find ourselves" (*The Nation-State and Violence* [Berkeley: Univ. of California
Press, 1985] 33). As we are shown later in the volume, the real nature of that world is
the constant threat of "totalitarian" abuses, surveillance, and mass violence.

2. The real myth is still with us, and it is a myth of origins.

This is the chief theoretical relationship I hope to unmask. Any myth of apocalypse is grounded in a myth of origins. The *end* is intimately tied to the *beginning* of any story. The apocalyptic narration of decline and fall presupposes that there was, once upon a time, something specific that we have now lost. To live in an "after-time" requires some sense, however vague, of what came "before." To speak of our spiritual losses makes sense only if there is another place and time, of which we can still catch fleeting glimpses, that had in abundance the very things we allegedly no longer have. A pessimistic present needs an optimistic reading of the past to sustain itself.

If the problem is the breakdown of traditional societies that enjoyed an extraordinary level of common agreement on values and virtues, then we need to be shown such a world—a world where the kind of divisive social conflicts that call these very virtues into question did not arise. There simply never was such a society. That there are meaningful *degrees* of conflict and consensus is beyond dispute. But modernism does not content itself, by and large, with this more moderate claim. Modernity needs a myth, needs, in fact, a world devoid of such conflict. Such a world never existed, save in our most postured antimodern fantasies.

If the problem is the steady rise of an amoral individualism, and the emotive relativism that it brings in train, then here again, we need to be shown a world where collective identity and collective practices are the *only* valid moral norms. In such a world, civil disobedience (to say nothing of something a little less than civil) would not be a meaningful activity—would in fact be utterly senseless—because there is no place *outside* of the social matrix where one may stand in order to be critical of the social roles that are taught to us. We need to be shown a world, in fine, where civil disobedience—and the "individuals" who participate in it—did not exist. Again, there simply never was such a world. Here again, there certainly *are* meaningful degrees of civility and obedience. But here too, modernity feeds itself on myth—the myth of a world where there were *no* such problems.

If the real problem is the alleged collapse of traditional religious belief in the present day—that centuries-long proclaimed "death of God"—then we need some sense of a religiosity which was not tinged with conflict and doubt, a faith which puts the world together so seamlessly that the moral of Humpty-Dumpty remains hidden from us. In short, the dis-ease that comes from knowing how difficult religious faith is today assumes that there was another time and place where faith was somehow easier, where the confrontation with mortality and injustice was somehow less divisive than it is now. That there are those who depend upon their faith in this manner—on what Simone Weil called "the armor of a lie" — is doubtless true. "Modernity" itself often depends upon a faith in just this fashion — faith in the conviction that there were other periods and places when everyone believed in much the same way, when the "sacred canopy" that religion provides had no visible seams or tears. Religious faith raises at least as many — if not more — problems than it solves, and has always done so. Religion does not have utility; it is not simply "good for you." It is, or at least it means to be, "true" — and its bracing truth is *tragic* in a manner I hope to illumine here.

Finally, if we are claiming that *the* modern problem is technology — our own confrontation with abortions, computers, and the Bomb — then we are subtly assuming that the premodern period was happier insofar as it was blissfully unaware. That the antique world did not face some of our dilemmas is plain enough. But by the same token, we no longer face many of theirs. At a time when more children died by their second year than survived it, in a world where death and hard work and communal isolation were the rule, rather than the exception, technology itself would not have been viewed with the same desperate urgency. The pessimistic foundation on which we build our arguments leads inevitably, so we say, to the toppling of every idol. Only the past gleams with a glitter and a happy innocence that continue to elude our frustrated grasp. Many people today — and I am tempted to say *most* people, particularly our scholars — love a good crisis. It is attractive somehow (in the way car-wrecks are) to believe that we are living at *the end* of something. Apocalypticism has been the bread and butter of cultural discontent in every age. Ours is no novelty.

3. One's normative ideas about *tragedy* — whether as a literary genre or as a philosophical idea — are very largely determinative here.

Of all the difficult ground I will be covering, this is without question the most difficult. It will take this entire book, I expect, to get this right, but there are some observations worth making here at the outset. Tragedy simply does not submit to easy definition; it is not that kind of concept anymore than Eros is. The two ideas are, in fact, deeply related. Tragedy lays extraordinary demands on the person who would understand its hard lessons. It is, moreover, a concept that is integrally related to the profound cultural pessimism we have been discussing. Tragedy is extremely easy to misread. Existentialists misread it as often as antimodernists do. Most of the misreadings lead to the very caricature that characterizes so much "modern" thought, what I have for this reason elected to call "the *tragic* posture." Tragedy is, it seems to me, an invitation to suggestive new ways of thinking about our world.

Tragedy speaks to an experience so profound, so unsettling, that our contemporary therapeutic concepts can hardly contain it: the experience

of *redemptive,* rather than merely radical, suffering. Tragedy presents us
with a curious paradox, none more so. We witness tremendous human
suffering on a stage, yet we derive pleasure in the process. *Tragedy turns
our agony into ecstasy.* It is an ennobling estate — in the theater and in
the streets — despite its description of and fascination with the hardest
problems of human life. It refuses to accept the counsel of Humpty-
Dumpty. It dwells with the cracks, but insists on making things whole.
It presents a vision where oversimple categories like "optimistic" and
"pessimistic" simply do not apply.

As such, authentic tragedy flies in the face of most of the very canons
of our posturing modernity. Where the modern dramatist despairs of
a world that is our *Fate,* tragedy counsels us to shape a *Destiny* for
ourselves out of this cracked creation: Humpty-Dumpty patched and
pasted, not scrambled. Finally — and here is surely the most jarring
claim to our apocalyptically attuned modern ears — *tragedies do not
necessarily end badly. They begin badly.* They originate at a point of
calamity and outrageous human suffering. But they can be, and often
are, *resolved.* It is a point worth pausing over — I will pause over it
several times in this book — that nearly half of the surviving Greek
tragedies *end well.* An air crash is not "tragic" because it ends badly,
nor because it seems a "fated" occurrence that rests entirely in other
hands. That makes it a disaster, nothing more. Tragedy, unlike disaster,
involves a choice. Tragedy is something harder, infinitely rarer, a challenge thrown in the face of the brute facticity of the world. If Hamlet
is tragic — and he most assuredly is — then it is not because of what
the world does to him; it is because of what he is, what he does, and
how he does it. His tragedy derives, in large measure, from who he is.
"Character *is* destiny," said Heraclitus, some three millennia ago.

**4. The religious perspective is not antitragic by definition, nor is it
comic, Dante notwithstanding. Christianity, for its part, is a *tragic* faith.**
Any faith that preaches a "saviour" who died on a cross cannot be so
naively quick to laughter or comic conclusions as is normally alleged. It
is not insensitive to the very real agony of embodied suffering, nor does
it cheapen such experiences with religious romance. Religious faith *does*
fail to be broken on the wheel of the world, finds profound reasons for
rejoicing even in the midst of life's hardness. It is not antitragic because
it attempts to put a broken world together again. This refusal of the
parable of Humpty-Dumpty makes it antimodern, to be sure, but hardly
antitragic. Tragedy itself, properly understood, stands at an infinite remove from the postured pessimism that so characterizes our modern
style. *Tragedy subverts "modernity."* The gospel does so as well — but
that is a topic for chapter 4. Christianity cannot be discounted because

it tells a story that seems to end well. The tradition tells many differ-ent stories that end in a variety of ways. 'Gospel' and 'tragedy' are not necessarily antonyms. In fact, the two words resonate profoundly and seem to me to invite a similar, and challenging, perspective on the mod-ern situation. Both present precisely the challenges and correctives that the modern posture so grossly fails even to recognize *as* an alternative. They lie, in any case, at the heart of the vision, and embody the very constellation of themes, that I will attempt to draw out in this book.

II

The best way to illustrate the pervasiveness of these "modern" convic-tions I am highlighting might be to find some book, or books, that look at the world through the lens I have been describing — something more postured, more recognizably "modern." It is my primary contention that such books abound and that the schools of thought which circle around the themes of such books share something essential, different as they otherwise doubtless are. This superabundance is itself a chief constituent of our "modernity." This is one story we have all been taught to tell.

Two books in particular are exemplary for my purposes, in that all four elements are in place there. Their authors later give up one or more of these assumptions, and in so doing realign themselves in relation to the tragic posture. But by understanding the nuances of the tragic pos-ture first, I am arguing, one comes to a richer understanding of these thinkers, as well as a critical awareness of what is at stake in their ques-tions. I will return to both thinkers throughout this book, *not* to make them seem more important than they are, but rather to use them as the most vigorous exemplars of a regnant self-understanding.

The first book that introduced me to the tragic posture was entitled, appropriately enough, *The Death of Tragedy,* and was written in 1961 by George Steiner, one of the most eloquent and provocative of moder-nity's many cultural interpreters. Steiner is bracingly pessimistic about the modern situation. The experience of two world wars in this cen-tury — and at least one holocaust — was more than enough to kill any lingering optimism in him.[3] His pessimism is still more pervasive than that. Tragedy has died, Steiner wants to say, because it is no longer *pos-sible* in the modern world. Fate eventually collects its own. The gods are all dead, and tragedy died when they did.[4] For tragedy requires more

---

3. See George Steiner, *In Bluebeard's Castle: Some Notes toward a Redefinition of Culture* (New Haven: Yale Univ. Press, 1971) 29–56, as well as two essays, "The Hollow Miracle" and "A Kind of Survivor," in *George Steiner: A Reader* (New York: Penguin Books, 1984) 207–234.
4. See George Steiner, *The Death of Tragedy* (New York: Hill and Wang, 1961)

than a theater; it requires an audience, all of whom share something in the way of common beliefs and dramatic expectations, all of whom share a moral language in common. Tragedy, first and foremost, requires *community*.

Such a community, Steiner claims, once existed far off in the Greek past. Here we meet the nostalgic romance for the Greek *polis* that so characterizes the tragic posture. Sixth-century Attica, where tragedy was born — or some other place very much like it — represents a measure of our fall from grace, and innocence, and spiritual endowment. That world was a seamless web of common meanings and collective myths. Now Humpty-Dumpty has had his great fall; and the age of the kings is gone for good.

Such a construal of the present as a Fall from the paradise of the past invokes tragic language explicitly. Eden *and Babel* are the only myths we all still know. Back of all these stories stands the paradigmatic myth of a Fall — our natural inclination for unhappy endings, again.[5] "Babel was a second Fall," Steiner observes, "in some regards as desolate as the first."[6] We know these stories, at a level deeper than memory, at a level of spiritual *recognition,* because they tell us what we all believe — the story of what we have lost, of what we can probably never have again. It is all *very* simple. Tragedies end badly.[7] That is the sober fact of life that they attempt to describe. We fail to live in "tragic" fashion to the degree that we are unwilling to bear the burden of tragedy's heavy truth.

Christianity and Judaism are unwilling, perhaps even unable, to do so.[8] Christianity is "comic" precisely because it does not and cannot do so. Dante was right, and Shakespeare was, in a curious way, misguided. Christianity is about redemption, about paradise regained. Eden...*ends.* It ended temporarily when we "fell" and lost our patrimony. But in the grander scheme, the story that began in the Garden *will end well.* We will regain our paradise, or rather it will be given back to us. The prodigal will have a homecoming. Babel will be built on a surer foundation next time, when we all learn to speak a better, common language. The *polis* will be reborn in the guise of a much larger, perhaps even universal, church. Heaven is a Fate, not a Destiny — we

353; *Antigones* (New York: Oxford Univ. Press, 1984) 303; but also *Real Presences* (Chicago: Univ. of Chicago Press, 1989) 218–219, where he is suddenly out to resurrect these ancient gods and their myths.

    5. See Steiner, *In Bluebeard's Castle,* 4ff., and *The Death of Tragedy,* 8–13.

    6. George Steiner, *After Babel: Aspects of Language and Translation* (New York: Oxford Univ. Press, 1975) 59.

    7. That is the *leitmotif* to Steiner, *The Death of Tragedy,* 7–10, 16, 19, 98, 128–135, 166–169, 291. For a most insightful counter to this overgeneral claim, see Walter Kerr's remarkable *Tragedy and Comedy* (New York: Simon and Schuster, 1967) 36–56.

    8. Steiner, *The Death of Tragedy,* 3–7.

are heading there through God's grace, and no real action of our own. In a world defined by gravity *and* grace,[9] the earth tends to drag all things down — but God pulls the arrow irresistibly upward. This mythology makes Christianity as "antitragic" as it could possibly be, according to Steiner.[10] It also makes religious faith sound rather naive and optimistic, where it is not actually silly. This narrative account of Christian convictions tends toward this kind of silliness — I will argue this point in chapter 4 — precisely because it misses all the nuance and complexity of tragic texts like Mark's gospel.

III

I mentioned that there was another book that makes much the same case and does so by thematizing this same constellation of issues. That book is *After Virtue*,[11] written twenty years later in 1981 (second edition, 1984) by Alasdair MacIntyre. It is ironic indeed that this thinker should see himself chiefly as a polemicist and a diagnostician of modern culture — he did, after all, entitle a collection of occasional essays *Against the Self-Images of the Age*.[12] MacIntyre turns out, on closer inspection, to be one more symptom of what I take to be a far more fundamental, and pervasive, "modern" problem, the self-image against which *tragedy* stands. That problem is, quite simply, the tragic posture.

Now, having said this rather sharply, it needs to be reiterated that neither Steiner nor MacIntyre can manage to be as desperate as the logic of their own arguments invites them to be.[13] That is part of what makes both thinkers, and their books, so exciting and so rich. We are witness to very supple minds at work on very deep problems. This point is an important one because it illustrates again the importance of the tragic posture. These men, like Hegel and Nietzsche, are involved in critical conversation with themselves, but unlike the latter, the tragic *posture* sets the parameters of their thinking. This may help to explain the very uncharacteristic and rather flat ending of Steiner's more recent work. In an exhaustive study of the myth of Antigone, he concludes, rather simply, that "new 'Antigones' are being imagined, thought, lived now; and

---

9. The phrase is Simone Weil's, from the posthumous collection *La pesanteur et le grâce* (Paris: Librairie Plon, 1948).

10. Steiner, *The Death of Tragedy*, 11-13, 323-324.

11. Alasdair MacIntyre, *After Virtue*, 2d ed. (South Bend, Ind.: Univ. of Notre Dame Press, 1984).

12. Alasdair MacIntyre, *Against the Self-Images of the Age: Essays on Ideology and Philosophy* (South Bend, Ind.: Univ. of Notre Dame Press, 1978).

13. Steiner, *In Bluebeard's Castle*, 97-98, 106; and *The Death of Tragedy*, 351-355. Citations in MacIntyre's case prove somewhat more difficult, if only because the tension and paradox — or less kindly, the inconsistency — are all-pervasive.

will be tomorrow."[14] But this simple fact — it *is* a rather odd way to conclude such a monumental study — represents an astonishing conceptual breakthrough. Steiner has denied its very possibility up until now. Here is a sudden, and rather unexpected, vote of confidence for the future of Western culture — which he has elsewhere seen degenerating, particularly in America, into a "museum culture"[15] — and a far less despairing account of the present. Tragedy is not dead, and the rich cultural resources of the West are all still available. The myths still move us, probably always will.

This chastened, tentative optimism does not last. It is, in fact, little more than a passing moment. In the second full-length book to emerge out of an earlier lecture,[16] Steiner comes very close again to the thematics that concern me here. He is worried first and foremost — the lecture makes this even clearer than the book — about what he takes to be the moral bankruptcy of recent trends in "modern" thought.[17] But he cannot really challenge this position so long as he accepts the shape of the debate as his modernist opponents have defined it. This is most apparent in the facile apocalypticism that wants to see "modernity" as the end of something, as an "after-time." Steiner wants to begin, it seems, by calling this assumption into question: "Fundamental breaks in the history of human perception are very rare,"[18] he says. He even admits that apocalypses (his term is, appropriately enough, 'the *afterword*') are "also prefaces and new beginnings."[19] In fact, he concludes that there are only two really distinct epochs of human thought: "the first which extended from the beginnings of recorded history . . . to the later nineteenth century" and "the second phase *[that] comes after*."[20] The conclusion is sudden and inescapable. There is only one genuine apocalypse — and we moderns are living in its "aftermath."

If Steiner's work is fraught with a deepening academic desperation — bowing to the irresistibility of cultural gravity and the seductiveness of the posture — then MacIntyre, to his credit, is becoming more ambivalent. He himself seems to sense this.[21] What I find remarkable, then, is

---

14. Steiner, *Antigones,* 304.

15. Steiner, *In Bluebeard's Castle,* 110–111.

16. See Steiner, "Antigones," the Twelfth Jackson Knight Memorial Lecture delivered at the University of Exeter on 2 March 1979, and "Real Presences," the Leslie Stephen Memorial Lecture delivered at the University of Cambridge on 1 November 1985.

17. Steiner, *Real Presences,* 132.

18. Ibid., 87.

19. Ibid., 94. But that is *all* he says.

20. Ibid., 93, emphasis mine.

21. MacIntyre's *Whose Justice? Which Rationality?* (South Bend, Ind.: Univ. of Notre Dame Press, 1988) seems to me to represent the same odd twist: a chastened and cautious vote of confidence in the contemporary situation where virtues — and, of course, vices too — are as possible now as they ever were.

the degree to which his readers have not acknowledged this, or at the very least have failed to sense the disparity between claims that span a four-year interval. The tragic posture, so eloquently presented in *After Virtue,* is what has excited the scholarly community, in a way that his later modulations and nuances have not.

MacIntyre initiates his argument with an important word of caution. *"Pessimism,"* he says, "will turn out to be one more cultural luxury that we shall have to dispense with in order to survive in *these hard times.*"[22] All to the good, we are wont to say. Yet, in the final analysis, the times prove to be a little *too* hard, and the whole epic movement of MacIntyre's narrative is "a decline and fall"[23] designed to demonstrate how we have lost touch with a past that was pretty surely better and is now pretty surely irrecoverable. His book concludes with a slightly unexpected, and surely abbreviated, discussion of the Marxist tradition, in which he returns to these same fundamental premises. Marxism is grounded in an inescapably "optimistic" worldview, he says — presumably because it is invested in a "happy ending." Its very optimism — that distinctly "liberal" emotion — renders it "exhausted as a *political tradition*" ... as is "every other political tradition within our culture."[24]

MacIntyre now returns to a very old, and very natural, next question: "Does it then follow ... that my argument commits me and anyone else who accepts it to a generalized social pessimism? Not at all." Yet the only ray of hope that MacIntyre offers us, on the concluding page and in a single paragraph, is the possibility — slim though it be — that small, sectarian forms of *local* community will survive in these imminent Dark Ages: a cataclysm that is in fact not merely imminent, but already upon us, if we only had the eyes to see it for what it is. This *is* pessimism, of a high order, and it is grounded in the very nostalgia for small, face-to-face, *pre*modern communities that I am arguing is one of the chief trademarks of the tragic posture.

It is with regard to precisely this mythology that MacIntyre possesses one virtue that Steiner does not. He is clearer about his romantic investments. Steiner talks in general terms about cultural myths — Eden and Babel, primarily. He even seems to suggest that some such mythologizing is *necessary.*[25] We cannot do without it, *for life itself has a narrative char-*

---

22. MacIntyre, *After Virtue,* 5, emphasis mine.

23. Ibid., 3.

24. Ibid., 262. He faces this issue head-on in *Marxism and Christianity* (South Bend, Ind.: Univ. of Notre Dame Press, 1968, 1984) 115–116, 142, where he notes an interesting similarity in the stories that Marxists and Christians tell: from corruption to redemption. In this early essay, MacIntyre speaks far more favorably of the virtue of hope than he will in his more recent work. For more of the same see Steiner's *The Death of Tragedy,* 323–324, and *In Bluebeard's Castle,* 43–47.

25. Steiner, *In Bluebeard's Castle,* 8, 71, 134.

acter. On this point MacIntyre seems inclined to agree.[26] But MacIntyre also *names* his ideal. It is Greek antiquity, in the Agora rather than the theater of Dionysus.[27] More specifically, it is Greece in the Homeric and preclassical age; then again, it is Greece when this Golden Age was immortalized later in the encyclopedic philosophical summations we get from Aristotle.

I intend to use MacIntyre's idiosyncratic reading of the Greek legacy to illustrate just how symbiotic is the relationship between a postured pessimism about the "modern" situation and a romantic myth of (Greek) origins. Modern problems are not what MacIntyre makes them out to be, precisely because the past is not what he claims it was. MacIntyre claims for the past a harmony that now eludes us, claims that the past was a place where the community, *not* the individual, determined what counted as appropriate action, defined what were the relevant social roles and duties. The "individual," MacIntyre claims, is "a new social and cultural artefact,"[28] precisely because he or she can exist only in a world that — much like Humpty-Dumpty — has come apart. We have come undone today, have been dislocated, cast out of Eden. We have lost what the Greeks had in such marvelous abundance.

My strategy will be to turn MacIntyre's portrait of the past upside down, to insist that there is indeed a remarkably contemporary portrait of "the individual" already in Homer, the earliest Greek epic narrative we possess, and that this legacy finds new and enduring life in the tragic theater.

At one level, my disagreement with MacIntyre — insofar as it is a disagreement with his sentimental reading of the past — is a disagreement over what the Greeks were all about. Moral community? Or the individual? The city-state (*polis*)? Or the great-souled individual (*megalopsychos*)? In point of fact, the Greeks were concerned to the point of obsession with *both* ideas — community *and* individuality — but it is clear enough that all of their notions of moral community were informed by their tragic sensitivity. They lived between the mountaintop and the Agora and did not worry so much about that rhythmic movement as we do today. Human socialness is a drama, a dance, a *tragedy.* Attendance at the semiannual dramatic festivals was a principal civic duty, the heart and soul of communal obligation with all its attendant

26. MacIntyre, *After Virtue,* 121.
27. I suspect that this is almost universally true in contemporary theological and philosophical writing. It is interesting to see Steiner moving in this same direction in his latest work. He also has a fascinating, if slightly psychedelic, theory about why this should be the case — namely, that certain Greek myths are actually encoded in our grammar. See *Antigones,* 300–304.
28. MacIntyre, *Whose Justice? Which Rationality?* 339.

pomp and ritual.[29] And this is what makes MacIntyre's tragic insensitivity so damning to his argument. The Greeks in their tragedies celebrate the individual, in some ways, more than they do the *polis*.

There are two rival interpretations of the Greek tragic vision with which I will be dealing at some length — Hegel's and Nietzsche's — as well as a variety of more contemporary ones, chiefly Martha Nussbaum's and Simone Weil's. All are characterized by an explicit interest in tragedy. Hegel and Nietzsche were both deeply concerned by what they took to be the uncritical cultural pessimism of their own day (actually, Nietzsche's views changed on this point, as I will try to show in chapter 3). Both sought to subvert the myth of harmonious origins, which eighteenth- and nineteenth-century German philology had itself been so instrumental in creating. Classical Greece, while an exceptional *cultural* and *aesthetic* moment, was no *political* Eden. Both thinkers insisted that this magical world had been created largely as a haven from the secular and "modern" present that scholars no longer wanted — an academic escapism of the worst sort, which Nietzsche called "Quixotism."

Hegel and Nietzsche press further still. They are, in fact, unique, in that they did not confine their analyses simply to what tragedies make us feel; they both sought to articulate what constitutes a tragedy. The analysis of tragedy that I present here is the fruit of their labor primarily and represents a truly remarkable level of agreement between two philosophers who are diametrically opposed in most every other way. Theirs is a denial, not of answers, but of *simple* answers. It is a denial of simple *endings*.

In what, then, does their tragic philosophy consist, and where does it diverge? Respective chapters, the second and third, will seek to answer this question, but the tragic topography is plain enough. Both read tragedy as an essentially *affirmative* genre. It is the realm of great individuals, individuals involved in a Destiny of their own devising, not crudely doomed to an equally crude and abstract Fate. Both read it as *beyond* optimism and pessimism, categories that are far too shallow for tragedy's tremendous depth. Both see tragedy, through authentically Greek eyes, as profoundly uninterested in "the end." How a tragedy "ends" is an issue that did not concern the Greeks too much. Of the nineteen plays of Euripides that survive, five of them end exactly the same way. The question of an ending is a virtual obsession with most moderns, however, given our own apocalyptic version of the world. It was not, and is not, Greek.

---

29. See Oddone Longo, "The Theater of the Polis," trans. John J. Winkler, in *Nothing to Do with Dionysus? Athenian Drama in Its Social Context,* ed. John J. Winkler and Froma Zeitlin (Princeton, N.J.: Princeton Univ. Press, 1990) 12–19, and other essays in the same volume.

Now, Hegel and Nietzsche diverge on only one point, but this one simple point changes a great deal. The question concerns the relationship between tragedies and gospels, between pagan Greece and classical Christianity. Where Hegel sees exciting similarity, Nietzsche declares war. Nietzsche issues an ultimatum: in the battle between Dionysus and the Crucified, only one god can survive. If the Christian world wants to maintain its integrity in the face of the modernist challenge, it must do away with the Greeks. Luther and Augustine sensed this quite clearly. Not so, says Hegel: the two traditions may be synthesized in ways that are uniquely challenging and intellectually truer to our spiritual life. Aquinas had said this much, and more, centuries before.[30]

To my mind, the best way — the only way, really — of mediating this dispute is to read a gospel. In so doing, I am concentrating twice over: on the story of the Passion and particularly on its performance in Mark's gospel. This reading is a task for chapter 4. Here, the tragic dimension of the story is drawn out in sharp relief. It is a depiction of extraordinary human suffering, but that is precisely the point — it is *extraordinary*. It is elevating, ennobling, and the present is infinitely more exciting because these things have taken place. The past, so far from being romanticized, is made a prelude to the present disaster. Religious faith — so far is it from making the world and its horrors intelligible, so far is it from taking our pain away — culminates in the desperate cry from the Cross: "My God, my God, why have you abandoned me?" This tragedy does not end badly, but ambiguously ... particularly Mark's gospel, which ends with an empty tomb and a failure that is (almost) complete. The fact is that Mark believes in the infinity of God's power, in the principle of tragic resolution, which is to say (in his idiom), in *resurrection*. Mark has, in fact, staked his whole spiritual life upon these things. Yet he chooses to end his story without showing us any of this, and *that* strikes me as one of the profoundest dramatic moments available to us in any language. It is a denial, as I say, not of answers, but of *simple* answers. It is a denial of simple *endings*.

These, then, are the thematics of the argument: the pessimistic worry about the present; the optimistic, and very nearly mythic, regard for the past; the attempt to move beyond such simplistic dichotomies, which lies at the very heart of *both* classical *and* Christian tragedy. These texts

---

30. And not only Aquinas. It is surely telling that some of the most exciting cultural moments in "Western" thought have relied on this same synthesis (Greek and Christian), among them: the Eastern church's attempt to create a "new culture" in the fourth and fifth centuries, a venture embodied in the writings of the Cappadocian Fathers; the revolution of Renaissance humanism, heralded by the simultaneous development of Italian popular theater and the birth of "modern" philology; and nineteenth-century German Romanticism, perhaps symbolized best in the figure of Hölderlin.

depict a difficult world, to be sure. But their better insights are things that we have forgotten much too well. There is a crying need in the midst of our own crushing modernness for an authentic *tragic* witness — to counter the tragic posturing that is, as nearly as I have been able to tell, the only real or imagined "modern" catastrophe.

Chapter 1

SOPHOCLES' TRAGIC VISION
Antigone; or, The Niece Was Not

> Thus play I in one person many people,
> And none contented. Sometimes am I a king.
> Then treasons make me wish myself a beggar;
> And so I am. Then crushing penury
> Persuades me I was better when a king.
> Then am I kinged again; and by and by
> Think that I am unkinged by Bolingbroke,
> And straight am nothing. But whate'er I be,
> Nor I, nor any man that but man is,
> With nothing shall be pleased till he be eased
> With being nothing.
> [music plays]
> Music do I hear.
> Ha, ha; keep time! How sour sweet music is
> When time is broke.
>
> —*Richard II*, V, 5

It is always most difficult to know how to begin. Descartes, as is well known, made that insight the mainstay of his method.[1] He began by doubting everything, so he said, and then determined what remained certain even when all else had been doubted. He was left with the *fact* of human consciousness, he believed. *Cogito, ergo sum,* "I think, there-

---

1. I am particularly indebted to Alasdair MacIntyre's *Whose Justice? Which Rationality?* (Notre Dame, Ind.: Univ. of Notre Dame Press, 1988) 360–361, for making clear to me the centrality of this methodological claim. While I have found MacIntyre's discussion most illuminating, that assistance has taken the form primarily of helping me see what I do not believe. I turn to Hegel for a suppler analysis of the (apparent) contingency of every philosophical starting point and the way that contingency is resolved in a necessity, of sorts, at the end. To these narrative and tragic notions—questions of beginning and ending—I will return throughout this book.

fóre I am," as he so succinctly put it. That is his starting point, his philosophical beginning.

It is doubly difficult to know how to begin an extended study of a topic so broad and multifaceted as "tragedy." So many of these discussions, too many in fact, are abstract in the extreme, never dealing with the concrete, staged theatrical reality of tragic drama. Philosophical accounts of "the tragic" are too abstract; topical discussions of particular plays are too narrow, more the stuff of the Drama section of the *New York Times*. Still, one must make a beginning, however doomed to a certain arbitrariness such a beginning may seem to be. I have chosen to begin this study of tragedy particularly, with a single play, Sophocles' *Antigone*.

Why this play and no other? The reasons are varied. It is a very well-known play, deeply influential (however intermittently) for two and a half millennia. It has been staged and adapted perhaps more than any other single Greek tragedy,[2] and continues to be so in the present day. Of the three surviving Attic tragedians, Sophocles stands somehow over the other two in a rarified air of serenity and especially bracing tragic vision. This was true already in antiquity. Aristophanes — when a contest is staged in Hades (sponsored by Dionysus, no less) between the shades of Aeschylus and Euripides, for the coveted prize of returning to Athens to play again in the theater that bears his name — tells us that Sophocles would not deign to compete in such a contest because he is as content in one place as any other.[3] Sophocles' vision of tragedy is paradigmatic — for Aristotle[4] and, to an admittedly lesser degree, for us.

That said, my choice of Sophocles, and more specifically the *Antigone*, has a lingering arbitrariness about it. I prefer Hegel to Descartes on this question. There is something profound at stake in Hegel's assertion regarding arbitrary beginnings, and it involves this same (*tragic*) theory of philosophical beginnings. Granted, he admits, there *is* an apparent (and probably inescapable) arbitrariness and contingency to every decision about how to begin — so much so that it seems impossible to begin at all.[5] Yet we all do, ever and again, *begin*. At the end of any philosophical inquiry, or at the end of a human life, certain beginnings that had an inescapable arbitrariness at the time are seen now in a new light. They are seen as *necessary*, in fascinating if ultimately inexplicable ways. At

2. George Steiner, *Antigones* (New York: Oxford Univ. Press, 1989) 107–110.

3. Aristophanes, *The Frogs*, scene V, trans. Dudley Fitts (New York: Harcourt Brace Jovanovich, 1962) 119.

4. Aristotle, *The Poetics*, §§5, 14–16, 24, 26, trans. Gerald Else (Ann Arbor: Univ. of Michigan Press, 1965) 19, 41, 44, 47, 66, 74.

5. Hegel, *The Science of Logic*, §1, trans. William Wallace (Oxford: Oxford Univ. Press, 1975) 3.

the end, the beginning is read in a new light — as *necessary,* not merely arbitrary. So, too, here. I cannot adequately defend my decision to begin with the *Antigone* here, at the beginning. At the end of the book, however, both reader and writer will ideally have more to say.

I

It was, so far as we can tell, Heraclitus who first said that "character is destiny,"[6] implying that each of our inner worlds impacts far more profoundly upon the outer world than any of us might like to admit at a glance. We have had occasion already to observe how far this view stands from what passes for an academic orthodoxy in the present age. We today are fascinated by how the outside shapes the inside, not vice versa.[7] It is one of the chief tenets of that modernist perspective that MacIntyre represents so well that our "selves" are little more than what society — with its roles and expectations, habits and practices — and a lifetime of experiences make them out to be. We are in crisis because, as moderns, we live in *an age* of crisis. Whatever this view is, modern or antimodern, it is decidedly *not* Sophocles' view. And it seems small wonder that today we have so little to say about "Destiny" — we, who have given over the search for the destin-ations lodged within our natures in order to concentrate upon a Fate that is ineluctably ours in the "modern" world.

We should note that one crucial Greek term for Destiny, *moira*[8] —

---

6. *Ēthos anthrōpōi daimōn.* This fragment may be found in Charles H. Kahn's *The Art and Thought of Heraclitus: An Edition of the Fragments with Translation and Commentary* (Cambridge: Cambridge Univ. Press, 1979) #114. The classic edition of Diels, *Fragmenten der Vorsokratischer,* lists this as #119. In citing these fragments, I will refer to Kahn's numeration of the fragments, including Diels' in brackets. So here: Heraclitus, Fragment #114 [D-119]. The fragment was originally found in Plutarch's *Quaestiones Platonicae,* 999e. Upon closer inspection, I have found a number of fascinating parallels between key Heraclitean fragments and Sophocles' arguments in this play. Tracing these out will be one major theme of this chapter, as it was in E. R. Dodds' "On Misunderstanding the *Oedipus Rex,*" in *Greek Tragedy* (Oxford: Oxford Univ. Press, 1983) 187. It is perhaps worth noting that there is one essential divergence between Heraclitus' perspective and Sophocles' in this play, where the philosopher is being intentionally iconoclastic and provocative. Calling into question the very natural piety that alone makes sense of this tragedy, Heraclitus argues that "corpses should be thrown out quicker than dung!" [Fragment #88].

7. See Iris Murdoch, "The Idea of Perfection," in *The Sovereignty of Good* (London: Routledge and Kegan Paul, 1970) 1–45, esp. 24–25, 36, 44.

8. It is worth mentioning that when Hesiod anthropomorphizes these goddesses — the *Moirai* — he calls them the daughters of Zeus...and of *Themis* (*Theogony,* 904ff.). *Themis* is a crucial idea in classical thought and especially in this play. I explore the concept in some detail in my "The Tragic Posture in the Modern Age: An Essay on Tragedy — Classical, Christian and Modern" (Ph.D. diss., Emory University, 1990) 47–62. See also my "In the Aftermath of Modernism: On Present Postures and Their Portrait of the Past," *Soundings* 75:2/3 (1992) 255–285, esp. 267–268.

like the term *daimōn,* which is used here by Heraclitus — originally connotes a sense of "portion" and of "personality." Thus, character, like Destiny itself, is that which is distinctively our own — our portion from the cosmic till.[9] If this is true of a concept as abstract as character (*ēthos*), how much the more will it be true of something as personal as our name. In any case, the Greeks, who were fascinated by Destiny in every guise, reveled in the uncanny idea that names, too, are Destiny.[10] This is one of those tantalizing classical beliefs that is still barely visible in contemporary Greek society. Far more important than one's birthday is one's "name-day" (*yiortē*), the day of the saint who serves as one's patronym or matronym. The point, if one cares to reflect upon it, is that the bestowal of this name has done something to one's *character,* something that birth alone did not do. For us, who cannot hear the Fates' or Graces' echo quite so clearly in a name — and who moreover have been schooled on the notion that names cannot, after all, alter the sweet smell of a rose — this idea must seem as foreign as the alphabet of that distant age.

It is for this reason that this chapter is divided *topically,* to introduce ideas that are, on the surface, most foreign and strange to a modern audience. This play helps introduce us to the tragic vision, as the Greeks understood it. There is nothing postured about it. In succeeding sections this chapter will explore the following themes: the Destiny involved in the process of *naming;* the importance of *first words* that characters speak; the concept and function of a dramatic *chorus;* and finally the concept of *stichomythia and dialectics.* At that point, we will be well-positioned to discuss what Hegel *did* with this (Sophoclean) tragic vision.

Her name, then, is Antigone. It is her character; it is her Destiny. She is defined by what she is not, what she can never be. She is *anti-gonē.* The richness of the resonances that her name invokes is difficult to ren-

---

9. This is the essential point of Gerald F. Else's *The Madness of Antigone* (Heidelberg: Carl Winter Universitätsverlag, 1976), where he uses this same Heraclitean fragment to point out how the Aeschylean view of Fate as an external *Atē* descending on a family from above has been internalized by Sophocles, made personal, made an issue of *character,* and nothing more. Antigone is not destroyed passively, so much as she destroys herself.

10. Thus Helen is the "ship-destroying," "man-slaying," and "city-destroying" woman, all at once (*Agamemnon,* 681–690); Prometheus sees the future (*Prometheus Bound,* 85–87); Ajax is, quite simply, the embodiment of "agony" (*Ajax,* 430–433); Admetus is the man who has "not been yoked" to necessity (*Alcestis,* 416ff.); Hippolytos is the breaker of horses who will himself be broken by them (*Hippolytos,* 110–112, 228–235, 1215–1254, 1355–1359); and Medea's name calls to mind the Delphic injunction (*mēden agan,* "nothing too much") for precisely the moderation that she so sorely lacks (*Medea,* 125ff.). For another interesting, if characteristically overdrawn, discussion, see MacIntyre, *Whose Justice? Which Rationality?* 376–379.

der immediately. And we need to reflect upon those resonances first, at the beginning. "Anti-" is a prefix that means "instead of"; thus, Antigone is being defined in terms of certain essential Greek social norms from which she will diverge dramatically. It is interesting that we, who have inherited this prefix (*anti-*) from the Greeks, have subtly altered its meaning. What to the Greeks suggested *substitution*, "instead of," suggests *opposition* to us, "against, opposed to" — suggesting, finally, I think, that the Greeks may have been far more comfortable with difference than we are, and may have much to teach us still about looking at, and even reveling in, that which seems strangest to us. Tragedy is one essential realm in which that Greek confrontation took place.

Now I certainly recognize that this claim, beyond the risk it runs of romanticizing the Greeks, also flies in the face of what is commonly held to be true about premodern cultures and about classical Greek culture in particular. Their world is supposed to have been much smaller than our own, certainly not larger. Naturally enough, MacIntyre's work is again what I have chiefly in mind. For the romantic belief, that heroic and classical Greek society may be used as a model for those very homogeneous, and seamless — *and* deeply xenophobic — societies he considers barely recoverable today, is simply violated too often by these tragic texts. The Greeks whom Herodotus and Xenophon describe are fascinated by differences, in whatever form, and do not seem in the least disturbed by them. Their use of the term 'barbarian' (*barbaros*) originally denoted simply a person who did not speak a Greek dialect and whose speech therefore sounded like senseless chatter (*bar-bar*). The word was originally onomatopoetic, nothing more. It is *we* who attach moral valence to the term, as did MacIntyre in the concluding pages of *After Virtue*.[11] His warrant for doing so comes from Aristotle, for whom "barbarian" was also a category of derision, in the first chapter of *The Politics*. But this well illustrates the obvious point that the resurrection of Aristotle may not represent the recovery of Greek thought at its best. I turn to tragedy rather than to moral philosophy, Sophocles rather than Aristotle. Among the Archaic and Homeric Greeks, the highest god, Zeus himself, was first and foremost a god of *philoxenia*, "the love of the strange," a virtue that also receives preeminent praise from Pindar in his Victory Odes, from all the surviving tragedians without exception, and even by so late a "classical" thinker as St. Paul (in *Romans* 12 and elsewhere).

In fact, it is the character of Paul who helps us draw this argument around upon itself. Recall what we are told about his reception

---

11. Alasdair MacIntyre, *After Virtue* 2d ed. (Notre Dame, Ind.: Univ. of Notre Dame Press, 1984) 263.

in Athens, after he had been exiled or spirited away from very nearly every self-respecting city in the Hellenistic world:

> And the Athenians took him and led him to the Areopagus, saying, "May we know what this new teaching [*kainē didachē*] is which you teach? For you bear some strange things [*xenizonta*] to our ears, and we want to know what they mean."
>
> Now all the Athenians and the foreigners [*xenoi*] who lived there delighted in nothing so much as the telling or hearing of the latest new thing [*ti kainoteron*].[12]

Strangers within the gates, strange ideas pouring in from the outside — in this milieu the boundary-line between insider and outsider, between enemy and friend, becomes difficult to draw. It is a chief tenet of this new faith that Paul brings with him that such lines must never *be* drawn. We are *all* related in ways we only vaguely understand; there is no "outside." And the Athenians, in their best moments, refused to draw it. *Antigone* refuses to draw it.[13] The exception to this lovely rule will not surprise us. It is Aristotle. He claims that such lines *must* be drawn, often with devastating effect. "Taking our analogy from warfare [*polemois*], where the dividing line of a ditch, however small it may be, makes a regiment scatter in crossing, we may say that every difference [*diaphora*] is apt to create a division [*diastasin*]."[14]

Leaving this issue to one side, let us return to this woman's name. There is, indeed, a sense of negation, of not-ness, which resides in the prefix *anti-*, even if the Greeks did not, broadly speaking, attach the same moral valence to such negations as do we today. Short of reading the play in Greek, it is impossible to communicate how deeply saturated the language of Sophocles' play is in the rhetoric of negation.[15] So I will simply assert here at the outset that this play contains a clear and un-

---

12. *Acts* 17:19–21. We cannot make too much of this passage, since it is a description at least four hundred years *younger* than the times I mean to discuss. Still, there *is* a power in the stories people tell about themselves and about others. And the story that is told here appears much older than Luke's telling of it.

13. This is essential to Antigone's rejection of the sham heroic doctrine of "helping friends and harming enemies." See Mary Whitlock Blundell, *Helping Friends and Harming Enemies: A Study of Sophocles and Greek Ethics* (Cambridge: Cambridge Univ. Press, 1989).

14. Aristotle, *The Politics*, 1303b.13–15.

15. This insight, too, is an essential one for Heraclitus. To borrow a phrase from Martin Heidegger, *there is a privative that is prior to the positive.* It is in the very nature of things — since we live in a world of conflict and flux (#82, 83 [D-53, 80]) — to generate their own oppositions, "to become other than they are" ([*alloioutai*], #123). Heraclitus had previously remarked: "*Hidden* harmony is better than *revealed*" (Fragment #80 [D-54]). Actually in Greek, it is clear that the negative term has been given priority. *Harmoniē aphanēs phanerēs kreittōn*: in the interplay between *in*visible (*a phanēs*) and visible (*phanerēs*), the *in*visible is more primordial.

deniable subtext of negation, and will attempt to provide some sense of what this means as the chapter progresses.

There are no fewer than eight negations in the first five lines of Antigone's opening speech, and no fewer than fourteen in the first seventeen lines exchanged between her and Ismene. Here at the outset, Sophocles has underscored something for us, inviting us to take a closer look at the idea, and he will continue to play and pun with negative language throughout the tragedy.[16]

We are not the first to notice this. In fact, this reading, this angle, was originally the result of a truly extraordinary exercise in youthful collegiality and romantic philhellenism. Hegel, Hölderlin, and Shelling were students together at the seminary in Tübingen; one of the things that first drew them together was a common love of the Greek classics, Sophocles' Theban trilogy preeminently.[17] The results of that collaboration were dramatically to shape the mental landscape of contemporary German life and letters. The effect of the play on all three men, and through them on all of Germany, even all of Europe, was extraordinary. Shelling grew increasingly entranced by the figure of Antigone, particularly the principle of *themis* that she dies defending. Her natural piety, her intuitive sense of what is right, her genius if you will, all lend substance to his later philosophy of "intellectual intuition." Hölderlin returned to the play at the end of his all-too-brief intellectual career and used his attempt at a translation of the play as an opportunity to demonstrate his own mature views on translation and interpretation,[18] views that anticipate much of what we today call "hermeneutics." Hegel's attraction and fascination with the play were lifelong. Of the play's heroine, he remarked, "[She is] celestial,...the most resplendent figure ever to have appeared on earth." And he called the play itself quite simply "the pre-eminent, the most satisfying...of all splendors of the ancient and modern world."[19] Hegel's tragic vision derives largely from his reading of this play, as we shall see in some detail.

It is not simply the case that Hegel loved this play, perhaps loved it beyond all others. In fact, Hegel favored Shakespeare, and *Hamlet*

---

16. See also G. F. Else, *The Madness of Antigone*, 29.

17. George Steiner, *Antigones*, 7–8, 22–36; John D. Barbour, *Tragedy as a Critique of Virtue: The Novel and Ethical Reflection* (Chico, Calif.: Scholars Press, 1984) 22–29; Clark Butler, ed., *Hegel: The Letters* (Bloomington: Indiana Univ. Press, 1984) 45–47, 50–51; René Girard, *Violence and the Sacred,* trans. Patrick Gregory (Baltimore: Johns Hopkins Univ. Press, 1977) 155–158; and Georg Lukács, *The Young Hegel: Studies in the Relations between Dialectics and Economics,* trans. Rodney Livingstone (Cambridge, Mass.: MIT Press, 1966, 1975) 4–7, 46–49, 411–413.

18. See *Hölderlin: Werke und Briefe* (Frankfurt: Insel Verlag, 1969) 2:737–790.

19. Henry Paolucci, *Hegel: On the Arts* (New York: Frederick Ungar, 1979) 190; and Steiner, *Antigones,* 39–40.

was, on his view, arguably the greatest single work of dramatic poetry. Rather, the *imagery* of this play and the myth that lay behind it stuck with Hegel, imagery that recurs in much of his later work. There is, of course, the image of two brothers locked in a life-and-death struggle before the gates of Thebes, which clearly anticipates the dialectic of mastery and servility. But chief among these images, these rhetorical tropes, is his view that the true task of philosophy is "looking the negative in the face, and dwelling with it."[20] As for what 'the negative' finally entails, it will take an entire play, and a good deal more than this, to begin to make this clear.[21] Hegel rather cryptically calls it "the magic power which converts itself into being" — first and foremost in our existential encounter with the fact that we must all die someday. This is "the highway of despair" that both Antigone and Creon are destined to traverse. Another important clue comes from Nietzsche, who was no less moved by Greek imagery and who, in his reflections on Greek drama, argued that the Greeks stared into the darkness (the negative?) for so long that they began, at long last, to see small specks of light, as though accustoming their eyes finally to the horror of it.[22]

Hegel would have concurred, I think, for this is precisely what he saw happening to Creon. Only at the end, after everyone around him has died and he too has been reduced to "nothing," is he eased or pleased with the emptiness that is himself. Hegel insists — and there is strong textual support for this belief, both in this play and in the gospels — that this is *necessary,* that human truths cannot be apprehended in any other way. If we are to find our life, we must lose it first — a view that is neither simple good news nor a recipe for quick success, but rather something that marks the beginning of what we will eventually want to call "tragic philosophy."

What, then, does this play actually say about negations? To begin with, Antigone, even at the level of her name, is defined as what she is not, a variety of things she can never be. In all of these negative definitions, she is defined primarily over against Creon, who will be — as Hegel saw so clearly — her dramatic foil throughout the play. She is not male, like him, which is to say that she is a girl. She is not mature, like him, which is to say, again, that she is a girl.[23] She is not lawful, at

---

20. Hegel, *The Phenomenology of Spirit,* trans. J. B. Baillie (New York: Humanities Press, 1966), §32, p. 93; *Werke,* III, 36.

21. For a related discussion, invoking Hegel explicitly, see Mark C. Taylor, *Nots* (Chicago: Univ. of Chicago Press, 1993) 1–27. Taylor's final chapter on the bodily negation that is disease (214–255) — what he calls "the betrayal of the body" — is also worth reading, however postured its final (viral?) conclusions.

22. Nietzsche, *The Birth of Tragedy,* §9; *The Gay Science,* §90.

23. And Aristotle would immediately want to add that, as a youth (*neos*), she must be impetuous and idealistic to a fault: "And they are more courageous [than the other

least not in his terms, and thus she stands at an infinite remove from him, heeding *other* obligations — the laws of the nether gods (*themis*, not *nomos*) and the law she recognizes within herself. The Chorus accuses her of being *autonomos*, or "self-ruled," and they do so in the masculine gender.[24] They do not mean it as a compliment. She stands for everything that lies *outside* the city; her abode lies beyond its too-narrow boundaries, in the wild precincts, where her beloved brother lies, unburied:

> It has, I believe, been given to only one literary text to express all the principle constants of conflict in the condition of man. These constants are fivefold: the confrontation of men and of women; of age and of youth; of society and of the individual; of the living and the dead; of men and of god(s). The conflicts which come of these five orders are not negotiable. Men and women, old and young, the individual and the community or state, the quick and the dead, mortals and immortals, define themselves in the conflictual process of defining each other. Self-definition and the agonistic recognition of 'otherness' (of *l'autre*) across the threatened boundaries of self, are indissociable.... To arrive at oneself — the primordial journey — is to come up, polemically, against 'the other.'[25]

What this play has to show us is nothing if not a polemical[26] conflict between a variety of selves and their combative attempts to define themselves in other terms. At the conclusion of the battle for political control of Thebes now comes... *another* war, even if this time it is warfare temporarily concealed.

---

age groups]; for they are impulsive and filled with good hopes, of which the former quality makes them lack fear, and the latter makes them brave; for no one feels fear when angry, and to expect something good is a source of confidence. And they are sensitive to shame; for they have been educated only by convention and do not yet understand other fine things. And all the mistakes they make are in the direction of excess and vehemence, contrary to the maxim of Chilon; for they do 'everything too much': they love too much and hate too much and all other things similarly" (*Rhetoric*, II, §12.9–10, 14, trans. George A. Kennedy [New York: Oxford Univ. Press, 1991] 165–166). I suspect that this description, and those of "elderly men" and "men in their prime" that follow it, are not so much reflective of Aristotle's own moral anthropology as they are reflective of the stock stage-conventions of the comic theater in his own day. Hence the ambiguity of the word 'character,' which can mean our own inner nature, as it does for Heraclitus, or merely the masks worn by actors and actresses on a stage.

Finally, it must be noted that — contrary to MacIntyre's reading of heroic and postclassical society — Aristotle feels that it is *only* youths who *fully* accept the stock conventions of their society; they are not yet old enough or sufficiently independent to disobey. Even this claim will be dramatically disproved in the exceptional case of Antigone. See Martha Nussbaum's *The Fragility of Goodness* (Cambridge: Cambridge Univ. Press, 1986) 337–340, for a complementary interpretation of this text from the *Rhetoric*, and MacIntyre's *After Virtue*, 27–31, for a discussion of "character" as little more than stock conventions of social roles.

24. *Antigone*, 821. See also Else, *The Madness of Antigone*, 60, 76–80.

25. Steiner, *Antigones*, 231–232.

26. *Polemos*, War, is invoked as a god by Heraclitus, Fragment #83 [D-80].

Given this chain of negations, as well as the polemic to which they
inevitably give rise, this play also has something else to show us about
our-selves. If, as this play suggests, the self and the other are mutually defined in such a way that their boundaries overlap; if, in fact, the
boundaries themselves are hopelessly blurred and impossible to sketch
out clearly,[27] then there is a fundamental identity that these characters
are thought to share, above and beyond their many differences. This
assumption is the very essence of dialectics. Recall the competition of
myths — Aristophanes' and Diotima's — that Plato presents in the *Symposium*.[28] If out of the primordial One, the Two emerge, then out of
the erotic conflict between these Two — and Eros *is* the animus in this
tragedy — a new and doubtless very different Third Thing, the "We,"
is born:

> In these Tragedies justice is grasped by thought. The collision between
> the two...is set forth in a plastic fashion in that supreme and absolute
> example of tragedy, *Antigone*. In this case family love, what is holy, what
> belongs to the inner life and to inner feeling, and which because of this is
> also called the law of the nether gods, comes into collision with the law
> of the State.
>
> [Antigone and Creon each] realizes only one of the moral powers, and
> has only one of these as its content; this is the element of one-sidedness
> here, and the meaning of eternal justice is shown in this, that both end
> in injustice just because they are one-sided, though at the same time both
> obtain justice too....
>
> It is only the one-sidedness in their claims which justice comes forward
> to oppose.[29]

From this polemical back-and-forth between Creon and Antigone — an
exploration of what they mutually *are not* — a truth emerges, a lingering
sense of what they are and what they need to become. Men become
women, and women men. The young and old are inseparable, the dead
are bound up with the living in the dialectics of Destiny. And the city,
for all of its grand pretensions, is ultimately nothing more — the point
that Creon and MacIntyre and arguably even Hegel are all in danger
of forgetting — than a collection of such individuals, sewn together at a
comparatively late hour.

---

27. See G. H. Mead, *Movements of Thought in the Nineteenth Century* (Chicago:
Univ. of Chicago Press, 1936) 74–75, 82–84, 415–417, on the "modern" fascination
with this notion of "the Self/Not-Self Dyad."

28. *Symposium*, 189c–193e, 203b–204c.

29. Anne and Henry Paolucci, eds., *Hegel: On Tragedy* (New York: Harper and
Row, 1962) 325. This passage appeared originally in *The Lectures on the Philosophy
of Religion*, II, 2, a. See also Steiner, *Antigones*, 37–42, and Th. C. W. Oudemans
and A. P. M. H. Lardinois, *Tragic Ambiguity: Anthropology, Philosophy and Sophocles'
Antigone* (Leiden: E. J. Brill, 1987) 107–117.

II

But all of this circles around the central truth embodied in her name. We must look even more closely at her name. She is "not-*gonē*." She is not *this*, but *that*, something else very different. Translation takes time.[30] For *gonē*, like *gen*, is a root that has given us words as diverse as 'gonad' and 'genesis,' 'genetics' and 'genealogy.'[31] So, too, it renders our 'gender.' She will have no gen-ealogy, no gen-erations after her own. The race, the gen-us, will die when she dies.[32] For she herself is gen-der-less. She is not of the family the way most of us are; her gen-esis is a very different thing. Or better, while she is emphatically *from* the family — she is without a doubt *Oedipus'* child — she *is not* familial, save in this regressive sense. Gen-etically speaking, she has no future; family, for her, resides in the dark shadows of the past, and only there. She will never marry, will never bear children of her own, and will go to her living death, a virgin still:

> Eros is invariably connected with Thanatos....Virgins in tragedy leave for the abode of the dead just as they might their father's home for the home of their husband.[33]

Now, however, comes the paradox. Antigone, who is destined to have no family of her own, will go to her death in the name of the family and all that is holy about it. She will defy Creon's edict[34] and will bury her brother's corpse where it now lies, abandoned, outside the city gates.

She knows that she will die for doing so. She wants to die. She claims, in fact, to be dead already.[35] But in the process of loving her dead

---

30. Richard Emil Braun, in his translator's introduction to the play (Oxford: Oxford Univ. Press, 1973) 7, 18, argues — for admittedly very different reasons than the ones I am offering — that we might well also hear *her mission* in her name. She is, on this reading, *gonē-anti*, "born to oppose."

31. Froma I. Zeitlin, "Thebes: Theater of Self and Society in Athenian Drama," in *Nothing to Do with Dionysus? Athenian Drama in Its Social Context*, ed. John J. Winkler and Froma I. Zeitlin (Princeton, N.J.: Princeton Univ. Press, 1990) 152. See also Seth Benardete, "A Reading of Sophocles' *Antigone*: I," *Interpretation* 4 (1975) 156–157.

32. Which is an important factor in seeing the curse on the Labdakid house through to its end, in that all of Oedipus' *and* Creon's children will be dead by the end of this play. See Else, *The Madness of Antigone*, 50.

33. Nicole Loraux, *Tragic Ways of Killing a Woman*, trans. Anthony Forster (Cambridge, Mass.: Harvard Univ. Press, 1987) 37.

34. The word is consistently *kērygma* in this play, which, for all of its New Testament resonance, speaks powerfully to the way we must think, and think again, about laws and their tenuous relationship to truths.

35. Actually, to be precise, she claims a liminal place for herself, on the threshold between the worlds of the living and the dead. Thus, as a citizen *between* two worlds, belonging to neither, Antigone is emphatically without a home, "apolitical" in the distinctively Sophoclean sense. As she is led to her (living) death, she sings:

brother so well, or rather so exclusively, she alienates every other person who could conceivably lay a claim upon her familial sympathies —
again because, as she herself observes, she is "already dead":

> There is a marked tendency among modern commentators to romanticize
> Antigone. She is treated like the heroine of a romantic novel. It seems to
> me that this kind of interpretation reveals the bias of these commentators
> for this kind of character. This is what they think a heroine should be. It
> is not objectively based on Sophocles' text....
>
> [Antigone] belongs to an exceedingly tough class of personage, one
> which we no longer meet in our society and are therefore liable to mis-
> understand. She is a woman for whom the family is everything, who lives,
> both personally and vicariously, through the family, who is prepared to
> regard herself, in the last resort, as the personification of the family. An-
> tigone is, we have no reason to doubt, loving and capable of love: but
> her love is bound up with, and inseparable from, an idea.[36]

Antigone will have nothing but contempt for her sister, Ismene — Ismene, who fails to share the deed with her, and yet is only too willing
to share the blame and the punishment at Creon's hands. For her fiancé,
Antigone gives not a thought, and indeed, it is Ismene, not Antigone,
who introduces his name into the text of this play.[37] Finally, ironically,
she is related to Creon himself — Creon, who is the brother of her
mother, Jocasta. Yet Jocasta was also the mother — *before* she was the
bride — of Oedipus, and this makes the familial relations all the more
confusing. Small wonder that she chooses another way to be in the
world, a way "instead-of-gen-erating." Not only does she represent an
alternative to it, she is *against* it. She is *not* en-gen-dering anything, has

---

> Alas, wretched!
> I am *neither* a corpse
> among mortals
> *nor* yet housemate to the dead.
> *Not* living.
> *Not* dead. (ll. 850–852)

36. J. H. Kells, "Problems of Interpretation in the *Antigone*," *Bulletin for the Institute of Classical Studies* 10 (1963) 50. See also Else, *The Madness of Antigone*,
100–101.

37. This last point, at l. 572, is disputed in the manuscripts. The codices all attribute
the line, "O dearest Haemon, how your father dishonors you!" to Ismene, yet later scho-
liasts attribute the line to Antigone. Their questionable reasoning insists that Antigone
surely would not go to her own death without ever having mentioned her lover's name.
But this is *precisely* what she fails to do: *surely* this reticence is a key part of Antigone's
character, what renders her incapable of understanding the love of a man who will,
like Romeo, kill himself at her lifeless feet. It is an aspect of Antigone's one-sidedness
that she can love in only one dimension; her love will allow for only two people in
the world—and one of these, her brother, is already a corpse. See Kells, "Problems of
Interpretation in the *Antigone*," 53.

no interest any longer in future gen-erations. She cares for, and loves,[38] a single family member — and he, after all, is dead. The only love she will allow herself is thus "impossible" — as everyone (save herself) knows only too well.[39] She, and all her race, *is* not, a paradox that disrupts the very contours of our language. She *has* no generation. She *is* no generation — for her father is her brother, and her brother is a corpse.

The antitheses and the poetic confusion of this whole dramatic set-ting are made with startling force in the first line of the play. The scene is set outside the Theban palace. As dawn breaks, two sisters, whose generation makes them more than sisters (if less than kind), be-gin to talk with one another. The first line is Antigone's, emphasizing the more-than-sisterliness of this pair. Their very kinship is excessive:

> Ō *koinon autadelphon Ismēnēs kapa.*
> [O kindred, sister-self! Ismene's head!]

They are common kin (*koinon*),[40] the same blood running through their veins. And even more than this, they are primordially linked, such that neither is merely "sister" (*adelpha*) but also "self" (*auta*) as well. This same strange, archaic word, *autadelphon,*[41] will be used several times in the play to refer to the primordial matrix of "self and second-self" by which Antigone finds herself bonded to her dead brother. Perhaps in the same manner, Creon is bonded to his city, for his name means, roughly, "Rule."[42] Next, Antigone refers to the head (*kara*) of her sister, not the

---

38. The words are *eraō* and *keimai*, which possess a none-too-subtle erotic implica-tion. This will be an important aid in understanding the profound feelings of loyalty that this young girl will feel for her older brother. And we must not lose sight of the fact that there is a most disturbing "Ode to Eros" at the very heart of this troubled play (ll. 781–801).

39. The word is *amēchanōn*, at *Antigone,* 90, and elsewhere. It is one of the chief, and frankly surprising, weaknesses of Hegel's reading of this play that he fails to notice the centrality of Eros in it. In point of fact, he goes so far as to use Antigone as a model of the very chastity her character lacks. Antigone, on this view, proves just how innocent and pure are the idyllic relations between brother and sister. See the *Phenomenology,* §457; Baillie, 464–482, esp. 477. In fact, Hegel goes even further and asserts an *historical* necessity for this. Classical art is not yet capable of expressing the interiority of true erotic commitments, all of which must wait for Christian subjectivity and the development of romantic ideals. See Paolucci, *Hegel: On the Arts,* 47–48.

40. This word, as well as its correlate, *xunon*, is essential for Heraclitus, Fragments #3, 6, 30, 31, 82, 99 [D-2, 80, 103, 113, 114]. In his turn, Heraclitus is recalling the sobering Homeric sense of cosmic justice (*Iliad,* 18:309): "Ares is just [*xunos*], and kills those who kill."

41. *Antigone,* 696. See Else, *The Madness of Antigone,* 27–28, and Seth Benardete, "A Reading of Sophocles' *Antigone,*" in *Interpretation* 4:3 (1974) 148–149.

42. In fact, we get some independent confirmation of this in Haemon's discussion with his father. At l. 733, Creon refers to Thebes as *homoptolis*, which we might render as "same-city," but taken in the sense of "same as yourself." Thus I do not think it inappropriate to translate this as "city-self," making the parallel to what Antigone has just said explicit. Her siblings *are* her self; for Creon, *the city* is.

face (*prosōpon*). In the eerie half-light of approaching dawn, two male actors, cloaked in the robes and masks of women, hail each other with an appeal to a relationship that transcends linguistic categories:[43]

> Literally and figuratively, Antigone's writ to Ismene springs at her sister and at ourselves out of receding darkness.... Polyneices is, he must be felt and seen to be, the brother whom Antigone and Ismene share in total symbiosis.... The grammar of Antigone lies prior to our classifications. ... Of these fusions, the Greek tragic chorus may itself have been a late vestige.[44]

The Greek language has one mode of discourse that we no longer possess, "the dual." Duality — as distinct from the singular as it is from the plural — possesses a completely distinctive form in this dialect.[45] To be two together is as different from being three as it is from being alone. This Sartre knew. Antigone will make abundant use of this archaic verb form until Ismene definitively rejects her appeal for assistance in the burial of their brother. After this, Antigone will reserve this rhetoric of relation — *autadelphon*, *kara*, and the dual voice — for her brother alone.

Antigone "rides into the play on a torrent of negatives"[46] and in so doing sets the tone for the rest of the play:

> Do you *not* know that Zeus brings to fulfillment
> all Oedipus' *sorrows* upon *us two*, living still?
> *No* thing — *neither* pain, *nor* ruin,
> *nor* shame, *nor* yet dishonor — *no* evil thing,
> whether *yours* or *mine*, have I *not* seen.
> And now, what new command [*kērygma*], murmured through
> out the city, is this the general has just laid down?
> Have you heard tell of it? Or did the news *fall short*
> of you, of enemies' *curses* bearing down on friends?[47]

43. This word (*kara*) as well, Antigone will use twice in saying farewell to her brother (ll. 899, 915), confirming once again that her attention has shifted decisively from her sister Ismene to her dead brother Polyneices.

44. Steiner, *Antigones*, 211–212.

45. See the remarkable chapter, "Men in Pairs," in Thomas MacCary's *Childlike Achilles* (New York: Columbia Univ. Press, 1982) 127–136. See also Charles Segal, *Tragedy and Civilization: An Interpretation of Sophocles* (Cambridge, Mass.: Harvard Univ. Press, 1981) 186. This same idea is the starting point for Hegel's dialectic of mastery and servility, where doubling (*Verdopplung*) does for his philosophy much the same thing that the dual voice does in this play.

46. R. P. Winnington-Ingram, *Sophocles: An Interpretation* (Cambridge: Cambridge Univ. Press, 1980) 128.

47. *Antigone*, 2–10. I have used the Greek text in *Sophoclis: Fabulae* (New York: Oxford Univ. Press, 1961). While I have highlighted the negative language in this first passage, I will not do so throughout this chapter. Thus, in reading the translations, one should note how central the negative language really is.

And in Ismene's response, we see the play upon notions of duality versus singleness that will dominate the relationship between these two sisters, and a whole host of other relationships in Thebes:

> To me [*emoi*][48] *no* stories come, Antigone —
> *neither* sweet *nor* sour — save that
> *we two* are bereft of our *two* brothers,
> *both* dead this *single* day, if by a *doubled* hand.
> Since the Argive army is fled this very night
> I know *no* further news —
> *neither* welcome *nor* ill-omened.[49]

And now the crucial parameters of this play — of negation and the theory of an identity-in-pairs that undergirds it — have already been set in verse.

III

This, then, is a play that is fascinated by what it means, linguistically, socially, and existentially, to be a self. Linguistically, the dual voice speaks of a primordial matrix in which self and some single other are not yet completely differentiated. Communally, the *polis*, as least as Creon seeks to understand it, underwrites this same idea. And yet Creon's view, much like the antimodern posture, is significantly overdrawn. For all of our relationality, each of us acts in some measure alone, claiming "responsibility" for our own actions. Nowhere is this point made more dramatically than in the case of civil disobedience — or else in the act of suicide, which is the peculiar Destiny of so many characters in this passion-play.

The theme was to be definitive for Hegel. In point of fact, his two most popular works, *The Phenomenology of Spirit* and *The Philosophy of Right,* might best be read as rigorous analyses of the implications of this theory of negation and its role in the formation of authentic human selves, the definition of authentically *civil* disobedience. The *Phenomenology* explores the existential dimension — and in particular how it is that one fashions one's identity in a (largely negative) encounter with some one other — and the larger Fate of the world. Here, the dialectic of mastery and servility is fundamental. *The Philosophy of Right,* by

---

48. As I introduce other characters into this analysis, it will be seen how each of them begins with a reference to him or her self (*emoi*), only to turn around and define this self in terms of some one other. Here we find a stunning confirmation of the fact that Sophocles really is concerned, among other things, to help us see what it means to be a self.

49. *Antigone,* 11–17.

contrast, becomes fascinated by the question of the *polis*, or more accurately, by the nature of modern bourgeois civil society. Elsewhere, in
his aesthetic lectures, Hegel distinguishes two kinds of classical tragedies: the "horizontal," of which the archetype is *Antigone*, in which the
self comes into conflict with the social and political powers that be; and
the "vertical," of which the *Oedipus* is best representative, and which
explores the individual's conflict with Destiny, the gods, and the will
of the world. This is but another, and more refined, way of making
the same point. The important thing is that these ideas are not original with Hegel. They — and particularly the concentration upon the
concept of negation that drives the dialectic — are already abundantly
clear in Sophocles. Hegel, so it seems to me, is one of the most sensitive
readers Sophocles ever had.

Now, along this path from the dual to the singular, from the city to
the self, each of us is first defined in "other" terms. What is remarkable
here is how frequently the *Antigone*'s characters' first words on stage
make this collective identity explicit. In discussing ourselves, we very
often begin by appealing to others. In defining who we are, we often
begin by saying what we are not. Antigone's first words, as we saw, were
for her sister, who is, in the very strictest sense, her sister-self. So too
with Creon, whose first words seek self-definition in relationship, albeit
a very different kind of relationship. His name vaguely means "Rule,"
and he speaks, not surprisingly, of the city:

> *Gentlemen,* after shaking *the city* with pounding
> waves, *the gods* have calmed our seas again.[50]

In his first words, Creon has appealed to a whole range of relationships and civic attachments — his peers, his city, his gods. After seeking
to rationalize his own assumption of royal power (not surprisingly, according to the ties of kinship that bind him to the house of Oedipus),[51]
Creon goes on to describe the essence of what political identity means
to him. In a word, it means law — his word is *nomos*, not *themis* — and
an obedience that, like his justice, is very nearly blind:

> Impossible [*amēchanon*] to learn from any man
> spiritedness, nor mindfulness, nor wisdom,
> until he proves himself in *ruling* and in *law* [*nomoisin*].
> To me [*emoi*], whoever steers the entire *polis,*
> but fails to grasp the noblest plans,
> and rather holds his tongue confined in fear —
> he seems to me *the basest sort* [*kakistos*] of man.

---

50. Ibid., 162–163.
51. The irony of this appeal is clear, in that Creon is about to deny the validity of
these self-same rights to Antigone. See *Antigone*, 164–174.

> And whosoever loves something other than [*anti*]
> *the fatherland:* him I won't discuss at all.[52]

As we shall see, Creon's own one-sidedness resides precisely in this narrow view of what loyalty and law entail.[53] In the first place, law is a purely negative category; it prescribes limits outside of which the actor may not go, beyond which membership itself may allegedly be denied. It will be left to Antigone to say that membership can *never* be denied, that our obligations to one another transcend even the bad infinity of death. Creon's law entails a host of "thou shalt nots," negations, with no parallel account given of the "thou shalts" that are indispensable and inescapable in any genuinely human society. It is, once again, left to Antigone to articulate this *positive* dimension of the law (as *themis*, not *nomos*).[54] Antigone insists that the law also requires that certain things be done — like burying and mourning for a dead brother, rites that are implicitly owed to *all* the dead. Finally, there is some question of how genuinely "social" this law is, after all. There are times when Creon's own agenda seems to make of the law little more than the arbitrary mandate [*kērygma*] of a single power-hungry man. For Antigone, the law is something else again, and she will, in any case, die defending it.

That is a point that needs to be emphasized: she *dies* in its defense. What is fascinating about this fact is not only that it makes her disobedience genuinely "civil" in the sense we customarily give the term. More important to the rhetoric of the play is the explicit linkage between Antigone's "rights" and the nether gods. There is a distinction between Olympian and chthonian deities that lies at the conceptual heart of this play.[55] It is a duality that is as old as Aeschylus' Prometheus trilogy: the upstart gods, new to power and as jealous of their position as Creon is of his, enchaining the older gods whom they have supplanted — even Prometheus, who has helped them achieve everything they finally do achieve. In the name of new "laws" (*nomoi*), Prometheus says, these gods rule "lawlessly," without *themis*.

Hades functions significantly in a number of Sophoclean plays.

---

52. *Antigone*, 175–183.

53. For other excellent examples of this extremity, see Nietzsche's *The Gay Science*, §43.

54. *Themis* is invoked twice, by the Chorus at ll. 880 and 1259. For a nice discussion of the complex relations between *themis*, *dikē*, and *nomos*, see Steiner, *Antigones*, 247–251, and James Redfield, "Drama and Community: Aristophanes and Some of His Rivals," in *Nothing to Do with Dionysus?* 319–322. So too, Thucydides, who describes the collapse of moral reason in the bloody aftermath of the Corcyrean Excursus in terms that directly recall the *Antigone*: "Family relations were a weaker tie than party membership" (*The Peloponnesian War*, III, 82).

55. See Charles Segal, "Antigone: Death and Love, Hades and Dionysus," in *Tragedy and Civilization*, 152–206, esp. 177–181, 197–201.

Hades, like all the chthonian gods who come from the nether realm, is a symbol of the radical equality of persons whose final destination is ultimately the same. Achilleus is driven to the brink of madness by the thought that death comes to the noble and the base alike. His commitment to an heroic code of noble aristocracy cannot survive the encounter with this cold fact. Sophocles dealt with the subject directly in his *Ajax* — a play that is absolutely indispensable for a proper understanding of the *Antigone*. In the first half of that play, we are shown Ajax's excruciatingly slow movement toward suicide.[56] He has been horribly shamed by the gods. When he set out to murder Agamemnon, Odysseus, and his other enemies, Athena blinded him, drove him mad, such that he butchered a herd of cattle, not his enemies. But then the play breaks off at midpoint with the death of Ajax, and an entirely new issue emerges. Where the first half of the play operated within the strict economy of the heroic shame-culture — the old doctrine of helping friends and harming enemies — the second half suddenly finds a place, and even a vocabulary, for compassion.[57] In it, we are witness to the equally slow and drawn out process whereby Odysseus gradually wins *the right of burial* (more successfully than Antigone!) for his former enemy. It is a brilliant piece of theater. Agamemnon, the dullard spokesman for the doctrine of helping friends and harming enemies, insists that "even in death, *he* is no friend."[58] Odysseus sees things very differently, sees something that Agamemnon cannot see. "I look upon him," says Odysseus, "and I also see my self."[59] He had said this in the opening scene when Athena had invited him to laugh at his vanquished enemy; he underscores the point here. It is also a brilliant rhetorical move — one that we will see again shortly when Haemon squares off against his father. He appeals to the very *selfishness* that animates Agamemnon's universe.[60] Someday, Odysseus warns us, *I* will stand in need of the same service, someone who will see *my* body into the ground. But his deeper insights transcend this and explode this whole way of dividing up the world: "I look upon *him,* and I also see *my self.*" Hades, the great equalizer, symbol of our *common* Destiny, whose gods defend a brand of *universal* justice: *themis.*

We have dwelt at length upon the many implications of Creon's first speech. Let us glance briefly at two other characters' first words before

---

56. See Herbert Golder, "Sophocles' *Ajax:* Beyond the Shadow of Time," *ARION,* n.s., 1:1 (1990) 9–34.
57. See Blundell, *Helping Friends and Harming Enemies,* 60–105, for her analysis of the *Ajax.*
58. *Ajax,* 1348–1361.
59. Ibid., 124–126.
60. Ibid., 1366–1368.

moving on to an analysis of the central conflicts in the play. Haemon's Destiny is also apparent in his name. He is "blood," meant in the sense of blood-ties, of kinship, and when he emerges on stage to speak with his father, who is also the king — in the very first words that leave his lips — the seeds of his own destruction are already sown:

> Father, *I am yours. Your* good judgment
> steering *me* straight, most useful to *me* —
> this shall *I* ever follow.
> *For me* [*emoi*] no marriage-ties can be
> worth more than *your* tender guidance.[61]

It is painfully apparent how exclusive is Haemon's self-definition in relation to the other, a single other, a definitively masculine other. And it is precisely the singleness of this devotion to his father, ruptured now by the love he holds in his heart for his affianced, that will lead him ultimately to suicide. He loves his father, to be sure; but he is not now, nor was he ever, "his."

The case of Teiresias, the blind seer, who comes to warn Creon of his own impiety and impending doom, confirms this last point. And it does so with a particularly stunning poetic image. We must imagine Teiresias, led on stage by the hand of a small boy who serves as sight to him — Teiresias, the aged, the blind prophet of Thebes, whose inner sight and knowledge so far exceeds the one-sidedness of all the other sighted characters in this play:

> *Theban Lords, we two* are come along a *common* [*koinēn*] way,
> *two* men seeing with *a single* eye. Among the blind
> this is the way of *wandering*.[62]

He is a symbol of our common condition. His very dramatic presence speaks of a relationality and genuine interdependence that far exceed that sham society of which all the other characters speak. Antigone can really love only a corpse. Creon, too, respects the city and his son only insofar as they do not cross him, which means so long as they do not have a thought of their own. Haemon is finally too young and inexperienced to know what romantic love is all about; he dies for all the wrong reasons. Teiresias, by subtle contrast, is entirely dependent upon the *polis* for the very stuff of life. And yet without him, the ship of state drifts irresistibly toward the shoals of self-destruction. He is a genuine individual, great-souled but not autonomous. He has understood the Delphic injunction — *mēden agān*, "nothing too much"; and in the images of blindness, wondering, and wandering, he finds compelling symbols for

---

61. *Antigone*, 635–638.
62. Ibid., 988–990.

the essence of how we all live out our days. In recognizing and living within these limits, in contentment to be one needy individual among many others, Teiresias possesses a breadth of vision, a clarity, and a sobriety (*phrēn*) that far exceed that of any other character. He becomes the symbol of what they have lost, or better, that which they have given over in their passionate excesses.

IV

Leaving the province of Destiny and of naming, then, let us return to the first scene, where Ismene and Antigone are speaking still. We are briefly told the story of the past day's events, and then the Chorus punctuates this conversation with its own description of the battle, this time in strophic verse.[63]

Upon Oedipus' banishment from Thebes, rule of the city fell to his two sons, Eteocles and Polyneices, who agree to share rule of the city in alternate years. The year of Eteocles' rule is now at an end, yet he has refused to relinquish the throne.[64] Thus, Polyneices has assembled an enormous Argive force to storm Thebes and wrest control of the city from his brother. The battle is a particularly bloody one and lasts an entire day; as dusk approaches, the Argives are at last repulsed.[65] Polyneices and Eteocles meet at last in single combat before one of the seven Theban gates, and slay each other there. Now, as dawn of the following morning approaches, the city is safe from attack, but, as so many times since Oedipus first erupted upon Thebes, she finds herself without a leader. Creon steps into this unenviable vacuum, taking the tiller of the ship of state. He justifies this seizure of power through claims of kinship (*genos*) with the former rulers. The Theban queen, Jocasta, was, after all, his sister. Strange indeed, that the man whose very authority derives from bonds of kinship and family ties will presently deny these same sacred rights to others, his niece and nephew chief among them. It is a memorable dramatic feature that delighted Hegel:

---

63. Ibid., 100–162.

64. Sophocles does not, and really cannot, make much of the fact that Polyneices' reasons for launching his attack are, at least in the abstract, reasonably just. Here again, Creon's allegiance to the *polis* and to civic virtue — to the exclusion of every other form of loyalty — is excessive. It is not our business to choose between Eteocles and Polyneices in this play, but rather to recognize the virtues of both — something that neither Antigone nor Creon is capable of doing. They both demand that we make a choice. See Else, *The Madness of Antigone*, 18–26, 37, 40–41.

65. Again, Sophocles does not elaborate on this dimension of the myth, but other poets tell us that it needed the sacrifice of Creon's eldest son, Megareus, to turn the tide of the Argive advance. Thus, "saving" this city-self will finally have cost Creon two sons, a niece, a wife, and finally, himself. See Euripides' *Phoenissae*, 930–1018.

They are then both, as individuals, clearly in the power of the very thing they are fighting, and they therefore violate what, by the law of their own existence, they should be honoring. Antigone, for example, lives under the political authority of Creon; she herself is a king's daughter and the betrothed of Haemon, so that she undoubtedly was bound to pay obedience to the sovereign's command. Yet Creon, too, as father and husband, was bound to respect the sacred ties of blood, and not command anything that violated their pious observance. Immanent in each of these figures, therefore, is the very thing against which each rebels, and they are both, for that reason, seized and broken by what pertains essentially to the sphere of their own existence.[66]

These characters consume themselves. And such self-division, alienation really, lies at the very heart of their tragedy.

For Creon's first act of state is to announce an edict (*kērygma*) commanding burial with high honors for Eteocles, as an heroic defender of the *polis*, and denying any burial whatsoever to Polyneices, as a cursed enemy of the state who sought to rain fire down upon the city's hearths and household gods. Impiety shall be met with impiety; Polyneices' alleged crimes against the state will be answered by crimes against nature, his corpse, and the nether gods.

It is news of this edict that Antigone brings to Ismene. Already she has set herself upon a path leading away from the city, decisively outside — out to where her brother lies unburied. She intends to perform these symbolic rites herself, thereby fulfilling her filial obligations and releasing her brother's soul to Hades. It is exactly here that the problem comes into focus. Antigone has impetuously decided upon a rash act — an eminently *male* act, according to the peculiar prejudices of the times — and Ismene rejects it on this basis. She is a woman; her *gender* will not allow it:

IS: You must keep this in mind: we are born
women, and can not wage war with men.
Since, then, we are ruled by our superiors,
we must heed [*akouein*] these commands, and any even worse....
To act beyond measure has no sense in it at all [*ouk echei noun oudena*].

AN: I would not urge you now — not even if later
you gladly wished to help,
Still no.[67]

---

66. Paolucci, *Hegel: On the Arts*, 189.

67. *Antigone*, 61–64, 68–70. I will not be able to explore this dimension of the play, but there is a profound examination of the meaning, subjectivity, and significance of *sanity* here as well. A whole host of characters accuse one another of insanity, that is, of *not* possessing their mind (*nous*), of *not* thinking straight (*orthōs*). This too is a marvelously contemporary issue, highlighted in the works of Goffmann and Foucault among others, who wonder: By whose standards shall we call some persons insane

The problem with Ismene — as Claudius was a problem for Hamlet — is that she, too, is "a little more than kin, and less than kind."[68] No sister of Antigone, we want to believe, could deny the filial obligations imposed upon her by a dead brother; no daughter of Oedipus could so willingly and with such docility accede to the restrictions imposed upon her by a society's definition of gender and its limitations:

IS: You have a hot heart for cold deeds.

AN: I know enough to ease those I ought to please.

IS: If you are able. But you lust for the impossible [all' amēchanōn erāis].

AN: Well then, when my strength fails, I shall give over.

IS: Not proper, to begin an impossible [amēchana] mission.

AN: If you say so, then you are hateful to me,
and you shall go to justice [dikēn], an enemy of the dead.
Now leave me to my folly
to suffer this awful [deinon] deed alone.[69]

The break is complete, from Antigone's perspective, although it is all a little less clear to Ismene. Ismene accuses Antigone of being *anous* — "mad," literally "of no-mind" — but she seems to be implying only that Antigone is rash and headstrong. *Creon* uses this word as a technical accusation, a pernicious judgment of criminal "insanity" that will cost Antigone her life. Be this as it may, for Antigone, the break is final; she will not use the dual voice in relation to her sister again. This special intimacy she now reserves for Polyneices alone. And Ismene has spoken more truly than she knows when she accuses Antigone of "lust-

---

and incarcerate them on the basis of this alleged deviance from some equally suspect social norm? We have all been sensitized to these dimensions of what Foucault calls our "carceral society," given the manner in which Soviet (and other) political dissidents were indefinitely hospitalized on the basis of their alleged mental lapses. To criticize the party, just as to criticize Creon, is to be "mad," almost by definition. For the *only* "objective" reality is the state. That is decidedly *neither* Sophocles' *nor* Hegel's view of the matter.

68. Shakespeare, *Hamlet* I, 2.

69. *Antigone*, 88–96. This last word, *deinon*, is particularly significant. It will appear shortly in the choral "Ode on Man," perhaps the best-known single piece of Greek poetry. It spans an enormous range of connotative meanings, from the most positive to the most starkly negative. To be *deinon legein* is to be "terribly [skilled] in speech." Here it is akin to the French *formidable* and the German *unheimlich*. But *deinon* can also be awe-full in the negative sense. Perhaps the best way to get some sense of the range this word possesses is to reflect on the aphorism that "the *fear* of the Lord is the beginning of wisdom" and then to translate this into a Greek idiom. We should say that the realization that God is *deinon* is the beginning of wisdom. The Chorus itself makes this point explicitly: "The power of destiny is *deinon*" (ll.951–952). And so does Aristotle, who argues that the tragedies concern themselves always with *deina* things, which inspire fear (*phobos*), as well as *oiktra* things, which inspire pity (*eleeos*). See *Poetics*, 1453a.22, 1453b.14–15, and Gerald F. Else, *Aristotle's Poetics: The Argument* (Cambridge, Mass.: Harvard Univ. Press, 1957) 376, 412–413.

ing" (*erāis*) for impossible things.[70] She wants the one man she cannot have — both because he is her brother and because he is a corpse. There is a clear subtext of incestuous passion, well befitting a child of Oedipus, that runs through every scene that follows.

Antigone storms from the stage. The Chorus then sings a mournful dirge reflecting upon the storms of war. At its conclusion, Creon erupts onto the stage, storming in a peculiar frenzy of his own.

After legitimating his own force of rule — and force *is* the heart of the matter — Creon announces the edict concerning the two fallen sons of Oedipus.[71] No sooner has he concluded his *kērygma*, and commanded the Chorus to watch over the corpse, than a messenger comes on stage to inform him that the corpse has already been mysteriously and ritually interred. The messenger (Guard) takes his time in describing first the wide-wandering way that has led him to this moment,[72] and his own ambivalence about being the bearer of such unhappy tidings:

GU: Awful things [*deina*] bring reluctance in their wake.

CR: Won't you speak, and be released at last?

GU: I say it to you. Someone has come and buried
the corpse, just now, strewing thirsty dust upon
his skin, and honoring him with the necessary rites.

CR: What are you saying? There is a man who dared this?

GU: I simply do not know.[73]

We know — what neither Creon nor the Guard yet know — that there is no man who dared do this, but there is a woman who did. It is interesting that the Chorus is first to wonder if this mysterious deed, so

---

70. The erotic language is in itself a fascinating dimension of the play (recall what Aristotle said about the fickleness and passion of youth, at Note 23). As mentioned above, at the midpoint of this tragedy the Chorus sings an "Ode to Eros" (ll. 781–805), whose conclusion is remarkably stirring and pertinent:

> Eros, unconquerable [*anikate*] in battle! . . .
> You it was who twisted just minds [*phrenas*]
> upon the path of injustice.
> You it is now who has sown
> dissension among common kin [*xunaimon*].
> Longing conquers [*nikāi*], armed with
> the fluttering eyelids of the bride's
> beauty, enthroned with power equal to
> unwritten laws [*thesmōn*]. Impossible to fight [*amachos*],
> for the goddess, Aphrodite, is playing. (ll. 791–801)

Thus, she who lusts for impossible (*amēchanon*) things is fighting a battle against impossible (*amachos*) odds.

71. *Antigone*, 192–208.
72. Ibid., 223–236.
73. Ibid., 243–249.

manifestly full of awe (*deinon*), might not have been ordained by the very gods whom *everyone* thus far has invoked in their own defense. At the conclusion of the Guard's report, the first response is not Creon's, but the Chorus's:

> CH: My lord, the thought suggested itself to me [*emoi*] many times
> that this deed might be some god's devising.

> CR: Stop! Before with talking you enrage [*orgēs*] me
> and show yourself reckless [*anous*] as well as old.
> You speak unbearably when you say
> that the gods give this corpse a thought.[74]

Creon quickly puts an end to all such speculation. All too certain of his own opinions (which are, by his definition, "the law"), Creon is convinced that such "thirsty dust" came, not from the gods, but from some anonymous, profit-seeking rebels whose "necks are not yet fitted in the yoke."[75] He will be wrong in every conceivable way. The portrait Creon paints is one of remarkably unstable rule; a single day in power — not even this — and he is already finding plots and intrigue under every rock, potential revolt hovering over a single, war-torn, "enemy" corpse.

V

As the Guard exits, thankful still to be in possession of his life, the Chorus erupts into a strange and mantic poesy of its own. It is not clear at first why they are singing at all. They thought to find the *gods'* handiwork in a mysteriously buried corpse; they now find *human* handiwork in everything:

> Many are the awful [*deinon*][76] things, but nothing
> more full of awe [*deinoteron*] than Man.[77]
> This the race which crosses
> the surging seas in winter
> storms, cutting through waves
> billowing all around.
> The greatest of all gods, Earth —

---

74. Ibid., 278–283.

75. Ibid., 291.

76. Emanuel Viketos, in his "Study of *Deinos* in its Dramatic Context," *Platon* 40 (1988) 79–81, displays how the Chorus's words are intended one way and are taken in another way by the audience. Essentially, they are saying, "How *awful* it is for someone to break the law,..." but we also hear: "How *awesome* are heroes and heroines like Antigone!"

77. I have opted to translate this ode without the use of inclusive language because it seems essential to the careful contrasts that Sophocles is constructing between man and woman that this ode be heard as a statement about the manner of being Man, not Human. I apologize for any insensitivity it may convey to the contemporary ear.

undecaying and laborless — *we* wear her away,
pushing our plows ever forward
year by year [*etos eis etos*],
driving the race [*genei*] of horses.

The race [*phylon*] of nimble-minded birds
he hunts with casting nets,
hunting too the races [*ethnē*] of wild beasts.
And salty succour sown by the sea
he harvests in the net's double folds —
this ever-clever Man [*anēr*]. He rules
the mountain-ranging beasts
with craft and skill [*mēchanāis*].
Both shaggy horses and tireless bulls
he yokes about the neck.

Now speech [*phthegma*] and wind-swift
thought and a passion [*orgas*] for
civic law [*astynomous*] ... we teach ourselves.
We learn to flee
the storming pelts of Heaven.
With a way for everything [*pantaporos*],
he meets no future
without a way [*aporos*].[78] Past Hades only
he cannot find a way.
He even controls disease
impossible [*amēchanōn*] before.

Wisdom and devising [*machanoen*]
with a skill beyond our dreams,
he is at once base [*kakon*] and noble [*esthlon*],
fulfilling the laws [*nomous*] of earth [*chthonos*]
and the justice [*dikan*] of the gods.[79]
High is his city [*hypsipolis*]!
But citiless [*apolis*] is the base man
in his daring [*tolmas*].
May that man never
share my hearth, or thoughts [*phronōn*],
who can act this way.

---

78. This concept of *aporia*, literally "lack of a way," will be extremely important for Plato. While his dialectic takes us down the long, circuitous paths of reason, it leads us to a deadend, past which our reason cannot go. Reason encourages us finally to lose our way. It is, then, by dwelling upon our "lostness" that another way gradually emerges — through dialectics, and through erotics. It is arguable that Sophocles' notion of the *amēchanon* is the tragic counterpart of this same essential Platonic idea.

79. Note that the dichotomy here is precisely what it was for Heraclitus, earthly *nomoi* over against the *Dikē* of heaven.

My mind is split by this demonic sight.
Can I see this and deny [antilogēsō]
it is the child [paid'],[80] Antigone?
O wretched,
born of a wretched father — Oedipus.
What now? Surely not you they bring in chains
for disregarding royal laws [nomois]
and debasing yourself with folly [aphrosunē]?[81]

This ode is a marvel of construction, and well deserving of its reputation as a distilled statement of the humanism that characterized
the Great Age of Pericles. Still, it has its self-consciously darker side.
The deep ambivalence of the portrait that Sophocles has taken such
pains to paint reminds one of Van Gogh — a surging vividness that,
for all of its splendor, borders on the demonic and suggests the la-
tent, barely restrained power of chaos. It is, finally, an ambivalence that
far transcends the rather trite humanistic notions of progress and civic
virtue.[82]

The first images are those of "mechanics," or technē. In point of
fact, each of these technai — sailing the sea, tilling the ground, building
cities — was specifically associated in traditional mythology from Hesiod onward with the Fall of humanity, a decline from the Golden Age
of primal innocence.[83] Nature harnessed to human purposes, animals
snared and yoked to a "higher" human will. While humans are themselves animal, merely one "race" among many others — as the Chorus
says countless times — they are sovereign over all others, boundlessly
creative, cunning, and resourceful. Violence percolates to the skimming
surface of language, the violence that is done to birds and beasts not
only in yoking them, but in the very process of negating them, of insisting that men and women are "a race apart." This Chorus, especially,
plays with the language of negation as it explores the manifold ways in
which all other races become subject to this one. This is all made explicit
when the greatest and most tireless of gods, Earth (Gē) herself, is men-

---

80. I think that the frequent references to Antigone as a child (pais) are designed, as
I indicated earlier at note #23, to make an issue of her extreme youth.

81. Antigone, 332–375.

82. For a helpful reading of the deep ambivalence of this ode and the Sophoclean anthropology in general, see Laszlo Versenyi, Man's Measure (Albany: State Univ. of New
York Press, 1974), 208–215, and Martin Heidegger's An Introduction to Metaphysics,
trans. Ralph Manheim (New Haven: Yale Univ. Press, 1959) 146–165; Oudemans
and Lardinois, Tragic Ambiguity, 118–131, and Benardete, "A Reading of Sophocles'
Antigone: I," 187–196.

83. Robert Coleman, "The Role of the Chorus in Sophocles' Antigone," Proceedings
of the Cambridge Philological Society 198 (1972) 10.

tioned. It was Hesiod who remarked that Earth knows all things because she has suffered all things.[84] Now we see the culprit. It is (a) Man.

Beyond our profound technical skills, humanity is the proud possessor of other precious gifts, speech and wind-swift thought chief among them. As in Akira Kurosawa's films, the wind will always be a divine symbol in this play. It was to a gust of divine wind that the Chorus attributed the original burial of Polyneices. These characteristics speak of the special favors granted to the human caretakers of their primal mother, the Earth. And yet not all things come from gods; civic laws (*nomoi*) and civic passion (*orgē*) itself are things we teach ourselves.[85] Here again a fundamental ambivalence emerges: between the comparative divinity of Man, who is sovereign over all other races upon the earth and who yokes them just as surely as Creon seeks to yoke his city; and the corresponding earth-i-ness of all the vain, that is, mortal, endeavors of these "creatures of a day."[86]

This is the fundamental Sophoclean perspective that makes humanity a problem to itself *and* the gods, awful and awesome by turns. The vision is *tragic*, not a posture. Two ways always: *hupsipolis* and *apolis*, in the city but not of it; *pantaporos* and *aporos*, lost and found; *hāmerion* and *periphradēs*, the ever-clever creatures of a day; *kakon* and *esthlon*, capable of the best and the worst; demonic (*deinon*) in every double-sense. There is a law (*nomos*) that we make for ourselves, of necessity, to order our common life. Like every erotic yoke (which is how Creon describes it), this law is primarily negative, prohibitive, appropriate to the animal nature in us. Yet there is also a divine law (*dikē, themis*) that inheres in Nature itself, to which even Olympians are answerable, and which we ignore at our peril. The gods have set limits to all human

---

84. And has been endlessly violated. The sexual resonance of the language of harnessing and yoking is clearer in Greek. It will be made explicit when Creon remarks that Antigone's death should not be too much for his son to bear—there are, after all, "other fields for his plow" (l. 569). Martha Nussbaum, *The Fragility of Goodness*, 57–58, makes much of this line in her reading of the play, arguing that Creon fails finally to realize the particularity of genuine *erōs*, that no two fields are ever entirely alike. And in any case "plowing" is not the chief point, in love. See also Charles Segal, *Interpreting Greek Tragedy: Myth, Poetry, Text* (Ithaca, N.Y.: Cornell Univ. Press, 1986) 146, 154.

85. There is admittedly a verbal ambiguity here. The verbal form *edidaxato* possesses a range of meanings that are both self-referential and passive. Thus, it could be the case that "Man teaches these things to Himself," or rather that "they all are taught to Man." The former meaning, which allows greater agency to Man as subject, seems warranted to me. For a precisely opposite reading, an *anti*humanist reading, see Martin Heidegger's *Introduction to Metaphysics*, 156–157. For more on Heidegger's antihumanism, see Luc Ferry and Alain Renaut, *Heidegger and Modernity*, trans. Franklin Philip (Chicago: Univ. of Chicago Press, 1990).

86. Prometheus was punished by the gods precisely for taking too great an interest and granting too many favors to his human charges. In his *Prometheus*-play, Aeschylus makes much of this dichotomy between the immortals and the creatures of a day.

endeavor; for all of our craftiness, Hades still sets the parameters, the boundaries past which we have "no way." Thus are we *pantoporos* and *aporos* — infinitely resourceful, yet lost nonetheless. Thus are we *hypsipolis* and *apolis* — governed by the best of all states, always striving for the highest forms of community, yet oddly and fundamentally without a home, without a way past one another or past death. In essence, Sophocles reminds us that "we are capable of anything." We are painfully well aware of this simultaneously marvelous and terrible fact today — we, for whom technology has been both a source of boundless confidence and speculation, yet at the same time a curse that threatens to undo the globe. It is no accident that this ode has been fertile ground for philosophers of technology in every age; and it ends on a telling note of tortured ambiguity.[87]

As the Chorus rightly concludes, Antigone has been led on stage in chains as the very culprit Creon seeks. The Guard, who had just moments ago been accused by Creon himself, is only too eager to tell the tale. After having so shortly expected never to see Creon's face again, "change of mind proves thought a liar."[88] In accord with Creon's orders, the Guard and his fellows returned and uncovered Polyneices' corpse. They then sat guard over it. Around midday, as the grim summer heat made their collective senses dull, a strange windstorm (sent by other gods?) arose and concealed the corpse again. When it subsided at last, Antigone was spied hovering over the corpse, shrieking like some unnatural bird — the very bird, be it noted, that is "netted" by human craft (that is, the *law, Creon's* law). As Antigone initiates her feckless rituals over the corpse again, the guards approach and seize her, taking her at once to Creon.

VI

And now, at this pivotal dramatic moment, comes the first in a series of exchanges that are the chief convention of the Greek theater, the stichomythia. The term means, literally, a "divided story," and that is precisely what it is. As two characters present their alternate view of events, rhetorically and poetically and combatively by turn, the agonistic dimension of this genre becomes most explicit.[89] Greek culture was, in its own way, an obsessively competitive culture. We would do well to remember that, no sooner had the war been temporarily suspended

---

87. See Jean O'Brien's "Sophocles' Ode on Man and Paul's Hymn on Love: A Comparative Study," *Classical Journal* 71 (1976) 138–151.

88. *Antigone*, 389.

89. Josiah Ober and Barry Strauss, "Drama, Political Rhetoric, and the Discourse of Athenian Democracy," in *Nothing to Do with Dionysus?* 259–263.

on the plains of Troy, than the Greeks organized competitive games to occupy their leisure.[90] In any case, every Greek tragedy possesses, often even culminates in, this kind of rivaled exchange:

> The symmetry of the tragic dialogue is perfectly mirrored by the stichomythia, in which the two protagonists address one another in alternating lines. In tragic dialogue, hot words are substituted for cold steel. But whether the violence is physical or verbal, the suspense remains the same. The adversaries match blow for blow, and they seem so evenly matched that it is impossible to predict the outcome of the battle.... Tragedy now assumes its proper function as a verbal extension of physical combat.... The indecisiveness of the first combat spreads quite naturally to the second, which then sows it abroad. The tragic dialogue is a debate without resolution.[91]

The Greeks, long before they made this agonism explicit in their textbooks on rhetorical argument, took special delight in seeing something argued, and argued well. The cult of political oratory and their pervasive litigiousness — both of which Aristophanes parodies so brilliantly — are reflections of the same thing. "The contest [*Wettkampf*] of the Greeks is even evident in the symposia," Nietzsche observed, "in the form of rich spiritual talk."[92]

What is curious about these ritual contests is that they seldom resolve anything, and they seldom, if ever, end.[93] Normally, the stichomythia is simply a forum for characters to shout one another down. Martha Nussbaum has done much to remind us that Plato himself cannot be genuinely understood apart from his own immersion in this tragic tradition.[94] It is precisely here, at the locus of the stichomythia, that the battle lines are drawn between Plato and the poets. Plato, I think, wants to take this privative tragic inheritance — the stichomythia — and to turn it into something positive: the *dialektika*.[95] If the stichomythia is a primarily negative category, in which no resolution can occur — and in

---

90. *Iliad*, XXIII. See Nietzsche's essay, "Homer's Contest," published posthumously in *The Portable Nietzsche*, trans. Walter Kaufmann (New York: Penguin Books, 1954, 1985) 32–39. See also *The Birth of Tragedy*, §12; *Human, All-Too-Human*, §170, and *The Gay Science*, §§80, 86. Finally, see Kells, "Problems of Interpretation in the *Antigone*," 54ff.

91. René Girard, *Violence and the Sacred*, 44–45, also 71, 150–153.

92. Nietzsche, *Wir Philologen*, 5[101]; *Sämtliche Werke*, VIII, 66.

93. There are, of course, exceptions to this. Perhaps most notable is Sophocles' *Ajax*, which we have already discussed, where Agamemnon is finally convinced to permit the burial of Ajax's corpse. It should be noted that it needs Odysseus' — Agamemnon's friend (*philos*) — urgings to convince him of this; the self-same arguments in Teucer's — his enemy's (*echthros*) — mouth move him not at all. See Steiner, *Antigones*, 299–300.

94. Nussbaum, *The Fragility of Goodness*, 122–135.

95. It was Nietzsche's genius to recognize this, although he quite naturally opposed it, arguing that Socrates is the very decadent who has subverted the healthy agonism of the heroic age. See especially his *Twilight of the Idols*, "The Problem of Socrates,"

which tensions are more often than not actually heightened — then Plato (much like Hegel) wishes to "negate this negation" in order to derive some positive value from it: the emerging ideal of dialectical speech.

We are today ill-served by the mystification that the word 'dialectic' has undergone in its Hegelian and Marxist guise. The word derives from a Greek root, *dialegō*, and it simply means "to talk something through," presumably to a (tentative) conclusion. Plato — and the portrait of Socrates that he paints in such flattering colors confirms this — is trying to develop a dialogical model of human being that asserts, with tremendous faith in reason and a more chastened political optimism, that if we engage in dialogue seriously, committed wholly to the process, to our partners, and to the search for truth, then our dialogical exchanges need not end, as does the stichomythia, in tragic dissolution.[96] Optimistic, to be sure, but this does not make it wrong. In point of fact, it is one Hegel's chief insights into the tragic genre that polarities such as optimism and pessimism ill-serve our understanding, as we shall see in detail in the next chapter. Greek tragedy — like Hegel's dialectic — is as optimistic as it is pessimistic, which is to say that it is neither. It points toward a reconciliation with reality without necessarily, or finally, achieving it. The tragic vision, as opposed to our modern posture, believes in the possibility — not the inevitability — of redemption, come what may.

This dialectical vision is, in any case, hopelessly violated by the play. As Antigone and Creon begin, it is painfully apparent that they are not interested in agreeing. They know only that they hate one another, that they must come into irredeemable conflict. They live in entirely separate worlds and possess not a single interest in common.[97] Their debate and disagreement begins, as we saw in the last chapter, with a "point of law":

---

§§5–8, although the thesis appears already in his *Birth of Tragedy* and *Wir Philologen*, 6[13].

96. Again, these insights are remarkably contemporary. Heir to these ideas, by way of Hegel, Marx, and the Frankfurt school, is Jürgen Habermas, whose "ideal speech situation" is a profound elaboration of this Platonic idea. And it is precisely this idealism that inclines critics, from Nietzsche to Foucault, to take the position to task, with the reasoning that conversation is not about the search for truth, but solely about domination and power. Says Foucault: "Here I believe one's point of reference should not be to the great model of language and signs, but to that of war and battle. The history which bears and determines us has the form of a war rather than that of a language: relations of power, not relations of meaning.... 'Dialectic' is a way of evading the always open and hazardous reality of conflict by reducing it to a Hegelian skeleton, and 'Semiology' is a way of avoiding its violent, bloody, and lethal character by reducing it to the calm Platonic form of language and dialogue" (Paul Rabinow, ed., *The Foucault Reader* [New York: Pantheon Books, 1984] 56–57).

97. See Vincent J. Rosavitch, "The Two Worlds of *Antigone*," *Illinois Classical Journal* 4 (1976) 16–26.

CR: Did you know these things were forbidden?

AN: How could I help but know? It was clear.

CR: Yet you dared overstep the laws [*nomous*]?

AN: For me [*moi*] it was not Zeus who commanded [*kēruxas*] this
nor Justice [*Dikē*] which resides among the nether gods
and orders all the laws [*nomous*] among the people.
Nor do I consider your commands [*kērugmath'*] to be
so binding as the unwritten and changeless laws [*nomima*]
of gods — nor you, mere mortal [*thnēton*], able to throw them over.[98]
Not for now, nor yesterday, but for-ever,
no one knows from whence they came — only that they are.[99]

Antigone and Creon cannot converse because they mean to talk about different kinds of laws. "Time does not answer or bandy words with eternity":

> No meaningful communication takes place. Creon's questions and An-
> tigone's answers are so inward to the two speakers, so absolute to their
> respective semantic codes and visions of reality, that there is no exchange.
> Where, in essence, does the chasm lie? Creon's idiom is that of tempo-
> rality. Like no other speaker previous, perhaps, to the Fourth Gospel,
> Antigone speaks or, rather, endeavors to speak, out of eternity.... It is
> in this very sense that the unwritten laws of loving care which Antigone
> cites, and which she places under the two-fold aegis of Olympian Zeus
> and chthonian *Dikē*, are "natural laws." They embody an imperative of
> humaneness which men and women share before they enter into the mu-
> tations, the transitory illusions, the divisive experiments, of a historical
> and political system. Creon does not and cannot answer.[100]

Thus it is that, while they speak at great length to one another, they fail to converse at all. The stichomythia remains what it seems to have been from the beginning — a shouting match that emphasizes nothing so much as the infinite distance between and the penultimate triumph of political power. It is part of Sophocles' genius, in this play and others, to convert the stichomythia into something else. He does it in the *Ajax* and the *Philoctetes,* almost as if he were himself questioning the common

---

98. The word-choice here returns us to the choral "Ode on Man." For 'mortal' (*thnētos*) stems from the same root as 'death' (*thanatos*), and Hades, we will recall, is the final boundary that no one can outrun. Thus, Creon too is *deinon*, particularly when he tries to hide this fact from himself.

99. *Antigone,* 447–457. See Charles Segal, *Interpreting Greek Tragedy,* 140, for an excellent presentation of the ambiguity in the very language Creon and Antigone use: where Creon talks about *kērygmata*, which are his own very personal ideas, Antigone speaks of *nomima*, the eternal laws of gods. And while both appeal to justice, *dikē*, they mean entirely different things by it.

100. Steiner, *Antigones,* 247–248, 251.

wisdom that a tragic dialogue — like tragedy itself — must be a "debate without resolution."

VII

I want to propose that this play is, in fact, best understood if it is read primarily in the light of its three extended stichomythic exchanges. This is said by way of side-stepping an enormous and complex question about the origins of Attic drama. The general consensus has been that Greek tragedy emerged out of some sort of poorly documented rural festivals in which choruses sang and danced in carefully choreographed performances. When one character detached from the group — and was called the "protagonist," so the thesis runs — a dialogue (rather than a song) became possible between him and the choral group. In this way, staged drama, as we understand the term, was born. By the time Aeschylus appears, two actors with speaking parts are tolerated on the stage simultaneously. With them, stichomythia becomes a dramatic possibility. Sophocles, among his many other dramatic innovations, added a third speaking part. What is significant for my purposes is that in the great age of classical Athenian drama, tragedy is a highly structured interplay of choral ode and stichomythic exchange. Of the two, it is the stichomythia that is new. Its novelty is part of what is most central (and Sophoclean) about it.

In saying this, I am disagreeing with those — most notably Martha Nussbaum — who want to attend first and foremost to certain of this play's choral odes.[101] These odes do certainly all set a tone — and it was that *tone* that I attempted to trace out in the "Ode on Man." Its ambivalence will be important for understanding the overall dramatic movement of the play. Nonetheless, by concentrating exclusively on the Chorus, it seems to me that we may well lose sight of the care with which Sophocles has crafted his stichomythia. In the choruses, we tend to get a one-sided and harmonious reading of events. Everyone in the Chorus is in general, if simplistic, agreement. We never really see a Chorus divided against itself — except on matters of factual interpretation of what has transpired off stage. In the stichomythia, by contrast, Greek drama sets pairs of opposites over against one another. In addition to emphasizing the real depth of the conflict, Sophocles also seems to point to the possibility — slim though it seems at times — that such deep divisions may in fact be mediated. It is precisely this aspect of the

---

101. Nussbaum, *The Fragility of Goodness*, 52. There is a long tradition of doing so. See also Robert Coleman, "The Role of the Chorus in Sophocles' *Antigone*," 4–27, as well as R. W. B. Burton, *The Chorus in Sophocles' Tragedies* (Oxford: Oxford Univ. Press, 1980) 85–137.

play — which has not been discussed in most contemporary readings, which remain at the level of a "Creon versus Antigone" interpretation of the dramatic action — that fascinated Hegel and sharpened his own philosophical instincts. It is what makes the play something more than pessimistic, something other than a simple wallowing in the inevitability of an unhappy end.

In this play, every stichomythic exchange orbits around Creon, that dense immovable mass, who is the dramatic centerpiece and the king. Creon the tyrant, Creon the king, Creon who, as such, is the sole authority in this play — he speaks first with Antigone, then with Haemon, then finally with Teiresias, descending ever deeper into himself, ever farther removed from any even nominally "civil" society and any genuine willingness to listen. It is nothing short of fantastic that, in these short, rapid-fire exchanges, Sophocles shows us how one thing generates its opposition, how the polarities and negations with which we began are potentially resolved or dissolved in human discourse. Man and woman, young and old, law and conscience — all meet in the dialogical space that the poet has created. It remains to his son to explain why *Creon's* words must fail, why, ultimately, stichomythia cannot become dialectics under Creon's rule: "You wish to speak [*legein*] and, speaking, not to listen [*kluein*]."[102] If this is Creon's condition, it is hardly his alone. He is no more, and no less, one-sided than his niece. If he is totally political, then she is totally filial. Moreover, she is *erotically* filial, in the most damnably Oedipean way imaginable.

Between Creon and Antigone — it is Sophocles' first truly stichomythic exchange in the play — the fundamental issue concerns the nature and extent of the law, whether human or divine. When the divine law erupts into the all-too-human world, then "everything stands on its head."[103] We are told in Hebrew scripture that God does not judge as humanity judges — while we gaze upon the stature, God gazes upon the heart.[104] Antigone's point is relevant: if human virtues divide the world into enemies and friends, the nether gods do not see things quite so simply:

CR: Are you unashamed, to think this way alone?

AN: No shame at all, to honor common kin.

---

102. *Antigone,* 757. While he uses different words, Heraclitus expressed basically the same insight: "Not knowing how to listen [*akousai*], neither can they speak [*eipein*]" (Fragment #17 [D-19]).

103. *Antigone,* 1165. This image plays a central role in Hegel's philosophy, for he asserts that natural consciousness must be taught to stand on its head, that this "inverted world" is where things really start to get interesting. We must lose our bearings, it would seem, in order to see our world, really, as if for the first time.

104. *1 Samuel* 16:7.

CR: Did he not have the self-same blood [*homaimos*]
    who stood opposite this corpse?

AN: Self-same blood, from one mother and a common father.

CR: How can you honor Honor [*charin*], when you dishonor *him?*

AN: A dead corpse does not see things this way.

CR: He will if you honor irreverence more than him.

AN: Not some slave, but a *brother,* who is dead.

CR: Died ravaging this land. But *he* opposed it.

AN: All the same, Hades longs for equality of laws [*nomous*].

CR: Surely not that the noble share a destiny with the base!

AN: Who knows how these things look, below?

CR: The enemy, even in death, is not a friend!

AN: Not born for hatred, I was born for love.[105]

The rhetorical question with which Creon begins bears directly on the whole question of insanity that every character brings to his or her defense. For Creon, to fail to think as the majority does is already to be clinically insane. It is to break with the story, the *mythos*, which alone lends coherence and meaning to one's world. For Antigone, like Achilleus before her, the larger question remains unaddressed: What *kind* of coherence? What price coherence? If this argument can only rarely be resolved at all, how much slimmer are the hopes that it will be resolved in Creon's city. Antigone is led off summarily in chains, death her only Destiny now — the equality of the laws below. The misogynist in Creon has failed to listen, and failed to learn. Were he a little slower to equate compassion and generosity with femininity and weakness, he might have seen that there is something essentially *right* about what Antigone is saying. While he does indeed have a city to govern, by law, *themis* is hardly irrelevant to his royal tasks. *Themis* is, as Antigone rightly points out, the very lifeblood of the *polis*. Men and women, in this passage, and the respective laws for which they stand, never really meet, as meet they eventually must.[106]

It is at this point, after the departure of Oedipus' two children, that another child enters the stage, Haemon, Creon's own. Here again there is a dialogue (*stichomythia* is what Haemon later calls it) moving in a single direction — Creon's monologue, really, conducted in the cowed presence of others. Haemon's profession of dutiful loyalty — "Father,

---

105. *Antigone,* 510–523. See Blundell, *Helping Friends and Harming Enemies,* 106–107.

106. I take this to be part of the significance of the Chorus's invocation of Dionysus in the last ode of the play (ll. 1115–1152). He is, after all, the only emphatically androgynous god in the entire Greek pantheon.

I am yours!" — inspires Creon to a brief lecture on the nature of true virtue:

> There is no evil worse than anarchy [*anarchias*]!
> Anarchy destroys cities.
> Anarchy makes homes desolate.
> Anarchy, too, turns the spear to rout.
> It is obedience [*peitharchia*] which saves
> the very lives of those who are thinking straight.[107]

On the surface, Haemon seems to agree, but through a brilliant rhetorical move, similar to the one we saw in the *Ajax,* he manages to introduce a new perspective — that of mutuality — into what is, on the surface, the same idea. In rejecting it, Creon rejects his son, his city, and his own better judgment, thus meeting Antigone at last in self-destruction:

> For me [*emoi*] the fact that you are doing well, father,
> is greater richness than anything else could be.
> What trinkets could be more valuable to children
> than a father's flourishing —
> or still more a *child's* flourishing, for a *father?*[108]

Here is the mutuality demanded of the dialectic, violated and finally done to death by Antigone and Creon alike. If obedience commands concern from a son for a father, then surely fairness and piety — the equality of *themis* that Antigone invoked before she was so summarily silenced — command the converse. Haemon's warning words are genuine: the city is, at best, ambivalent about the decree concerning Antigone; at worst, civic unrest glows now like the hot embers that still smolder by the war-torn city gates. In this second stichomythic exchange, the polarities of age and youth, femininity and masculinity, civic order and civic excess, circle one another but fail to touch:

CR: Shall we who are so old learn mindfulness [*phronein*]
     from the nature of one so young?

HA: Not at all unjustly. While I am young,
     you should not look at my years more than my deeds.

CR: Your "deed" is the honoring of disorder.

HA: I would never recommend honor to the base [*kakous*].

CR: Is *she* not suffering from this very illness?

HA: Thebes, your city-self [*homoptolis*], does not say so.

CR: Shall the *polis* teach me how to rule?

---

107. *Antigone,* 672–676.
108. Ibid., 701–704.

HA: See how you have spoken? How like a child!

CR: Shall I rule this land for an other than myself?

HA: The *polis* is not a single man's possession.

CR: Is the *polis* not under a single ruler's law [*nomizetai*]?

HA: You would rule a desert well — *alone.*

CR: He, so it seems, allies himself with Woman.

HA: If you are a woman. I take thought for you.[109]

Again, the outcome might be different were Creon a little less of a misogynist and were Thebes a little less a war-torn desert-city. We are not in classical Athens — that much is clear — but in Homeric Thebes, moreover a Thebes besieged. Creon's one-sidedness prevents the expression of a mature civic consciousness. Everyone has a place and a role, and the boundaries that Creon has taken such care to draw — between young and old, man and woman, good and evil, order and chaos — have hardened into barriers that prevent any genuine movement at all. It was Antigone who recognized that "equality of law" demands that we never draw such lines so sharply, if ever we draw them at all.

And so Haemon storms offstage — trapped in his Destiny, just as surely as his name — leaving his father to consign his bride to her Destiny. Alone, unmarried, affianced solely now to her dead brother, their consummate embrace to be presided over by the nether gods, Antigone is entombed, or perhaps en-wombed, in a desolate cave that will be birthplace, marriage bed, and final resting place for her.[110] At this point Teiresias is led to the palace gates, by the hand of his younger, second-self, with words of dire warning for the new-old king. At the outset, Creon seems inclined to listen; at last, it looks as if stichomythia may yet be transformed into dialectics, the tragedy eluded at the last:

TE: I will teach, and you obey [*pithou*] the prophet.

CR: May I never veer from the straightness of your mind [*phrenos*]!

TE: That is how you steer the city straight [*orthēs*].

CR: I am convinced, am witness to your profit.

TE: Know, then, that you are walking Fortune's razor.[111]

---

109. Ibid., 726–741.
110. As we saw at note #35, Antigone speaks of herself (850–852) as a liminal figure, caught between the living and the dead. While she is leaving the sight of the very world she has long since forsaken, in a strange erotic commitment to her dead brother, she still lives and breathes and suffers. She has become what Bossuet saw in the rotting corpse: "cet objet qui n'a de nom pas dans aucune langue" (René Girard, *Violence and the Sacred,* 256). As for Antigone and what is happening to her, the words have failed us too, as though she has already become a corpse.
111. *Antigone,* 992–996.

If indeed Creon is inclined to listen to this man, then he hears only what he wants to hear. Convinced that the gods would not dare oppose his cause — *his* sense of what justice and piety entail — Creon believes that any opposing prophecy cannot be founded upon anything more than the crassest kind of self-interest. Profits, not prophecy.[112] If it is not that, then it is something even worse — the sort of civic insanity he has worried about before:

CR: I do not wish to speak against [antieipein] a prophet.
TE: You already did, when you said I divine lies.
CR: All prophets are a race of money-lovers.
TE: And the race of kings, lovers of dirty money.
CR: You realize you are speaking to a king?
TE: I know. I it was who saved the city you now rule.
CR: You are a wise prophet, but a lover of injustice.
TE: You move me from motionlessness to speak against my mind [phrenōn].
CR: Move then, only do not speak for profit.
TE: Do I seem concerned with money, or with you?
CR: You no longer seem such a treasure, to my mind [phrena].
TE: Know well and sure that the sun
will not trace many circles more before
you yourself, on account of your own passion,
will trade [antidous] corpses of your own for this one,
in place of [anti] those you hurled above and below.
You send one living soul dishonored into burial,
and you keep a corpse alight, against the gods,
against destiny, without rites, without right.[113]

After all that he has said about the necessity of the young learning from the old, Creon should have been the first to heed the prophet. It is by now an all-too-familiar pattern. We have been shown the avenue toward genuine mediation only to have it promptly closed off to us, and to them. Now, alienating to the last, Creon has drawn the curtain down upon his own strange civic play. Little left for him to do, but a great deal left to learn:

My heart scarcely knows what it is to do.
I cannot wage war on Necessity [Anangkē] any more.[114]

---

112. For more on this image of Teiresias as profiteer, and the classical ambivalence about mercantile values, see Jean-Christophe Agnew, *Worlds Apart: The Market and the Theater in Anglo-American Thought, 1550–1750* (Cambridge: Cambridge Univ. Press, 1986) 18–27.
113. *Antigone*, 1053–1071.
114. Ibid., 1105–1106.

The play ends in a predictable, which is to say necessary, "domino-chain of death."[115] In this regard, it feels a little more like Shakespeare in his middle period, with the relentless dénouement-in-destruction (how many die, for instance, at the end of *Hamlet* or *Macbeth?*). Antigone has been led off to living death. Yet she rules in Hades in a way that Creon cannot begin to understand. She, a young girl, knows far more than he about the equality of Destiny, equality before the law.

Too late, Creon relents and orders her released from her entombment. It is a critical dramatic moment that is overlooked far too often. For Sophocles is very carefully and deliberately restoring Creon at least partially to our favor, as he must do if he is to equalize the moral forces in this play. If Antigone enjoys an heroic stature at the outset, she is ruthlessly cut down to size by Sophocles' honest portrayal of her excessive and strangely erotic character. At this same moment, Creon is finally on the rise. Surely he has been bombastic in the past. No longer. And in this chiliastic movement, the two meet on an equal footing at the end, in figurative and literal death.[116] This moment is crucial to Sophocles' purposes in the play, as it is to Hegel's reading of it.

In any case, it is still too late. Relenting and release only reveal another corpse. She has already hung herself.[117] In a frenzy, Haemon responds in kind, thrusting first at his father and then killing himself at her feet.[118] Upon hearing the news of this fresh calamity, Eurydice (Creon's wife, but more importantly, Haemon's mother), like the city itself, can bear no more of this living death and opts to be more honest, choosing to make the death that now haunts her city a little more explicit. She, too, dies by her own hand.[119]

In this setting, which anticipates the awful grandeur of *Richard II* or *King Lear,* as I indicated in the epigraph to this chapter, Sophocles leaves us with the parting image of suffering — Creon's, not Antigone's — in the guise of a broken, embodied, and eminently human king.[120]

---

115. Else, *The Madness of Antigone,* 70.

116. James C. Hogan, "The Protagonists of the *Antigone*," *Arethusa* 5 (1972) 93–100, esp. 97. See also Else, *The Madness of Antigone,* 48–49.

117. Nicole Laroux, in her *Tragic Ways of Killing a Woman,* 15, 32–33, points out that the tragedies tend to reserve death by hanging for newly married brides (*nymphai*), while a suicide that sheds blood is associated with virginity (*parthenia*). Thus, there is an additional irony here: even in death, Antigone is blurring the conventional categories, taking upon herself a death and a Destiny that, technically, she should not have.

118. Else, *The Madness of Antigone,* 57–58.

119. Ibid., 52.

120. To my mind, one of the most effective renditions of "the tone" of this play's end is Shakespeare's:

> No matter where. Of comfort no man speak.
> Let's talk of graves, of worms, and epitaphs;
> Make dust our paper, and with rainy eyes

Time, and the course of his own cruel curses, have broken him. Dialectic dies; there is no one left to talk to. And yet it is precisely here, in calamity, in the sheer brutality of being broken, that Creon has at last found his true voice. All mention of gods, of passions, of personal vendettas — even of Fate itself — has disappeared from what has until now been pretentious and self-important talk. In the sheer purity of his negation, hints of a positive self begin to be visible:

> Oh me, me [omoi moi]! No other mortal is yoked
> to these crimes as their cause — only me [emās].
> For I [egō] did this to you. I [egō] did.
> Heedless.
> I [egō] did, I say it clear. Alas, servants,
> lead me away, quickly,
> take me away on foot —
> I who now am nothing more than nothing
> [ton ouk onta māllon ē mēdena].[121]

While we may despair, and rightly so, of ever adequately defining what constitutes a "tragedy," there are things that tragedy surely cannot be. It is not simply about suffering, which is spectacle or *pathos*, nor is it simply a depiction of the radical absence of closure in human matters, which is *farce*. Rather, pathos and farce are converted into tragedy when they are read in the light of deeper meaning, in the light of values that are "absolute," and the conviction that we all still inhabit a common universe of such values.[122] Tragedy needs *themis* and the gods; it is a *religious* undertaking. The gospel of Mark and the *Antigone* qualify as tragedy; *Godot* does not.[123]

> Write sorrow on the bosom of the earth....
> Throw away respect,
> Tradition, form, and ceremonious duty;
> For you have but mistook me all this while.
> I live with bread, like you; feel want,
> Taste grief, need friends. Subjected thus,
> How can you say to me I am a king?
>
> (*Richard II*, III, 2).

121. *Antigone*, 1317–1325.
122. Steiner, *The Death of Tragedy*, 353, and *Antigones*, 302–304. His point in these passages is close to Nietzsche's in *Wir Philologen*: "Is tragedy possible for us, who no longer believe in a metaphysical world?" (5[163]).
123. Becket himself seems painfully aware of this. The chief point of his theater is that modern concepts of humanity lack the very stature that they would need to make genuine tragedy possible. There is no such thing as tragic stature; we are pathetic today, if we are anything, not tragic. Tragic drama thus has something illegitimate and dishonest about it. Becket's drama seems to me to have embodied, however eloquently, nothing so well as the tragic posture. His genius derives from the fact that he knew this, presenting his plays as a problem, not a triumph.

VIII

To appreciate something of the awful grandeur and strange seriousness
of Greek tragedy — even on a first reading, and even in translation —
would be difficult indeed apart from one very obvious point. All of
these plays — the *Antigone* in particular hinges on this — appeal to
something very like a constant human nature and a naturally credible
human "law." This is one area in which the Greeks' tragic vision diverges sharply from the modern posture. Many go so far as to claim
that the overcoming of this very sentimentality and naïveté is precisely
what constitutes the "modernness" of our own age. We do not believe
such fables any more. And yet it was this common (*koinon, xunon*) dimension to the experience of being human that alone — at least for the
Greeks of the Archaic and classical period — could account for our astonishing ability to talk with one another across the barriers of culture
and of language, across the semipermeable membrane of time.[124]

The contemporary academic posture, as I say, denies all this in emphatic terms. We have seen fit — here is where MacIntyre is most
representative and significant — to emphasize our *differences* as social
creatures and to concentrate upon the manifold cultural boundaries that
serve to keep us apart. Our world needs to be made smaller, more man-
ageable, not larger. Naturally, there is much to commend this view to us,
and I do not mean to be naïve. Still, like so many other things that pass
for orthodoxy in the academy, the view is overdrawn. Taken to its logical extreme, such a perspective makes nonsense of the very texts it tries
to read. And it is a pernicious myth. For, as even Aristotle knew well,
any such barrier is a violent thing, no matter how well intentioned, and
will eventually lead to "division." The root metaphor is always military.

Even language itself is part of the problem, on this view, more of
a hindrance than a help in our attempts to communicate with one another. Language, said Nietzsche, is a prison-house — a view that we shall
have opportunity to discuss in some detail in the third chapter of this
book. Concentrating upon this Nietzschean image (to the exclusion of
Heidegger's objection that language is also our "home"), most moderns
view language itself as the brickmason that lays down walls between us,
that lays its heavy hand upon any and every attempt to perceive reality
unmediated and whole.[125]

Here, the experience of Greek drama seems to me to prove the modernist false. For if translation is an art that is never completed, it is by

124. Stanley Rosen, "A Modest Proposal to Rethink Enlightenment," in *The Ancients
and the Moderns: Rethinking Modernity* (New Haven: Yale Univ. Press, 1989) 1–21.

125. See Hans-Georg Gadamer, *Hegel's Dialectic: Five Hermeneutical Studies,* trans.
P. Christopher Smith (New Haven: Yale Univ. Press, 1971) 115–116.

no means "impossible."[126] It is a task that our differences make difficult and never-ending; it is a task that our identity renders both necessary and acutely meaningful. This is one of the points at which Hegel seems most "classical" and Nietzsche most "modern." Building upon Sophocles, Hegel is so bold as to claim in his *Phenomenology of Spirit* that he has pretty well laid out for us, in broad strokes to be sure, most all of the paradigms with which human consciousness responds to its world. Now it is surely one thing to claim this, to claim that there is some meaningful similarity in a variety of human responses to the world, and that this similarity is in its turn grounded in a human "nature" or "consciousness" which we all share. It will be another thing to make good this rather idealistic claim, as Hegel attempts to do in the *Phenomenology*.

We will not undertake a validation of Hegel's claims here, yet we should probably pause at least long enough to point out what they were. In so doing, we will be better equipped to discuss the nuances of Hegel's tragic vision in the next chapter. In the first place, it needs to be recognized that Hegel's *Phenomenology* attempts to trace out, not one genealogy, but two. Hegel attempts to trace out a phenomenology of human consciousness, articulating the manner in which each of us develops to the point of self-awareness, a sense of ourselves as the other might see us. Yet this is only half the story that Hegel seeks to tell, and the lesser half at that. The second, much more difficult, half of the *Phenomenology* is a phenomenology of spirit, *Geist,* the dawning self-consciousness of

> an individual who is also a world. At a certain stage along the way, the particular consciousness not only *has* reason, it has itself *become* reason — it is Hegel himself who established this distinction between having and doing.[127]

Both halves are of the essence, yet it is only the first half that concerns me in this book. Only the first half appeals directly to what Hegel learned from this play; in the second half of the *Phenomenology,* Hegel attempts to move beyond anything that Sophocles could, or would, have said. In fact, this second level of abstraction — Hegel's curious vision of "an individual which is a world" — presents enormous problems, particularly for his moral and political thought, as we shall see more clearly in the next chapter.

---

126. This is one of the themes of George Steiner's *After Babel: Aspects of Language and Translation* (New York: Oxford Univ. Press, 1975). For a remarkable discussion of this same idea, by a translator who is also a poet, see W. H. Auden's introduction to Rae Dalven's translation of *The Complete Poems of Cavafy* (New York: Harcourt Brace Jovanovich, 1959, 1974) vii–xv.

127. Jean Hyppolite, "L'Etat du Droit," *Hegel-Studien, Beiheft* 4 (1966) 181.

All that needs to be demonstrated here is how critical the concept of negation — of separation, annulment, and mediation — is for Hegel's understanding of the manner whereby consciousness emerges. There are four "moments of the whole," says Hegel, "consciousness, self-consciousness, reason, and spirit."[128] As I have said, only the first three concern us here, and only the first three may be derived from Sophocles. In this evolution of consciousness from the naïve simplicity of sense-certainty to the complexity of self-consciousness, three *negations* are essential.[129]

In the first, which Hegel lays out in the opening paragraphs of the *Phenomenology*, consciousness posits itself over against the world. The subject-object dichotomy is itself grounded in a negation. I am *not* that. I am "here," over against a world that is "out there." Only then does consciousness emerge:

> In sense-experience pure being at once breaks up into the two "thises,"
> as we have called them, one this an *I*, and one an *object*. When *we* reflect
> on this distinction, it is seen that neither the one nor the other is merely
> immediate, merely *is* in sense certainty, but is at the same time *mediated*:
> I have the certainty through the other, viz. through the actual fact.[130]

As consciousness reflects upon the status of these various "thises," the "I" becomes more and more of a problem to itself. It may no longer be taken for granted. The true self is born by standing outside of *and over against* itself. In this second negation, we find the emergence of *self*-consciousness:

> Consciousness is *for itself* and on its own account, it is a *distin-*
> *guishing of the undistinguished*, it is *Self-Consciousness. I distinguish*
> *myself from myself;* ... I, the selfsame being, thrust myself away from
> myself.... Consciousness of an other, of an object in general, is indeed
> itself necessarily self-consciousness, reflectedness into self, consciousness
> of self in its otherness. The necessary advance from the previous attitudes
> of consciousness ... brings to light this very fact that not merely is con-
> sciousness of a thing only possible for a self-consciousness, but that this
> self-consciousness alone is the truth of this attitude.[131]

Self against the world, self divided against itself. Now the ground has been laid for the third negation (and for Hegel this is the really defin-itive experience of negation), which occurs when the conscious self is confronted by "some conscious other" that is undeniably *the same as*

---

128. *The Phenomenology of Spirit*, §679; Baillie translation, 689; *Werke*, III, 498.
129. Stanley Rosen, "*Sōphrosunē* and *Selbstbewusstsein*," in *The Ancients and the Moderns*, 83–106.
130. *The Phenomenology of Spirit*, §92; Baillie, 150; *Werke*, III, 83.
131. *The Phenomenology of Spirit*, §164; Baillie, 211–212; *Werke*, III, 134–135.

it is. In the negation afforded by some conscious other, the realm of reason first becomes accessible. Hegel's is a philosophy grounded in the experience of stichomythia:

> A self-consciousness has before it a self-consciousness. Only so and only then *is* it self-consciousness in actual fact; here for the first time it comes to have the unity of itself in its otherness. . . . When a self-consciousness is the object, the object is just as much ego as object. With this we already have before us the notion of *Geist*.[132]

Now this last negation, whereby the self slams up against the boundaries imposed upon it by another equally conscious self — Eteocles and Polyneices, Antigone and Creon — represents the experiential crisis known as the dialectic of mastery and servility. For now, I simply want to observe how potent the imagery of the *Antigone* has been in clarifying Hegel's thought. Not only is Hegel a sensitive reader of Sophocles; Sophocles sharpened his own philosophical instincts. This is the assumption that underwrites the next chapter. For this latter negation is precisely what was at stake between Eteocles and Polyneices when they fought to the death, and it is also what animates the spiritual warfare in which Creon and Antigone find themselves engaged. Now, Hegel is after something very elusive and profound. A confrontation of this kind must initially take the form of a battle. Upon first meeting an other, a life-and-death struggle for self-constitution takes place, even if we are not always aware of it.[133] War and negation — both essential aspects of the tragic stichomythia — are the most primordial reality. And yet — here is the turnabout — such conflicts are *constitutive* of the self. In the absence of others, we ourselves will never fully realize ourselves. In point of fact, it is only when I open myself to the presence of other people, when I in fact hand over my life to a him or a her, that I begin to understand the things I most need to know: *der Begriff des Geistes,* "the notion of Mind, or Spirit."[134] Mutuality is an ideal so severe and demanding that we can scarcely bear it. We must lose life to find it. Suffering teaches. Only now does it become clear that "the Ego is a 'we,' a plurality of Egos, a 'we' that is also a single Ego. Consciousness discovers in self-consciousness its real turning point."

These are audacious claims, and the *Phenomenology* is nothing if not an audacious presentation of experiences that Hegel claims to be universally "ours." At this stage, I hope only to have sketched in broad strokes where these claims come from, and especially how essential the *Antigone* was for Hegel in formulating them. But Hegel's claims are finally no

---

132. *The Phenomenology of Spirit,* §177; Baillie, 226–227; *Werke,* III, 144–145.
133. *The Phenomenology of Spirit,* §187; Baillie, 232–233; *Werke,* III, 148–149.
134. *The Phenomenology of Spirit,* §177; Baillie, 227; *Werke,* III, 145.

more audacious, and pretty surely less so, than the claim — which as far
as I can tell *is* the "modern," the postured, claim — that we share nothing in common, neither human "nature" nor *thematic* justice.[135] What
Hegel discovered in his own formative encounter with Sophocles' *Antigone*, in 1795 and 1796, animated a lifetime of profound thinking.
The play itself provides a vital clue to what will be the mainstay of his
mature method: this universal experience of negation, and the *thematic*
justice that it first brings to consciousness.

What I want to argue is simply this: if we want to come to terms with
any thinker of real substance, we need first to get the questions right.
This is the old issue of *beginnings and endings*. If we want to end well,
then we need to begin properly — in order to avoid asking questions the
text is not designed to answer. "The beginning," says an ancient Greek
proverb, "is half of everything." This will be another dividend to take
with us gratefully from Sophocles: not just a way of thinking about the
world — a distinctive tragic vision, very different in its way from the
modern posture — but also an eloquent introduction to some of Hegel's
deepest questions. If we do not do this, then we are like Creon. "We
wish to speak, but speaking, not to listen."

In listening carefully and at length to what Sophocles has to say,
perhaps now we are better equipped to speak of Hegel's tragic vision.

---

135. Says Alasdair MacIntyre: "There are no such [natural human] rights, and belief
in them is one with belief in witches and in unicorns" (*After Virtue*, 69).

Chapter 2

HEGEL'S TRAGIC VISION
Athens and Jerusalem

Anyhow you had to perish Hamlet you were not for life
you believed in crystal notions not in human clay
always twitching as if asleep you hunted chimeras
wolfishly you crunched the air only to vomit
you knew no human thing you did not know even how to breathe

Now you have peace Hamlet you accomplished what you had to
and you have peace The rest is not silence but belongs to me
you chose the easier part an elegant thrust
but what is heroic death compared with eternal watching
with a cold apple in one's hand on a narrow chair
with a view of the ant-hill and the clock's dial

Adieu prince I have tasks a sewer project
and a decree on prostitution and beggars
I must elaborate a better system of prisons
since as you justly said Denmark is a prison
I go to my affairs This night is born
a star named Hamlet We shall never meet
what I shall leave will not be worth a tragedy.

—Zbigniew Herbert, "Elegy of Fortinbras"

One justification for taking as much time with the *Antigone* as we have is that this play, and Sophoclean tragedy more generally, is perhaps uniquely representative of authentic Greek tragedy, as the classical Athenian Greeks wrote it and lived it. It stands at a rather shocking remove from that constellation of modern assumptions I am calling "the tragic posture."

Sophocles is a visionary, a *tragic* visionary. So too was Hegel. While one need not defend the desire to read a great dramatic work in some detail, there are pointed reasons for having done so here. Hegel spent a lifetime reading and rereading this play, and we see the fruits of this rereading in his mature philosophical-theological system. I do not mean to say that he pored over the Greek text of Sophocles' play, although he did in fact study Greek and spent some time with this manuscript in seminary. What I want to suggest is that Hegel's mature intellectual career might be very helpfully viewed as a continuous dialogue with the *Antigone,* an attempt to wrest ever-fuller meaning from the play.

Hegel emphasizes several things that become essential to his tragic vision. First and foremost, as we have seen, he emphasizes that the Greek tragic heroes (and here Oedipus is truly father to his daughter) always have a hand in their own destruction. *Tragedy is the realm of Destiny, not Fate.* I will spend a great deal of time in this chapter with that distinction and will return to it at the conclusion of the book. Hegel's tragic ruminations also offer two tentative definitions, of sorts, that taken together neatly summarize his mature views. The first is that *there is no gain without a commensurate loss.* That sobering insight lies behind much of the negative rhetoric in Sophocles' play and in Hegel's philosophy. Tragic negations are an essential, and probably inescapable, step along the way to spiritual maturation. A second point is directed with equal specificity to Antigone: *tragedy derives from the fact that there is more than one will in the world.* As such, tragedy becomes a permanent feature of human life, both in society and before God, yet it is not necessarily beyond redemption. Stichomythia is an essential step along the way to *dialektika,* not its antithesis.

Now, in his later work, allusions to the *Antigone,* and to other Greek dramas, become more muted. The gospels gain a prominence they had not enjoyed since his seminary days. There are reasons for that, I suspect, or, to couch it in an Hegelian idiom I have used before now, such movement might actually have been *necessary.* 'Necessity' is neither a concept nor a word to be bandied about lightly. It is an idea that takes on full meaning only at the end of a book, or a lifetime, never in the middle. In order to begin to defend what may still seem an arbitrary starting point (namely, Sophocles' *Antigone*) I want now to discuss the manner in which Hegel's mature writings reflect his lifelong relationship, his intellectual dialogue, with this play. Our own close reading mirrors Hegel's, then, in ways that will be, I hope, probing and ultimately illuminating.

I

The most natural question that emerges from a careful reading of the *Antigone* — at least in Hegel's day, and it *was* the question with which he began — is: Who is right? or Who is *more* right? In a word, Is it

Creon or Antigone? This was the question that everyone was asking when Hegel lived and wrote, and it would surely have been the question with which he began when he was first exposed to Sophocles in *Gymnasium,* then again at the Tübingen seminary between 1788 and 1793. It is also the question he finally rejected as woefully inadequate to understanding the true moral meaning of the play.[1] At that time, as I mentioned briefly in the last chapter, most everyone — but chiefly the Romantics, and Kant who anticipated them in this — was reading Antigone's as the clearly superior moral position, as the *only* truly "moral" position. Creon's position, as it turns out, is "legal," not "moral" at all. In a discussion of the moral conscience, Kant could not be clearer:

> But what is a man [or in this case, a woman] to do when a positive and a natural law conflict? . . . The verdict of natural conscience being in conflict with the verdict of instructed conscience, he [and she] must obey the former. All positive laws are conditioned by the natural law, and they cannot, therefore, rightly contain anything which conflicts with it.[2]

Such statements suggest that where there is duty, there is always only one. That which we call singleness of purpose might also be called one-sidedness. Hegel's objection could not be more fundamental, for what he sees in the play is a dramatic description of the *necessity* of moral conflict in the arena of social life, where each of us has given over a large portion of ourselves (even our conscience, it would seem) to the state. Antigone, on Kant's reading, becomes an heroic spokeswoman for the autonomous individual and the timeless validity of natural laws, over against the demonic force of an oppressive state. And she is this. But she is also something else. In countering this one-sided reading, in insisting that there is nothing inherently demonic in the state, Hegel's own mature philosophy, and particularly his *Philosophy of Right,* begins to take shape.

It would take us too far afield to dwell for an extended period on Hegel's *Aesthetics,* specifically, his late theories of tragedy. Still, he *did* develop one, and it was a central philosophical concern of his to do so.[3] His tragic theories are, moreover, of a piece with his dialectical philosophy. For now, it is enough to single out its chief feature, which is also

1. See Hegel, *The Phenomenology of Spirit* (New York: Humanities Press, 1966) §§466, 468–469; Baillie translation, 486, 488–489. Throughout this chapter, I have consulted the critical edition of *Hegels Werke in 20 Bänden* (Frankfurt am Main: Suhrkamp Verlag, 1971) — so, here, *Werke,* III, 344, 346–347. For a different — philological, rather than philosophical — presentation of this same essential insight, see James C. Hogan's "The Protagonists of the *Antigone,*" *Arethusa* 5 (1972) 93–100.

2. Immanuel Kant, *Lectures on Ethics,* trans. Louis Infield (New York: Harper and Row, 1963) 133, emendation mine.

3. George Steiner, *Antigones* (Oxford: Oxford Univ. Press, 1984) 21–37.

the source of its stunning originality. Hegel insists that tragedy involves a certain kind of *Kollision*, a *necessary* collision between opposed moral powers, both of which lay a claim upon our sympathy, both of which lay a claim to being "right." Nowhere does Hegel insist upon a collision between "*equal* and opposite" moral powers (whatever that would mean) — a theory that is more physics than poetics, more Newton than Hegel. And this omission is an important one. Most of Hegel's contemporaries imported notions of "equality" into their readings that were quite foreign to the substance of the play,[4] and thus converted the play into something other than what Sophocles intended:

> There are two tragedies unfolding simultaneously: the tragedy of Creon and the tragedy of Antigone. Why have so many scholars insisted on the primacy of Antigone? There is a simple, significant, sufficient answer, which is that the tragedy of Creon is "Aeschylean," whereas it is the tragedy of Antigone which raises the great Sophoclean issues.[5]

Hegel insists — quite correctly, I think — that the fundamental issue here is not so much equality as *opposition*, and the conception of politics that emerges from trying to hold both protagonists' claims together in a single moral vision, a single moral universe.

The Romantic encomium of Antigone has been most recently propounded by no less a critic than Martha Nussbaum. In her writing on this play — where she too is, oddly enough, highly critical of Hegel, who receives mention nowhere else in her book[6] — Nussbaum pretty clearly lays out what she feels is at stake in Hegel's question, as well as what is wrong with his answer. She recognizes that both characters are one-sided, yet Antigone's remains, in her view, the clearly superior moral position. Antigone is the *only* truly "moral" character in the play.[7]

Nussbaum's reasons are essentially threefold. First, a violation of civic law is obviously less egregious than a violation of the dictates of natural

---

4. Brian Vickers, in his *Towards Greek Tragedy: Drama, Myth, Society* (London: Longman, 1973) 526–552, undertakes a systematic criticism of Hegel's reading, and he does so by emphasizing something that Hegel *never* said, namely, that Creon and Antigone are *equally* in the right. This statement, Hegel explicitly denied. For the same misrepresentation of Hegel, see also Gerald F. Else's *The Madness of Antigone* (Heidelberg: Carl Winter Universitätsverlag, 1976) 99–100.

5. R. P. Winnington-Ingram, *Sophocles: An Interpretation* (Cambridge: Cambridge Univ. Press, 1980) 147.

6. Martha Nussbaum, *The Fragility of Goodness: Luck and Ethics in Greek Tragedy and Philosophy* (Cambridge: Cambridge Univ. Press, 1986) 51–52, 67–68, 72–75, 79, 81. While more careful in other places, she concludes by saying that "it is one thing to say that the state will in general respect these claims, and quite another to say, with Hegel, that the very possibility of conflict or tension between different spheres of value will be altogether eliminated" (p. 68). Clearly, Hegel never said anything of the sort. His philosophy of "the negative" disallows it.

7. Nussbaum, *The Fragility of Goodness*, 63, 66–67.

piety, she suggests. *Nomoi* are answerable to, and finally less binding than, the demands of *themis*. Nussbaum agrees, with Heraclitus and Kant among others, that there *are* unwritten laws in the moral universe, and that they *are* timelessly binding.[8] It is in deference to them that Antigone defines herself, and in defense of them that she dies. Second, Nussbaum insists that Antigone's unwavering commitment to certain principles, no matter how one-sided and excessive they may be, does no real harm to anyone else, as Creon's commitments most assuredly do. Antigone's will, unlike Creon's, is not armed with police force or the state. Third, Nussbaum argues, Antigone remains willing to take moral risks in a manner that Creon has rejected. Creon seeks an illusory security through a simplification of all personal attachments — as is simply never possible in a real human life. Antigone ventures all; she risks everything on the firm commitment, not to be denied, she has made to the reality of certain eternal truths. In the name of these things, she is even willing to risk, and then to lose, her life.

Now, couched in these terms, we are witnessing an elegant and sophisticated restatement of the Romantic point of view (I mean this in a technical, and not a disparaging, sense). It is precisely this interpretation that Hegel abandoned when he began to develop his own distinctive philosophical voice in the late 1790s and immediately thereafter in Jena. I think that we can criticize each of these three points in Hegelian terms, and that, moreover, we shall be true to the Sophoclean text in doing so.

The issue of risk-taking, and of Antigone's allegedly greater vulnerability, is, I think, most easily dispensed with. In fact, my reading of the play in the last chapter highlights the degree to which *Creon's* experience of negation, and *not* Antigone's, is the most pregnant and enduring image in the play. It is the final image with which Sophocles leaves us. It is, in fact, just as risky, just as agonizing, for Creon to live as it is for Antigone to die. Many other dramas make this same point, as we shall see: Sophocles' *Philoctetes* and his *Oedipus,* but most explicitly the *Herakles* of Euripides. Creon and Ismene, Herakles and Oedipus may choose life, yet their pain is in no way diminished and is surely no less real than Ajax's or Antigone's grief. As the Hegelian/Marxist literary critic Lucien Goldmann points out with appropriate candor:

> First of all, from a purely textual and dramatic point of view, the character of Creon is far more important than that of Antigone — he is on the stage much longer, and says much more than she does.

---

8. See her fascinating comments at *The Fragility of Goodness,* 14–15, especially the long note on the latter page.

Secondly, Creon is exactly like the other tragic heroes of Sophocles —
Ajax, Philoctetes, Oedipus — who live in illusion and discover the truth
only at the end of the play, when it kills or blinds them.[9]

Crassly put, at the end of this play, Creon is still there, still thinking, still growing, and most important of all, he is still speaking to the
audience. While Antigone may be preferable *to us,* given our own romantic and bourgeois prejudices, we must recognize that Hegel — at
least early in his career — wants to call these very things into question
and has undertaken a revaluation of them precisely in his reading of the
play.

There is the second issue of "doing harm." It, too, is simply belied too
many times by the text. Antigone's commitments, as we saw in the last
chapter, do *enormous* harm to everyone around her. The reckless singularity of Antigone's blind devotion to one dead brother (there is, after
all, also Eteocles, another dead brother, for whom she seems to give not
a thought — and it is *Creon* who tells us this) makes her a particularly
unsavory character, however much a heroine she may also be. She completely alienates her sister, denying finally that very bond that ought to
bind her as tightly as it binds her to Polyneices' corpse. The singularity
of her affections makes Haemon entirely irrelevant to her — Haemon,
her betrothed, who loves her and who himself chooses death rather than
a longer life without her. She even kills herself too soon; and Sophocles
means us to see that, had she waited but an hour, the whole "domino-
chain of death" could have been avoided. Creon yielded, in fact, in a
way that Antigone could not. And the reasons for Antigone's surprising
one-sidedness in all of this are not far to seek. Sophocles identifies them
explicitly:

> Eros! Unconquerable Eros!
> You who seize upon possessions,
> who take lodging in the soft features
> of a young girl,
> you who stride the sea into
> wild and lawless [*agronomois*] lairs.
> Nowhere to which immortals can flee
> still less so creatures of a day —
> nor any whom you once have driven mad [*memēmen*].
>
> You it was who turned just minds
> upon the paths of injustice.

9. Lucien Goldmann, *The Hidden God: The Tragic Vision in the Pensées of Pascal and the Tragedies of Racine,* trans. Philip Thody (London: Routledge and Kegan
Paul, 1952, 1964) 45, note #2. See also Robert Coleman, "The Role of the Chorus in
Sophocles' *Antigone,*" in *Proceedings of the Cambridge Philological Society* 198 (1972)
26.

You it is now who have sown
dissension among common kin.
Longing conquers all, armed
with the fluttering eyes of
beauty, seated in power equal to
unwritten laws [*thesmōn*]. Impossible to fight —
for the goddess, Aphrodite, is playing.[10]

Shakespeare was not the first to recognize that "As flies to wanton boys, are we to the gods, / They kill us for their sport."[11] Sophocles already knew well how difficult it is to assess the motives of the human heart, how enslaved we often are to the passions that undo us, how difficult it is *to know.* Antigone does indeed appeal to the timeless validity of unwritten laws — and she is *right* to do so. Yet Eros sits "equal in power to these same laws [*thesmōn*]," and Eros undoes her just as certainly as it undoes everyone else in Sophocles' passion-play.

That leaves us with the primary, and far more controversial, argument about natural piety and natural law. It is this question that serves as the fulcrum around which Hegel's mature ethical thought revolves. I suspect that it would go too far to say, at least at this early stage of his career, that Hegel was out to ground the rights of a concrete, absolute state. This is after all aesthetics, not political science, and not the philosophy of history. Yet he surely *is* out to validate Creon's legal claims and his whole dramatic stature in the play:

Creon is not a tyrant, but rather stands for something which is likewise a moral power [*sittliche Macht*]. Creon is not unjust [*hat nicht Unrecht*]; he asserts that the law of the state [*Gesetz des Staats*] and the authority of the government must be maintained and that punishment follows offense.[12]

Hegel is careful to do so only because Creon's right had been ignored by all the Romantic accolades that elevate the figure of Antigone to such celestial heights (ironically enough, his own comments concerning her "celestial" nature included). If her "disobedience" is to be truly "civil,"

---

10. Sophocles, *Antigone,* 781–801. It is the chief shortcoming of Gerald Else's otherwise very fine analysis, *The Madness of Antigone,* 53–58, that he fails to apply this ode to Antigone's character at all. He argues instead that the Chorus is only talking about Haemon here. Yet surely *her erōs* is a chief, if not *the* chief, source of the madness (*mania*) that stalks *everyone* in this play. See also Winnington-Ingram, *Sophocles: An Interpretation,* 92–98, and Th. C. W. Oudemans and A. P. M. H. Lardinois, *Tragic Ambiguity: Anthropology, Philosophy and Sophocles' Antigone* (Leiden: E. J. Brill, 1987) 140–144.

11. *King Lear,* IV, i.

12. Anne and Henry Paolucci, *Hegel: On Tragedy* (New York: Harper and Row, 1962) 325. This passage originally appeared in *The Lectures on the Philosophy of Religion,* II.2.a; *Werke,* XVII, 133.

then it can be and will be punished. As much as he wants to legitimate Creon, I suspect that Hegel really wants to prune the figure of Antigone down to human size:

> Each of these two sides realizes only one of the two [moral powers], and has only one of these as its content. That is their one-sidedness, and the meaning of eternal justice [*ewigen Gerechtigkeit*] is precisely this: that both are unjust [*haben Unrecht*] because they are one-sided, yet both are at the same time right [*recht*]. Both would be recognized in a calmer setting of morality [*Sittlichkeit*]; here both would enjoy their validity, but a balanced validity. It is only one-sidedness which justice opposes.[13]

In this early period, when Hegel first discovered the play — and later, in Frankfurt, growing out of his own disaffection with the French Revolution that had gone so badly and lopsidedly wrong[14] — he has opted to give the state, and modern society more generally, another long look. It was an important moment in his intellectual development, when Hegel averted his own temptation to the tragic posture. He had been rather desperate about "modernity" in the past; his perspective now becomes more temperate. Hegel here corrects himself, speaking of "freedom, not anarchy." Freedom in the modern period — and this is the greatest legacy of the French Revolution, which even survived the Terror — depends upon and presupposes a very high level of social order. We should recall that one of Creon's chief concerns was the problem of anarchy and the death it must inevitably do to any kind of state.[15] Hegel never saw it quite this way, but in Jena he is no longer a blind devoté of Antigone either. "Anarchy has been distinguished from freedom now," he says, "the notion that a firm government is indispensable for freedom has been deeply engraved on men's minds."[16] Much later, Hegel gave fuller expression to this same idea:

> Freedom as the *ideal* of that which is original and natural, does not exist as *original and natural*. Rather must it first be sought out and won, and that by an incalculable medial discipline of the intellectual and moral powers.... The perpetually recurring misapprehension of Freedom consists in regarding that term only in its *formal,* subjective sense, abstracted from its essential objects and aims.

---

13. Paolucci, *Hegel: On Tragedy,* 325; *Werke,* XVII, 133.
14. Georg Lukács, *The Young Hegel: Studies in the Relations between Dialectics and Economics,* trans. Rodney Livingstone (Cambridge, Mass.: MIT Press, 1966, 1975) xxvi–xxvii, 93–106, 234–235, 314–317.
15. *Antigone,* 672–676.
16. Quoted by Lukács, *The Young Hegel,* 308ff.

We should on the contrary look upon limitation as the indispensable proviso of emancipation. Society and the state are the very conditions in which freedom is realized.[17]

I suspect that Hegel did not always keep his own counsel; in fact, I would read *The Philosophy of Right* as a far less satisfying account of the *twinned* necessities at work in this play. In his later writing, Hegel loses much of the richness and dialectical nuance of this contrast between personal freedom and political limit — that which had animated all of the best insights in his interpretation of the play. Is it so difficult to imagine that Hegel, who was, early on, possessed of a brilliant intuitive insight into the play — as well as into the Greek respect for the strict *necessity* of political order — defended Creon against the caricatures, defended him for so long that he began finally to caricature his *own* better dialectical insights, began to lose sight of the fact that Antigone, too, is right?[18]

These questions haunt every Hegelian text, just as they haunted Kant, just as they haunted Sophocles: What is the relation of *nomos* and *themis*? How are disputes — that is, tragic collisions — between them ever to be resolved? We will want to look at Hegel's answer to these questions in some detail.

II

Gerald Else has argued persuasively that among the many allusions which Sophocles makes in the *Antigone,* those that appeal to Aeschylus' Theban trilogy are by far the most important. With great philological sensitivity, Else has culled a remarkable number of Aeschylean words, phrases, and images from the text. On his view, the *Antigone* might best be understood as the next step in an Aeschylean narrative that had been considered "finished":

> The *Seven Against Thebes* shows us a doom, an *atē* from the gods, in the final process of fulfillment.... *The doom is now completed* with the death of the brothers. Thus the message of the *Seven* could not be clearer: *it is finished.* The doom from the gods and the curse of Oedipus have reached their destined term: the race of Labdakos and Laius is wiped out. I now propose to argue that the *Antigone* offers a radical amendment to this view. The matter is *not* finished.[19]

---

17. Hegel, *The Philosophy of History,* 40–41; *Werke,* XII, 58–59. See also the comments by T. M. Knox in his translator's forward to *The Philosophy of Right* (Oxford: Oxford Univ. Press, 1952) x.

18. For more on what it means for both characters to be "right," see Lukács, *The Young Hegel,* 48–49, 410–413.

19. Else, *The Madness of Antigone,* 26–27. Also Winnington-Ingram, *Sophocles: An Interpretation,* 150–178.

What Aeschylus meant to show us, on this reading, was how a sober and intelligent ruler, Eteocles himself, may be very suddenly and completely maddened by the gods and driven to his own unwitting destruction.[20] In Eteocles' rash decision to engage his brother in single combat — the headlong pursuit of his own undoing — we are meant to see what the gods, not men, have wrought. And what the gods will, no mortals may undo, as Herodotus already knew.

Antigone's madness is something else again. In the first place, we never see her any other way. Her soul is a lyre strung so tightly that, even from its opening notes, we are sure that it must eventually snap. In essence, the grand, cosmic Fate of Aeschylus' dramatic imagination has been internalized, made an issue of personal character. "Character *is* destiny," we recall. We do not see Antigone go mad, as Aeschylus showed us her brother; we simply see her manic, as she has presumably always been. Madness, like the lust and dark confusion that surround her, runs in the family and is dormant in her name. It is all a matter of character:

> Sophocles has moved irrevocably onward from the Aeschylean vision — grandiose though it was — of an external fate descending upon the generations. Fate now operates in the blood, the genes; or, in the cases of Haemon and Creon, through the mind. Haemon is reduced by the power and truth of Antigone's ideas, Creon by the half-understood glamor of a great, imperious, regal personality (Oedipus); both are swept away. The gods are impartial in their reign of destruction — except that they give Antigone what *she* truly wanted: death.[21]

This insight, and it is a crucial one, is Hegelian to the core. In fact, in the same text from his lectures on religion where Hegel seeks to counter the romantic idolization of Antigone with a more balanced and positive view of Creon, he makes an essential distinction between Fate and Destiny[22] — a distinction that lies at the very heart of *everything* he tried to say. The verbal distinction that Hegel seems to maintain is that between Fate (*Schicksal, Fatum*) and Destiny (*Bestimmung*). In addition, he makes frequent use of "necessity" (*Notwendigkeit*) as a transitional category: that is, he attempts to demonstrate how it is transformed from something "blind" into something that is rational and self-aware. Hegel

---

20. And that in a sudden, single line, *Seven against Thebes,* 653, and then through 719.

21. Else, *The Madness of Antigone,* 101.

22. I am aware of the unfortunate mystification that Hegel's thought suffers when we capitalize every word of importance. Baillie's translation has done much to perpetuate this mystification. I have chosen to maintain the capitalization of these two terms, Fate and Destiny, in order to highlight their presence for the reader, and I will maintain this practice throughout the book.

speaks of Fate, more often than not, as something blind, something that possesses no conscious necessity *for us*. Some things just happen; that is the way of the world. Classical Greek even has a verb to express this very thought: *tynchanō* (from the same root as *tychē*, blind chance). Over against this Hegel posits Destiny, the realm of spirit, which is a realm of dawning self-consciousness, that philosophical point of view which recognizes the spiritual *necessity* of all that really is. To give an example: the fact that I am mortal is no more and no less than that, a brute (and blind) *fact*. Mortality is my, and all of our, Fate. The *manner* of my dying will, by contrast, someday, be *uniquely* my own, my Destiny.

It was, appropriately enough, in this same section, entitled "The Tragic and Reconciliation," that Hegel makes this distinction best:

> Fate is unconscious [*Begriffslose*], where justice and injustice disappear in abstraction; in tragedy, on the other hand, Fate [*Schicksal*] moves within a sphere of moral justice [*sittlicher Gerechtigkeit*]. The noblest form of such tragedies we find in Sophocles. It is precisely here that Fate [*Schicksal*] and Necessity [*Notwendigkeit*] are discussed: The Fate [*Schicksal*] of individuals is presented as something incomprehensible, but Necessity [*Notwendigkeit*] is recognized as true justice [*wahrhaftige Gerechtigkeit*]. For this very reason every tragedy is an immortal spiritual work of moral [*sittlichen*] understanding and conceptualization, the eternal pattern of the moral [*sittlichen*] concept. Blind Fate is something unsatisfying. In these tragedies, justice is grasped by concepts.[23]

It seems to me that Hegel's thought may be simplified considerably once we recognize how very Homeric, and Sophoclean, are its roots.[24] In point of fact, the concern for the relationship between contingency and necessity, between Fate and freedom, hardly began with Kant. It runs throughout Homer as well as the tragic and philosophic literature that supersedes and builds upon him. The Greek language is extraordinarily rich in the modal language of necessity.[25] The very manner in which Greek sets the problem reflects an acute sensitivity to its multivalence.

---

23. Paolucci, *Hegel: On Tragedy*, 325. Originally this citation also appeared in Hegel's *Lectures on the Philosophy of Religion*, II.2.a.; *Werke*, XVII, 132.

24. This is the chief methodological assumption of W. Thomas MacCary's suggestive study, *Childlike Achilles* (New York: Columbia Univ. Press, 1982), which attempts to bring the *Iliad* into conversation with both Freud and Hegel on the issue of the emergence of the conscious individual. MacCary argues (p. 19) that there are four essential texts in this psychological canon: Homer's *Iliad*; Plato's *Symposium* (or *Phaedrus*); Hegel's *Phenomenology of Spirit*; and Freud's essay "On Narcissism." I deal only with the first three.

25. For a highly suggestive discussion of the various linguistic "modes" of classical Greek, see William Arrowsmith's introduction to his translation of Euripides' *Alcestis* (New York: Oxford Univ. Press, 1974) 4–11.

The Sophoclean solution to this Oedipean riddle of existence, as it presents itself in "fated things," was to distinguish between Fate and Destiny, much as Hegel does. The language of necessity is initially the rhetoric of Fate. Each of the *Iliad*'s heroes is *fated* to fight, to kill, and very often to die, before the walls of Troy, "far from their homes, and families, far from warm baths and children's laughter." Each hero was *fated* to be born Greek or Trojan; each was *fated* to be born male. Nevertheless, every hero remains free to act and to live within the parameters set by these fateful facts, and in so doing, remains free to create a Destiny uniquely his own. We would never — Homer insists that we *could* never — mistake an Achilleus for a Hektor, a Sarpedon for a Patroklus. Their Fate is identical: they *all* die at Troy. There the similarity ends, however, and it is this unique *Destiny* that makes each of them undeniably individual, distinctively who they are. We need constantly to remind ourselves of this, even better than Hegel did: we are in Homer's universe, not the blind fatalism of Icelandic saga.[26] Surely it is no accident, but rather a philosophical necessity, for Homer to take such endless pains, and such endless delight, in displaying for us the inner debate in which each and every hero indulges at some point — envisioning a different world, imagining what it would be like to turn away from Troy, simply to leave. Now, in very nearly every case these heroes choose to stay; yet the fact remains that they have *chosen,* and in so doing, have changed everything, have converted the brute realities of Fate into a Destiny uniquely their own.

In his last lectures on aesthetics, Hegel makes this point very elegantly in a discussion of epic poetry, which contains, so he argues, "the world view of a people in its entirety."[27] As such, epic is the product of a *Zeitgeist,* a dramatic portrait of the spirit of its age. Yet the *Iliad,* the *Ramayana,* and *The Divine Comedy* are not "simply" the products of a blind Fate. Rather, they are predestinate, *necessary,* the unique products of a distilled poetic genius — they represent *the Destiny of a single poet* living in absolutely singular times:

> We must take care not to mistake the historical actuality here. As a truly unified work of art, an epic poem can come to be through one individual only. The spirit of an age, of a nation, is no doubt the essential operative

---

26. An excellent example is *Njal's Saga,* trans. Magnus Magnusson and Hermann Pálsson (New York: Penguin Books, 1960) 227, 250. Hegel himself admitted "I must acknowledge that I have little taste for the savagery and dark confusion of such narratives." See Henry Paolucci, *Hegel: On the Arts* (New York: Frederick Ungar, 1979) 157. This book is a greatly abridged translation of the massive three-volume *Lectures on the Philosophy of Fine Art.* Running to only one-sixth the length of the original, these lectures nevertheless present the essential structure of Hegel's aesthetic thought and are a fine introduction to it.

27. Paolucci, *Hegel: On the Arts,* 149.

cause; but that spirit can produce an actual work of art only when it is concentrated in the individual genius of a single poet.[28]

Hegel goes on to distinguish between epic and tragic poetry, far less convincingly — here he sounds more like Alasdair MacIntyre than he does himself at his best. The reason for this inconsistency, which we have had occasion to mention before, is that Hegel never finally made up his mind about the Greeks. In fact, long after the *polis* had ceased to be a living political ideal, the classical moment continued to represent an aesthetic ideal, never to be surpassed.[29] Here is another dimension of his break with the tragic posture — from here on out, Hegel's romanticization of the classical moment is not politically informed. The *polis* is not to be, and ought not be, resurrected. This passage well illustrates that what most concerned Hegel was his distinction between brute facticities, blind Fate, and the Destiny that is slowly beginning to understand itself. In a word, epic portrays Fate, whereas tragedy portrays Destiny:

> Given the world situation, [epic] heroes seem to have an absolute right to be precisely what they are.... Achilleus simply is what he is, and, so far as epic poetry is concerned, the matter ends there. It is, after all, in the epic, and not, as is commonly supposed, in drama, that Fate is absolutely dominant. The dramatic hero's Fate is tragic because he knows that he *creates* it *for* himself. In the epic, however, what befalls an Achilles or an Odysseus is rooted in the necessity of a total state of affairs.[30]

Leaving the epic to one side, the epic that Hegel had treated so much more fully and adequately in his earlier lectures, let us turn to the tragedies and the doctrine of Destiny that Hegel articulated there.

The story of Oedipus in particular, which Hegel discusses in this same section on "tragic reconciliation," is essentially mythopoetic philosophy — fully consonant, so I am arguing, with the *Iliad*. Oedipus has been cast into a world he did not choose, a world where he is doomed to commit certain fateful crimes. Yet he could not have become a Destiny apart from the peculiarities of his own character. The Fate he enacts is, strictly speaking, the Fate he always was, his character. A man a little less passionate might have thought twice about killing an elder man at the side of the road, and would surely have refrained from marrying a regal woman so many years his senior.[31]

---

28. Ibid., 150.

29. Lukács, *The Young Hegel,* 51, 86–88, 162, 301.

30. Paolucci, *Hegel: On the Arts,* 152–153.

31. Aristotle may well have had a similar view in his discussion of the tragic flaw (*hamartia*), see *The Poetics* 1453a.10, 16, and Gerald F. Else's *Aristotle's Poetics: The Argument* (Cambridge, Mass.: Harvard Univ. Press, 1957) 375–376, 378–385. Else argues that the notion of *hamartia* is directly linked to Aristotle's overall formal treatment of tragedy, specifically to his ideas about tragic recognition (*anagnōrisis*), such that the

Fate and freedom, "in no wise incompatible,"[32] *both* are of Destiny's essence.

Pascal had earlier addressed himself to this same set of concerns. His Oedipus is like Hegel's:

> Man is a reed, the feeblest in nature. But he is a *thinking* reed. And even if the universe were to crush him, he would still be nobler than what kills him, since he knows that he is dying and the universe knows nothing of the advantage which it has over him.[33]

Nietzsche is, characteristically, even pithier:

> Can an *ass* be tragic? To perish under a burden one can neither bear nor throw off?
> The case of the philosopher.[34]

For Hegel, we are neither asses nor thinking reeds, but poets — something as grand and as dignified as an Oedipus, at the *end*, at Colonus:

> Stars, animals, plants have no knowledge or experience of their laws; but man is truly man only when he knows what he is and what surrounds him. He needs to know what the powers are that made him be what he is and do what he does; and that is the kind of knowledge that poetry, in its original substantive form, provides.... Poetry is man's original grasp of truth.[35]

In a remarkable early essay — "The Spirit of Christianity and Its Fate," written between 1798 and 1799 — what almost might be considered *Hegel's* original grasp at truth, he was already toying with this eminently Greek distinction.[36] The formula is less clear and consistent than in his later lectures on religion and aesthetics, yet it is perhaps all the more noteworthy for that. Here we are meeting a germinal insight, not yet fully formulated, that was to be of lifelong concern:

> A Fate [*Schicksal*] appears to arise only through another's deed; but this is only the occasion of the Fate. What really produces it is the manner

---

question of moral culpability is a secondary concern, if it is a concern at all. This is theater, after all, first and last. "We may debate over which caused the killing of Laius, Oedipus' ignorance or his hot temper, but there can be no argument about what he recognizes: it is the identity of the man he killed" (p. 385). Thus, in all fairness, to argue as I am arguing, and as I think Hegel did, is in one sense to go well beyond Aristotle. See also the *Nicomachean Ethics* 1110a.30–1111b.3.

32. Herman Melville, *Moby Dick,* §47, "The Mat Maker," is one of the most remarkable dramatic descriptions of this idea in American literature.

33. *Pensées* #347, E-391. For a discussion of this and related texts, see Lucien Goldmann's *The Hidden God,* 81–82.

34. Nietzsche, *Twilight of the Idols,* "Maxims and Arrows," §11.

35. Paolucci, *Hegel: On the Arts,* 145.

36. Georg Lukács, *The Young Hegel,* devotes an entire chapter to this manuscript, 179–208, yet he seems to miss what is at stake in Hegel's notion of Fate, at note #37.

of receiving and reacting against the other's deed. If someone suffers an unjust attack, he can arm and defend himself and his right, or he may do the reverse. It is with his reaction, be it in battle or submissive grief, that his guilt [*Schuld*], his Destiny [*Schicksal*], begins....

Courage, however, is greater than grieving submission, for even though it succumbs, it has first recognized this possibility [of failure] and so has consciously made itself responsible for it; grieving passivity, on the contrary, clings to its loss and fails to oppose it with all its strength.[37]

The passage is noteworthy for some revealing comments that it makes about the nature of right (*Recht*), as well as its dubious accessibility in the real world. The text also clearly anticipates the famous dialectic of mastery and servility in the *Phenomenology of Spirit*. More to our present point is Hegel's distinction between activity and passivity — which we will take up again in a moment, and which is directly tied to his rejection of optimism and pessimism as meaningful tragic categories. Toward the end of this stirring essay, Hegel applies these Greek categories, quite appropriately I think, to the gospel.[38] He argues that Jesus could not have been simply *fated* to die in Jerusalem. Such a fatalistic reading of the "historical" facts misses all the force and contingency of his character. Jesus *chose* to go to Jerusalem, *opted* for his Destiny there, fully cognizant that, nature and the prevailing political realities being what they were, his life might well be lost. To construe this grand drama as a foreordained cosmic event makes an ass of Jesus, in Nietzsche's terms, and fails to remember that Gethsemane came *before* Golgotha. Jesus — much like Homer's heroes — anticipated it all in the Garden, debated its meaning within himself, and finally was reconciled to it. To talk about Jesus' will as if it took shape in a vacuum[39] is, by contrast, to take all the passion out of the Passion, and to make the gospel little more than an embellished story of a fanatic suicide. It is rather the manner in which a world-historical figure of tremendous power and insight interacts with a world he did not make that converts the Fate of Golgotha into a Destiny. It is only in the light of *Gethsemane* that Golgotha takes on its truly *tragic* significance, as we shall see at length in the last chapter.

---

37. Hegel, *Early Theological Writings*, trans. T. M. Knox (Philadelphia: Univ. of Pennsylvania Press, 1948) 233–234; *Werke*, I, 347–348. It is worth noting that Hegel uses the single word *Schicksal* for both ideas here — Fate and Destiny — although within several years, and the publication of the *Phenomenology*, the verbal distinction has become explicit.

38. Hegel, *Early Theological Writings*, 288–289; *Werke*, I, 403–405.

39. Which is precisely what Albert Schweitzer did in his bizarre interpretation of the life of Jesus, *The Quest of the Historical Jesus: A Critical Study of Its Progress from Reimarus to Wrede*, trans. W. Montgomery (New York: Macmillan, 1968) 328–395.

Perhaps now we are in better position to appreciate the stark and somber tones of that much-maligned Hegelian "reconciliation."[40] Hegel did not say, naïvely, that tragedy works out in the end, nor even, simply, that it is left to us to make sense of it all. Rather, "reason is reconciliation with ruination."[41] Not every collision can be resolved, nor is every instance of suffering a tragedy. In fact, very few *ever* are. For every Hamlet who dies with poetry on his lips, twenty Ophelias drown in their own senseless chatter, and a hundred Fortinbras choose to live on, toiling at their tasks and sewer projects. For every Christ crucified on Golgotha, there are countless innocents slaughtered without a sound, save the lingering notes of Rachel's weeping — or, as in Mark's gospel, other criminals on other crosses who join in mocking Him. The rarefied air of tragedy, says Hegel, remains the province of the few. There is an aristocracy in our capacity to feel. "There are degrees in our high estate of pain."[42] Tragedy must be one's *Destiny*. It must be *earned*:

> In this way the end of tragedy is reconciliation [*Versöhnung*] — not blind necessity but rather rational necessity, the necessity which here begins to mediate itself [*sich erfüllen*]. It is justice which is in this way satisfied with the saying — "There is nothing which is not Zeus" — that is, eternal justice. Here we have an active necessity, which is however completely moral. The misfortune endured is perfectly clear. Here is nothing blind or unconscious.
>
> To such clarity of insight and cultural vision did Greece come at her highest cultural stage.[43]

If Kant was always a radically dualistic thinker,[44] a prober into paradox, then this too is a point at which Hegel diverges from his master.

---

40. We also cannot miss the essential religiosity of the notion, for Hegel. *Versöhnung* is, after all, the capacity to recognize God in oneself and one's sonship in God: "Every individual has in him the vision of his own reconciliation with God — not as a mere possibility, but as a reality which, for that very reason, had to appear as accomplished, as actually realized, in this one man" (Paolucci, *Hegel: On the Arts,* 40).

41. Hans-Georg Gadamer, *Hegel's Dialectic: Five Hermeneutical Studies,* trans. P. Christopher Smith (New Haven: Yale Univ. Press, 1971) 105–106, 110–111.

42. Edith Hamilton, *The Greek Way* (New York: W. W. Norton, 1930, 1942) 142. She continues, "It is not given to all to suffer alike. We differ in nothing more than our power to feel."

43. Paolucci, *Hegel: On Tragedy,* 326, also from *Lectures on the Philosophy of Religion,* II.2.a; *Werke,* XVII, 134.

44. And it is precisely this — the positing of two worlds that never meet — that makes him the first *tragic* philosopher, according to both Lucien Goldmann, *The Hidden God,* 15, 20–25, 33, 41–47, 52, 57–58, 67, 91–93, 145, 195, 271, 278, 333; and Georg Lukács, *The Young Hegel,* 21, 146–147, 285–300. See also George Steiner, *Antigones,* 2ff. I am no Kant scholar, and yet ironically I will speak a good deal about Kant in this chapter. I am *not* entering into a debate about what Kant did or did not mean, nor am I asking how his views might be defended. I am only interested in how Hegel was taking Kant, how he saw himself going beyond Kant — rightly or wrongly.

For Kant insisted upon the radical discontinuity between two realms — the realm of necessity, which is Fate, and the realm of freedom, which is Destiny's own. Hegel argues, by contrast — and I think that both Homer and Sophocles support him in this — that "all the world's a stage," where necessity and freedom are merely two masks worn by the evolving human consciousness. By weaving both necessity and freedom, the universal and the individual, into a single dramatic fabric, Hegel believes that he has articulated the spiritual manner in which "necessity begins to mediate itself" (*sich erfüllen,* another essential Christian category), the manner in which reality is recognized, and accepted, as "necessary." "*Love* Fate," said Nietzsche, "*Become* what you are." Hegel would have heartily concurred, and he leaves us, as so often, with a parting dramatic image.[45] Oedipus, broken, cursed, and exiled, yet clinging to the one shred of dignity and autonomy left to him — the one thing, moreover, that turns the gods' fateful curse into a Destiny unmistakably his own. After *blinding himself,* a brilliantly appropriate aesthetic act, Oedipus is intransigent, more himself than he has ever been:

> Apollo, it was, Apollo
> my friends
> who brought to fruition
> each and every thing I suffer.
> Save one.
> I — I, alone — and no one else
> with mine own hand
> did this.
> What need had I of eyes,
> I, for whom no sight on earth is sweet?[46]

It is Oedipus himself who chooses to live, much like Herakles in the Euripidean drama of that name, in a world that "calls out to the hero to die and tells him that there is no hope and no moral order at all."[47] Or again, even more poignantly, there is Christ, soon to be crucified, yet clinging to the tatters of a world that he, too, has had a hand in making: "Lo, *I came* to do thy will."

III

I have spoken already of Hegel and Nietzsche — both of them in a single breath, as it were — in a way that must seem strange to those who were

---

45. It is surely significant that the *Phenomenology* itself concludes with *an image* of Consciousness crucified, on its own absolute Golgotha.

46. Sophocles, *Oedipus Tyrranos,* 1329–1335.

47. William Arrowsmith, "A Greek Theater of Ideas," *Tulane Drama Review* 3:3 (1959) 55.

raised on the sweet milk of the assumption that they represent wholly incompatible ways of thinking about philosophy. It is time and past time to be weaned from this assumption. Who could possibly be more dissimilar, we are taught to ask, than Hegel, that arch-systematizer whose encyclopedic mind was matched only by the audacity of his system, and Nietzsche, that premier philosophical skeptic who insisted in countless places that "the will to a system is a lack of integrity"?[48] On the one hand, there is Hegel — Hegel, whose profound commitment to the scientific method is of a piece with his faith in the concrete historical reality of certain universal human categories. Taken together, these beliefs informed his conviction that "the system" can and should illuminate an order that is potentially valid for everyone:

> The systematic development of truth in scientific form can alone be the
> true shape in which truth exists. To help to bring philosophy nearer to
> the form of science — that goal where it can lay aside the name of *love*
> of knowledge and be actual *knowledge* — that is what I have set before
> me.[49]

How far removed from all of this must Nietzsche's perspectivism seem![50] Not only does Nietzsche call the integrity of systematic thinking into question; he calls the very legitimacy of *science* into question. "Aesthetics, not metaphysics" is his chief philosophical rejoinder, the petard upon which he claims to have hoisted the history of Western thought. "Existence and the world," says Nietzsche, "seem justified only as aesthetic phenomena."[51] More even than this, Nietzsche puts the very value of *truth* to the question: "The concepts 'true' and 'untrue' have, it seems to me, no meaning in optics."[52] Where we stand determines what we can see. Perspective, like ripeness, is all.

By returning to a point that I have already made a number of times, however, a remarkable and really very exciting similarity between the two thinkers begins to take shape.[53] It is more than the images of con-

---

48. Nietzsche, *Twilight of the Idols*, "Maxims and Arrows," §26.

49. *The Phenomenology of Spirit*, preface, §5; Baillie, 70–71; *Werke*, III, 14.

50. Developing the matter of this "perspectivism" is Alexander Nehemas' chief task in *Nietzsche: Life as Literature* (Cambridge, Mass.: Harvard Univ. Press, 1985), which we shall examine in more detail in the next chapter. Suffice it to say at this point that I believe the seeds for Nietzsche's "perspectivism" were sown in the unpublished essay, *Wir Philologen*. There, his reading of "the Greeks" forced him to address a prior question: *Which* Greeks do I mean? Plato and Aristotle? . . . Or something earlier, something *tragic?*

51. *The Birth of Tragedy*, §24, and see §17.

52. *The Case of Wagner*, epilogue. But see *The Phenomenology of Spirit*, preface, §§39–47; Baillie, 98–106; *Werke*, III, 40–47.

53. One of the only studies that I know that examines these "truly amazing parallels" is Walter Kaufmann's *Nietzsche: Philosopher, Psychologist, Antichrist*, 4th ed. (Princeton, N.J.: Princeton Univ. Press, 1974) 80–85, 198–200, 236–246, 353–354, 394.

flict, of contests in power — Homeric images, all — in which both men took such an infinite delight and from which they derived so many mature insights. It is more than the rhetoric of negation, which they both used with tremendous rhetorical force. (Hegel is not nearly the stylistic buffoon many would make him out to be. He is, in his own very distinctive way, and at his best moments, crystal clear.) Rather, it is *the source* of these images that Nietzsche and Hegel share so deeply.

Both thinkers drank deeply at the well of Greek literature, Homer and the tragedies in particular. Both men returned to these texts, and to these images, throughout the rest of their creative lives. These myths provide the source of much that is best and most enduring in their work. As I already stressed in the first chapter, both men were classicists *before* they were moral philosophers, and their classical training made an indispensable contribution to the quality of their mature moral and political thought. Neither of them is really accessible apart from the Greeks, whom they held up as spiritual ideals (aesthetic, not political, ideals), invoked as constant conversation partners, and, at least in their youth, related to as spiritual contemporaries. If the Greeks are, as the Egyptian priest would have it, perennially children,[54] then Hegel and Nietzsche both share a vision of cultural second childhood, what Paul Ricouer has called "a second naïveté." If it is not quite so naïve as was the first, if it is chastened and "mature," it is no less childlike for all of that. In the cases of both Hegel and Nietzsche, it is surely no less *Greek*.

And it is precisely when they are worrying about how to make Greek tragedy accessible to the modern world — in the face of its most sharply distorting postures and prejudices — that the two thinkers sound most nearly alike. It was in their writings on tragedy that they were both most penetrating and profound. Even Aristotle's seminal work pales by comparison.[55] For the *Poetics* is, finally, a strictly *formal* treatment of the genre. "Tragedy in its greatest days comported things that were not dreamt of in Aristotle's philosophy."[56] As Edith Hamilton has observed so keenly, Aristotle analyzes what a tragedy *makes us* feel; only Hegel

---

Even here, Kaufmann analyzes their metaphysics, not their aesthetics, and claims that both thinkers attempted to move beyond earlier dualisms in the direction of a "dialectical monism." My own view is, I hope, simpler. Both caught sight of a crucial, and authentically classical, insight: that tragedy is neither optimistic nor pessimistic and that this very way of putting the dramatic question is a reflection of nothing so much as "modern" prejudices.

54. See *Wir Philologen*, 5[84], 5[186]; *Sämtliche Werke*, VIII, 63, 93.
55. A. C. Bradley, "Hegel's Theory of Tragedy" *Oxford Lectures on Poetry* (London, 1950) 69–95, reprinted in Paolucci's *Hegel: On Tragedy*, 367–388.
56. Else, *Aristotle's Poetics: The Argument*, 446.

and Nietzsche endeavored to show what *makes* a tragedy.[57] And all of their manifold insights seem to me to converge upon a single point.

In a word, both Nietzsche and Hegel insist that tragedy is somehow, almost magically[58] and in spite of its subject matter (which is awful suffering), an *elevating* genre. There is something undeniably ennobling about it. The paradox is apparent to anyone who has ever reflected upon what he or she feels in the theater: "Tragedy shows us pain and gives us pleasure in the process":

> It is illuminating to consider our everyday use of the words tragedy and tragic. Pain, sorrow, disaster, are always spoken of as depressing, as dragging down — the dark abyss of pain, an anguishing sorrow, an overwhelming disaster. But speak of tragedy and extraordinarily the metaphor changes. Lift us to the tragic heights, we say, and never anything else. The depths of pathos but never of tragedy. Always the height of tragedy. A word is no light matter. Words have with truth been called fossil poetry, each, that is, a symbol of a creative thought. The whole philosophy of human nature is implicit in human speech. It is a matter to pause over, that the instinct of mankind has perceived a difference, not of degree but of kind, between tragic pain and all other pain.[59]

As Hegel saw so clearly, tragedies often *do* end badly — his favorites all did — but tragedy is itself essentially the forum for a certain kind of conflict, which he called *Kollision*.

Already, in framing the issue this way, Hegel is a world away from the tragic posture. Tragedy, so we moderns tell ourselves, is about "pessimism," pure and simple, a dramatic picture of the agony that is our common lot. The best gift of all, Sophocles has his Oedipus say, is never to have been born at all — and the second-best is to die young.[60] The briefest perusal of the newspapers, the most casual glance at the evening news, confirms the distance between Hegel, to say nothing of the classical Greeks, and ourselves. Today, everything is a "tragedy" — planes hijacked by terrorists, children trapped in lunatic cross fire, earthquakes, famines, floods — *catastrophe* in any form. Tragedy seems to connote catastrophe, pure and simple, but in the process of telling ourselves this so many times we have trivialized, through overuse, a word that was originally anything but trivial. As I said in the last chapter, whatever else he does allow, Hegel does not allow the overly simple.

---

57. Hamilton, *The Greek Way*, 140.

58. Hegel was not above speaking about "the magic power [*Zauberkraft*] of the negative" (*The Phenomenology of Spirit*, preface, §32; Baillie, 93; *Werke*, III, 36).

59. Hamilton, *The Greek Way*, 139.

60. *Oedipus at Colonus*, 1224ff. See Nietzsche's *The Birth of Tragedy*, §3; Plutarch, *Moralia*, 115; and MacCary, *Childlike Achilles*, 196–216. For an analysis of the way such texts are misused, especially by Alasdair MacIntyre, see my "After Virtue? On Distorted Philosophical Narratives" (forthcoming in *Continuum*, 1994).

Tragedy is not about earthquakes, famines, or floods. Such things can provide no more than the material conditions of a tragedy. One can no more imagine an earthquake staged — although Shakespeare once tried to stage a tempest — than one can imagine the future as a mirror image of the past. That is precisely Hegel's point. There is a world of moral difference between tragedy and pathos; our aesthetic and moral understanding simply is not served by blurring the genres or failing to be discrete in our choice of words. That tragedy involves suffering is indisputable. Yet tragedy cannot make do with any kind of suffering. Related to his distinction between Fate and Destiny, Hegel insists that, while we all may suffer, not all suffering is tragic. A fatalistic genre, like *Njal's Saga* and others in that vein, is deeply pessimistic to the core; Homer and the tragedies are not — precisely because they have supplanted Fate with Destiny. There are many more disasters than there are tragedies in the world, and we are ill-served by the denial of this difference. It is what I am equipped *to do* with my suffering, the Destiny that I carve out of my Fate, that defines, and alone is capable of defining, the tragic. As in so many other areas, Nietzsche was able to take an eminently Hegelian insight and to lend it an aphoristic luster it had not possessed before: "Can an *ass* be tragic? . . . The case of the philosopher." Hegel is, naturally, much kinder to the philosopher; indeed, it is only our philosophy, the dawning universal competence of a certain sort of reason, that makes us more than pack animals set to work in the world. There may be a special providence in the fall of a sparrow; but there can be genuinely affirmative greatness only in the suffering of the authentically tragic hero.

To put it another way, Hegel is out to distinguish two very different kinds of *pessimism* — as was Nietzsche, explicitly, in the new preface he wrote for the 1886 edition of *The Birth of Tragedy*. In this later edition, Nietzsche changed the subtitle to read "Hellenism and Pessimism," and we would do well to wonder why. To use the biblical idiom of which Hegel remained so fond, there is an elevated and a degenerate form of pessimism, an active and a passive degree.[61] The acceptance (Schopenhauer's word was 'resignation,' embodying the very pessimism that Hegel and Nietzsche reject) born of a "pessimistic" view of the world may be of two completely different types: passive, it speaks with the broken Job, "Here *I sit* in dust and ashes"; active, it speaks with Christ on the road to Jerusalem, "Lo, I come *to do* thy will."[62] We will have much

---

61. See *The Birth of Tragedy*, §9.
62. I do not intend this observation to argue for the superiority of one tradition over another. Such arguments are senseless. It needs to be said, however, that Kant, like the Hegel of the *Early Theological Writings* (211–216, 232, 247, 278–279), bore a strong streak of anti-Jewish feeling. It was a philosophical rather than a racial disdain in both

to say about this only superficially simple idea when we turn to Gethsemane in a subsequent chapter. "Surrender is the mystic's way, struggle
the tragic man's," and, according to Georg Lukács, "the one, at the
end of his road, is absorbed into the All, the other shattered against the
All."[63] Hegel's pessimism, insofar as it is meaningful to speak of it — and
this whole chapter means to put precisely this question — tends toward
this latter, tragic type. For Hegel, "World history is the very advance of
freedom into consciousness — a progress which needs to be seen in its
necessity [Notwendigkeit]."[64] Optimistic indeed, or so it seems until we
read on. History itself is viewed in a far more chastened light, "as the
slaughterbench at which the happiness of peoples, the wisdom of states,
and the virtue of individuals have been sacrificed."[65] Hegel's notorious
"reconciliation with reality" (Versöhnung mit der Wirklichkeit)[66] — his
own self-confessed theodicy — steers a clear and careful course between
the Scylla of overconfidence and the Charybdis of infinite resignation.

It is clearer, now, how far Hegel meant to stand from such simplistic
dichotomies as "optimistic" and "pessimistic." It is as if he is looking
for a word that will describe the person who, like Socrates, is neither,
or both at once. The Greeks characteristically enough had such a word,
sōphrosunē.[67] The whole force of the preface to The Philosophy of Right
hinges on Hegel's attempt to collapse what he considers this meaningless
and misleading pseudodistinction. In this he is explicitly developing the
political implications of his tragic-aesthetic insights. This is Sophocles
and Shakespeare translated into the political sphere. In the distinction
between romantic and classical art — as Hegel says quite explicitly, between Sophocles and Shakespeare[68] — Hegel has latched on to a crucial
insight for his own emerging tragic theory. In actual fact, Hegel's aesthetic writings present a threefold system of symbolic, classical, and

cases, tied to a belief in something — equal parts reason and love — that goes beyond
"the Law."
    As we have seen, part of Hegel's movement beyond Kant in his first years at Jena
began when he took a second long look at the value of law and attempted at the
same time to rehabilitate the battered caricature of Creon in Sophocles' play. This is
the decisive point, I think, marking the great shift in his moral thought. See Steiner,
Antigones, 24.
    63. Georg Lukács, "The Metaphysics of Tragedy," in Soul and Form, trans. Anna
Bostock (Cambridge, Mass.: MIT Press, 1974) 160.
    64. Hegel, The Philosophy of History, trans. J. Sibree (New York: Dover Publica-
tions, 1956) 19; Werke, XII, 32.
    65. The Philosophy of History, 21; Werke, XII, 35.
    66. Hegel, The Philosophy of Right, preface, §13; Werke, VII, 27.
    67. William Arrowsmith has suggested to me that this word is perhaps best
translated by the far from simple phrase "skill at being human."
    68. For a historical discussion of this dichotomy in post-Renaissance theater, see
George Steiner, The Death of Tragedy (New York: Hill and Wang, 1961) 33, 188–190.

romantic art.[69] His lectures drive home this schematic and historicist point with impressive, if at times overdrawn, range and erudition. Still, it is not the nuance of Hegel's aesthetics that concerns us, but rather the simple observation that Hegel makes a clear and really rather emphatic distinction between the classical form of the Greek tragedies and the romantic world of Shakespeare, who has introduced us to the subjective realm of inner thoughts and feeling. His characters, much more so than Aeschylus' or even Sophocles', live and breathe with an undeniable inner life. I am not quite so sure as Hegel was of this, since Homer's characters already possess an extraordinary inner depth. That is the self-same ambivalence we have met before in Hegel, an excessive historicism. I would like to use this same polarity — Sophocles and Shakespeare — to draw out another point that is implicit if not really explicit in Hegel's contrasts.

The "modern," more postured approach to tragedy tends to be as simplistic as the optimism/pessimism dichotomy on which it depends for its very life.[70] We have neatly, all too neatly, divided the Shakespearean canon into *tragedies,* all of which end in calamity, and *comedies,* in which everything works out in the end, usually with everyone married and off to bed. What is particularly striking about this construal is that Shakespeare, who in most other ways fits so nicely into the formal Aristotelian schema[71] that is laid out in the *Poetics,* draws our attention to a lingering inconsistency exactly here. On the one hand, Aristotle *seems* to have a normative view of "the tragic," and it *seems* to require that the play end in disaster. As Lucien Goldmann puts it, tragedy "defines a universe of agonizing questions to which man has no reply."[72] In this regard, it becomes meaningful to speak of dramas that are "more and less tragic," and in fact Aristotle does so. He goes so far as to call Euripides *"the most tragic"* (*tragikōtatos*) of all the Attic poets for much the same reason.[73] Yet here again, Aristotle's analysis is a strictly formal one. For Aristotle's theory of tragedy up to this point has insisted upon three things: (*a*) a simple, rather than a complex, plot; (*b*) a fall from good fortune (*eutychea*) to ill (*dustychea*);[74] and (*c*) the fall being motivated

69. Paolucci, *Hegel: On the Arts,* 36–37.

70. For a remarkable survey of epic history, which is also the history of a "mixed style" of high seriousness and low comedy — from Homer, through Callimachus, to Virgil and Dante and Boccacio, then through Chaucer and Milton, and on into the contemporary epic forms of Tolstoy or Thomas Mann — see John Kevin Newsom, *The Classical Epic Tradition* (Madison: Univ. of Wisconsin Press, 1986).

71. Ibid., 37–72.

72. Goldmann, *The Hidden God,* 42, note.

73. *Poetics* 1453a.30.

74. Recall that these were the very terms used by Herodotus in his discussion of the truly happy man, terms that Aristotle accepts *prima facie* in the *Nicomachean Ethics.*

by a tragic error (*hamartia*).[75] It is entirely possible that Aristotle simply means to say that Euripides is clearest in staging such a formal typology. On this view, Aristotle would be saying simply that Euripides is structurally closest to his own ideas, and therefore "the most tragic" of the three. Moreover, he has done so to defend Euripides against the sharp criticisms that had been made against the poet in Aristotle's own day.

What Aristotle cannot be saying is that Euripides is "the most tragic" of the poets simply because more of his plays end in disaster.[76] For Aristotle goes on to say, almost immediately, that the best of all tragic plots, and clearly the ones he himself prefers, are those in which disaster is averted, usually at the last moment.[77] To insist that tragedy must "end badly" is as pandering to the modern posture, which finds tragedy under every fallen sparrow or airplane, as it is alien to an understanding of the deeper issues with which Greek tragedy means to deal.

And upon closer inspection, this dichotomy does not even hold for Shakespeare, as Hegel knew only too well. It is *our* typology, not his — as the late "comedies" amply attest. On the "modern" view, how are we to understand *The Tempest*, Shakespeare's penultimate dramatic labor, the whole dramatic movement of which culminates in the essential bittersweetness[78] of its end?[79] To be sure, Prospero "wins" in the end, achieves revenge upon his enemies and recognition for all the wrongs he has suffered. Yet the whole dramatic force of *The Tempest* is that it, like the gospel before it, calls into question what it is to win and what it is to lose. To achieve his victory, what a cost Prospero has had to pay — the handing over of all his many hard-won powers:

> Now my chances are all o'erthrown
> And what strength I have's mine own —
> Which is most faint.[80]

---

75. Else, *Aristotle's Poetics: The Argument*, 399–406, 446.

76. *Eis dustychian teleutōsin*, *Poetics* 1453a.26.

77. *Poetics* 1454a.5–9, and see Else, *Aristotle's Poetics: The Argument*, 421, 450–452. With this Hegel concurs: "[T]ragic resolution of tragic conflicts can be dramatically justified only where its necessity, whether objective or subjective in essence, is made intelligible by the dramatic action itself. But where the necessity of suffering and misfortune has not been demonstrated, audiences have a right to prefer something else" (Paolucci, *Hegel: On the Arts*, 196).

78. This word — the Greek is *glykypikron* — was traditionally coined by Sappho, as a description of Eros. See D. A. Campbell, *Sappho and Alcaeus* (Cambridge, Mass.: Harvard Univ. Press, Loeb Classical Library, 1982) Fragment #130. The word works equally well, I think, as a description of tragedy.

79. For an excellent discussion of this play, and for its resonances in Euripides, see William Arrowsmith's introduction to the translation of the *Alcestis*, 3–4. An excellent analysis of the late Shakespeare appears in Nikos Kazantzakis' travel notes from *England* (New York: Simon and Schuster, 1965) 262ff.

80. *The Tempest*, epilogue.

There is a heaviness, an oppressive heaviness, about this play that attenuates its comic dimensions, no matter how "happily" it may have ended. The same poet who exclaims,

> O wonder!
> How many goodly creatures are there here!
> How beauteous mankind is! O brave new world
> That has such people in't,[81]

was painfully aware of a contrary truth:

> we are such stuff
> As dreams are made on, and our little life
> Is rounded with a sleep.[82]

This play, which could be read as half a *Hamlet* and half *A Midsummer Night's Dream*, is a penetrating piece of theater. Not only this. It points out, with stunning clarity, just how simplistic this distinction between comedy and tragedy — both Greek *and* modern — has been until now.[83] It fails to recognize — what Hegel emphasized — that Shakespeare was a master at blurring genres:

> We find a much more suitable and richer interplay of the tragic and comic in modern drama since, in its development, the principle of subjectivity that so freely reigns in comedy, as we have seen, becomes a dominant feature in tragedy too.[84]

One thinks of the Fool in *Lear*, the comic interludes in *Hamlet* or *Othello*. These are not, as the scholars might have us believe, mere sop to whet the degenerate appetites of the Globe's groundlings. They are, as far as Shakespeare and Hegel were concerned, the very stuff of the subjective (and epic) life.

We have forgotten too well that marvelous ending to Plato's *Symposium*.[85] After an evening rich in discussion, those few Greeks who are still awake — Agathon, the tragic poet, and Aristophanes, the comedian — are caught up in further conversation with Socrates. He is gradually winning them over, this man who is himself the archetype for

---

81. Ibid., V, 1.

82. Ibid., IV, 1.

83. One of the most intelligent discussions of this relationship is Walter Kerr's *Tragedy and Comedy* (New York: Simon and Schuster, 1967). In a more historical, less theatrical idiom, see Newsom, *The Classical Epic Tradition*, 3–36.

84. Paolucci, *Hegel: On the Arts*, 184. Again, at the risk of repetition, the only problem I have here is the overt historicism, where Hegel feels the need to find *progress* — where later arts possess what was unavailable in an earlier age. Shakespeare is surely different than Sophocles. Whether he is superior in any sense is quite another matter. And in any case there are other places where Hegel does *not* say this.

85. *Symposium*, 223c–d. See Diskin Clay, "The Tragic and Comic Poet of the Symposium" *ARION*, n.s., 2:2 (1975) 238–261.

modern tragicomedy, to the view that the master in one genre must be master in the other. Tragedy and comedy are flip sides of a common coin. They need one another and flow from a common source. Our laughter, much like a second naïveté, takes on a profundity and depth when it emerges on the far side of tears. That which we call "suffering," or "tragedy," might also be called maturation, a coming of age.

This distinction *by way of an ending* would have been senseless to the Greeks. It is not even so compelling in more modern literature, as anyone who has once considered Goethe's *Faust* will confess. That *Faust* is a *Trauerspiel* — Hegel calls it "the one absolutely philosophical tragedy"[86] — is true in spite of the fact that both Gretchen and Faust are redeemed in the end.[87] The idea that tragedy is to comedy as tears are to laughter, or disaster to celebration, is a thoroughly medieval idea. It was immortalized, of course, by Dante — for whom the *fact* of redemption is the world's ultimate *commedia*.[88] But it was not always so. And it certainly was not so for the Greeks in the classical age. Aeschylus, so far as we know, wrote only trilogies. That is to say, a deep crisis in the moral order is presented in the first play, but it is resolved in the third. Resolution provides a dénouement. Sophocles, too, began by writing trilogies, none of which survive intact, but later took to composing single plays. All the more telling, then, that three of his seven extant tragedies also *end well*. It is only with Euripides that disaster begins to play a larger role in tragic drama. I suspect that this is precisely what many Athenians considered so decadent about him (as Aristophanes makes clear in *The Frogs*). Still, and in any case, Euripides has also left a number of tragedies, or "tragicomedies," that scholars worry so about classifying precisely because of the way they end: the *Helen*, the *Iphigeneia at Tauris*, and the *Alkestis* preeminently.

Tragedy was recognized as the forum for serious questions, for the timeless, metaphysical reflection upon the condition of our humanity. By contrast, the classical comedies were a frankly sexual and scatological business, designed to make pointed political commentary on the current events of the day. "There are no lavatories in tragic places," according to George Steiner, "but from its very dawn, comedy has had use for chamber pots."[89]

Hegel now takes this analysis to one further remove. Tragedy latches on to the essential category of *divinity*, and the absolute ethical demands

---

86. Paolucci, *Hegel: On the Arts,* 194.
87. George Steiner misses this point, as indeed he must, when he accuses Goethe of trying to "evade" tragedy at the end. See *The Death of Tragedy,* 133–135, 166–172.
88. Ibid., 11–19.
89. Ibid., 247. Alasdair MacIntyre's failure to distinguish the genres this way leads to profound interpretive problems in *Whose Justice? Which Rationality?* 56–59.

that the divine lays upon every dramatic actor. Comedy concerns itself primarily with the essence of *subjectivity*, which it presses, more often than not, to laughable extremes. A divine world and a human one... it is both a measure of Shakespeare's greatness as well as a necessary historical development of tragic drama in his day that both of these elements coalesce more and more — precisely as they do in the bittersweet conclusion of *The Tempest*. And if *The Tempest* is a play that has a foot in two worlds, Hegel seems to suggest, how much more so does Mark's gospel?

It will be a little clearer now how far the Greek theater was from thinking teleologically, from asking questions of an ending, questions about the relative "optimism" or "pessimism" of a play:

> The true development consists, in other words, in the annulment of contradictions *as contradictions,* in the reconciliation of the substantive powers which in their conflicts have struggled to destroy one another. Only then can the final point of the thing lie not in the misfortune and suffering but in the spirit's satisfaction.[90]

"Tragedy shows us pain and brings us pleasure in the process." Which is to say that suffering teaches, and *that* really is the tragic in tragedy. *You never gain something but that you lose something.*

Clearly, one of the things I am arguing against is the very teleology that Alasdair MacIntyre has turned into a canon of moral criticism, the notion that every moral philosophy, and indeed every human thought, contains an implicit end.[91] Our personal demand for closure is seldom as rigid as the academic need for it seems to be. Nietzsche's criticism is trenchant: "We have invented the concept of 'end': in reality there is no end."[92] And here again, it seems to me, we are very near to another surprising affinity between Nietzsche's and Hegel's reading of the intellectual phenomenon that we call Greece. Tragedy, not teleology — for tragedy has *no* interest in the end.

The parallels between Hegel and Nietzsche run still deeper, for both defined themselves over against Arthur Schopenhauer, or at least against the pessimistic posture that he represents. Hegel was a colleague at the University of Berlin, and Nietzsche a disenchanted pupil. Schopenhauer had done much to popularize the notion of Greek tragedy as a profoundly pessimistic genre. It counsels despair — his word is 'resignation' — in the face of the brutal fact of the world, hardly an Hegelian "reconciliation" with reality, still less a Nietzschean "Yes-saying" to

---

90. Paolucci, *Hegel: On the Arts,* 188; also 74, 184–191.
91. However arbitrary such a narrative ending may in fact be. See Alasdair MacIntyre, *After Virtue,* 2d ed. (Notre Dame, Ind.: Univ. of Notre Dame Press, 1984) 52–55, 148, 185, 215–219, 226, 243.
92. Nietzsche, *Twilight of the Idols,* VI, §8.

all of life's hardest problems. "The purpose of tragedy," Schopenhauer insists:

> is the description of the terrible side of life. The unspeakable pain, the wretchedness and misery of mankind, the triumph of wickedness, the scornful mastery of chance, and the irretrievable fall of the grand and the innocent are all here presented to us; and here is to be found a significant hint as to the nature of the world and of existence.... [Tragedy] produces resignation, the giving up not merely of life, but of the very will-to-live itself....I will allow myself only one observation more concerning the treatment of tragedy. The presentation of a great misfortune is alone essential to tragedy.[93]

Now Hegel had opposed this view eloquently in Berlin — had Schopenhauer helped him see what it was that he did *not* believe about "modernity"? It was Schopenhauer, along with Shelling in his notorious later lectures, who popularized the idea that Hegelianism is a cheap way out, a philosophical "optimism" achieved only by refusing to look at the world at its "tragic" worst. The depth of the misunderstanding — grounded as it is in the tragic posture — is uncanny. "The tragic worst" was a contradiction in terms for Hegel, as Schopenhauer failed to see, and Nietzsche regrettably seems to have inherited this prejudice. All the more extraordinary, then, that Nietzsche should have come to a view so close to Hegel's in all its particulars:

> Precisely their tragedies prove that the Greeks were *not* pessimists: Schopenhauer went wrong at this point as he went wrong everywhere.... How high had I jumped with [my] insights above the wretched and shallow chatter about optimism versus pessimism!... In this sense I have the right to understand myself as the first *tragic philosopher* — that is, the most extreme opposite and antipode of a pessimistic philosopher.[94]

There is much that is right here, but one point is overdrawn. Nietzsche was not the first tragic philosopher; Hegel had charted out this territory well before him.

In one regard, the chief tragedy of Nietzsche's intellectual career — and it *was* both a gain and a loss, for him as well as for all of us who are heir to his insights — is that he never felt inclined to take Hegel more seriously. In breaking with Schopenhauer, Nietzsche felt compelled to

---

93. A. Schopenhauer, *The World as Will and Representation,* trans. E. F. J. Payne (New York: Dover Publications, 1969) 1:252–254. This passage is quoted favorably by Martha Nussbaum at *The Fragility of Goodness,* 79, where she deems it "more nearly correct than Hegel's." I have challenged that claim and her reading of Hegel as a whole in my "Martha Nussbaum: On Tragedy and the Modern Ethos," *Soundings* 72:4 (1989) 201–217.

94. *Ecce Homo,* III, 1, § 3. See also the extraordinary statements at *The Will to Power,* §851, also written in 1888.

reject his categories, yet Hegel he opted merely to ignore. Of all things, and in contrast to very nearly everyone else, Nietzsche censures Hegel's philosophy for its *pessimism!*

> In the face of nature and history, in the face of the thorough *immorality* of nature and history, Kant was, like every good German of the old stamp, a pessimist; he believed in morality, not because it is demonstrated in nature and history, but in spite of the fact that nature and history continually contradict it. To understand this 'in spite of,' one might perhaps recall something similar in Luther, the other great pessimist … *credo quia absurdum est:* — it was with this conclusion that German logic first entered the history of Christian dogma. But even today, a millennium later, we Germans of today, late Germans in every respect, still sense something of truth, of the *possibility* of truth behind the celebrated dialectical principle with which in his day Hegel assisted the German spirit to conquer Europe — "Contradiction moves the world, all things contradict themselves" — for we are, even in the realm of logic, pessimists.[95]

Never mind that this doctrine of contradictions sounds eminently Heraclitean, and very much like Nietzsche's own. The point here is simply that it matters little if Hegel is censured as a pessimist, as by Nietzsche, or as an optimist, as by Schopenhauer and Nussbaum and very nearly everyone else. Both extremes miss the mark, which, for Hegel, was to recognize that tragedy stands at an infinite remove from either extreme. It is neither, or both at once, precisely because it is profoundly uninterested in the end.

IV

The history of the reception of Hegel's tragic thought has not been an altogether happy one. Penetrating reviews like A. C. Bradley's "Hegel's Theory of Tragedy" have been few and far between. In order to highlight just how pervasive has been this misconstrual of what Hegel actually said about tragedy, even by those steeped in his work, I would like to pause briefly and to look at what is in every other regard a remarkable book. The text, to which I have had occasion already to refer, is *The Hidden God,* intended as an exercise in "dialectical" (that is Hegelian-Marxist) literary criticism, by Lucien Goldmann. Goldmann is interested in historicizing a particular moment of profound literary productivity, thereby demonstrating his own Hegelian conviction that art, too, reflects its time and its place, that works of great art are without exception the products of profound cultural crisis.[96] More specifically,

---

95. From the 1886 preface to the reprint of *Daybreak,* §3.
96. Although in this fascination with "crisis" we are already close to the tragic posture. See Goldmann, *The Hidden God,* 23–25, 48.

Goldmann wants to describe the manner in which Racine's tragedies and the philosophical writings of Pascal reflect their immersion in the Jansenist controversy and the broader theological disputes of the age. In what is an extremely careful and tightly argued book, there is one glaring oversight — one that calls into question its chief thesis and that amply illustrates how commonplace it is, even for those immersed in Hegel's thought, to miss the essential point that he, and now I, have been so long in making. That is, the temptation always remains to slip back into the very categories that Hegel denies — optimism and pessimism — and in so doing to violate the very essence of the insights that make the Hegelian dialect true kin to the tragic thought of the classical period.

Goldmann is, by his own admission,[97] building upon the analysis of Georg Lukács, who had himself attempted to come to terms with Hegel many times, as the *first* dialectical thinker and as a *necessary* prelude to Marx. Yet Lukács' work bears the same mark of inconsistency, combining as it does a really extraordinary sensitivity to Hegel's early development with a frank hostility to the Christian faith.[98] Lukács attempts to read this antipathy back into the young Hegel, rather unconvincingly, and precisely where Hegel is appealing most explicitly *to* the faith. He does so, I suspect, because he fails to appreciate how it was that Hegel himself finally became "reconciled" to Christianity — namely, by discovering in Jesus, at long last, a figure of truly classical and *tragic* proportion.[99] The gospels became authentically tragic for Hegel some time after he finished seminary; only *thereafter* do his mature dialectical views begin to take shape. Failing to see or say this, Lukács claims that Hegel discovered only "an insoluble tragic contradiction in the life and teaching of Jesus."[100] The misconstrual is absolutely fundamental; Goldmann shares it, even if he does not share Lukács' general hostility to religious thought. This phrase — "an *insoluble* tragic contradiction" — would have been an oxymoron to the mature Hegel. His whole doctrine of tragic reconciliation points to the dialectical advances that potentially emerge out of substantive moral collisions. Tragedy does not need to end unhappily, although it does always begin that way.

Now, there is a standard question in Christian theology that has been as vexing as it has been recurrent: How seriously must one take *sin* in order to have taken it seriously enough?[101] And the standard orthodox answer has been to say that we must take sin so seriously that we are fi-

97. Ibid., 22.

98. Lukács, *The Young Hegel*, 16, 23, 227.

99. Despite what Lukács notes at *The Young Hegel*, 62.

100. Lukács, *The Young Hegel*, 123; see also 165, 184, 200–202, 403–405, 416–419, 566.

101. I am indebted to Jon P. Gunnemann for couching the theological question in

nally forced to the confession that a *God* is necessary to set the problem right. Sin is so pervasive, so deeply problematic, that grace is necessary. Naturally, such an answer is rather hollow, in that it leaves the central question unanswered:

> The need to think of the Absolute as subject, has led man to make statements like "God is the eternal," "the moral order of the world," or "love," etc. In such propositions the truth is just barely stated to be subject, but not set forth as the process of reflectively mediating itself with itself. In a proposition of that kind we begin with the word God. By itself this is a meaningless sound [*sinnloser Laut*], an empty name [*blosser Name*]; the predicate says afterwards *what it is,* gives it content and meaning; the empty beginning becomes real knowledge only when we get to the end.[102]

It is one thing to say that we recognize the *necessity* of grace, of help from the outside, and that we recognize the insufficiency of our own powers to overcome our baser nature. "Man cannot bear this *Angst,*" said Hegel; "from the terrifying reality of evil and the immutability of the law he can fly to grace alone."[103] It is one thing to say that we cannot help ourselves; it is another thing to believe it or to wallow in this *Angst.* And, in any event, it is as tempting to slip into some sort of deterministic passivity — like so many followers of Calvin — as it is to press forward with our own claims to autonomy and inner goodness, as seems to have been the case with Kant. Steering a pious and careful course between fatalism and naïve confidence has been the endless task of philosophical and theological reflection alike in the Christian era.

There is a parallel here to an important Hegelian issue with which we are now at last ready to deal. According to Hegel, tragedy's essential question may be formulated in a similar manner: *How seriously must we take* suffering, *and* fragility, *in order to assure ourselves that we have taken these things seriously enough?* This is the question with which each of us is left at the conclusion of a tragedy. Who can speak of "reconciliation with reality" in the face of so much agony without inevitably minimizing someone else's pain, without making Oedipus' or Antigone's suffering a mere spectacle for our own cathartic desire? Naturally, it is the chief criticism of Hegel's view (although, oddly enough, the same criticism is seldom ventured against Nietzsche) that he *answered* this question, that he presumed to attempt an answer:

---

these terms, as well as for leading me to consider how it might be extended to dialectical thought. See also Gadamer, *Hegel's Dialectic,* 49–51.

102. *The Phenomenology of Spirit,* preface, §23; Baillie, 84; *Werke,* III, 26–27. See also Paolucci, *Hegel: On the Arts,* 8.

103. Hegel, "The Spirit of Christianity and Its Fate" (1798–1799), in *Early Theological Writings,* 227; *Werke,* I, 341.

> In contemplating the fate which virtue, morality, even pity, experience in history we must not fall into the Litany of Lamentations [*die Litanei der Klagen*] that the good and pious often fare ill in the world, while the evil-disposed and wicked prosper.[104]

As I noted in the introduction, and as Alasdair MacIntyre's very deceptive blending of Homeric and Icelandic epics makes clear,[105] the modern posture has tended to view "tragedy" as a battle against impossible odds, a war we are all fated to lose from the beginning. We are cast into a world that lays waste our labors, into a body that is doomed to die, engaged in a battle with entropy that we can never hope to win. Such is our "litany of lamentations." Goldmann himself notes that, while tragedy does not avail itself of easy definition, there is one principle of which it cannot let go: "a deep crisis in the relationship between man and his social world"; and "questions to which man cannot reply."[106] To attempt to resolve this crisis would be to move "beyond tragedy," so the argument runs.

Thus, the tragic posture would answer Hegel's questions in strictly negative terms: we must resist the temptation to speak of reconciliation; we must, if we are to be honest with ourselves, resist any "blessed rage" for order, or closure, in human life. In order to take our own fragility seriously enough, in order to dwell long enough with the reality of human suffering, we must simply accept the radical brokenness of the world. Theodicy, as Nietzsche saw quite early on, gives way to pessimism in turn.[107]

On this view, failing to heed what I have been calling "the parable of Humpty-Dumpty," Hegel tried to outdo all the king's horses and men. He refused to see what the tragedians have always told us; he tried to put a hopelessly broken world back together again. His doctrine of "reconciliation" refuses to acknowledge — what we all know in our hearts — that some things need *to stay* broken, perhaps always

---

104. Hegel, *The Philosophy of History,* 34; *Werke,* XII, 51. He continues: "The real world is as it ought to be.... God governs the world; the actual working of his government, the carrying out of his plan — is the History of the World" (*The Philosophy of History,* 36; *Werke,* XII, 53). See also Peter Fuss and John Dobbins, *Three Essays, 1793–1795* (Notre Dame, Ind.: Univ. of Notre Dame Press, 1984) 26–27, for a theological explanation of this idea.

105. MacIntyre, *After Virtue,* 121, 128. See also my "After Virtue? On Distorted Philosophical Narratives."

106. Goldmann, *The Hidden God,* 41, 42. For more in this same vein, see Alexandre Kojève, *An Introduction to the Reading of Hegel,* trans. James H. Nichols, Jr. (Ithaca, N.Y.: Cornell Univ. Press, 1969) 34–35, *passim.* Finally, see *After Virtue,* 142–145, for an interesting discussion that, while sensitive to the complexity of the issue, still concludes that Sophoclean tragedy "systematically explores rival allegiances to incompatible goods," a rivalry that can be *ended* (by a *deus ex machina*) but never *resolved.*

107. Nietzsche, *The Birth of Tragedy,* §3.

were broken, always had a place where they would eventually crack and shear. Hegel gets his reconciliation too cheaply, so the criticism runs; he has failed to pay the full price that tragedy demands. He has, ironically enough, not dwelt long enough with the negative himself. In our tenuous transactions with divinity, the unknown remains eternally unknowable. The tragedy, and the fissures that such tragedy introduces into our world, *stay.*

This criticism, which has become a commonplace, is dangerously close to Njal's fatalism, which emphasizes an ideology at the expense of a far more complex reality. It is not Hegel who imposes his concepts (*Begriffen*) on the world so often as it is his detractors.[108] Just as sin must allegedly be considered the last word in Christian affairs (not the first?), so too here — the claim is that suffering and failure must have the last word in a tragedy, as they do in life. Short of this, neither the sin nor the suffering has been taken seriously enough. This all boils down to the customary criticism that Hegel is "too optimistic." And this, precisely in so doing, fails to acknowledge what was essential for Hegel — that this whole way of setting up the problem is what he is out to subvert.

Another way of illuminating this same point might be to reflect on the theological virtue of *hope.* Hegel's theory of tragedy insists that hope — not merely despair and paralysis — is an entirely appropriate, and even essential, tragic emotion. This is where Goldmann's analysis becomes relevant and illustrative:

> Where [Hegel and Marx] differ from [the tragic vision], however, is in replacing the tragic wager on eternity and a transcendent divinity by an immanent wager on man's future in this world. It is this wager which, for the first time since Plato in the history of Western thought, shows a deliberate break with intelligibility and transcendence, and reestablishes the unity of man with the world, thus raising *the hope* that we may return to the classicism abandoned by the Greeks.[109]

Quite naturally, Goldmann wants to distinguish the "tragic" from the "dialectical" vision. He does so for very good historical reasons, as one who believes — with Hegel, although Hegel's views were more complex than this — that thought itself evolves. As such, "the tragic vision" represents an historical mediation between the rationalism (Descartes) and empiricism (Hume) that preceded it, and the dialectical idealism (Hegel) and materialism (Marx) that followed. The essential figures in this "tragic moment" are Kant and Pascal and, to a lesser extent, Racine. Tragedy *gives birth to* dialectics. What remains unclear, however, is where the difference between these two modes of vision — tragedy and

---

108. Hans-Georg Gadamer, *Hegel's Dialectic*, 9–10.
109. Goldmann, *The Hidden God*, 48; also 56–59, 174–180.

dialectics — is supposed to lie. I suspect that Goldmann is attempting to be *too* historical in reading intellectual progress this way. He insists that the tragic vision, with the absolute demands it places upon the world, "is incapable of seeing itself in this historical perspective... as essentially a transitional phase."[110] By contrast, the dialectical vision recognizes the essential historical location of every human thought. Like MacIntyre — although he is willing to use concepts like "timelessness," "global vision," and "the human condition" — Goldmann wants to particularize a phenomenon that simply is not so particular.

For the essence of tragic thought, according to Goldmann, is captured by the concept of "the hidden God" and the theodicy of which it is the essential ingredient.[111] We are never faced with a simple choice between a Yes or No in this life. "God is always absent and always present,"[112] which is to say that God both answers and does not answer our prayers. That is the gospel of Gethsemane. To hear God clearly is to move "beyond" tragedy; to meet God face-to-face is to die.[113] Yes and No, always together, and always simultaneous. Were we to achieve our Yes too cheaply, we would fail to take sin and suffering seriously enough. Were we to wallow in the No, we would fall prey to a posturing brand of *Angst* that is the decadent legacy of existentialism popularized among effete cafe-style intellectuals. A perspective and balance are sorely lacking.

This balanced perspective, the simultaneous Yes and No, is not only dialectical; it is tragic, too. Goldmann himself seems to suggest as much when he calls Pascal *both* "the creator of dialectical thought" *and* "the first philosopher of the tragic vision."[114] The great temptation — Gold-

---

110. Can "dialectical" thought limit itself any better, we well may ask? See ibid., 34, 41.

111. I am indebted to my colleague, Wendy Farley, and her book *Tragic Vision and Divine Compassion: A Contemporary Theodicy* (Louisville: Westminster/John Knox Press, 1990) 53–59, for the helpful distinction between "radical suffering" and other, less urgent, theodicial challenges. My concern is less her claim that the Holocaust, like other twentieth-century genocides, cannot really be discussed. Words fall short; language breaks under the strain to speak of it. Rather, my concern is that, in calling ourselves a post-Holocaust generation (p. 31), we lose the meaningful (and quite biblical) distinction between *radical* and *redemptive* suffering. It seems crucial to me to insist on this difference, to insist that tragedy means to speak of redemptive suffering, not radicalness for radicalness' sake. As Farley rightly notes, "Compassion is a power to redeem from suffering" (p. 116). But as Hegel would be quick to add, tragic compassion is a power to redeem *through* suffering, not *from* it. Farley's most suggestive comments, to be carried on in a subsequent book, are those on a *divine eros* (p. 124), God's longing for the other, and the power of redemption as "the non-finality of evil" (p. 130). These are all eminently Hegelian categories.

112. Goldmann, *The Hidden God*, 11, 36, 48, 50–52, 68, 169, 247, 277.

113. Ibid., 36–39.

114. Ibid., 55. He also refers to "the tragic dialectic" at pp. ix and 11.

mann calls it "the great sin" — that both traditions argue against is the same:

> The one great sin which all dialectical [and here we should add 'tragic' as well] thought must avoid is that of saying definitely either Yes or No. Engels once said that to write "Yes, Yes" or "No, No" was to go in for metaphysics — and this was not intended as a compliment. The only way to discover human reality — Pascal realized this two centuries before Engels — is to say both "Yes" and "No," and to bring the two opposite extremes together.[115]

In passages like this one, dialectical thought is true heir to its tragic legacy. That there are differences is certain, and Goldmann elucidates them nicely. Tragedy deals only with the radically isolated individual; it is left to dialectics to deal with the concept of collectivity, and class.[116] Tragedy makes absolute demands of the world, cannot accept compromise, and experiences a constant frustration at the imposition of limits and finitude. By contrast, dialectical thought is "reconciled with reality," has made its peace with the narrower demands of *relative* progress, goals that will themselves be superseded in turn.[117] In addition, Goldmann suggests (a bit disingenuously, as we have seen) that dialectics has rescued a chastened optimism from tragedy's pessimistic maw, from the refusal of the world on its own terms.[118]

Finally — and this is the essence of his thesis — tragedy thinks ahistorically; it was left to Hegel and Marx, Engels and Lukács, to focus upon the essential fact that human consciousness itself evolves.[119] Goldmann is trying to defend an historicist perspective that insists that the tragic vision cannot be a timeless option available to human thought. It can only have existed for a relatively short period, and then it must have given way to something else. Tragedy is *itself* nothing but a more or less fleeting historical moment. And yet Goldmann himself is forced to admit — and he is honest enough to do so explicitly — that if tragedy is a mere moment, it has been a long time a-dying:

> Authentic tragedy makes its first appearance with the work of Sophocles. ...It is an unbearable world, where man is forced to live in error and illusion, and where only those whom a physical infirmity cuts off from normal life can stand the truth when it is revealed to them.... Only those who are blind can really live in this world, since as long as they keep their physical sight they can see only illusion and not truth. For the others —

115. Ibid., 169, emendation mine.
116. Ibid., 16, 240.
117. Ibid., 48, 51, 57–59, 62, 71, 90–95.
118. Ibid., 174–180.
119. Ibid., 34, 41, 215.

Ajax, Oedipus, Antigone — their discovery of the truth does nothing but condemn them to death.[120]

This comment — strong resonances of Schopenhauer here — must sound odd, given everything we have said up to this point. How seriously are we to take sin and suffering in order to assure that we have taken them seriously enough? So seriously, it would seem, that we must let them have the last word in human affairs. Any Yes that we utter subsequent to the No of the world is merely the myth that dialectics tells itself in order to hide the truth of tragedy from its open eyes. Reconciliation, like redemption, is tragically impossible. Yet, as such, "authentic tragedy" becomes a very nearly impossible and quite terrifying thing. Surely it cannot have been Aeschylus' vision — Aeschylus, whose trilogies were *always* resolved.[121] In an astonishing footnote to this same discussion, Goldmann admits as much:

> It goes without saying that this refers to *Oedipus Rex,* since *Oedipus at Colonus* is, like *Philoctetes,* an attempt to go beyond tragedy.[122]

We would need to add the *Ajax* to this list...and even *Antigone,* if Hegel's reading is right. Sophocles himself, so it seems, was seldom up to the awful (*deinon*) demands that the tragic vision places upon the human spirit.

This inconsistency must seem strange in a book that devotes itself to mapping out "the tragic vision." The one thing that may explain this, it seems to me, is Goldmann's philosophical commitment to articulating an historical development that *progressed through* a tragic moment on its way to dialectics. In so doing, he slips back into the very categories of optimism and pessimism that fly so wide of Hegel's clearer marks. My own view, while deeply sympathetic with Goldmann, is simpler. The dialectical vision that Hegel wants to articulate *is* precisely "the tragic vision," as he understands it. By this I mean that it stands "beyond optimism and pessimism," beyond a fixation upon happy and unhappy endings, beyond the skimming surface where sin, suffering, and fragility must be given the last word. That is Hegel's view, so it seems to me, and I find it a compelling one, both as a reading of Greek drama and as a necessary corrective to the tragic posture.

V

Not that it is without its problems, some of them severe. Yet what I find most compelling about Hegel is the degree to which one may venture an

---

120. Ibid., 44.
121. Ibid., 41.
122. Ibid., 44, note #1.

internal critique of his thought — that is, we may criticize Hegel's work with an appeal to standards he himself has been instrumental in establishing.[123] I think that this is perhaps best demonstrated by continuing in a vein we have already begun to explore, namely, to use Hegel's interpretation of the *Antigone* as a resource for an immanent critique of his later work, particularly his political writings such as *The Philosophy of History* and *The Philosophy of Right*.

Two issues emerge most prominently when we do so, and they are essentially linked — as will not surprise us in Hegel's system, which is, as he himself tells us time and again, a closed circle.[124] The first concerns the distinction between Fate and Destiny, or more precisely, the subtle relationship between them. In order to frame this issue accurately, we need to remind ourselves again of what we already know — namely, that within the larger framework of Hegel's thought, his aim is to describe not one phenomenological development, but two.[125] In the first, Hegel describes the emergence of self-consciousness out of a series of negative, that is, conflictual, encounters: with the objective world; within one's conscious self; and finally with some equally conscious other person, who destines us finally to mastery or servility. The outlines of this development we examined briefly in the last chapter. The end of the road is well known: "the unhappy consciousness," which seeks to reestablish a lost unity within itself yet is unable to do so in its own inescapably one-sided terms. It remains for the second, the larger, half of the *Phenomenology* to articulate a concept of "free concrete *Geist*," whereby reason at long last understands that it is "a concrete totality":

> From the fact that self-consciousness is reason, its hitherto negative attitude towards otherness turns round into a positive attitude.... *Qua* reason, assured of itself, it is at peace so far as [others] are concerned, and is able to endure them; for it is certain that its self *is* reality, certain that all concrete actuality is nothing else but it.... Reason is thus the conscious certainty of being all reality. This is how Idealism expresses its notion.[126]

To put it simply — and the issue *is* simple, at least conceptually, for Hegel — the individual requires a world, *and* the world requires an individual. Much like the master needs the servant, the state needs individuals — for *recognition*.[127] Hegel's is a very earthy and realistic

123. On this point see Georg Lukács, *History and Class Consciousness*, trans. Rodney Livingstone (Cambridge, Mass.: MIT Press, 1968, 1971) 17.
124. *The Logic of Hegel*, trans. William Wallace (Oxford: Oxford Univ. Press, 1975) §§15–18; Wallace, 20–23; §§79–90; Wallace, 244ff.; *Werke*, VIII, 60–64, 168–196.
125. Jean Hyppolite, "L'Etat du Droit," *Hegel-Studien, Beiheft* 4 (1966) 181–182.
126. *The Phenomenology of Spirit*, §§232–233; Baillie, 272–273; *Werke*, III, 178–179.
127. *The Phenomenology of Spirit*, §475; Baillie, 497; *Werke*, III, 353.

idealism, where "ontogeny recapitulates phylogeny": the path of development through which each individual consciousness evolves precisely
mirrors the development of the community at large.[128] The two are, in
fact, one: "This universal spirit is itself also an individual";[129] and "the
individual... is himself a world."[130]

The part *and* the whole, the particular *and* the universal — it is the
chief tenet of the dialectical method that these things be related, that
they mutually define one another.[131] The free, autonomous individual
and the "concrete ethical substance" that Hegel calls "the state" — that
is to say, Antigone *and* Creon — are *both* necessary moments in the
larger, tragic narrative that Hegel wants to tell. This was his essential
insight, even if he did not always maintain the rare dialectical balance
that was his hallmark.

The relevance of this duality to his comments on Fate and Destiny
is not far to seek. The world, which is to say *Geist,* has a will. Certain
things are meant to happen, *need* to happen, "*love* to happen."[132] This,
and only this, is cosmic necessity. So, too, each of us possesses a will, as
autonomous moral agents. In the collision of these two disparate wills,
in the space generated by their conflict, Destiny emerges — neither exactly what the world wills nor exactly what we will, but something else
again. It is as if, in Gethsemane, Christ had said, "Not my will, and not
yours either, but *ours!*" And that alone — Hegel is as insistent on this as
Sophocles and Homer were — constitutes a Destiny.

Both Creon and Antigone, *both* the whole and the parts (which are
each a whole in themselves), *both* Fate and free will — anything less
than this is one-sided and fails to grasp the notion of Destiny, of what
is truly necessary, *bestimmt.* Yet Hegel himself, at times, expresses this
pretty badly. At his most unsatisfying, in *The Philosophy of Right,* he
argues that *warfare* is "necessary" — as, of all things, an essential "ethical moment." Warfare and violence are one essential language in which
nations, past a certain point, commerce with one another.[133] We should
keep in mind the unsettling idea that we met already in the *Phenom-*

---

128. *The Phenomenology of Spirit,* preface §28; Baillie 89–90; *Werke,* III, 31–33. This
is also the crucial methodological assumption that allows MacCary, in *Childlike Achilles,*
to apply Freudian categories to Achilles and to claim that what we see in the *Iliad* is
both a picture of an earlier social world — heroic society — as well as a picture of
everyone's childhood memories. The Greeks, so the Egyptian priest would have it, are
"always children."

129. *The Phenomenology of Spirit,* §354; Baillie, 378; *Werke,* III, 267.

130. *The Phenomenology of Spirit,* §441; Baillie, 460; *Werke,* III, 326.

131. Goldmann, *The Hidden God,* 3–21.

132. *Philei touto ginesthai.* This statement represents the zenith of fatalistic philosophy, as represented in Marcus Aurelius, *The Meditations,* X, §21.

133. *The Philosophy of Right,* §324; Knox, 209–210; *Werke,* VII, 491–494.

enology,[134] namely, that freedom is obtained only on the far side of a life-and-death struggle, that the person who has not risked everything may claim to be a person, but not a free or fully rational moral agent. We are meant to recall the gospel in that: "You must lose your life to find it."

In any case, Hegel returns to Fate and Destiny precisely here, in his discussion of warfare:

> This Destiny [*Bestimmung*], whereby the rights and interests of individuals are established as a passing moment, is at the same time the positive moment — namely, the positing of their absolute [*an und für sich*] individuality, not merely something accidental [*zufälligen*] and unstable.[135]

But Hegel's own careful dichotomy eludes him here. Everything has become Fate in a grand cosmic sense — almost as if Hegel had finally come to take his own dramatic imagery too seriously, invoking a divine script that preexists its players, thereby eliminating all the richness and contingent nuance of world history. History and warfare have been subsumed into the system. After claiming that "war is *not* to be regarded as an absolute evil *nor* as a pure, external accident [*eine bloss aüsserliche Zufälligkeit*]," but rather as an historical *necessity,* Hegel defends his claim in the following manner:

> It is to what is by nature accidental [*Zufälligen*] that accidents [*Zufällige*] happen, and this Fate [*Schicksal*] whereby they happen is a necessity [*Notwendigkeit*]. Here as elsewhere, the point of view from which things seem purely accidental [*blossen Zufälligkeit*] vanishes if we look at them in light of the notion and of philosophy, because philosophy knows this to be mere *appearance* [*Schein*] and recognizes its essence to be necessity [*Notwendigkeit*].[136]

While the same constellation, the same play of forces, appears to be at work here — Fate and freedom, contingency and necessity — the emphasis is all wrong. Destiny is missing. Whereas it had been the chief principle of Hegel's system that the universe *requires* an individual,

---

134. *The Phenomenology of Spirit,* §§187–188, Baillie, 232–233; *Werke,* III, 148–150. See also Kojève, *An Introduction to the Reading of Hegel,* 11–21.

135. *The Philosophy of Right,* §324; Knox, 209; *Werke,* VII, 491.

136. *The Philosophy of Right,* §324; Knox, 209; *Werke,* VII, 492. Hegel continues: "It is *necessary* [*notwendig*] that finite things — property, and life itself — precisely *should be* accidental [*Zufälliges*], because that is the notion for finite things. This necessity [*Notwendigkeit*] has on the one hand a natural authority; everything finite is, after all, mortal and passing. But in the ethical substance [*sittlichen Wesen*], in the state, nature is robbed of this authority, and necessity [*Notwendigkeit*] is elevated to the status of a work of freedom, that is, to the status of something ethical [*Sittlichen*]."

needs a contingent, finite being[137] — God *must* eventually become a person[138] — he seems not to say this here. The parts have been subsumed into the whole; Antigone has been lost, absorbed into the totality of the "ethical substance," Creon's Thebes:

> At this point in his argument Hegel is close to claiming the self-revelation of Absolute Spirit, the almost autonomous resolution of the contradictory moments in the notion itself. . . . In Hegel's system the final revelation of Absolute Spirit seems to turn the tables on us, to make us witness to an epiphany, whereas all along we had felt like antagonists in a drama under our own direction.[139]

Goethe had ventured much the same criticism — in the guise of Mephistopheles — as he seems to have anticipated much of the future decadence of systematic idealism, even before Hegel had popularized the idea:

> The philosopher comes with analysis
> And proves it *had* to be like this:
> The first was so, the second so,
> And hence the third and fourth were so —
> Were the first and second less than sure,
> The third and fourth were nevermore.
> Thus are students made to believe.
> They learn to paste, but not to weave.[140]

Perhaps it really *is* still left to us — as Marx and countless others have said — to negate Hegel's negation. Tragically speaking, "It is necessary that everything *not* be necessary," if we are to do full justice to the complex and very *un*systematic Destiny of the world.

---

137. Actually, the issue is a bit more complex than this, given Hegel's interest in the phenomenon of world-historical figures, men such as Alexander, Caesar, and Napoleon. Such figures, in pursuing their own wills and desires, accomplish something that *needs* to happen in the theater of the world. For Hegel, Julius Caesar is the archetype. Caesar "did the Right, from a world-historical perspective," which is to say, he unified the Roman Empire under a single, subjective will and imposed this subjectivity on the empire. This, too, needed to happen: "This important change must not be regarded as a thing of chance [*etwas Zufälliges*], it was *necessary* [*notwendig*]." See *The Philosophy of History*, 311–313; *Werke*, XII, 377–380.

138. *The Philosophy of History*, 249; *Werke*, XII, 305.

139. Thomas MacCary, *Childlike Achilles*, 32. It is worth noting again that MacCary concludes by arguing that the first half of Hegel's project (the phenomenology of human consciousness) is of far greater value and significance than the second half (the phenomenology of *Geist*), which was clearly *Hegel's* chief concern.

140. Goethe, *Faust*, 1928–1935. One might also see Aristotle's *Metaphysics*, 1026b.1–1028a.4 and 1064b.15–1065b.4.

VI

We have now come to the heart of the matter. It is a commonplace to comment on Hegel's exceedingly slow development as a thinker. He did not publish a serious philosophical work until 1802, and he was thirty-seven years old when his *Phenomenology of Spirit* finally appeared. The rewards for this patience were many. Not the least of them is that Hegel's intellectual development was largely complete by the time he ventured his first systematic study. On this view, he spent a lifetime simply fleshing out and broadening the scope of a system of critical thought whose essential shape was never seriously altered. When Hegel's first manuscript bursts onto the philosophical stage in 1807, the world was privy to a vision that had crystalized into maturity. Hegel's system had been presented; it would be nuanced and fine-tuned, but not substantially altered.

Now, up to a point, this is all true enough. Hegel *did* have a remarkably keen sense of himself and of what he wanted to accomplish at an unusually early age. But the romanticism of this view in its extreme form is of a piece with the capitalization of all his favorite words. It mystifies the man and his method. And it would be strange indeed if this thinker, who was graced with a voracious and encyclopedic appetite for new knowledge, really failed to develop *any* substantively new ideas in the second half of his life.

We are indebted to Georg Lukács for mapping out so clearly some of the trajectories of Hegel's early development. By dealing with the juvenilia, the writings of a young man still in seminary, Lukács lends a very human dimension and an essential element of fluidity to the portrait of a very late-blooming philosopher. He does so by no means simply to shatter the mystique. He is far more interested in making the essential point that Hegel's mind *was* changed on any number of important issues, that Hegel was *passionately* engaged in the political life of Europe and therefore necessarily changed his views as events themselves changed. Moreover, and there is no great surprise in this, as an old man he gave up a great deal of the revolutionary zeal that had — along with a love of Sophocles, and of the *Antigone* in particular — first drawn him into the orbit of Hölderlin and Shelling.

Among Lukács' many noteworthy insights, one stands out to my mind as by far the most significant.[141] Not only did Hegel's political thought develop, says Lukács, but it generated, in good dialectical fashion, its own oppositions. It would be impossible to assume that Hegel, in the preface to the last book he ever saw to press, should uncon-

---

141. Lukács, *The Young Hegel*, 454–461.

sciously turn on its head the critical assumption of his first major work, also nicely laid out in *its* preface. Rather, Hegel is engaged in sticho-mythic dialogue with himself. In *The Phenomenology of Spirit,* Hegel makes explicit what he views as essential in the relationship between his philosophy and world history:

> It is not difficult to see that our epoch is a birth-time and a time of transition to a new period. Spirit has broken with the former world and its ways of thinking.... Spirit is never at rest, but is rather always in progress, on the move. But here it is like the birth of a child: after a long period of nutrition in silence, the continuity of gradual growth in size, the quantitative change is suddenly cut short by the first breath drawn — there is a break in the process, a *qualitative* change — and the child is born. In like manner the spirit of the time, growing slowly and quietly ripe for the new form it is to assume, disintegrates one fragment after another of the structure of the previous world.... This gradual crumbling to pieces, which did not alter the general look and aspect of the whole, is interrupted by the sunrise [*Aufgang*], which, in a flash and at a single stroke, brings to view the form and structure of the new world.
>
> But this new world is perfectly realized just as little as the new-born child; and it is essential to bear this in mind.... A building is not finished when its foundation is laid; and just as little is the attainment of a general notion of the whole the whole itself.[142]

Playing with an idea that is as old as Plato — philosophy as a midwife, which slowly brings new and difficult ideas to birth — Hegel argues that the world has passed through a revolution, and that everything has been made new. Revolution, then, is the *Fate* of the modern world. Philosophy — by giving us the necessary understanding of this and the categories with which to think about it — enables us to convert this blind Fate into a *Destiny*. In the new world that is even now becoming visible, at sunrise, we all have an essential role to play. The revolution will be our Destiny, only when its fateful dimension is understood; then and only then will it become what *we* make of it. Like Homer's heroes, we must choose it, be willing to fight and even to die for it.

Fifteen years later, in Berlin, this has all changed — *all* of it, down to the very imagery Hegel uses. Contrast this rhapsodic description of daybreak with what Hegel now says, in one of his best-known remarks:

> One word more on the *teaching* of what the world ought to be: philos-ophy in any case always comes on the scene too late to give it. As *the thought* of the world, it first appears only after reality [*Wirklichkeit*] has fulfilled its process of development and thus has completed itself. That which the concept teaches, that which history has shown to be necessary [*notwendig*], is that the ideal appears over against the real for the first

---

142. *The Phenomenology of Spirit,* §§11–12; Baillie, 75; *Werke,* III, 18–19.

time only when reality [*Wirklichkeit*] is matured.... When philosophy
paints its grey in grey, then a form of life has already grown old. With
grey in grey, it may be understood but it may not be made young again.
The owl of Minerva begins her flight only when dusk [*Dämmerung*] falls.
Surely it is time now to close this preface.[143]

"The extraordinary vividness with which Hegel expresses his ideas in
each passage points up the contrast in his views even more sharply,"
Lukács notes.[144] "In the first case he speaks of the dawn, in the second
of dusk; the *birth* of a new epoch in the first case, the *end* of an era in
the second." What has happened? we are wont to ask at this juncture.[145]
Two things, it seems to me. In the first place, Hegel is attempting to take
with full seriousness his own doctrine of the "reconciliation with reality" that tragic insight provides. He introduces the idea again in this
same passage.[146] What will be will be; philosophy's task is to understand it, not to change it. Philosophy cannot change anything, anymore
than it can restore lost vigor to the weariness of old age. Hegel's imagery
here comes dangerously close to Schopenhauer's doctrine of tragic "resignation," despite what Hegel says about "the cold comfort" of such
views. The comfort Hegel offers is "warmer," so he says.[147] But whether
Hegel's late views are more resigned than reconciled is a question we
can no longer avoid.

What is clear is that there *is* a fatalism in these notes and images that
is not merely a far cry from the ebullient tone of the *Phenomenology*;
it is a violation of the very concept of Destiny he himself has been so
instrumental in articulating. Now we are told that there is no undoing
what has been ordained — shades of Herodotus again or an Oedipus
without a will and a character of his own. The world has a will and
realizes itself in spite of our resistance, no matter how heroic — shades
of *Njal's Saga. Amor fati,* while not necessarily a counsel of despair, is
still a clear concession to Fate that the young Hegel stubbornly refused

143. *The Philosophy of Right*, §§15–16; Knox, 12–13; *Werke*, VII, 27–28.
144. Lukács, *The Young Hegel*, 456.
145. Lukács has his own answer, which seems warranted to me. He argues (*The
Young Hegel*, 456–457) that Hegel has reconstituted his own view of world history. The
past remains intact. Greece and Rome continue to play the role they always played, as a
beginning. The medieval middle continues to get remarkably short shrift, if only because
the Romantics gave it too much attention. It is *the present* that is completely different
now. In Jena, while writing the *Phenomenology*, Hegel had been captivated by the French
Revolution as the inauguration of a new human era, and by Napoleon as its fulfillment.
Recognizing, finally, that this made too much of an episode whose philosophical import
simply *could not* be evaluated at the time, Hegel later located the decisive turning point
of the "modern" era in the Reformation, where Luther accordingly becomes the first
"modern man."
146. *The Philosophy of Right*, preface, §13; Knox, 12; *Werke*, VII, 26–27.
147. *The Philosophy of Right*, preface, §14; Knox, 12; *Werke*, VII, 27.

to make. It is for this reason that the passage I cited earlier from *The Philosophy of Right* is really so essential. It illustrates precisely what has changed, and does so in Hegel's own terms. When Destiny, with all of its unpredictability, becomes a simple Fate again — when necessity is blind, as it has to be, at dusk — then the authentic tragedy at the heart of *human* history has been lost.

We are on essentially religious ground here, for we are talking about apocalypse, and apocalypses have primarily religious roots. It is an extremely complex idea that has been expressed in a variety of ways:

> Whether apocalypse is perceived as "the end" or "the new beginning" of the world has everything to do with what side one is on in the war of myths.[148]

On the one hand, this insight is a concise summation of Hegel's tragic vision. There is no gain without a loss, and the really significant civilizations from a world-historical perspective are *those that have died.*[149] But there remains a lingering question of emphasis. Hegel *has* changed sides in the great war of myths. Moving from Antigone to Creon, from dawn to dusk, the apocalyptic trumpet he means to sound now signals, not the *beginning,* but the *end.* If Hegel is not the reactionary he is sometimes made out to be, he *has* moved decisively to the right — toward Creon — in the endless war of tragic myths.

Now, the reasons for this startling change in a thinker who has been on the whole so remarkably consistent should at least be mentioned. As the passages we have set off against one another indicate, Hegel no longer sees his own age as a novelty, as a new beginning. He now believes that he is living at the end. This is, it seems to me, Hegel's late temptation to the tragic posture. Is *this* the "pessimist" Nietzsche criticized? Our own age is, he tells us time and again, *das letzte Stadium der Geschichte,* "the last step in History."[150] The owl has flown, dusk has fallen, and the history of human consciousness is drawing to its *necessary* close. Hegel insists at any number of places that the true order of things can be seen only at the end. Only hindsight is perfect, or in his own terms, "absolute." To live at the end of an era is to be capable of vision impossible before. Now, Hegel is quick to add that there is no cause for self-congratulation in this fact. It is "merely" a fact, and a contingent one at that. This man, Hegel, *just so happens* to be living at the end, and has therefore been vouchsafed a perspective from which

148. Ched Myers, *Binding the Strong Man: A Political Reading of Mark's Story of Jesus* (Maryknoll, N.Y.: Orbis Books, 1988) 414.

149. *The Philosophy of History,* 72–74, 173; *Werke,* XII, 96–100, 215.

150. *The Philosophy of History* 442; *Werke,* XII, 524.

the happenstance of history may be seen at last as an intelligible whole, a drama with a beginning, a middle, and now an end.

"To accept the starting point *necessarily* leads to the final result,"[151] Hegel believes. But that is the point; the beginning must be *accepted*. This point was pivotal for all his philosophical undertakings. It was perhaps a little premature of me to say that Hegel intended to do "tragic" philosophy in a Sophoclean idiom, and that the words 'tragic' and 'dialectical' are synonymous in his writings. There is indeed much in his work that suggests this equation. Still, it is unfortunately not that simple. Perhaps it is better to say that Hegelian dialectic *becomes* tragic once it is shorn of its teleological pretensions. Had Hegel been a little less interested in the end, had he been just a little less certain that his own era was in fact the era of closure and fulfillment (*Erfüllung* being another explicitly theological category), then perhaps the tragic dimension of his thought — which *is* so clearly there — would have come to fuller expression. And I think that Hegel can be fully appropriated today, despite what Marxist philosophers such as Kojève and Lukács may say, only when we separate the tragic wheat from the chaff of a pretentious teleology. An open-ended dialectic, without a closure and without an end — what I am arguing is that one need not take sides in the war of myths if one refuses to admit that a war is necessary, if one finally refuses to fight. For it is precisely this war-waging banner that Nietzsche picked up where Hegel left it, and carried into our own century.

Nonetheless, for Hegel himself, only when the curtain is drawing down, and the lights are going up, do we know that the play is ending. And, once this has been recognized, then the task of interpretation begins. Only now may we begin to speak of the "sense" the play has made, the inner necessities that have driven it, what Hegel himself, in a discussion of the concept of teleology, calls "the cunning [*List*] of reason."[152] The issue is one of closure, pure and simple — both in logical syllogisms and in human history. Are we participating in a play, with a complete script and an implicit end? Or must we rather view life, with Lukács, as "an anarchy of light and dark"?

> Nothing is ever completely fulfilled in life, nothing ever quite ends; new, confusing voices always mingle with the chorus of those that have been heard before. Everything flows, everything merges into another thing.... To live is to live something through to the end; but *life* means that nothing is ever fully and completely lived through to the end. Life is the most unreal and unliving of all conceivable existences; one can describe it only

---

151. Kojève, *An Introduction to the Reading of Hegel,* 82; see also 34–35, 90–93, 194.

152. *The Logic of Hegel,* §209; Wallace, 272; *Werke,* VIII, 365.

negatively — by saying that something always happens to interrupt the flow.[153]

It was largely through the hugely influential lectures that Alexandre Kojève gave on the *Phenomenology* in Paris between 1933 and 1939 that we have come to see how methodologically crucial was Hegel's later assumption that human history is now complete, that no *paradigmatically* new events can take place.[154] After the French Revolution and the rise of the modern bourgeois state, history will be largely "more of the same," Hegel seems to suggest. And here at the end, accidents may finally be seen for the necessity that was in them.

We should recall Herodotus' story of Cleobus and Biton,[155] the two dutiful sons whose "reward" from the gods is an early, and entirely painless, death. Alasdair MacIntyre misreads this text as he misreads much Greek literature.[156] His is an Hegelian misreading, as he seems to be vaguely aware.[157] And it is all the more ironic since so much of Hegel's *aesthetic* thought hinges on the rejection of a crass teleology. "Look to the end," Herodotus tells us, for only at the end of a life will all of its randomness and happenstance be resolved into the unity of a single narrative plot. Only at the end can consciousness be truly "happy" — until that time, there are only the various stages of unhappiness that Hegel traces out with such elegance and finesse. Hegel is convinced that he himself lives at a moment of ending and therefore that he may understand what could not have been understood before him. It is not that his wisdom is absolute, but his perspective is — for he is living at the end. And he intended to be the philosophical spokesperson for his times. How much of this tragic vision falls by the wayside when we give up the postured fixation on the end? — there is no more important question in all of Hegel's thought.

VII

In point of fact, there may be some truth to the view that Hegel is the first "modern" philosopher.[158] In saying this, I do not mean to suggest that Hegel is the spokesperson for a world-order that was decisively and

153. Georg Lukács, "The Metaphysics of Tragedy," in *Soul and Form*, trans. Anna Bostock (Cambridge, Mass.: MIT Press, 1974) 152–153.
154. See Gadamer, *Hegel's Dialectic*, 101ff.
155. Herodotus, *The Histories*, trans. David Grene (Chicago: Univ. of Chicago Press, 1987) I, §§30–33.
156. MacIntyre, *After Virtue*, 34.
157. See ibid., 3.
158. Jürgen Habermas, *The Philosophical Discourse of Modernity*, trans. Frederick Lawrence (Cambridge, Mass.: MIT Press, 1987) 51.

irrevocably changed at some point in the not-so-very-distant past. I do not want to talk about the end at all, nor do I mean to speak of Hegel in strictly "historical" terms. For all of his historicism, Hegel had a profound regard for the category of the *timeless,* that element in the human experience that has not changed so very much over the millennia — as I think his writings on tragedy and the Greeks illustrate best. "The great works of the past are not to be denied their universal validity," he says. "[Sometimes] we get the beginning and perfection all at once."[159] Rather, in speaking of Hegel's "modernity," I would like to appropriate his tragic vision as an astonishingly relevant and contemporary constellation of ideas — whose questions, and answers, are perhaps uniquely suited to our own day.

In order to do so, the tragic dimension of Hegel's thought is essential. I would like to conclude this chapter with four occasional observations that will suggest something of the timeliness of Hegel's tragic vision. We need to be clear about this: Hegel's *tragic* vision, not simply his dialectics. In bracketing his fixation upon the end, in divorcing his dialectics from an overdrawn teleology, I think that we are left with a much more sophisticated, a much richer, Hegel. He is, moreover, a thinker who can provide a lovely balance and perspective on a host of allegedly "modern" predicaments. He is, along with Nietzsche, our single greatest ally in the great war of myths that comprise so essential an ingredient of the modern situation.

1. We have witnessed a fascinating development in the moral thought of the past decade — the "rediscovery" of the moral philosophy of Aristotle. The writing of Stanley Hauerwas in Christian ethics, as well as Alasdair MacIntyre's and Martha Nussbaum's work in philosophical ethics, are three of the most eloquent presentations of this tension between the new and the old, between tradition, loosely so-called, and translation. They have all called, to an admitted variety of intellectual purposes, for a recovery (read: retranslation) of the Aristotelian account of the virtues — a view that emphasizes, among other things, their embeddedness within an intellectual and cultural *tradition.* No virtues exist in a vacuum, it is said, as virtues "in themselves." It is even a mistake to speak of rationality-as-such, MacIntyre adds. Rationality itself takes on thickness and real meaning only within the parameters of the tradition in which we just so happen to find ourselves. Hollow appeals to universal ideals — like "human rights" and "natural law" — must be dropped

---

159. Paolucci, *Hegel: On the Arts,* 59, 122. For an excellent discussion of the tension between the new and the old, of tradition and translation, in Hegel, see Gadamer's *Hegel's Dialectic,* 7ff.

in favor of more concrete realities: "is" before "ought," *nomos* before *themis*. Only by returning, by recovering our sensitivity to the richness of our own intellectual traditions may we in the West make sense of (and perhaps negotiate a way out of) our contemporary moral perplexity. As I have said, I view the return to our Greek origins as a decisive and appropriate move, yet I do so for very different reasons than these latter-day Aristotelians. I am leery of wishing Aristotle to be our sole guide along these complex paths of thinking. We have other guides, thankfully, on our journey backwards into the tragic Hellenic past — Hegel and Nietzsche chief among them. And there are, in any case, two points at which Aristotle's account of the virtues is profoundly wanting by comparison.

First, there is his much-touted Mesotes Formula, the problematic doctrine of the mean,[160] which scholars have gone to such tortuous lengths in defending, yet which really was as simple as it sounds. Aristotle seeks to define every virtue in terms of two related vices. A virtue is a mediation between bad extremes, an alleged avoidance of the twinned temptations to one-sidedness. Hegel criticizes this method explicitly at the beginning of the *Phenomenology*. He argues that "the extremes, on both sides, are nothing *in themselves* ... [but are rather] only vanishing moments, an immediate transition of each into its opposite." Dialectics demonstrates that

> the two extremes ... are now merged together; and since they have disappeared as extremes, the middle term, the mediating agency, as something other than these extremes, has also vanished.[161]

The neither/nor reasoning that animates Aristotle's ethical thought represents a very different concept of negation than the one Hegel is after (and I think that Nietzsche agrees). For Hegel, just as tragedy is in its essence an affirmative genre, so too is the dialectical collision of extremes actually *constitutive* of the moral life. Extremes are not to be avoided, but rather are to be embraced. It is not that Antigone and Creon are both *wrong* because they are extreme, as Aristotle's definition of the "tragic flaw" (*hamartia*) would seem to suggest. Rather, Hegel is after an idea much more difficult to conceptualize — an interpretation where Antigone and Creon are both in the *right,* and thus *necessarily* find themselves enmeshed in the dialectics of constitutive, tragic conflict. This is a difficult reading, hard to conceptualize, and I do not claim to have grasped it fully. Still, what *does* seem clear is that Hegel's entire tragic vision hinges upon it.

---

160. *Nicomachean Ethics,* 1106a.13–1107a.27.
161. *The Phenomenology of Spirit,* §§140, 165; Baillie, 188, 212; *Werke,* III, 114, 135. For a more concrete application of this reasoning to the phenomenon of cultural syncretism, see *The Philosophy of History,* 173, as well as Paolucci, *Hegel: On the Arts,* 27–28. Finally, see Kojève, *An Introduction to the Reading of Hegel,* 9–10.

It should also be clear how far this all stands from Aristotle's "negative" reasoning. The same simple ideas that led to the Mesotes Formula also led him to the theory of the tragic error in the *Poetics*, as I have just said.[162] Since Aristotle does not appear to have considered the meaning of tragedy apart from its *formal* considerations, he could not articulate what Heidegger called the "positive in the privative," the *constitutive* notions of negation and conflict that we explored in the last chapter. For Aristotle, tragedy requires that something be *missing;* he fails to say — what Hegel highlighted — that in tragedy something is also *discovered.*

Finally, we need to confront the related issue of Aristotle's notorious sectarianism. It is surely the most provincial and least compelling dimension to Aristotle's thought — Aristotle, who genuinely believed that it was Greece's *racial* Destiny to rule over Persia.[163] Hegel, whose universalism could not have been more explicit, will clearly have none of this. Again, an example makes the point nicely. St. Paul insists that, in the new world that is dawning under God's bright new day, there will be *"neither* Jew *nor* Greek."[164] It is a subtle detail, but an infinitely telling one, in terms of illuminating the tempting iconoclasm implicit in such a thought. In the new age which is emerging — and Hegel certainly shared this explicitly Christian apocalypticism, where the end is prelude to a marvelous new beginning — there must be *both* Jew *and* Greek. These cultural extremes must be mediated. As Hegel always insists — he returns to this point in nearly all of his lectures — the very essence of Christianity is *Vermittlung,* mediation, the heroic holding together of things that seek to separate. Cultural syntheses take place in no other way, save conflictually, as we shall have occasion to say many times in the next chapter. That phenomenon that we know as the Eastern Orthodox Christian world is precisely such a synthesis, a rich combination of Jew and Greek, worlds away from the negations Paul described:

> John. Christ. Let me
> sing the latter like a Hercules, or
> like the island which clung to Peleus, rescuing him
> from the wide desert of cool
> ocean waves. But it
> doesn't work. A fate is something else.
> More wonderful.
> Richer to sing. Unfathomable...[165]

---

162. See also René Girard, *Violence and the Sacred,* 292–293.

163. Aristotle, *The Politics,* 1254a–1255b.

164. *Galatians* 3:27–28. See also *Galatians* 6:15; *Ephesians* 2:14–16; *Colossians* 3:9–11.

165. "Patmos," fragments from a later version found in *Hölderlin: Hymns and Fragments,* ed. Richard Sieburth (Princeton, N.J.: Princeton Univ. Press, 1984) 102–105. As

What is fascinating about the Greek Orthodox tradition — which Hölderlin found on "Patmos" — is how explicitly its liturgy and ritual bear
this out. Without the affirmation of *both* traditions, the richness and determinate power of their collision will be lost. "Athens *and* Jerusalem,"
that is Hegel's formula — Hegel, who "tried to do from a Protestant
point of view what Aquinas attempted six hundred years earlier: a synthesis of Greek philosophy and Christianity, making full use of the
labors of his predecessors."[166]

2. For Hegel distinguished very clearly between determinate and
indeterminate negations,[167] tragic collisions in which positive truths
gradually emerge, and calamities or polemics in which disaster and destruction laugh last. Failing to appreciate this distinction — it lies at the
very heart of the dialectic of mastery and servility[168] — we suffer the cultural consequences. And this leads us to a second consideration. Much
has been written in recent years about "the death of tragedy" in the
modern world, a view I have touched on several times already and will
return to in conclusion. While such talk is usually couched in terms of
the very apocalypticism I mean to reject, there *is* insight to be gleaned
from all the talk. The cultural despair is itself hardly novel, as even Aristotle can attest.[169] Aristotle was just as concerned as Plato was with the
degeneracy of the theater in his own day. It had all been reduced to
the level of a spectacle, where what the audience wanted were great individual performances and stunning scenery, where actors were public
figures in a way that writers and choreographers no longer were.[170] The
essential truth had been forgotten: the poetry is what makes or breaks
a tragedy. Aristotle could almost be describing Hollywood in the 1990s;
for the cinema is as close as we ever get to a "national theater" in Amer-

---

Hegel says himself: "The sensuous [Athens] and the spiritual [Jerusalem] are both essential to art. The contest or struggle of the two in the mind of man makes him, it has been
said, an amphibious animal forced to live in two contradictory worlds at once.... When
the cultural experience of an entire age sinks into this contradiction, it becomes philosophy's task to show that neither side possesses truth in itself, that each is one-sided
and self-dissolving, that the truth lies in the reconciliation and mediation of the two"
(Paolucci, *Hegel: On the Arts*, 5).

166. Walter Kaufmann, *From Shakespeare to Existentialism* (Boston: Beacon Press,
1959) 88, reprinted in MacIntyre's *Hegel: A Collection of Critical Essays*, 21.

167. *The Phenomenology of Spirit*, §§52–53, 59, 79; Baillie, 111–112, 117–118, 137;
Werke, III, 51–53, 56–57, 72–73. It should be noted that 'determinate' might here be
rendered 'destined' (*bestimmt*) — the negation whereby we become conscious of our real
Destiny in the world. See also Aristotle's *Metaphysics* 1055a.5.

168. Kojève, *An Introduction to the Reading of Hegel*, 8.

169. See *The Poetics*, 1461b.26–1462b.18, as well as Gerald Else's *Aristotle's Poetics:
The Argument*, 633–641. Finally, see Paolucci, *Hegel: On the Arts*, 177–178.

170. See Niall W. Slater, "The Idea of the Actor," in *Nothing to Do with Dionysus?*
385–395.

ica. And he could almost be bemoaning the phenomenal success of films like the *Rocky* tetralogy. What is clear, given the extraordinary success of such films, is that our society does not consistently demand authentic tragedy of itself or of its cultural heroes. It is not that we are incapable of tragedy, whatever that would mean; in point of fact, the technology of celluloid offers us some really exciting aesthetic opportunities. The Greeks knew that they could not stage a spectacle as impressive as the one created by the mind's eye. Thus they narrated their most jarring scenes, in long messenger speeches, and invited our imaginations to wander. We today are capable of creating things even wilder and more spectacular than anything the Greek poets or their audiences imagined. To say it again, our problem is not that we are incapable of tragedy; we have simply failed to meet its demands, failed to understand what its deeper truths have to teach us. Tragedy is *not* something that "dies"; that is the posture, the enduring cultural myth. *Tragōidia* was indeed born — somewhere in Attica in the sixth century B.C.E. But it does not, cannot, die. A beginning, yes; but no end.

Compare Herakles, whose suffering knew no bounds and yet who (as Euripides is careful to tell us, in the play that bears his name) *endured* in the face of life's inevitable conflicts, with Rocky — another, very different, sort of cultural icon — who crashes and careens from one inevitable victory to another, battered and bruised, but always, cruelly, triumphant. Herakles is the great Greek symbol of the Aeschylean conviction that "[tragic] suffering teaches." By contrast, we like our drama "neat," simple conflicts between good and evil, not the tragic shades of grey, in which Hegel said philosophy always paints its portraits. How far our own drama normally stands from any moral collision such as Hegel envisioned — between two forms of right — is well attested by Stallone's films, where no expense is spared to present the opponent — products of a ruthless quest for success and technical will-to-power — in a completely unsympathetic light. Of the opponent, these "heroes" can say only, "If they die, they die" — what no Hegelian master (and precious few Homeric heroes) could *ever* say. For the master knows what Stallone does not, namely, that he *needs* the slave just as much as, if not more than, the slave needs him. He does not *lord over* the slave; he *gives himself over*[171] to him. Without that, we do not achieve recognition.

The problem with our films is not simply that the outcome is so often certain. The Greeks knew the stories long before they ever came to the theater, as Aristotle reminds us.[172] They filled the theater of Dionysus not to learn the stories, which they already knew, but rather to learn

---

171. *The Phenomenology of Spirit,* §194; *Werke,* III, 152–153.
172. *Poetics,* 1453b.24–25.

something essential about themselves. The moral potential of such a genre is lost on most of us. Thus we are left with a hollow spectacle of brutality and blood, something closer to the Roman gladiatorial arena than it is to the Athenian stage.[173] What triumphs is simply a philosophy of might making right — which is the ethos of a Rambo and which is as far from Hegel's tragic vision as it is from the Greeks who taught the tragic vision to him.

3. What is glaringly absent in our theater, as this all makes sadly apparent, is any serious account of love — an idea that is usually sentimentalized in Hollywood — where it is not caricatured as an acutely bizarre form of violence and will-to-power. *Erōs* is certainly not usually considered a topic for serious philosophical discussion, despite the fact that it is the only thing Socrates claims he ever knew anything about.[174] Where it *is* discussed, as it is by Sartre in his answer to Hegel,[175] the issue is raised only to be deflected. Love, Sartre insists, is the ultimate exercise in bad faith, the last lie consciousness tells itself in order to hide the inevitability of failure from our eyes. Failure, *échec*, which is such an important Sartrean idea, is one of the chief catchwords of the tragic posture.

Hegel begins with the "fact" of self-consciousness, a fact that he took for granted and that was not to be seriously questioned until Freud. To be self-conscious is to be already, in Hegel's sense, 'dialectical,' a potentially tragic being engaged in stichomythic exchange with oneself and with others. To be self-conscious is to be both a self and an alien, second sort of self — a self that looks at itself and reflects, half-externally, upon what it sees. We are divided within ourselves, self-alienating, a doubled (*verdoppelt*) sort of self. "I don't know what to do; I'm torn in two [*duo*]," says Sappho.[176] And yet at the same time, we are capable of bringing these two moments together, mediating them, as each of us in fact does every day.

There is a further implication here. To be tragically, dialectically self-conscious is also *necessarily* to be capable of loving. To become, at least in part, an object to oneself is to be capable of taking on the role of another, some one inescapable other whom we love. And *that* is what allows our spirit to roam freely, to transcend the animal nature that is in

---

173. Simone Weil notes, "The Romans despised foreigners, enemies, vanquished peoples, their subjects, their slaves; thus they had neither epics nor tragedies. They replaced tragedies with the sport of gladiators" ("L'Iliade, ou, Le Poème de la Force," in *La Source Greque* [Paris: Editions Gallimard, 1953] 41).
174. Plato, *Symposium,* 177e, and elsewhere.
175. Sartre, *L'Etre et le Néant* (Paris: Editions Gallimard, 1948) 361–364, 428–441.
176. Campbell, *Sappho and Alcaeus,* Fragment #51.

us, the pure egoism of survival. We are capable of sacrifice, compassion, and care. We, and perhaps we alone, *love* — erotically, passionately, and to the death.

Hegel's views crystallize, unsurprisingly, around a constellation of Greek myths. I think that his views on love might best be grasped by considering the image of the Amazonomachy — the war between men and women, a theme that adorns more classical temples than any other (the labors of Herakles being the only serious rival). Here, as in all Hegelian things, reconciliation — like tragedy itself — begins at a point of conflict and collision. Hegel is no sentimentalist. He tells us in no uncertain terms that where there is love, there must already have been a war, a stichomythic contest for self-definition and *mutual* recognition. Sappho speaks of Aphrodite as her "ally" (*symmachos*), not simply her inspiration.[177] In Sophocles' "Ode to Eros," the warfare is invoked as often as the tenderness. Our differences and conflicts are the *necessary* conditions, the starting points, for any erotics that will be worthy of the name. Laughter — *love's* laughter — emerges only on the far side of tears:

> Even feeling, bodily [*leiblich*] as well as spiritual [*geistlich*], has its dialectic. Every one knows how the extremes of pain and pleasure pass into each other: the heart overflowing [*erfüllte*] with joy seeks relief in tears, and the deepest sadness will at times betray its presence with a smile.[178]

Love appears only on the slaughterbench of what we originally thought we wanted. According to one version of this particular Amazonian myth, Achilleus killed Queen Penthesileia in battle — only to fall hopelessly in love with her in the moment when their eyes met, that moment that was her last.[179] This dramatic image seems to me a little closer to the idea Hegel has in mind. If all is fair in love and war — something Hegel certainly did *not* believe — then it is so only because the two are inseparable. Reconciliation and harmony, to be sure, but not in a manner that erases the necessities, or the agony, of the conflict. There is no gain without a loss — and in love we lose *ourselves*. True love is arguably the *most* tragic of all dialectical human facts:

---

177. And that in the only complete poem of hers that we possess. See Campbell, *Sappho and Alcaeus*, Fragment #1.

178. *The Logic of Hegel*, §81, *Zusätze*; Wallace, 118; *Werke*, VIII, 175.

179. This is at least one variant of the myth. For a review of the others, see René Malamud's essay on "Amazons" in *Facing the Gods*, trans. Murray Stein and ed. James Hillman (Dallas: Spring Publications, 1991) 47–66. Heinrich von Kleist produced his stunning *Penthesileia* in 1808; Hegel surely knew it when he came to Berlin, if not earlier. And in Kleist's version, it is Penthesileia who kills the enraptured Achilleus. For the text of this play, see *The Classic Theater*, vol. 2, ed. Eric Bentley (New York: Doubleday, 1959) 313–419.

Love completely *negates* [*aufhebt*] objectivity and thereby *annuling* and transcending reflection, *depriving* man's opposite of all its foreign character, and discovering life itself without further defect. In love the separate still remains, but as something united and no longer as something strictly separate; life [in the subject] senses life [in the object].[180]

In an age that has become ever-more sensitive to the necessity of taking "otherness" seriously, and particularly of being sensitive to the *necessary* differences between men and women, this tragic vision of love's Destiny seems peculiarly apt and pressing.[181] We must be careful, Hegel seems to say, not to conflate equality and sameness. Men and women are equal, but hardly the same. Likewise, we cannot worry about whose experience is "more authentic," "more real." Such hierarchical value judgments are Aristotle's, not Hegel's, as the first book of *The Politics* sadly attests.

Hegel tried to move in a different, more complex, direction. Women and men are decidedly different, he suggests, and would do well to accept this fateful fact. Two ways, again, however. On the one hand, we are fated to be eternally dissimilar. Yet we are not destined to eternal warfare. The battle between the sexes can have an end. Ours is not a conflict *beyond* redemption. There is a constitutive hope that lies at the heart of such tragic differences. After we collide, we can become less strange to one another. It seems to me that the best definition of this tragedy of erotic longing and intersex dialogue comes from a contemporary French feminist. She expresses it in an Hegelian idiom:

> You will always have the touching beauty of a first time, if you aren't congealed in reproductions. You will always be moved for the first time, if you aren't immobilized in any form of repetition.... And if I have so often insisted on negatives: not, nor, without, it has been to remind you, to remind us, that we only touch each other naked. And that, to find ourselves once again in that state, we have a lot to take off. So many representations, so many appearances, separate us from each other. They have wrapped us for so long in their desires, we have abandoned ourselves for so long to please them, that we have come to forget the feel of our own skin. Removed from our skin, we remain distant. You and I, apart.
>
> You? I? That's still saying too much. Dividing too sharply between us: All.[182]

Feminism is to my mind, along with the theologies of liberation in a third world context, one of the most exciting areas of authentically

---

180. *Early Theological Writings*, 305; *Werke*, I, 246. Also 211–216, 232, 247, 278–279. And Lukács, *The Young Hegel*, 112–118.

181. Steiner, *Antigones*, 17.

182. Luce Irigaray, *This Sex Which Is Not One*, trans. Catherine Porter (Ithaca, N.Y.: Cornell Univ. Press, 1977, 1985) 217–218. See also Paolucci, *Hegel: On the Arts*, 40–43; and Gadamer, *Hegel's Dialectic*, 72.

tragic thought today. It is also, of necessity, the greatest temptation to the tragic posture, with its alternating postures of nostalgia (for a pure matriarchy) and despair (for eternal warfare and endless domination). The suffering, the negations, that make our being together as men and women tragic need not end badly. In fact, it may one day end well. The peace between the sexes is at least as interesting, and probably a good deal more so, than the war has been.

4. In his best moments, Hegel could be just as inspired, just as lyrical, particularly in his theological speculations. He speaks of "the life of God" as "an elaborate game of love" (*ein Spielen der Liebe*).[183] And it is, in any case, with the theological implications of his tragic vision that I should like to conclude this chapter. Hegel is deeply committed to the idea that God sacrificed omnipotence in the very moment of creation. Creation is a self-giving, self-emptying act. This is a radically historical fact; and Hegel's most explicit comments on this idea appear, appropriately enough, in *The Philosophy of History*. The Fall is already implicit in creation, insofar as God divided Godself there:

> This is a deep truth, that evil lies in consciousness: for the brutes are neither evil nor good; the natural man just as little.... For the state of innocence, the paradisiacal condition, is that of the brute. Paradise is a park, where only brutes, not people, can remain. For the brute is one with God, but only implicitly [*an sich*]. Only Man is *Geist*, which means, only He is himself self-aware [*für sich selbst*].... The Fall is therefore the eternal mythos of Man — in fact, the very manner by which he becomes human.[184]

There is something that keeps Hegel's fascination with the Fall from the tragic posture, however. In a word, this divine act of self-division was itself "necessary." Alienation alone makes reconciliation possible. Theodicy, according to Hegel, teaches us that there *needs* to be a rift, a wound, in order for there to be healing. War before love, always — even for God:

> The Oriental antithesis of light and darkness is transferred to *Geist*, and the darkness becomes sin. For the negation of reality there is no compensation but subjectivity itself — the human will as itself universal; only thus does reconciliation [*Versöhnung*] become possible. Sin is the recognition of good and evil as separation [*Trennung*]; but this recognition also heals an ancient hurt, and is the source of infinite reconciliation [*unendlich Versöhnung*].[185]

---

183. *The Phenomenology of Spirit*, §19; Baillie, 81; *Werke*, III, 24.
184. *The Philosophy of History*, 321–322; *Werke*, XII, 389.
185. *The Philosophy of History*, 323; *Werke*, XII, 391.

As he himself insists so many times, the part and the whole must not be viewed as separate; they are indivisible. The world needs individuals just as surely as individuals need the world. God needs humanity just as inescapably as humans need one another and need God. One might almost say — Hegel's views of dialectical self-alienation demand as much — that God needed humanity, *needed* to divide Godself, to crucify Godself upon the infinite subjectivity of the world.

It is in this sense that God "sacrifices Godself." In creation, a self-transformation has taken place. *Geist* evolves. God learns. "Redemption consists in God's reconciliation with the world and thereby with himself, *through man.*"[186] Hölderlin, again:

> But their own mortality
> suffices the gods. Heaven
> requires one thing only—
> heroes and humans,
> mortals all. Since
> the gods feel nothing
> themselves (if to say so
> is permitted), they need
> some other to share and feel
> in their name.[187]

God creates free beings whom God remains free to love, but is no longer free to control. God has created, in effect, the rock too large to lift. This, then, is a setting ripe for tragedy — our world, a stage, the theater for tragic collisions. Both God's claims and our own are, in a sense, just; we are both "right." That extraordinary thesis is the essence of Hegel's real radicalism. Once again, it was nowhere Hegel's contention that these claims are "equal" in any sense — whatever that would mean — only that they are *both* valid and that they will *necessarily* come into *Kollision*. In this collision, a theodicy begins to emerge:

> God actually descends into finite, temporal existence, so as to mediate and resolve what are the inherent contradictions in the absolute's own understanding of itself.[188]

God's will, which is Fate; Christ's will, which is negated; the agony in the Garden, which is the heart of the tragedy — reconciliation, *Destiny*, on the cross. At that spot, Jesus becomes Christ. At that spot, God learns

---

186. Paolucci, *Hegel: On the Arts,* 39.
187. "The Rhine," in *Hölderlin: Hymns and Fragments,* 74–75.
188. Paolucci, *Hegel: On the Arts,* 39. It remains unclear to me that Hegel has provided an adequate theodicy, although it *is* clear that he intended to, and believed that he had. What *is* clear is that it was explicitly incarnational, and here again, there is a fascinating convergence with the early Nietzsche: "Thus do the gods justify human life: they live it themselves—the only satisfying theodicy!" (*The Birth of Tragedy,* §3).

what God cannot know in any other way, namely, what it is to suffer pain, the agony of doubt, the frustration of finitude. And at that spot, says Hegel, we are all learning still.[189] Tragedy changes things, and our friendship now takes place on a deeper and surer foundation.[190]

Thus do the gospels participate in the heady realm of tragedy. Where there is love, there has always already been a war. Jesus is on the cross, or rather *in* the cross, long before Golgotha, and until the end. "Christ will be in torment of death until the very end of the world," said Pascal. "For all that time we must not sleep."[191] In conflict with Fate, in conflict with others, divided within himself, Jesus is as are we all. That there is good news, even and especially here, that *both* the tragedies *and* the gospels teach this same somber truth, is the chief implication of Hegel's tragic vision. This is what Nietzsche finally will not allow. For Nietzsche, Jehovah and the Olympians are locked in a battle that cannot be mediated and that can have no end.

---

189. Paolucci, *Hegel: On the Arts*, 33–34, 107, 157.

190. It is perhaps relevant to note that Aristotle explicitly denies that friendship with the gods is possible, at *Nicomachean Ethics* 1159a.5–10, although he seems to contradict himself at 1162a.5. See, by way of contrast, *John* 15:15.

191. Pascal, *The Mystery of Jesus*, as quoted by Goldmann, *The Hidden God*, 76–82: "In the last analysis, Christ's acceptance of reality, his 'Yes' to fate extends not only to his own suffering and to his sleeping disciples, but also to the whole of the universe which crushes him."

Chapter 3

NIETZSCHE'S TRAGIC VISION
Dionysus against the Crucified

Such a spirit who has *become free* stands amid the cosmos with a joyous
and trusting fatalism, in the *faith* that only the particular is loathsome,
and that all is redeemed and affirmed in the whole — *he does not negate
any more.* Such a faith, however, is the highest of all possible faiths: I
have baptized it with the name of *Dionysus.*
— Nietzsche, *Twilight of the Idols*
"Skirmishes of an Untimely Man," §49

Three points emerge most clearly from Hegel's rich, though often wandering, philosophical discussions. Or rather, two related *definitions* of
"tragedy" emerge from his more disciplined reflections — two definitions, and one essential distinction. The distinction is that between *Fate
and Destiny,* so essential to this book. The first definition is that *there
is no gain without a commensurate loss.* But this rule, tragedy's lesson,
emerges from an even more essential insight into the nature of reality:
namely, *that there is more than one will in the world.* This fact implies,
and even necessitates, tragic conflict. Conceived in this manner, tragedy
is a permanent feature of human collective life — as it is in the erotic life.
Yet such a life is not beyond redemption, or in Hegel's terms, *reconciliation.* Tragedy is the very stuff of life in a morally, erotically, religiously,
and will-fully plural universe. It was so in antiquity. It was so in Hegel's
Europe. It remains so today.

In tracing out some of the timelier implications of Hegel's tragic vision, I expect the treatment of Aristotle to be of rather narrow interest
to some philosophers and some classicists. Certainly, the implications for
feminist thought, and for erotic thought, are more topical and digestible,
however incomplete and even controversial they may seem. Taking on
the endless series of *Rocky* and *Rambo* films will hardly seem an act
of courage on my part — and it is not — least of all in a "cultured"

and "academic" environment such as my own. But the christological and "crucifixionary" musings with which the last chapter concluded are bound to raise a few eyebrows, and not only among the Nietzscheans.

The jarring impact of that language, so very like Hegel's own, centers around the problem we moderns seem to have with the category of *redemptive* suffering. Radical suffering, meaningless suffering, and innocent suffering we think we know, all too well. But the tragedies dare to speak of a peculiar kind of suffering that is redemptive in nature. It is on this fact—which seems really inescapable in Sophocles' texts and in a variety of biblical sources—that my thesis hinges. That thesis is that *the gospels, at least some of them, are Christian tragedies.*

What I find positively bizarre in Nietzsche, careful reader that he is, is his tremendous unfairness to Hegel on the one hand, whom he probably had not read, and to the gospels on the other, which he surely *had* read. Nietzsche knows this message well and insists upon the tragic reality of redemptive suffering. His own mature tragic vision hinges on the idea just as surely as Hegel's did. He knows redemptive suffering to be the essence of Dionysus. Yet he denies it any relevance to an understanding of Christ's Passion. Why?

Nietzsche surely agrees with Hegel that tragic conflict, the conflict of wills, is a permanent feature of human life in *every* age. "Those who insist upon a sharp juxtaposition between Hegel and Nietzsche," says Stanley Rosen, "have understood neither the one nor the other."[1] The Greeks' honesty about such matters, particularly the tragedians' honesty, is one reason Nietzsche returns to them, time and again, with such evident relish and contagious enthusiasm. Yet there are differences, to be sure. First and foremost, unlike Hegel, Nietzsche is not really a systematic thinker.[2] In fact, a more *anti*systematic thinker is scarcely imaginable. While it would be perverse to make Nietzsche a thinker of systematic pretensions and rigor, nevertheless his mature doctrine of "*the* will to power" has a curious systematicity about it. It is as though, however briefly, Nietzsche is flirting with a philosophical system.[3] He seems to suggest, at times, that tragedy exists not because there is a willful pluralism in the world,[4] but rather because the will to power is itself conflictual and deeply divided against itself. Such a view seems to qual-

1. Stanley Rosen, *The Ancients and the Moderns: Rethinking Modernity* (New Haven: Yale Univ. Press, 1989) 204.
2. For a decisive contribution to this period in Nietzsche's intellectual development, I am indebted to James J. Winchester's discussion in *Nietzsche's Aesthetic Turn: Reading Nietzsche after Heidegger, Deleuze and Derrida* (Albany: State Univ. of New York Press, 1994) preface.
3. Ibid., chapter 2.
4. Gilles Deleuze, *Nietzsche et la philosophie* (Paris: Presses Universitaires de France, 1962) 86–88. See also Winchester, *Nietzsche's Aesthetic Turn*, chapter 3, and in

ify (where it does not deny) Hegel's contention that tragic conflict, while
necessary, may yet be redeemable conflict. Nietzsche, anti-Christian that
he is, has no tolerance for the rhetoric of "redemption" or "reconciliation." He speaks of conflict; he speaks of accepting it. He speaks not
of individual wills, but of their absorption into the whole. He speaks
insistently of Dionysus, not Christ — and of an irredeemable conflict
between them that can have no end.

That idea — *the tragic proclamation that "there is no end"* — seems
to constitute the essence of Nietzsche's corrective to Hegel's tragic philosophy, his essential (however tentative and incomplete) break with
teleology (and apocalypse), which was so essential in the last chapter.

Hegel helps us see that the gospels are another essential chapter in the
long history of Hellenistic tragic literature. And Nietzsche himself came
only slowly to his later theories of (Christian) *décadence*. His earlier
philological writings are very much in line with what Hegel is saying.[5] I
may prefer Hegel, in the final analysis, but I would not have been able
to say why without the challenge to teleological thinking that Nietzsche
represents and the perspective that he, too, invites. Positively, Nietzsche's
eloquence helps explain what Hegel's tragic vision also is saying. Negatively, Nietzsche's criticism of "Christian" *décadence* helps us see what
the gospels really do mean. In that sense, this chapter on Nietzsche's
tragic vision is a *necessary* bridge between Hegel and the Greeks, on the
one hand, and the gospels, on the other.

I

Have I been understood? Dionysus against the Crucified...

This is one of the last published lines Nietzsche ever wrote, and he did
not live long enough to see it into print himself.[6] With it, his autobiography is at an end. It appears in one of the most self-reflective

---

a very different way, Colin E. Gunton, *The One, the Three and the Many: God, Creation
and the Culture of Modernity* (Cambridge: Cambridge Univ. Press, 1993) 11–40.

5. See my "Nietzsche's Vision, Nietzsche's Greece," *Soundings* 73:1 (1990) 61–84;
and "Mark's Tragic Vision" *Religion and Literature* 24:3 (1992) esp. 13–16.

6. Nietzsche, *Ecce Homo*, "Why I Am a Destiny," §9. I have used two translations
of this book: the first by R. J. Hollingdale (New York: Penguin Books, 1979); and the
second by Walter Kaufmann (New York: Random House, 1969). In all cases, I have consulted Nietzsche's German before opting for a given translation, often modified slightly
where it has seemed warranted. The text I am using is *Friedrich Nietzsche: Sämtliche
Werke, Kritische Studienausgabe in 15 Bänden* (Nördlingen: Deutscher Taschenbuch
Verlag de Gruyter, 1967–1977). So, here, the citation would be *Sämtliche Werke*, VI,
374.

A final word is perhaps in order concerning the last feverish year of publication before
Nietzsche's collapse in January of 1889. In that last year (1888), Nietzsche completed
no less than five books: *The Case of Wagner, Twilight of the Idols, The Antichrist,
Ecce Homo,* and finally, *Nietzsche contra Wagner.* Of these books, the last is largely

passages he ever composed, in which he reflected brilliantly, if a bit madly, upon the significance of what he had attempted to say. Nietzsche saw himself, fancied himself in later life, as a philosophical apocalypse — as a beginning *and* an end. "[H]e breaks the history of mankind into two parts. One lives *before* him, one lives *after* him."[7]

This single aphorism nicely captures the twin poles of Nietzsche's thought. In the first place, Nietzsche, perhaps more than any other writer, feels himself to be an untimely thinker, *unzeitgemass*[8] and *zeitlos*, speaking to a world that is not yet able to comprehend him. He is alone, alienated, and misunderstood, and hence there is a plaintive quality to the question, *"Have I been understood?"*

But more to our present purposes, Nietzsche thinks of his untimeliness — that which makes "a Destiny" of him — in terms of his status as the first, and therefore also the greatest, anti-Christian: *Dionysus against the Crucified.*

> *Definition of morality:* morality — the idiosyncrasy of *décadents* with the hidden intention of *revenging themselves on life — and* with success. I attach value to *this* definition.
>
> The *unmasking* of Christian morality is an event without equal, a real catastrophe. He who unmasks it is a *force majeure*, a Destiny [*Schicksal*].[9]

Yet Nietzsche does far more than criticize; this is no mere "scratcher at a cracked creation."[10] To say No is the chief sign of smallness of spirit, what he calls "nihilism." Nietzsche attempts to replace a decadent, Christian morality with another more affirmative one — if not "more true," then at least healthier. He proposes, through Zarathustra, the doctrines of eternal recurrence (*ewige Wiederkunft*), of *amor fati*,[11] and of the will to power (*Wille zur Macht*), all as prospective theories

---

a collection of reworked passages from previous works, designed to demonstrate that there was, in fact, consistency in Nietzsche's criticism of Wagner and that his *Case of Wagner* was no cheap shot ventured at a dead rival. As such, that last work is hardly new. And it is the previous book, his personal and intellectual manifesto, *Ecce Homo*, which really puts the seal to the Nietzschean corpus.

7. *Ecce Homo*, "Why I Am a Destiny," §8; *Sämtliche Werke*, VI, 373.

8. William Arrowsmith translates this idea as "unmodern" in a recently edited volume of translations of Nietzsche's essays: *Unmodern Observations* (New Haven: Yale Univ. Press, 1990) xi. The relevance of that title for my thesis concerning the tragic posture is obvious.

9. *Ecce Homo*, "Why I Am a Destiny," §§7, 8; *Sämtliche Werke*, VI, 373. It wants only to be added that the verbal distinction between Fate and Destiny that was so definitive in the last chapter does not carry over. Nietzsche, like Hölderlin before him, speaks of *Schicksal* only, never *Bestimmung*. He does, however, make a great deal of Necessity (*Nothwendigkeit*) in all his later books.

10. This is the way Nickles (that is, Satan) describes the human character in Archibald MacLeish's remarkable play *J.B.* (Boston: Houghton Mifflin, 1956) 10.

11. This doctrine is first introduced in *The Gay Science*, trans. Walter Kaufmann (New York: Random House, 1974), the first aphorism of the fourth and final section of

to fill the moral void. These, and *not* a fawning Christian moralism —
in this, he argues, lies his courage and his greatness. Two things always together: an untimeliness (Have I been understood?) and a scathing
iconoclasm (Dionysus against the Crucified!). In these twinned notions
Nietzsche affirmed his Destiny.

As with Hegel before him, Nietzsche is best understood by first iden-
tifying his own recurrent questions. It is harder to do in this instance;
Nietzsche customarily fights on many fronts at once, and his aphoristic
style does not clarify matters. Clearly, the status of morality was one
recurrent Nietzschean question. The status of religion was another. The
genius of the Greeks — a *tragic* genius, at heart — was another still.

Most all of Nietzsche's *self*-definitions seem ironically negative at
first glance. They begin to appear positive only toward the end. He
called himself a philosopher (*against* Kant and Hegel, among others), a
philologist (*against* Wilamowitz-Moellendorf and an impressive host of
German pedants), a psychologist (*against* Schopenhauer and even Wagner, so he says) — and an "anti-Christian" (over against Ernest Renan,
Bruno Bauer, David Strauss, and all the contemporary "new critics" of
the gospels).[12] I would like to discuss Nietzsche as an anti-Christian[13] —
since this, of all his many masks, seems best to integrate the related
issues of morality, religion, and the Greeks that I mean to discuss.

There is a great deal at stake for Nietzsche in this fundamental polarity of Dionysus and the Crucified. Here, embedded in a single line, I
think, we find the real essence of what Nietzsche saw and of what he
tried to say. Dionysus *is anti-Christos*. This is not the same *anti-* we met
in the *Antigone*. Nietzsche is not suggesting that we opt for one god
"instead of" another. These gods are at war, and eventually one of them
must die. In order to understand the full force of this assertion, we can
do no better than to listen to Nietzsche's own further reflections upon
this polarity, which appear in his notebooks, the posthumous collection
entitled *The Will to Power*. He begins with the telling insight that it is all
too easy to speak, superficially so, about "the death of God."[14] For it is
virtually impossible to do away with the idea, to live as if we ourselves
really believed in such a death. Long after the concept dies, the need
and the necessity endure. This is his late fascination with "necessary

the original text, §276; *Sämtliche Werke*, III, 521. Nietzsche later added an important
fifth section to the book, which is among his most illuminating.

12. Nietzsche explicitly refers to this school of "Synoptic philologists" in *The
Antichrist*, §§28, 52, trans. H. L. Mencken (Torrance, Calif.: Noontide Press, 1980).

13. *The Antichrist*, see Mencken's introduction, pp. 11–13, where he makes a short
but well-balanced case for the centrality of this *nom de plume*, as well as for the project
that lies back of it.

14. Nietzsche puts that phrase in the mouth of a "madman" first, not a prophet. See
The Gay Science, §125; *Sämtliche Werke*, III, 480–482.

fictions."[15] At best, we can substitute one truth, one god, for another. This Nietzsche clearly means to do. Yet from the wheel of endless return there is no final escape. To be rid of God would be, in the strictest sense, sense-less:

> "Reason" in language — oh, what an old deceptive female she is! I am afraid we are not rid of God because we still have faith in grammar.[16]

Beyond the realm of sense lies madness. It is only "the madman," according to Nietzsche,[17] who is able to understand the full significance of this claim that others make with such decadent facility: *God is dead.*

It is not with theism that Nietzsche has a quarrel, but with the *Christian* God. It is not in religion that he finds the source of every cultural decadence, but in the *Christian* religion. In fact, he likes classical paganism a great deal — its pluralism, its agonism, its willfulness. It is not even the principle of resurrection that he rejects — for his own doctrine of the eternal return shares the same language and the same explicit concern for redemption (*Erlösung*). Dionysus, too, is resurrected. No, it is only the risen Christ that elicits his unaffected scorn. After this emphatic No, and by way of response, Nietzsche seeks to perform a resurrection, or revaluation, of his own.[18] In the "life-and-death struggle" of Dionysus and the Crucified, Nietzsche still holds to the earnest hope that it is Dionysus who will eventually triumph. It is clearly another sort of apocalypse, a different *Götterdämmerung* — only here the ending will be happy:

> Verily, that Hebrew died too early whom the preachers of slow death honor; and for many it has become a calamity that he died too early.
> As yet he knew only tears and the melancholy of the Hebrew, and hatred of the good and the just — the Hebrew Jesus: then the longing [*Sehnsucht*] for death overcame him.
> Would that he had remained in the wilderness and far from the good and the just! Perhaps he would have learned to live and to love the earth — and laughter too.
> Believe me, my brothers! He died too early; he himself would have recanted his teaching, had he reached my age.[19]

15. See *Beyond Good and Evil*, trans. Walter Kaufmann (New York: Random House, 1966) §§1–4; and Winchester, *Nietzsche's Aesthetic Turn*, chapter 4.
16. *Twilight of the Idols*, III, §5; *Sämtliche Werke*, VI, 78. See also *The Gay Science*, §354.
17. At *The Gay Science*, §125.
18. With the oddly ironic twist that his own prophet, Zarathustra, speaks in words that closely resemble those of Christ. See *The Antichrist*, §§32, 39.
19. Nietzsche, *Thus Spoke Zarathustra*, trans. Walter Kaufmann (New York: Viking Press, 1954, 1966) "On Free Death"; *Sämtliche Werke*, IV, 95.

In any case, Nietzsche presents himself as a prophet for the resurrection of this very pagan, necessarily *anti*-Christian, tradition. He has allied himself with the gods of Asgard, or Olympus, and he believes — or at least he did in his earlier phase — that they can win:

The Two Types
Dionysus and the Crucified

To determine: if the typical religious man is a form of *décadence?* The great contemporaries are, without exception, sick, and even epileptic.

But are we not forgetting another type of religious man, *the pagan?* Is the pagan cult not a form of thanksgiving and affirmation [*Bejahrung*] of life? Are its highest representatives not an apology for and deification of life? The type of an infinitely capable, ecstatic, overflowing spirit...The type which takes into itself the contradictions and questionable aspects of existence, the *liberated* [*erlösenden*] type...

Here I place the *Dionysus* of the Greeks: the religious affirmation [*Bejahrung*] of life, all of life, neither denied nor divided.[20]

In order to appreciate more fully what is at stake for Nietzsche in this polarity and polemic — it is, as I have said, a *war* that he is waging — we need to understand who these central characters are, what they embodied in Nietzsche's script. To do so, we are returned, almost in spite of ourselves, to the concept of negation, in which so much of his rhetoric, like Hegel's, resides. For these two terms orbit one another in an ellipsis of mutual nihilation. Paganism *is* anti-Christian. Christianity *is* antipagan. The choice could not be sharper, nor, from Nietzsche's perspective, clearer.[21] Christ, or more accurately, "the Crucified," is a symbol of the profoundest pessimism. The Christian religion is here construed as a simple case of nihilism, the saying No (*verneinen*) to life so allegedly characteristic of this martyr-tradition — No to all of its richness, sensuality, and fullness; No to all of its *jeunesse.* "World," says Nietzsche, "is a Christian term of abuse."[22] The Crucified is a symbol of pure suffering — suffering romanticized, sentimentalized, and in this very process, trivialized to the point of irrelevance.

Dionysus is opposed to all of this. "The tragic artist," Nietzsche reminds us, "is no pessimist. He says Yes to everything.... He is Dio-

20. *The Will to Power,* §1052; *Sämtliche Werke,* XIII, 265–266.
    21. See *Human, All-Too-Human,* trans. Marion Faber (Lincoln: Univ. of Nebraska Press, 1984), §114; *Daybreak,* trans. R. J. Hollingdale (Cambridge: Cambridge Univ. Press, 1982), §§58–59, 65, 69, 72, 76, 78, 168–172; *The Gay Science,* §§130–132, 135, 139, 277; *Beyond Good and Evil,* §46; *Twilight of the Idols,* IX, §47; *The Antichrist,* §§5, 29, 51, 59, 60; and *The Will to Power,* §§150, 187, 195, 204, 252, 1003–1052. In many instances, I will include large numbers of references such as I have done here. They are by no means exhaustive, but are meant to mark points that preoccupied Nietzsche consistently over a period of years.
    22. *The Case of Wagner,* epilogue; *Sämtliche Werke,* VI, 51.

nysian."[23] We will want constantly to reiterate this. Their opposition stems from a common starting point, for both Dionysus and Christ begin with the *fact* of semidivine suffering; they are both potentially tragic. From this single starting point, however, their paths diverge — and only Dionysus realizes his tragic potential. Jesus becomes merely negative, where he has not been made pathetic:

> Dionysus against the "Crucified": there you have the contrast. It is *not* a difference with respect to martyrdom — only here the same thing has a different meaning....
> *You guess: the problem is the meaning of suffering: whether a Christian meaning, or a tragic meaning.* ... In the first case, suffering is the road to a sacred existence; in the latter, existence is sacred enough already to justify a tremendous amount of pain.
> The tragic man affirms [*bejaht*] the harshest suffering: he is strong, full, divine enough to do so.
> The Christian denies [*verneint*] even the happiest lot on earth: he is sufficiently weak, poor, disinherited to suffer life in any form.[24]

Dionysus, like the tragic artist and also like every pagan, does what the free spirit does, what the Christian can never do: "He does not *negate* [*verneint*] any more."

II

Now, what does this all mean? To what tragic vision does it instruct or lead us? The answer to these questions is not easy, just as many of Nietzsche's foundational ideas are uneasy and unsettling. On the surface, they offer as cold a comfort as anything that Schopenhauer, or the Icelandic saga-writers, envisioned. Nietzsche himself seems to have recognized the vast burden of the challenge to free-spiritedness he was after, the sheer enormity of the task of saying Yes indiscriminately:

> That I have hitherto been a thoroughgoing nihilist, I have admitted to myself only recently: the energy, the nonchalance with which I advanced as a nihilist deceived me about this basic fact.[25]

He enjoyed sufficient self-possession, moreover, to recognize how much of his own writing relied upon an identical negation — "a Yes, a No,

23. *Twilight of the Idols*, III, §6; *Sämtliche Werke*, VI, 79.
24. *The Will to Power*, §1052; *Sämtliche Werke*, XIII, 266. See also *Daybreak*, §§62–96.
25. *The Will to Power*, §25; *Sämtliche Werke*, XII, 407–408. See also *The Gay Science*, §§344, 377; *On the Genealogy of Morals*, III, §24; *Twilight of the Idols*, "What I Owe to the Ancients," §1; *The Antichrist*, §18; and *Ecce Homo*, "Beyond Good and Evil," §1, "Why I Am a Destiny," §§1, 4.

a straight line, a goal"[26] — that is, the criticism and cavalier dismissal
of entire schools of thought, more often than not in a single line. His
grandest portrait, his Zarathustra, makes this point elegantly. The Yes
that Zarathustra knows to be his Destiny comes so uneasily to him.
"Destiny, not duty" is another central motif in this philosophical idiom.
Playing upon an old truism that is the same in German as in English,
Nietzsche resolves "to make a necessity [Noth] out of virtue":[27]

> Everything is necessity [Nothwendigkeit]; so says the new knowledge, and
> this knowledge is itself a necessity.
>   Everything is innocence [Unschuld], and knowledge is the way of
> insight into this innocence.[28]

Each of Zarathustra's many trips to the mountaintop, toward greater
self-presence and self-awareness, is punctuated by equally important periods of "going under" (Untergangen) — back to society, to others, to
the herd. Nietzsche's Gay Science originally concluded with a suggestive
aphorism entitled "Incipit Tragoedia," the tragedy commences. It was to
serve, almost verbatim, as the first section of his Zarathustra. The tragic
rhetoric is singularly fitting here — Zarathustra's presence with others,
after ten years of solitude, is a necessity, but a tragic necessity, the source
of all his gains and losses, the source finally of his tremendous spiritual
disquiet:

> When Zarathustra was thirty years old, he left his home and Lake Urmi
> and went into the mountains. There he enjoyed his spirit and his solitude,
> and for ten years did not tire of that. But at last his heart changed — and
> one morning he rose with the dawn [Morgenröthe], stepped before the
> sun, and spoke to it thus:
>   "You great star, what would your happiness be if you did not have
> those for whom you shine?... Bless this cup that wants to overflow in
> order that the water may flow from it golden and carry the reflection of
> your rapture everywhere. Behold, this cup wants to become empty [leer]
> again, and Zarathustra wants to become man [Mensch] again." — and
> Zarathustra began to go under.[29]

---

26. Twilight of the Idols, I, §44; Sämtliche Werke, VI, 66.
27. Sämtliche Werke, VIII, 290; and The Antichrist, §44.
28. Human, All-Too-Human, §107. For further references, see Human, All-Too-
Human, §§7, 39, 106; The Gay Science, §§1, 5, 56, 93, 109, 118, 205, 258, 276,
277, 335; The Antichrist, §§4, 40; Twilight of the Idols, "Morality as Anti-Nature," §6,
"The Four Great Errors," §§3, 7, 8, "Skirmishes of an Untimely Man," §29; and Ecce
Homo, "Why I Am a Destiny," §§1–9; the epilogue to Nietzsche contra Wagner; and
finally The Will to Power, §§288, 289, 545, 551, 552, 706, 707, 786, 1060, 1066.
29. The Gay Science, §342; Sämtliche Werke, III, 571.

It would be profitable indeed to analyze the variant strains of twentieth-century existentialism[30] — roughly equal parts tragedy and posture — as an extended *midrash* of this essential image from the *Zarathustra*. For one of the characteristic tenets of this modern philosophical style is its peculiar ambivalence concerning the status of other people — on the one hand, we find ourselves, much like Aristotle's "political animals," always-already in the presence of others, as *necessarily* social beings. You cannot have a "culture" (or a play) by yourself. On the other hand, "the They" represents a subtle temptation to a life of inauthenticity or bad faith, where all of life's fullness is experienced solely through the eyes of others.[31] These endlessly recurring *Untergangen* symbolize the fact that we cannot live at ease with others any more than we can live alone. The *polis, as so often rhapsodized,* is a romantic delusion: whether in Aristotle's terms or in Alasdair MacIntyre's. Moreover, Zarathustra is the prophet of destruction, nihilation, negation — yet in the very midst of this, the prophet for eternally returning natural life:

> "The god on the cross" is a flight from life, a signpost for how to break free; Dionysus cut to pieces is a *promise* in life: life will be reborn eternally and has a homecoming in destruction.[32]

III

Nietzsche's authorial life began with the topic of tragedy, and it was to be a concern — along with his related interests in culture, in morality, and in the aesthetic ideal of preclassical Greece — that dominated the horizon of his intellectual life. In the last analysis, Nietzsche wanted to be understood as the prophet for a tragic lifestyle, which he believed was as antipessimistic as it was anti-Christian. So he envisions the tragic philosopher *par excellence*. I will want to draw out Nietzsche's theory of tragedy in some detail, but before doing so, I would like to reflect upon how far Nietzsche's emphasis on tragedy places him from the tragic posture I outlined in the introduction. For now, one passage suffices: Nietzsche's definition of "tragic feeling," which is probably one of the most concise statements of his entire philosophy:

---

30. And they *are* variant, as Walter Kaufmann demonstrates in his extremely helpful introduction, *Existentialism: From Dostoevsky to Sartre* (New York: World Publishing, 1956) 9–50.

31. The canonical text for this idea is Martin Heidegger's *Being and Time*, trans. John Macquarrie and Edward Robinson (New York: Harper and Row, 1962), particularly IV, §§26–27 (pp. 153–168) where he discusses being-with-others at length.

32. *The Will to Power*, §1052; *Sämtliche Werke*, XIII, 267. See also *On the Genealogy of Morals*, where Nietzsche speaks of "that ghastly paradox of a 'God on the cross,' that mystery of an unimaginable ultimate cruelty and self-crucifixion of God *for the salvation of man?*" (I, 8); and *Beyond Good and Evil*, III, §46.

The psychology of the orgiastic as an overflowing feeling of life and strength, where even pain itself has the effect of a stimulus, gave me the key to the concept of *tragic* feeling, which had been misunderstood by Aristotle and especially by our modern pessimists. Tragedy is so far from proving anything about the pessimism of the Hellenes, in Schopenhauer's sense, that it may, on the contrary, be considered its decisive repudiation and *counter-instance*. Saying Yes [*Jasagen*] to life even in its strangest and hardest problems, the will to life rejoicing over its own inexhaustibility even in the very sacrifice of its highest types — *that* is what I called Dionysian, *that* is what I guessed to be the bridge to the psychology of the *tragic* poet. Not in order to be liberated from pity and fear, not in order to purge oneself of a dangerous affect by its vehement discharge — Aristotle took it that way — but in order *to be oneself* the eternal joy of becoming [*die ewige Lust des Werdens*], beyond all pity and fear — joy which even includes joy in destruction [*Vernichten*].

And herewith I again touch that point from which I once went forth: *The Birth of Tragedy* was my first revaluation of all values. Here again I stand on the soil out of which my will, my *ability* grows — I, the last disciple of the philosopher of Dionysus — I, the teacher of the eternal recurrence [*ewige Wiederkunft*].[33]

In this definition one sees a portrait of the very rich, and abundantly anti-Christian, ideas Nietzsche is after. What one sees less clearly is the place that the tragic man[34] occupies in such a world. Zarathustra makes most sense on a mountaintop; perhaps Nietzsche made most sense at his own peculiar kind of leisure in Sils-Maria.

Two things distinguish this tragic figure, however. First is the will to power, that is, the necessary, *biologically* necessary (*naturnothwendig*), egoism of all human life. "Our most sacred convictions," Nietzsche argues, "are judgments of our muscles."[35] This is the hard truth from which the moralist tries to hide:

When stepped on, a worm doubles up. That is clever [*klug*]. In that way he lessens the probability of being stepped on again. In the language of morals: humility [*Demuth*].[36]

---

33. *Twilight of the Idols,* "What I Owe to the Ancients," §5; *Sämtliche Werke,* VI, 160. See also *The Will to Power,* §§850–853, 1041, 1051.

34. And this figure is emphatically male for Nietzsche since woman is emphatically a locus of dis-ease and ill health. He was, as Alasdair MacIntyre points out, most concerned for a philosophy of cultural and spiritual *health* (*A Short History of Ethics* [New York: Macmillan, 1966] 223–224). Nietzsche's misogyny is, of course, legendary. One might consult *Human, All-Too-Human,* §§259, 426, and all of section VII, "Woman and Child"; *Daybreak,* §170; *Beyond Good and Evil,* §§84–86, 114–115, 127, 131, 139, 144–148, 194, 232–239. Finally, one can look almost at random through *The Gay Science,* a book that begins with the hypothesis that "truth is a woman" — namely, ever faithless and ever-changing.

35. *The Will to Power,* §314; *Sämtliche Werke,* XIII, 169.

36. *Twilight of the Idols,* I, §31; *Sämtliche Werke,* VI, 64.

Out of this solitary willfulness grows a second point, namely, that the tragic figure is a radically isolated individual with few, if any, strong attachments, save to himself and the *im*personal forces of the will:

> For one should not overlook this fact: the strong [*die Starken*] are as naturally inclined [*naturnothwendig*] to separate as the weak [*die Schwachen*] are to congregate. If the former unite together, it is only with the aim of an aggressive collective action and collective satisfaction of their will to power, and with much resistance from their individual conscience. The latter, on the contrary, *enjoy* this coming together — their instinct is just as much satisfied by this as the instinct of the born "masters" [*Herren*] (that is, the solitary, beast-of-prey [*Raubthier*] species of man) is fundamentally irritated and disquieted by organization.[37]

This element of the *Übermensch* is what Alasdair MacIntyre emphasizes in his own highly critical reading of Nietzsche, and we should perhaps pause to reflect upon the details of this criticism. MacIntyre wants to claim, in a nutshell, that Nietzsche cannot provide a social ethic since "socialness" is a bad word in Nietzsche's program. It is quite clear that MacIntyre objects to Nietzsche for the same reason that he objects to "modernity" in general: Nietzsche is a spokesperson for both the existentialism (hostility to others) and the emotivism (the crazy willfulness) that have allegedly been our modern undoing. Now, Nietzsche can be defended on this charge, and in fact Walter Kaufmann defends him at some length on precisely this point.[38] In defending him in this fashion, we are drawn to a fundamental question: Was the *polis* the chief focus of Aristotle's (and most Greek) moral philosophy? Or was Aristotle's view, and the Greek view more generally, focused upon *friendship*[39] — friendship between equals, and ideally between friends who are equal in their solitariness? Nietzsche *does* have a social ethic — and it is embodied in the very kind of deep, aristocratic friendships that Plato idealizes in the *Symposium* and elsewhere. It is, however, not a narrowly *political* ethic. It is in fact as *anti*political as it could possibly be. And *that* is precisely what MacIntyre disapproves.

There is thus a high degree of *ressentiment* in MacIntyre's criticisms. Nietzsche's "tragic" philosophy intends to be an explicit critique of every "virtue" — or, more to the point, a critique of the hypocrisy implicit in any tradition of the virtues, as well as a critique of the reactionary political agenda so often commensurate with that tradition:[40]

---

37. *On the Genealogy of Morals*, III, §18; *Sämtliche Werke*, V, 384.

38. See Kaufmann's *Nietzsche*, 251, 365–371, 412. Says Kaufmann, "He renounced Christian love for the sake of Greek friendship."

39. It is surely significant that the longest sustained discussion in the entire *Nicomachean Ethics* concerns *philia*, not the *polis*, in books VIII and IX (1155a–1172a).

40. See *Human, All-Too-Human*, §§67, 75, 83, 99, 226, 302; *Daybreak*, §§84, 98, 127–144; *The Gay Science*, §§8, 21; *Thus Spoke Zarathustra*, part II, "On the Virtu-

One cannot establish the domination of virtue by means of virtue itself;
with virtue itself one renounces power, loses the will to power.
    The victory of a moral ideal is achieved by the same "immoral" means
as every victory: force, lies, slander, injustice.[41]

Bearing all this in mind, there is much still to be gleaned in MacIntyre's
fields if we are careful and critical. I want to highlight one aspect of
MacIntyre's thesis here — a thesis that lies at the heart of his diagnosis
of "the modern problem" and one that seems astonishingly Nietzschean
to me.[42]
    As I have said before, MacIntyre's diagnosis of the modern predica-
ment (he intends to be as much a cultural diagnostician as Nietzsche
was) is grounded in his conviction that we have lost a coherent — which
is, for him, inescapably Aristotelian — tradition of social virtue. It is a
chief tenet of this view[43] that, where an Aristotelian teleology has been
lost, some version of Stoicism must arise to take its place. Where we are
no longer answerable to our political worlds, however large or small,
we are answerable to Fate. Where we no longer feel at home in small,
face-to-face communities, we must see ourselves as citizens of the world.
On the Stoic view, MacIntyre tells us, goods are now derived from the
model of nature since they may no longer be grounded in intelligible social practices. The good must be "naturally" good where it is not good
because society defines it this way. By the same token, the only relevant
narrative is now a narrative of the universe, of the whole, over against
the petty sectarianisms of any and every smaller community.[44]
    It is clear that MacIntyre reads Nietzsche as the most eloquent mod-
ern spokesperson for the Stoic tradition, or at least crucial aspects of
that centuries-long Greek and Roman tradition.[45] While Nietzsche is

---

ous"; *Beyond Good and Evil*, section VII, "Our Virtues" (where "honesty" is the only
one remaining); *The Antichrist*, §11; and *The Will to Power*, §§304–329, 552.
    41. *The Will to Power*, §§305, 306; *Sämtliche Werke*, XII, 273 and XIII, 25. It is
worth noting that Hegel offered much the same criticism of "virtue" in his own early
political writings. Of the French Revolution, he says: "Robespierre set up the principle of
virtue as supreme, and one may certainly admit that virtue was of the utmost seriousness
to this man. Virtue and terror are the order of the day; for subjective virtue, which is
ruled by conviction alone, brings the most fearsome tyranny in its train. It exercises
power without legal formalities, and its punishments are equally simple — death" (*The
Philosophy of History*, 450; *Werke*, XII, 533).
    42. Alasdair MacIntyre, *After Virtue* 2d ed. (Notre Dame, Ind.: Univ. of Notre Dame
Press, 1984) 52–56.
    43. See ibid., 168–169, 233–236.
    44. As I have said before, I believe *this* criticism can be turned around: Aristotelian-
ism, or at least MacIntyre's version of it, may be viewed as a petty and sectarianism
philosophy from the perspective of the Stoic or the natural lawyer — to say nothing of
the tragic perspective of Hegel or Nietzsche.
    45. For examples of Nietzsche's exceedingly complex relationship to the Stoic tradi-
tion, see *Human, All-Too-Human*, §§25, 80; *The Gay Science*, §§12, 131, 306, 326;

violently opposed to the apathetic virtues of Marcus Aurelius, as he is opposed to any brand of decadent (primarily Christian) "resignationism," his recovery of the principle of *amor fati* does lend itself to MacIntyre's observation. Nietzsche's *Übermensch*, says MacIntyre — we should perhaps again think of Zarathustra, despite Nietzsche's own ambivalence about him — lacks two essential things: he enjoys no genuine human relationships, no community;[46] and he has no meaningful social activities or practices.[47] On this view, the poetic image of Zarathustra, as well as Nietzsche's larger philosophical project, are embedded in a set of selfish conceptual categories, a tragic brand of what MacIntyre calls "moral solipsism."[48]

Now, as I say, there is a certain substance to this charge, although it paints in broad strokes, violating all of the richness of Nietzsche's texts and failing to recognize that Nietzsche knew well what he wanted and knew that he did *not* want to be "political." It is thus all the more significant that MacIntyre, who insists that these texts really are definitive, never actually reads any of them.[49] But I should like to backtrack a bit in order to understand more clearly the genealogy of MacIntyre's own position as well as its surprisingly Nietzschean affinities.

He begins, just as Nietzsche does, with a diagnosis of "the modern condition." In the absence of a coherent (read: Aristotelian) teleology, MacIntyre observes, only two parts of our inherited moral vision are still in place. We possess a short list of social virtues — things that our society has defined as "good" and "just" — and we also possess a vague notion of human nature as such. But there is something astonishing about this, and herein lies the heart of the modern problem. Absent a coherent teleology, these twin conceptions — of the virtues and of the human nature — are, in the predominantly Christian West, "expressly designed to

---

and *Beyond Good and Evil*, §§9, 227. In a word, the issue is this: Nietzsche wants a fatalism, but a joyous and affirmative fatalism. Thus, the same man who can proclaim the doctrine of *amor fati* can also complain of the pessimistic foundation of all classical Stoic thought: "Stoicism — which has only one sacrament: suicide" (*Sämtliche Werke*, XIII, 80).

46. See *Human, All-Too-Human*, §§351, 426, and Section IX, "Man Alone with Himself"; *Daybreak*, §§116–117, 177; *The Gay Science*, §§166, 182, 338, 342; as well as *The Will to Power*, §§766–793.

47. See *Human, All-Too-Human*, §§284, 439; *Daybreak*, §§97–101, 108; *The Gay Science*, §85; and *The Will to Power*, §225.

48. MacIntyre, *After Virtue*, 258.

49. Recall that MacIntyre confronts us with a choice: "Nietzsche or Aristotle?" In answering his own question, MacIntyre spends several chapters reading Aristotle for us (*After Virtue*, 146–164, 181–203). By contrast, he merely refers in passing to *two obscure passages* from Nietzsche (*The Gay Science*, §335, discussed at *After Virtue*, 113–114, and *The Will to Power*, §962 at *After Virtue*, 257–258).

be discrepant with each other."[50] Our vision of human nature renders us incapable of the virtues we say we want. But that is *precisely Nietzsche's criticism*! The *Christian* moral vision is grounded in the Pauline assumption that "I can will what is right, but I cannot do it. For I do not do the good I want; the evil I do not want is what I do."[51] The Christian doctrine of original sin lends a "tragic" pallor to all conventional moral discourse. This point is absolutely essential: sin, the paradigmatic tragic flaw,[52] renders the whole project of conventional morality a "tragic" battle that none of us can hope to win. Not only have we returned to the world of *Njal's Saga;* it should be clearer how closely MacIntyre's own diagnosis accords with Nietzsche's: Dionysus *against* the Crucified!

Now, how has this all come about? Whence this "radical incommensurability" within our moral traditions? The answer is not far to find. We are heir, says MacIntyre, to a fatally flawed attempt to synthesize two disparate moral traditions; we have attempted to combine an Aristotelian account of the virtues with a Christian view of human nature and original sin. We want our Greeks and our Christians, too. This is the heart of the problem: such cultural syntheses are self-deceptive and conceptually flawed.[53] It was precisely this synthesis that Aquinas attempted, and it was doomed from the start. This makes Aquinas, for MacIntyre, "an unexpectedly marginal figure to the history which I am writing."[54] The solution to the problem of modernity's cultural multivalence cannot be found in any such sham synthesis. Liberal pluralism is a dangerous myth. This is the root assumption that MacIntyre and Nietzsche *share.*

Rather, the solution to this duality — Greek *versus* Christian, Dionysus *against* the Crucified — can only be found in an equally rigid either/or:

Either, we recover a heroic view of human nature, which will better accord with our Greek list of the virtues — this was Nietzsche's answer;

Or, we translate our vision of the virtues into harmony with a Christian view of human nature and original sin.

---

50. MacIntyre, *After Virtue,* 55. See also his *Whose Justice? Which Rationality?* (Notre Dame, Ind.: Univ. of Notre Dame Press, 1988) 209.

51. *Romans* 7:18–19; also 7:22–23.

52. It bears noting that the Aristotelian term for the "tragic flaw" (*hamartia*) is the same term for "sin" in the *koinē* of the New Testament.

53. For an interesting discussion of this "conflict of values," see John Casey, *Pagan Virtue: An Essay in Ethics* (New York: Oxford Univ. Press, 1990) 211–226.

54. MacIntyre, *After Virtue,* 178–180. It is infinitely telling that MacIntyre completely backs off of this claim in his most recent writing, particularly since, in so doing, as I read him, he has undercut the chief (if unstated!) Nietzschean assumption of his entire diagnosis. See *Whose Justice? Which Rationality?* x, 164–182, and esp. 402–403.

This is MacIntyre's solution, I think: a *new* list of predominantly *Christian* "virtues." But how can such a "new" table of virtues be "traditional" at the same time? *That* is the antimodern dilemma. It is the essential point of contradiction in MacIntyre's work. At the end, one is uncertain whether Aristotle, Benedict, or someone else entirely (Aquinas?) has been the *telos*. What *is* clear is that our moral Destiny today is one of interminable *waiting*, "for another — doubtless very different — St. Benedict," and presumably his new table of Christian virtues.[55] It needs to be emphasized that, while Nietzsche and MacIntyre have very different answers to the riddle of modernity, their questions — like their diagnoses — are very much the same. And it is this way of setting up the problem — of claiming that there *is* a "problem," with *"modernity"* — to which I am objecting.

It remains only to be added that MacIntyre's solution is implicit already in his diagnosis. Now that in itself is hardly a novel claim. I have said many times that the beginning and the end of a story or an argument are always linked. This Hegel knew well. What *is* novel is the discovery of how similar Nietzsche's and MacIntyre's diagnoses really are — how sharp the contrasts, how emphatic their denial of the possibility of any cultural (read: Jew–Greek) synthesis. How absolute, finally, is their presentation of the antipathy between Greeks and Christians — what surely would have been news to St. Paul, the Cappadocian Fathers, Aquinas, or Hegel — and the incommensurability of the cultural choices we face today.

Why should this contrast be so sharp? Here again MacIntyre's answer is notable both for its tragic posture and for its Nietzschean flavor: the Christian tradition is a divine comedy; *it cannot account for moral tragedy.*[56] For MacIntyre, much like Nietzsche before him, Christianity has been defined as essentially *un*pagan and, consequently, *un*tragic.[57] Any resurrection of the pagan past must necessarily couch itself in terms

---

55. MacIntyre, *After Virtue*, 263. Charles Segal, in his *The Theme of the Mutilation of the Corpse in the Iliad* (Leiden: E. J. Brill, 1971) 11 note 1, points to a third possibility. He takes note of a fundamental divergence in Homeric scholarship between: (1) the Nietzschean will to power and delight in the forces of natural excellence; and (2) the anti-Nietzschean reaction against this view after World War II, best represented in Simone Weil's essay "L'Iliade, ou, le Poème de la Force." For Weil, power and force are hardly grounds for celebration or delight. What is surely relevant to observe here is that Simone Weil is as deeply committed to *harmonizing* the Greek and Christian vision as Nietzsche and MacIntyre would seem to be in rendering them totally incompatible. If there are in facts shades of the gospel already in Homer, then it is possible to choose *neither* Nietzsche *nor* Aristotle — Hegel, perhaps (MacIntyre, *After Virtue*, 3).

56. MacIntyre, *After Virtue*, 179, 243.

57. As we saw in the last chapter, Lucien Goldmann's *The Hidden God: The Tragic Vision in Pascal's Pensées and the Tragedies of Racine*, trans. Philip Thody (London: Routledge and Kegan Paul, 1956) 68, 76–79, makes the argument that the Christian faith can indeed, and perhaps really *must*, be read as a "tragic" and heroic call to

of the Antichrist. Any resurrection of the Christian tradition must make war upon the Greeks. One way, or not at all.

IV

We will return to this claim in some greater detail, but before doing so, let us return to Nietzsche and to a slightly more favorable reading of what he tried to say. Perhaps Nietzsche's greatest contributions to philosophy are "stylistic."[58] Nietzsche's style is a triumph, almost a triumph *over* the harsh cadences of the German tongue,[59] and his aphoristic genius is unsurpassed. It is the aphorisms,[60] above all, that make Nietzsche so memorable and so quotable — he, more than any other philosopher, fancied and intended himself in an *oral*, not primarily *written*, medium. His books, as he himself notes, all have light feet:[61]

> For I approach deep problems like cold baths: quickly in and quickly out again [*schnell hinein, schnell hinaus*]. That one does not get to the depths that way, not deep enough down, is the superstition of those afraid of the water, the enemies of cold water; they speak without experience. The freezing cold makes one swift.
>
> And to ask incidentally: does a matter necessarily remain misunderstood and unfathomed merely because it has been touched only in flight, glanced at, in a flash?[62]

It would not be an overstatement to say that where Heidegger gave philosophy back the hyphen, Nietzsche has, probably single-handedly, returned the exclamation point to modern thought. That is a matter of

---

resistance in the brute face of the world — the very antithesis of what Nietzsche, and MacIntyre, allege.

58. See Jacques Derrida's *Éperons/Spurs: The Styles of Nietzsche*, trans. Barbara Harlow (Chicago: Univ. of Chicago Press, 1978) for an explicit reading of Nietzsche's work in this light.

59. *The Gay Science*, §104. It bears mentioning that Hölderlin too saw himself as the first to break out of the painful constriction of the German language. See *Hölderlin: Hymns and Fragments*, trans. and ed. Richard Sieberth (Princeton, N.J.: Princeton Univ. Press, 1984) 130–133.

60. Something he learned from the French and German aphoristic tradition on the one hand (Marion Faber, introduction to *Human, All-Too-Human*, xiii–xix), and from Ralph Waldo Emerson, on the other (*Twilight of the Idols*, "Skirmishes of an Untimely Man," §13).

61. On the light feet of men and gods, see *The Will to Power*, §1038; *Sämtliche Werke*, XIII, 526.

62. *The Gay Science*, §381; *Sämtliche Werke*, III, 634. Nietzsche explains the "moral" imperative that his style places upon the reader in *Daybreak*, §454; *Sämtliche Werke*, III, 274: "A book such as this is not for reading straight through or reading aloud but for dipping into, especially when out walking or on a journey; you must be able to stick your head into it [*hinein*] and out again [*hinaus*] and discover nothing familiar around you."

tone, of style. His is a marvelous *intermezzo* of gaiety and high seriousness. Moreover, he has mastered a pose where one very nearly *sees* him, out ahead of us, beckoning us forward and upward in the name of learning some new thing, of seeing in a way we have not seen before. His domain is on the mountaintop; it is there that he means to wait for us. For Nietzsche above all — and this is the broader philosophic point — form and content are one. "What all non-artists call form is perceived by the artist as content, as 'the thing itself.' That is the price of being an artist."[63]

Nietzsche insists, in the name of stylistic taste, that we write slowly and carefully (*sic*) and that we read even more so:

> One of the greatest values of antiquity is the fact that its writings are the only ones which modern men still *read carefully*.
>
> Overstraining of memory — very common among classicists — and underdeveloped judgment.[64]

It is not enough to read thoughts; we must *think* them, again, for ourselves. That is the philology of critical thought:

> It is not for nothing that I have been a philologist; perhaps I am a philologist still, that is to say, a teacher of slow reading: in the end I also write slowly.... For philology is that venerable art which demands of its votaries one thing above all: to go aside, to take time, to become still, to become slow — it is a goldsmith's art and connoisseurship of the *word* which has nothing but delicate, cautious work to do and achieves nothing if it does not achieve its *lento*.... This art does not so easily get anything done, it teaches to read *well*, that is to say, to read slowly, deeply, looking cautiously before and aft, with reservations, with doors left open, with delicate eyes and fingers....
>
> My patient friends, this book desires for itself only perfect readers and philologists: *learn* to read me well![65]

Now, at one level, this is precisely the aspect of his thought that Heidegger seized upon.[66] But the point is Nietzsche's own. To generalize, he cautions, is always to violate the rich fabric of another's thought, the

---

63. From the *Nachlasse*, as quoted in Bernard Fenik's *Homer and the Nibelungenlied* (Cambridge, Mass.: Harvard Univ. Press, 1986) 47.

64. *Wir Philologen*, 3[25]; *Sämtliche Werke*, VIII, 22. At roughly the same time, he writes: "*Thinkers as Stylists*. Most thinkers write badly because they tell us not only their thoughts but also the thinking of the thoughts" (*Human, All-Too-Human*, §188); *Sämtliche Werke*, II, 163).

65. *Daybreak*, 1886 preface, §5; *Sämtliche Werke*, III, 17. See also *Wir Philologen*, 7[5].

66. Martin Heidegger, *What Is Called Thinking?* trans. F. D. Wieck and J. G. Gray (New York: Harper and Row, 1968); and *Poetry, Language, Thought*, trans. Albert Hofstadter (New York: Harper Colophon, 1971) 1–14, 91–142, 213–229. George Steiner, in his *Martin Heidegger* (Chicago: Univ. of Chicago Press, 1978), highlights this point well by noting that Heidegger is, first and foremost, a spokesperson for the phenomenon of

surest sign of smallness of mind: "The will to a system is a lack of integrity."[67] And we fail to understand Nietzsche's development if we do not read him as, among other things, a critic of the German university. It was Nietzsche, whose very career as a philosopher grew out of his disaffection with the classicists of his own day;[68] Nietzsche, who sought to bring a degree of self-awareness — what he calls "psychology" — to the process of academic thought heretofore unknown; Nietzsche, whom, finally, thinkers as diverse as MacIntyre and Freud feel compelled to applaud for nothing so much as his "intellectual honesty"[69] and his "more penetrating knowledge of himself than any other man."[70]

In spite of these accolades — and they could be endlessly, if curiously, multiplied — the fundamental inconsistency of it all is apparent. Who, after all, generalized and oversimplified more than Nietzsche? His aphoristic style *depends* upon generalities, and he is forever, himself, violating the richness and complexity of others' thoughts in the name of humor, and irony, as well as something more serious that he calls "culture." It is there that we find a more serious philosophical rationale for the peculiar genius, and peculiar one-sidedness, of Nietzsche's work. In a terribly significant early essay, written about the same time as his *Birth of Tragedy*, Nietzsche ventured a preliminary definition of "culture":

> The philosopher's mission when he lives in *a genuine culture (which is characterized by a unity of style [einheitlichem Stile])* cannot be properly derived from our own circumstances and experiences, for we have no such culture....
>
> A period which suffers from a so-called high general level of liberal education but which is devoid of *culture in the sense of a unity of style [Einheit des Stils]* which characterizes all its life, will not quite know what to do with philosophy and wouldn't, if the Genius of Truth himself were to proclaim it in the streets and market places.[71]

He published a similar sentiment slightly later, in his first meditation on David Strauss: "*Culture* is above all *the unity of the artistic style [Einheit des künstlerischen Stiles]* in all the expressions of the life of a people." Its opposite is barbarism, "which is a complete lack of style or else the chaotic mish-mash of every style. The German of our own

---

intellectual *astonishment,* beginning with the shock of recognition that there are *things* instead of *no*-thing(s). To be truly astonished takes time.

67. *Twilight of the Idols,* I, §26; *Sämtliche Werke,* VI, 63.

68. See William Arrowsmith's introduction to his translation of *Wir Philologen,* in *ARION* 2:2 (1963) 5–14, and 2:4 (1963) 5–11.

69. MacIntyre, *After Virtue,* 258.

70. Ernest Jones, *The Life and Work of Sigmund Freud,* vol. II (New York: Basic Books, 1953) 344.

71. Nietzsche, *Philosophy in the Tragic Age of the Greeks,* trans. Marianne Cowan (Chicago: Henry Regnery, 1962) 33, 37; *Sämtliche Werke,* I, 809, 812; emphasis mine.

day," he adds, "lives in this mish-mash."[72] In this crucial definition of "genuine culture" embodying "a unity of style," we find the kernel of a recurrent Nietzschean image. For Nietzsche — and this is really crucial if his thought is not to be grossly mistranslated — "unity of style" is a strictly cultural phenomenon, not a racial one at all.[73] It was never Nietzsche's point to say, merely in the name of brevity and wit, that "we all know how the English are,"[74] or the Italians, or his beloved French. Rather, it was Nietzsche's conviction that our ability to speak intelligibly and in general terms about a nation *as a people* (*Volk*) is the chief evidence of their own cultural health:

> So far the Germans are nothing, but they will become something; thus they have no culture yet — thus they can have no culture yet.... So far they are nothing: that means they are all sorts of things. They *will become* something: that means, they will some day stop being all sorts of things.[75]

In *The Birth of Tragedy*, as well as in his early writings on Wagner, we encounter the earnest belief that Germany is on the verge of *possessing itself*, culturally and spiritually, for the first time. If there is not now, there soon will be a genuine German culture, an authentic German *Volk*, a *unified* German style. Nietzsche intended to be a part of this cultural renaissance — as philologist, as philosopher, and as poet.[76]

It is only fair to admit that I have followed Nietzsche here, in moving rather quickly in and out of some pretty cold water — what is perhaps the most controversial, and certainly the most contemporary, issue in Nietzsche interpretation. The problem may be summarized in a single phrase: *"the style(s) of Nietzsche."* May we read Nietzsche's "style" as unitary, or is it essentially plural?[77] Jacques Derrida has insisted, in his own reflections upon Nietzsche, that "if there is going to be style, there can only be more than one."[78] By contrast, Martin Heidegger insists that Nietzsche's *ouevre* must be reduced to a *single* style — the fragment — just as his mature philosophy may be reduced to a *single* principle: the

---

72. Nietzsche, *The Untimely Meditations*, trans. R. J. Hollingdale (Cambridge: Cambridge Univ. Press, 1982) 5–6; *Sämtliche Werke*, I, 163.

73. See *Wir Philologen*, 5[198]; *Twilight of the Idols*, VIII, §4; and Kaufmann's *Nietzsche*, 298.

74. Although he was not above saying precisely this! "Man does *not* strive for pleasure; only the Englishman does that" (*Twilight of the Idols*, I, §12; *Sämtliche Werke*, VI, 61). See also *Beyond Good and Evil*, §§252–254.

75. *The Will to Power*, §108; *Sämtliche Werke*, XI, 572.

76. Stanley Rosen, "Poetic Reason in Nietzsche," in *The Ancients and the Moderns*, 209–234.

77. For a very sober and lucid discussion with which I largely agree, see Kaufmann's *Nietzsche*, 91–93.

78. Jacques Derrida, *Éperons/Spurs*, 139. See also his "The Ends of Man," trans. Sir Eduard Morot, in *Phenomenological Research* 30 (1969) 57.

will to power.[79] Alexander Nehemas has written a lengthy and provocative interpretation of Nietzsche that seizes upon precisely this point.
Nehemas observes:

> It is remarkable that, in a secondary literature essentially concerned
> with questions about the pluralism of interpretation, Nietzsche's *stylis-
> tic* pluralism has been almost completely overlooked. Once this pluralism
> has been noticed, however, the issue of its function can no longer be
> avoided.[80]

In making this claim, Nehemas does have the apparent support of
Nietzsche's own final views on the matter: "I have many stylistic pos-
sibilities — the most manifold art of style [*Kunst des Stils*] that has ever
been at the disposal of one man."[81]

The style(s) of Nietzsche...one or many? Upon this apparently
innocuous question hinges much of the interpretation of Nietzsche's
message and its meaning. Nehemas argues that Nietzsche's stylistic pluralism is a rhetorical mirror for his mature philosophical position, what
he calls Nietzsche's "perspectivism." Building upon the notorious claim
that "facts are precisely what there are not — only interpretations,"[82]
Nehemas sees Nietzsche's different voices and personae as a way to gal-
vanize this insight and to make it stick. While I will not pursue his
argument in detail here, it does have two problems that bear on our
discussion. In the first place, Nehemas relies far too exclusively upon the
first fifty sections of *Beyond Good and Evil* as well as the unpublished
notes for *The Will to Power*, and so he provides a less holistic reading
than the one I am trying to provide. Second, and perhaps more serious,
is Nehemas' interpretation of what Nietzsche's "perspectivism" entails.
We are asked to accept, largely on faith,[83] that, while Nietzsche believed
there are no facts and only interpretations, he still insisted that not all
interpretations are equally valid — a claim echoed by Derrida, among
others. "The problem of truth does not mean that there are not lies."[84]
Some interpretations are clearly better than others, so Nehemas argues,
in an attempt to defend Nietzsche from the charge that his philosophy
reduces in the end to a relativism of the simplest sort. His thought is shot
through with "emotivism," in MacIntyre's terms, *if* stylistic "plurality"
was Nietzsche's only point. I do not think that it was.

79. Martin Heidegger, *Nietzsche*, vol. I, 7ff.

80. Alexander Nehemas, *Nietzsche: Life as Literature* (Cambridge, Mass.: Harvard
Univ. Press, 1985) 18.

81. *Ecce Homo*, III, 4; *Sämtliche Werke*, VI, 304.

82. *The Will to Power*, §481; *Sämtliche Werke*, XII, 315.

83. Nehemas, *Nietzsche: Life as Literature*, 5, 36–37, 40.

84. For my application of this principle to political discourse, see "Of Coins and
Carnage: On Rhetorical Violence and the Macedonian Question," *Soundings* 77:3 (1994)
501.

The style(s) of Nietzsche...resolved into the quest for a stylistic unity. It seems undeniable to me that Nietzsche always pursued "a unity of style," whether he ever actually achieved this or not:

> One thing is necessary. To "give style" [Stil geben] to one's character — a great and rare art!...In the end, when the work is finished, it becomes evident how the constraint of a single taste [Geschmacks] ruled and formed everything, both large and small. Whether this taste was good or bad is less important than one might suppose — so long as it was a single taste![85]

Nietzsche grew less and less confident in this dream as a cultural goal — at least for his own day, and at least in Western Europe — but then he simply internalized it, made it a radically personal ideal, in the guise of Zarathustra.

Originally, Nietzsche the essayist wrote as a cultural analyst and diagnostician, a project that he *gave up* when he gave up his larger plan for the *Untimely Meditations*. This phase, if it was a phase, was succeeded by the phase of the aphorism, which began with the publication of *Human, All-Too-Human* and continued right up to the end. There are two glaring exceptions to this: *Beyond Good and Evil* and *On the Genealogy of Morals,* both of which give the appearance of being extended essays developing a single set of theoretical questions. It is no accident that these two texts, especially *Beyond Good and Evil,* enjoy a central place in Nehemas' work. They essentially make the case for Nietzsche's stylistic pluralism before we even get underway.

Now, I do not dispute the obvious fact that, for Nietzsche, one's genre may change. I may be a poet today, an aphorist tomorrow, an essayist or letter writer the day thereafter — although it is doubtful that I will be equally adept at all three, as Nietzsche surely was not. But what remains crucial for him is that I pursue the project of "becoming what I am" with my *whole* being, at each and every stage. Genre and style are not synonyms; and "style" needs to be unified. There is a bounded unity within the multiplicity of life's many masks. I cannot, and must not, be half an essayist and half a poet. Nietzsche's *ethos,* his heroic ideal, is that of self-constancy in a world of change — an eminently Heraclitean and Sophoclean ideal, particularly clear in Sophocles' *Ajax.* One must ever be what one is, and one can never be two things at once. We

---

85. *The Gay Science,* §290; *Sämtliche Werke,* III, 530. See also *Wir Philologen,* 6[4]; *The Antichrist,* §43; *Ecce Homo* III, 2, §3. The heading of this aphorism, *Eins ist Noth,* might best be translated in two different, but complementary, ways. On the one hand, "One thing is necessary," something that Nietzsche will now go on to describe in some detail. But note the description that follows — the old question of unity of style again. "*One* thing is necessary," which is to say, "Unity [Eins] is necessary." That seems to be Nietzsche's abiding point.

will be returning to this point in the subsequent discussion since it is
so central to Nietzsche's tragic vision. This concept, along with that of
stylistic unity, helps clarify Nietzsche's ultimate intellectual goals. Developing these ideas — what is right as well as what is overdrawn in
them — will be the focus of the rest of this chapter.

V

It might be helpful at this point to sketch out what I take to be the chief
trajectories of Nietzsche's tragic vision. I will not dwell on it quite so
long as I dwelt on Hegel's, largely because it would be redundant to
do so. Tragedy is, as I have said, the great area of conceptual overlap
between the two. Still, there *are* points to be marked out, and, as always, Nietzsche marks them with characteristic flair and insight. Rather
than do an exhaustive survey of Nietzsche's writing, I will simply concentrate on the collected notes for *Wir Philologen* — a book that would
have been, had he completed it, his most extended and sustained conversation with the Greeks.[86] It is also, as I have said several times now,
a seminal work in Nietzsche's own developing confrontation with the
tragic posture:

> Philologists are those who would exploit the stilted feeling of modern
> men concerning their own vast inferiority, all to earn a living.
> I know them. I am one myself.[87]

Over against the postured pessimism of the modern age, Nietzsche sets
the authentically *tragic* vision of the Archaic and classical Greeks. If
there is any lingering doubt about his desires to do "tragic philosophy"
under the aegis of a renaissance of the classical ideal, this essay amply
dispels it: "Clearly the Greeks were *in theory a higher type* of humanity from every earlier type — that is where the knife cuts. But it is all
confined to *their tragic age*."[88]

What then are the hallmarks of Nietzsche's tragic vision? I will concentrate on four themes that endlessly recur. First and foremost, there
is this concept of suffering — *redemptive* suffering — that we have highlighted several times before. It is the indispensable first step, as I say, the
beginning of any "tragedy":

> The passion in Mimnermus, the hatred of *age*.
> The deep melancholy in Pindar: only when a ray of light

86. For more on this pivotal essay — as a defense of Nietzsche's early unmod-
ernism versus his later antimodernism — see my "Nietzsche's Vision, Nietzsche's Greece,"
Soundings 73:1 (1990) 61–84.

87. *Wir Philologen*, 5[142]; *Sämtliche Werke*, VIII, 76.

88. *Wir Philologen*, 6[18]; *Sämtliche Werke*, VIII, 105.

streams down from above does human life shine.
The world is to be understood out of *suffering* —
that is the tragic in tragedy.[89]

Why is this so? we may well wonder. The answer is not easy, nor had Nietzsche fully articulated it in 1875 when he was working on this essay. Here, more often than not, he speaks of the excessive emotions of the Greeks,[90] that explosive capacity to feel and to feel deeply that demanded periodic release — in poetry:

How *real* [*wirklich*] the Greeks were, even in pure invention! How they made poetry out of reality [*Wirklichkeit*] rather than longed to escape it![91]

Tragedy is a safety valve, a *katharsis* more explosive than anything Aristotle ever imagined. Yet Nietzsche hints at far more than this, and we find here the very set of inchoate ideas that were to crystallize around his later doctrine of the will to power. Here, at last, the answer to tragedy's riddle was to be found:

What is good? Everything which increases the feeling of power, the will to power, the power itself in people.
What is bad? Everything which makes one feel weakness. What is happiness? The feeling which comes from being up to full power, from being able to overcome resistance.[92]

Here is a clue, whose importance cannot be overrated, to what Nietzsche has in mind. The *necessity* of suffering in "tragedy" is quite simple: it is here that life presents us with resistance; and tragic pleasure derives from the successful overcoming of such resistance. In saying Yes to suffering, in joyous affirmation, lies the only genuine human happiness — not so much pleasure as power. Life is an endless school of warfare, he tells us, with a single hard lesson: "What does not destroy me makes me stronger."[93] The health of any organism, both biologically and spiritually, is measured by the amount of resistance it can meet and affirm, digest and overcome.

There is an implicit conception of heroic stature here, and that is a second point. As I noted in the last chapter, tragedy is not for everyone, and there is a great deal more suffering than there is tragedy in the world. Very few of us are able to turn our agony into poetry, to

---

89. *Wir Philologen*, 6[20]; *Sämtliche Werke*, VIII, 106.
90. *Wir Philologen*, 5[78, 80, 147].
91. *Wir Philologen*, 5[63]; *Sämtliche Werke*, VIII, 58.
92. *Sämtliche Werke*, XIII, 480–481.
93. *Twilight of the Idols*, I, §8; *Sämtliche Werke*, VI, 60. See also Kaufmann's *Nietzsche*, 130–131, 272ff.

affirm the resistance with which the world has met our desires. The horror of the death camps lies precisely here: they very nearly made *tragedy* impossible; they systematically tried to deprive inmates of their individuality and dignity, the very stature that is a *necessary* prerequisite to tragedy. Resistance almost became a bad dream, save in a manner of such subtlety as to be as meaningless to oneself and one's fellows as to the enemy.

Now, those individuals who are not up to tragedy's hard lessons are *never* to be despised — that is the caricature of the will to power that has it that Nietzsche said other people are fit to be trampled, sacrificed upon the altars of our own excellence. Nietzsche *never* says this. In fact, he is quite clear about the *sympathy* — not Aristotelian pity — that the spiritual aristocrat will *instinctively* accord to those who are incapable of living at his sobering heights. Having defended Nietzsche in this manner, I should immediately admit how unfortunate it is that his thinking seems to have crystallized around the question of human slavery — not the symbolic image so poignantly described by Hegel, but the real thing — as a crucial phenomenon for understanding the antique world. How could such numerically inferior individuals have kept such large numbers of people in chains? Only by maintaining "their qualitative superiority," he thinks, which is to say, by keeping the masses in awe of them.[94] Developing this insight led him to some of his most nightmarish statements: such as those from *The Genealogy of Morals* on "slave morality" and the whole of section 9 — "What Is Noble?" — from *Beyond Good and Evil*.

Even still, Nietzsche's views, while polemical and sharply overdrawn, are impossibly far from the stereotypes. A tragic aristocracy cannot be grounded in nationality or race — he explicitly denies this countless times.[95] And if heroism is not an ethnic category, still less can a tragic aristocracy be defended militarily. It simply is not interested in that kind of power:

> The political defeat of Greece is the greatest failure of culture, for it brought in its wake the hateful theory that one may only nurture culture if one is at the same time armed to the teeth — that it is all done with boxing gloves....
>
> Sparta was the ruin of Hellas. It forced Athens to establish a centralized confederacy and to cast her lot completely upon politics.[96]

94. *Wir Philologen*, 5[199]; *Sämtliche Werke*, VIII, 96.
95. See *Wir Philologen*, 5[92, 198]; *Twilight of the Idols*, VIII, §4; and Kaufmann's *Nietzsche*, 384ff.
96. *Wir Philologen*, 5[91]; *Sämtliche Werke*, VIII, 64.

The point of this all is *cultural* superiority, superiority in those things that the Germans call *geistlich:* poetry, music, tragedy itself, the *Dionysian* arts. Tragedy portrays spiritual excellence because it is itself the creation of such excellence. And quite suddenly, we are back to an issue we touched upon in the first chapter and will meet again in the last. The spiritual legacy of Greece resides in its great individuals — its *cultural* and *aesthetic,* rather than its *political,* achievements. "The Greek *polis* and the *aien aristeuein* [great individual] emerged out of deadly enmity and opposition," he insists.[97] The great-souled individual, not the *polis* — that is the real legacy of Greece in the tragic age, for Nietzsche.

The reasons for this are clear enough by now. Such superior, authentically tragic individuals are capable of affirming life in its totality; they alone turn the subtle temptation to negation — what Nietzsche calls No-saying, or nihilism — into a Yes. The tragic hero is *resolute,* and I think that Ajax is Nietzsche's model here. As the first half of this tragedy in particular, and all of Sophocles' heroes in general, make clear, the chief heroic virtue is self-constancy in a world of flux. Where everything else is continually changing, the hero stands firm, as immovable as Ajax planted behind his shield. Nietzsche always loved Thucydides and even spoke, when reading him, of "the pleasant feeling with which one puts the key in the lock: gradual, reluctant, then slowly giving way."[98] We find a neat summary of the very heroic resoluteness Nietzsche seems to have in mind in Pericles' funeral oration:

> This is another point where we differ from other people. We are capable at the same time of taking risks and of estimating them beforehand. Others are brave out of ignorance [*amathia*]; and, when they stop to think, they begin to fear. But the man who can most truly be accounted brave is he who best knows the meaning of what is sweet in life and of what is terrible, and then goes out undeterred to meet what is to come.[99]

We meet this idea very early, in Aeschylus' Prometheus trilogy. There, suffering that is anticipated can be accepted, perhaps even embraced, by the tragic hero. Heidegger was to latch on to this same idea in his notion of "anticipatory resoluteness," and we will return to it in the next chapter, in Gethsemane, where Jesus' resoluteness is precisely at issue. For now, suffice it to say that Prometheus emphasizes something that Heidegger does not: that the tragic hero need not be resolute in the face of inevitable defeat. We are still a world away from *Njal's Saga.* Aeschylus

---

97. *Wir Philologen,* 5[100]; *Sämtliche Werke,* VIII, 66. See also 3[12, 49, 65]; 5[9, 11, 14].
98. *Wir Philologen,* 5[6]; *Sämtliche Werke,* VIII, 42.
99. Thucydides, *The Peloponnesian War,* II, §40, trans. Rex Warner (New York: Penguin Books, 1954) 147.

captured it all in a single line, which the Chorus of his *Agamemnon* repeated three times for emphasis: "Sing sorrow, sorrow — yet good may
win out in the end."[100]

And this is the single greatest contribution of Nietzsche's tragic vision, one fully consonant with Hegel's. Tragedy stands *beyond* optimism
and pessimism. It is not interested in the end. Actually, that formula is
Hegel's. Nietzsche states it a little differently, but his point is *precisely*
the same. In 1886, during a burst of creative activity that saw several
new books and a host of reeditions to print, Nietzsche took another long
look at his first work, *The Birth of Tragedy*. He changed the subtitle in a
way that is illuminating: *Out of the Spirit of Music* becomes *Hellenism
and Pessimism*. Why? Nietzsche is quite clearly rejecting his earlier fascination with and romanticization of music, *German* music, Wagner's
music most of all. But he is also out to prove that there are two very distinct kinds of "pessimism" in the world and that only one of them — the
Hellenic — is authentically tragic. This view was vaguely present even in
his first essay, but over the years it achieves philosophical prominence.
In his "Attempt at Self-Criticism," which Nietzsche composed as a new
preface to the book, this point is amply made:

> You will guess that the big question mark concerning the value of exis-
> tence had thus been raised. Is pessimism *necessarily* [*nothwendig*] a sign
> of decline, decay, degeneration, weary and weak instincts — as it once
> was in India, and now is, to all appearances, among us "modern" men
> and Europeans? Is there a pessimism of *strength?*[101]

"A pessimism of strength," the province of tragic individuals who are
strong enough to affirm life, even and especially in the face of its greatest resistance — this is the heart of Nietzsche's tragic vision. A great deal,
if not most, of his mature philosophy can be clarified by carefully reflecting upon it. Where I view Hegel's tragic vision as an invitation to think
about the world "beyond optimism and pessimism," Nietzsche accom-
plishes the same invitation by articulating a very "unmodern" sort of
pessimism — *tragic* pessimism.

In book 5 of *The Gay Science* (completed at roughly the same time
in 1885), Nietzsche addresses this issue head-on, in a manner that il-
luminates his own intellectual development, the true nature of tragic
pessimism, and his own stance vis-à-vis the "modern" tragic posture. It
is one of the most important texts in the entire corpus, and we need to

---

100. Aeschylus, *Agamemnon*, 121, 139, 159. See also *Wir Philologen*, 3[69].
101. *The Birth of Tragedy*, 1886 preface, §1; *Sämtliche Werke*, I, 12. See also §6, and
Wir Philologen, 5[21].

deal with it at length. The title already calls my primary thesis to mind: "What Is Romantic?"[102]

> At first I approached the modern world with a few crude errors and overestimations, but in any case *hopefully*. Who knows on the basis of what personal experiences, I understood the philosophic pessimism of the nineteenth century as if it were the symptom of a greater strength of thought, of more daring courage, and of a more triumphant *fullness* of life, than had marked the eighteenth century, the era of Hume and Kant.... Thus tragic insight appeared to me as the distinctive *luxury* of our culture,... as our *permissible* luxury.

Nietzsche is grappling with his own gradual disenchantment and final rejection of the "modern" world. That constitutes his own nod to the tragic posture. The rich irony of Nietzsche's position, like Hegel's, is that it generates its own opposites. The theory that fuels his criticism still seems authentically tragic to me. The categories are all right, even where the conclusions are overdrawn:

> You see, I failed to recognize at the time — both in philosophic pessimism [Schopenhauer] and in German music [Wagner] — what their true character was: their *Romanticism*.
>
> What is Romantic? Every art and every philosophy which may be considered a remedy and an aid in the service of growing and struggling life: they always presuppose suffering and sufferers. But there are two kinds of sufferers: on the one hand, those who suffer from the *overfullness of life* [*Überfülle des Lebens*], those who want a Dionysian art, a tragic perspective and insight into life; on the other, those who suffer from the *impoverishment of life* [*Verarmung des Lebens*], and seek redemption for themselves through art and knowledge, or else from intoxication, convulsion, anaesthesia, and frenzy....
>
> I ask in every single case: "Is it hunger or overflow here that has become creative?"

Nietzsche is no longer unmodern and untimely; he is *anti*modern. That, in a nutshell, is the posture. It goes too far to say that the "modern" world — with its Wagners and its Schopenhauers — is incapable of tragedy. That idea, Nietzsche's late philosophy of *décadence,* is, as I say, his nod to the tragic posture. But Nietzsche is so remarkably self-conscious as a thinker, and sees even this so clearly, that he goes on in the same passage to speak of his apocalypticism as *both* daybreak *and* twilight, a beginning *and* an end:

> Romantic pessimism [is] the last *great* event in the Fate [*Schicksal*] of our culture. (There *could* still be quite another kind of pessimism, one that

---

102. *The Gay Science,* §370; *Sämtliche Werke,* III, 619–622. All subsequent quotations are from this same section.

is classical... only the word "classical" antagonizes my ears — it is too trite, too round and unclear. I call it pessimism of the future — for it is coming! I see it coming! *Dionysian* pessimism.)

Elsewhere, he had already called it — *tragic.*

To say it again, I consider Nietzsche's categories to be quite right; it is only the cultural despair of his later writings — built as they are upon the very *ressentiment* he criticizes so well — that is postured and unhelpful. They represent his temptation to the tragic posture. And now that I have sketched out the main lines of Nietzsche's tragic vision — the doctrines of redemptive suffering, heroic resoluteness, and pessimism of a curiously unmodern sort — I should like to point to the two areas where I find it deficient.

The first is most easily dispensed with because I have already dealt with it at some length. The tragic hero, just like the healthy culture, according to Nietzsche, is characterized by a "unity of style." This is another key Sophoclean dramatic feature — heroines like Antigone are possessed of a single, burning idea that animates and crystallizes their whole being. Their character *is* their Destiny. My disagreements by now are obvious. Antigone *is* impressive and heroic; she is also one-sided and overdrawn, as Hegel knew. Sophocles clearly means us to see this. If she is an unsavory character, then Ajax — the most singular and obsessive of *all* Sophocles' heroes — is even more so. "Unity of style" is a dangerous ideal, and an even more dangerous cultural myth.

A final point is also the single most unsatisfying dimension of Nietzsche's thought. Christianity — he says this countless times — is the most *un*tragic, even *anti*tragic, thing in the world. He comes back to this issue time and again, but it was already his emphatic opinion when he wrote *The Birth of Tragedy* and *Wir Philologen*:

> We can generally say that the history of Christianity on earth is one of the most appalling chapters in history, and that it *must* be ended — once and for all.[103]

He never seriously qualifies this. What is so odd is that Nietzsche, who is so self-conscious and explicit in most every other way, always *asserts* this position and never *argues* for it. It is a posture, nothing more — a *tragic* posture. The closest one ever comes to an explanation is a single long note from *The Will to Power*, (§1052) that we examined at the outset of this chapter. Much more common — and it really is all over the place in his writings — are unfortunate moments like the following:

> What concerns *me* is the psychological type of the saviour.... If there is anything essentially unevangelical, it is surely the concept of the hero.

---

103. *Wir Philologen*, 5[16]; *Sämtliche Werke*, VIII, 44.

What the gospels make instinctive is precisely the reverse of all heroic struggle, all taste for conflict.... Imagine making Jesus a *hero!*[104]

Nietzsche's "reasons," insofar as there are any beyond a vague and ill-defined natural aversion, boil down to the belief that Christianity preaches the wrong kind of pessimism — it is criminally romantic, in the sense discussed above. Christianity finally can muster only a bleating No to the world and ventures a trembling Maybe on eternity. Christianity is never up to the terrible task of saying Yes. The irony of all this, as I said in the introduction, is by now abundantly, redundantly clear. Nietzsche's own reading of tragedy — as, much like Hegel's, *beyond* optimism and pessimism — is an elegant expression of the very movement we see in the gospels (particularly in Mark's gospel and particularly in Gethsemane, as we shall see in the next chapter).

VI

The history of Nietzsche's "turning" is well known. What has not been observed is how clearly Nietzsche's "turning" represents a partial nod to what he himself has been instrumental in combating: the tragic posture. What began as a gradual disaffection with his academic contemporaries grew gradually into the brooding pessimism that dominates Nietzsche's mature writings on Germany, on Europe, and finally on the "modern" world. Nietzsche's first book, *The Birth of Tragedy,* was a dismal failure. Yet Nietzsche's rise within the philological community had been unprecedented: he was nominated to his first academic appointment at the age of twenty-four, without having prepared a thesis, but solely on the strength of his recommendation from Albrecht Ritschl:

> *Never yet* have I known a young man...who was so mature as early and as young as Nietzsche. His Museum articles he wrote in the second and third year of his *triennium.* He is the first from whom I have ever accepted a contribution while he was still a student.... I prophesy that he will one day stand in the front rank of German philologists.... You will say I am describing a phenomenon. Well, that is what he is — and at the same time pleasant and modest.[105]

Nietzsche's first book was anticipated with high hopes and great eagerness. The philological community wanted a glimpse of this "phenomenon." But the academy was bitterly disappointed by what it saw. It seems that they were not yet ready to hear what Nietzsche had to say

---

104. *The Antichrist,* §29; *Sämtliche Werke,* VI, 199–200. See also §§40–41.
105. As quoted by William Arrowsmith in his introduction to *Wir Philologen,* ARION 2:2 (1963) 5–11. I am indebted to Arrowsmith's splendid essay for this cursory review of Nietzsche's early academic development. See also Kaufmann's *Nietzsche,* 24–30.

to them. He was genuinely fifty years ahead of his time as a classicist —
very "untimely," indeed — and far too certain of his own blossoming
convictions.

The scholarly community, oddly enough threatened by the upstart
Nietzsche (could they sense the essential *rightness* of what he was saying?), leapt to the attack. Wilamowitz-Moellendorf, a younger student
and contemporary of Nietzsche, destined finally to assume the mantle
Ritschl had reserved for Nietzsche, chose to make an academic reputation for himself at Nietzsche's expense. He published a scathing review
of *The Birth of Tragedy* (*Zukunftphilologie,* June 1872), saying that
whatever this book was, it was not philology, and if Nietzsche wanted to
do this sort of thing, he should do it elsewhere. The attack was so viru-
lent that it prompted a reply from Nietzsche's good friend Erwin Rohde
(*Afterphilologie,* October 1872), although Rohde himself had been none
too keen on Nietzsche's book. In any event, Nietzsche was effectively os-
tracized by the philological community, and enrollment for his classes at
the University of Basel dwindled away to almost nothing. Nietzsche's
Destiny — not his Fate, since he had an essential hand in it — had been
sealed, events conspiring now to see to it that he would be much more
than a "mere" philologist:

> Undisturbed, Nietzsche threw himself into the completion of his huge
> *Unzeitgemasse Betrachtungen* whose thirteen books were intended to in-
> augurate, under the aegis of Schopenhauer, Wagner, and the classics,
> a Renaissance of German culture. Above all this Renaissance was to
> be based upon a new reformed classical humanism,... and finally, a
> concerted effort to supersede or surpass classical culture.[106]

William Arrowsmith has pointed out that the number of essays is sym-
bolically deliberate: naturally, Nietzsche's renaissance was to be pagan
and virulently anti-Christian. The list of working titles clearly demonstrates the breadth and audacity of Nietzsche's plans.[107] Of these
"untimely meditations," only four were ever completed: the essays on
Strauss and on history, as well as two new ones entitled "Schopenhauer
as Educator" and "Richard Wagner in Bayreuth." Alongside of these are
the massive notes for *Wir Philologen.*[108] What is absolutely clear in all
of this is that Nietzsche had opted to leave the academy, or rather, to
leap over it and appeal directly to a wider German-speaking audience.
Far from giving up on his dream of a cultural renaissance, Nietzsche
simply redirected his energies to a different, more receptive, audience. It

---

106. Arrowsmith, introduction to *Wir Philologen,* 11.
107. *Sämtliche Werke,* VII, 699, 755.
108. Notes found in *Sämtliche Werke,* VIII, 11–130, all dated from the spring and
summer of 1875.

is only the *scholarly*, philological community on which he had given up hope. As his Zarathustra will later say of scholars, "My soul sat hungry at their table for too long."[109] But he had hopes still, in this early period, for the spiritual health and tragic potential of the German-speaking European world.

This dream dies in Nietzsche's later work. His soul, it would seem, was destined to hunger at every German table, and he finally leaves the "nation" far behind him. Small wonder, then, that in his later writings he will accuse Germany of having single-handedly, under the Reformative banner of Luther, destroyed the Italian Renaissance that in so many ways anticipated his own:

> From this moment forward all my writings are fishhooks: perhaps I know how to fish as well as anyone? —
> If nothing was caught, I am not to blame. *There were no fish* [*die Fische fehlten*].[110]

It would be fascinating to explore the degree to which Nietzsche's growing disaffection with Wagner fueled the development of this cultural skepticism: "That the poets in France have become sculptors, that the musicians in Germany have become actors and culture-mongers — are these not signs of *décadence?*"[111] He became physically ill at Bayreuth as he saw what had been intended as a celebration of the emergent tragic spirit in Germany reduced to the crass megalomania of a single, petty man. Moreover, he saw Wagner's late opera, *Parsifal,* as a betrayal and abandonment of the dream — as a retreat back into the redemptive fold of Christianity, on the part of this man who had sung so loudly, and so well, the *new* songs of Teutonic myth and legend.[112] With this dream too dies any positive comment on the concept of "culture." Taking the inward turn characteristic of much Stoic and Epicurean philosophy, Nietzsche will increasingly emphasize the "virtue" of self-constancy, the unity of style that derives from the heroic solitude of the individual free

---

109. *Thus Spoke Zarathustra,* part II, "On Scholars"; *Sämtliche Werke,* IV, 160. In *Wir Philologen,* the rejection is even more abrupt: philologists are all pessimists at heart.

110. *Ecce Homo,* "Beyond Good and Evil," §1; *Sämtliche Werke,* VI, 350.

111. *The Will to Power,* §838; *Sämtliche Werke,* XIII, 491. Some other relevant texts are the following: *Human, All-Too-Human,* §§161, 164; *The Gay Science,* §§99, 103–105, 357; *Beyond Good and Evil,* section VIII, "Peoples and Fatherlands," §§240–256; *Twilight of the Idols,* "Maxims and Arrows," §23, "What the Germans Lack" §§1-7; *Ecce Homo,* "Human, All-Too-Human," §§1-3, "The Case of Wagner," §§1-3; and finally, *The Will to Power,* §121, for a late distinction between "culture" and "civilization."

112. See *The Gay Science,* §357; "Wagner in Bayreuth," in the *Untimely Meditations;* see also *The Genealogy of Morals,* III, §§17, 26; *Ecce Homo,* "The Birth of Tragedy," §§1, 4; and, finally, most explicitly, *The Case of Wagner,* trans. Walter Kaufmann (New York: Random House, 1967). See also Kaufmann, *Nietzsche,* 36–41.

spirit. This freedom necessitates an isolation from the herd and finally
even from "culture" itself:

> Supposing that what is at any rate believed to be the "truth" really is
> true, and the *meaning of all culture* is the reduction of the beast of prey
> [*Raubthier*] "man" to a tame and civilized animal, a *domestic animal*
> [*Hausthier*], then one would undoubtedly have to regard all those in-
> stincts of reaction and *ressentiment* through whose aid the noble races
> and their ideals were finally confounded and overthrown as the actual
> *instruments of culture* [*Werkzeuge der Cultur*].[113]

He concludes the same essay with the observation that " 'autonomous'
and 'moral' are mutually exclusive."[114] This aphorism cuts to the very
heart of his moral philosophy.

Of a piece with Nietzsche's growing disappointment in Germany, and
in his times, is the emerging sense of untimeliness that characterizes his
later work. He is now appealing to *future* generations with ears to hear
what he is saying. Here we may place his call for "a gay science" to
combat the spirit of scholarly seriousness, this scholarly asceticism in
the name of "truth," and above all, to put an end to the priggishness of
the contemporary German bourgeoisie — their stagnation and spiritual
stupidity:[115]

> That *every* kind of swindle succeeds in Germany today is connected with
> the undeniable and palpable *stagnation* of the German spirit — the rea-
> sons for which I find in an exclusive diet of newspapers, politics, beer,
> and Wagnerian music, together with the presuppositions of such a diet:
> first, a national constriction and vanity, the strong but narrow principle
> "*Deutschland, Deutschland über alles,*" and then the *paralysis agitans* of
> "modern ideas."

Despite this rethinking and redirection, Nietzsche's *method* continues to
be aphoristic. He is the philosopher who, in the name of a unity of style,
will collapse key distinctions and commit the most egregious overgener-
alizations, almost in spite of himself. While he gradually overcame the
quest for "culture," the quest for "unity of style" endures, taking ever
more solitary — what he calls *übermenschlich* — forms. That the world
can be neatly bracketed and divided after a Nietzschean fashion points
to the emphatic rejection of any notion of *syncretism* — first law of
cultural anthropology — namely, that cultures are *always* growing and
changing, that no "indigenous peoples" and no "unity of style" ever
really existed, that there was nothing to be fragmented or lost in the

---

113. *On the Genealogy of Morals,* I, §11; *Sämtliche Werke,* V, 276.
114. *On the Genealogy of Morals* II, §2; *Sämtliche Werke,* V, 293
115. *On the Genealogy of Morals,* III, §§25–26; *Sämtliche Werke,* V, 407–408.

first place. "Culture" is always a manifold phenomenon. "Decadence" is finally a philosophical cheap way out:[116]

> But have you ever asked yourself sufficiently how much the erection of *every* ideal on earth has cost? How much reality [*Wirklichkeit*] has had to be misunderstood and slandered, how many lies have had to be sanctified, how many consciences destroyed, how much "God" sacrificed every time? *If a temple is to be erected a temple must be destroyed: that is the law* [*Gesetz*] — let anyone who can show me a case in which it is not fulfilled [*erfüllt*]![117]

We will need to take up Nietzsche's challenge. But first, I want to point out at some greater length what I have alluded to before — that the "modern" posture has seized upon this eminently Nietzschean idea, surely the least compelling component of Nietzsche's philosophy. Even Alasdair MacIntyre, as we shall see — and despite his own protestations to the contrary — is engaged in a very slippery kind of Nietzschean diagnosis.

VII

The "modern" posture entails a very Nietzschean dilemma: *whether to be unmodern or antimodern.* That is a key ingredient of the modernist schizophrenia.[118] This confusion derives from a broader theoretical principle: the explicit denial of cultural syntheses in favor of unity of style. Lack of style is a key to diagnosing modern times. Nietzsche defines "what is *modern*" as follows:

> Every age has, commensurate with its measure of strength, a measure of what virtues are permitted and forbidden to it. Either it has the virtues of *ascending* life: then it will resist from the profoundest depths the virtues of declining life. Or else the age embodies declining life: then it needs the virtues of decline, then it hates everything which comes from fullness, everything which justifies itself solely out of its abundance. Aesthetics is indissolubly tied to these biological presuppositions: there is an aesthetics of *décadence*; there is a *classical* aesthetics — the "beautiful in itself" is a figment of the imagination, like all idealism.[119]

---

116. See *Human, All-Too-Human,* §§158, 221, 224; *The Gay Science,* §§23, 86; *The Antichrist,* §§17, 38; and *The Will to Power,* §§40, 41, 43. See, too, the telling remarks made by MacIntyre in his *Whose Justice? Which Rationality?* 166–167, 346–348, 365.

117. *On the Genealogy of Morals,* II, §24; *Sämtliche Werke,* V, 335; emphasis of the words "temple must be destroyed" is in the original; otherwise emphasis is mine.

118. See Louis A. Sass, *Madness and Modernism: Insanity in the Light of Modern Art, Literature, and Thought* (San Francisco: HarperColllins, 1992) 1–16, 355–373.

119. *The Case of Wagner,* epilogue; *Sämtliche Werke,* VI, 50.

This myth of decadence — as a "decaying away" from some prior "unity" — lies at the heart of both Nietzsche's and MacIntyre's diagnoses of "the modern problem." It possesses an implicit sectarianism that is made explicit in a wide range of philosophical and theological literature today. 'World,' as Nietzsche noted, is too often a term of Christian abuse. But it is also a term of general philosophical abuse, if one appends the word 'modern' to it — even for Nietzsche, at times, later in his career. The "modern" world is an idea to be rejected. Pluralism and liberal democracy are to be despised; "unity of style" is the sole recipe for spiritual and cultural health. Perhaps a good way of illustrating this same constellation of ideas and their implicit problems will be to move outside the realm of philosophy altogether and to examine an enormously popular work in contemporary American theology, *The Nature of Doctrine*, written by George Lindbeck in 1984.[120] This examination will not be without relevance to my primary objection to Nietzsche's construal of "the modern problem," as well my discussion in the next chapter of what I am calling "Christian tragedy."

Lindbeck begins by taking the contemporary interest in language as a meaning-making canopy — another philosophical tradition that has deep roots in Nietzsche[121] — and attempts to apply it to religious traditions and "culture" more broadly:

> Stated more technically, a religion can be viewed as a kind of cultural and/or linguistic framework or medium that shapes the entirety of life and thought. It functions somewhat like a Kantian *a priori,* although in this case the *a priori* is a set of acquired skills that could be different....
>
> The Christian theological application of this view is that just as an individual becomes human by learning a language, so he or she begins to become a new creature through hearing and interiorizing the language that speaks of Christ.[122]

This so-called cultural-linguistic paradigm shares with Nietzsche the conception of language as "a prison-house":

> *We have to cease to think if we refuse to do it in the prison-house* [Zwange] *of language;*

---

120. George Lindbeck, *The Nature of Doctrine: Religion and Theology in a Postliberal Age* (Philadelphia: Westminster Press, 1984). It is interesting that this book was released in the same year as the much-revised second edition of *After Virtue.*

121. For his own more balanced treatments of language, see *Human, All-Too-Human,* §11; *The Gay Science,* §§58, 83; *Beyond Good and Evil,* §28; and *Twilight of the Idols,* " 'Reason' in Philosophy," §5, "Skirmishes of an Untimely Man," §26. The end of the matter for Nietzsche, and unlike his pseudoheirs, is clear: "*Untranslatable.* It is neither the best nor the worst of a book that is untranslatable" (*Human, All-Too-Human,* §184). Most contemporary language philosophers use only the occasional jottings and notes in *The Will to Power,* which are much more extreme. See §§482, 506, 522, 562, 625, 631, 634, 809, 810.

122. Lindbeck, *The Nature of Doctrine,* 33, 62.

for we cannot reach further than the doubt which asks whether the limit we see really is a limit.[123]

Lindbeck explicitly rejects the principle of translation — between languages *or* between cultures — and upon this rock he builds a most peculiar argument.

Lindbeck makes explicit the philological relevance of his theory (which is to say, its implications for a theory of translation) later in the book. Given the formative power of language — its role in making us human, in making our "meaning" for us — there is no neutral standpoint beyond it, no evaluative point from which one may survey the nuances of one's own language, and another's, in order to evaluate both. One cannot escape from this prison. There is, as MacIntyre never tires of telling us, "no neutral standpoint."[124] And there is, consequently — in the absence of any universal notion of language itself — no genuine translation. Translation is little more than an elaborate exercise in self-deception:

> In a cultural-linguistic outlook, in contrast, it is just as hard to think of religions as it is to think of cultures and languages as having a single generic or universal experiential essence of which particular religions — or cultures or languages — are varied manifestations or modifications. One can in this outlook no more be religious in general than one can speak language in general....
> The results of this particularity may be useful for the restrictedly ecumenical end of promoting unity within a single religion, but not for the broader purpose of seeking the unity of all religions.[125]

Lindbeck will later speak of "translation" — whether into newer "postliberal" categories or else globally across religious traditions — as the subtle temptation of the "modern" age. This criticism should recall Nietzsche's and MacIntyre's criticisms of Kant — his alleged presumption in claiming that others' languages and experiences may be accurately and meaningfully reflected in his own. My language is *nothing* like yours. Nor is my religion. Nor is my culture. We are suddenly, ironically, and irretrievably as isolated as Zarathustra on his mountaintop.

That view is overdrawn. The overstatement resides at two levels. The first is the level of language itself. While it *is* important to remind ourselves, time and again, of the enormous difficulties of translation —

---

123. *The Will to Power*, §522; *Sämtliche Werke*, XII, 193. Already in *Wir Philologen*, Nietzsche had observed that "words are the seductresses of philosophers — they squirm in the nets of language" (6[39]; *Sämtliche Werke*, VIII, 113).
124. See MacIntyre, *Whose Justice? Which Rationality?* 166–167, 346, 351, 368, 388.
125. Lindbeck, *The Nature of Doctrine*, 23.

translations are, after all, never "finished" products, but always only works in progress — it goes too far to insist that translation is therefore impossible. We need to be careful, Kant warns us, not to call a task "impossible" simply because it is difficult or because it has no end. *This* is the "subtle temptation" to which Lindbeck and MacIntyre — explicitly operating within the Christian tradition as they both do — should be more sensitive. A Christian *ought* to know that the end is always "now" and "not yet." The appeal to a "pure language" need not point to something that exists in the world. It exists in our minds, and it is on the basis of this that we attempt to make happen in our own language — always a vital and living language, admittedly, and never something static — what we see happening in another. Or better, we attempt to find the original "intended effect," what Walter Benjamin explicitly called the "pure language":

> Translation thus ultimately serves the purpose of expressing the central reciprocal relationship between languages. It cannot possibly reveal or establish this hidden relationship itself; but it can represent it by realizing it in embryonic or intensive form.... Languages are not strangers to one another, but are, *a priori* and apart from all historical relationships, interrelated in what they want to express....
>
> For to some degree all great texts contain their potential translation between the lines; this is true to the highest degree of sacred writings. The interlinear version of the Scriptures is the prototype or ideal of all translation.[126]

Benjamin is making the practical point that we *do* all translate texts, particularly those texts we call "classic" or "scripture" — or at the very least we rely upon belief in their inherent translatability. Benjamin refuses to accept the premise that all of our translations are nothing more than elaborate exercises in appropriation, deceit, and bad faith. And he does so for a very simple reason, elegantly drawn out by George Steiner. We must not mystify the translational act. It is difficult enough, already. Translations are the very stuff of human life; we all perform them, all the time. For even my own words, in the *same* language, need to be "translated" before they can "mean" to you. In short: "Inside or between languages, human communication equals translation. A study of translation is a study of language."[127] This brings us to the second issue,

126. Walter Benjamin, "The Task of the Translator," being his introduction to a translation of Baudelaire's *Tableaux Parisiens,* from *Illuminations,* ed. Hannah Arendt and trans. Harry Zohn (New York: Schocken Books, 1969) 72, 82. Benjamin is a crucial influence on George Steiner and has prompted some of his most penetrating comments. See *After Babel: Aspects of Language and Translation* (New York: Oxford Univ. Press, 1975) 63–65.

127. Steiner, *After Babel,* 47.

briefly alluded to by Benjamin, which is really fatal to the extreme case that Lindbeck is at such pains to make.

This second point is historical, not textual. It concerns the very history of his own Christian tradition. Christianity simply *cannot exist* apart from the possibility of translation. All of the early Christian fathers were philologists — *translators* — from beginning to end: Origen, Jerome, the Cappadocians, and so on. Augustine was the first who was not, and the implications of that fact for the cultural development of the Latin-speaking church were profound.[128] Jesus' Aramaic was translated — with whatever fidelity — out of his own idiom and into Greek, a language he seems not to have known. Moreover, as a proclamation explicitly offered to the entire world, these texts have been endlessly translated since then into foreign tongues and made — again, to a degree — at home in them. The parable of Pentecost is an interesting myth, but perhaps no more than that. Languages do not always translate so well; but cultures often do. It is in their very nature — *contra* Nietzsche — to translate, *and* to change in the process. It is this *cultural* equation, which Lindbeck makes explicitly, that is fatal to his argument.

Far more than words and phrases were translated by the Christians of the first century of the common era. A culture was, in part, translated and transplanted from its own Semitic soil to the much larger Hellenistic world where it firmly took root.[129] All of the churches to which Paul writes are in Greece or Asia Minor. *That,* and not Roman Palestine, was where this religious movement took off. This, it would seem, is precisely what Lindbeck's own picture — painted, as it is, in such harsh, Nietzschean contrasts — cannot allow. He fails to say that "culture" is an endlessly diverse, inherently syncretic enterprise. Culture borrows, culture learns, culture *translates*. His own Christian tradition is now Hebraic, now Hellenistic, enormously fluid and enormously complex. Theologians such as Rudolf Bultmann and Simone Weil, cultural critics like Czeslaw Milosz and even George Steiner, as well as virtually anyone who pursues the academic study of the New Testament, have made their careers out of reminding us of these central facts. Having forgotten them too well, we only very rarely recover the richness of the traditions whose contemporary custodians we ought to be.

---

128. For an interesting picture of this very early phenomenon of church fathers who were philologists — as best embodied in the figure of St. Jerome — see "Jerome on Translation: A Breviary," trans. and ed. William Arrowsmith, in *ARION*, n.s., 2:3 (1976) 358–367.

129. See *Daybreak*, §84 and *Antichrist*, §§28, 52, for Nietzsche's explicit criticism of what he calls "bad Christian philology" — which is to say, cultural translation in bad faith.

I take it to be far from accidental, but really a logically necessary outgrowth of his argument, that MacIntyre is drawn to this same
"cultural-linguistic" equation. His more recent work explicitly tackles
the question of translation, this time as an intellectual exercise between
"traditions in conflict." As I have tried to suggest, this conflictual image
is essentially Nietzschean. On the one hand, it assumes that two cultures
must come to blows as a necessary first step on the road to conversing,
a view apparently shared by the late Hegel. Power is the only pure language, the only thing that does not *need* translating. A healthy culture
is the one that seeks to overcome resistance and that reads *only* resistance in the existence of other cultures. *"If a temple is to be created
then a temple must be destroyed."* On the other hand, such a model —
based as it is on a deceptive definition of culture as "a unity of style" —
overlooks the very obvious fact that any "cultural tradition" contains a
whole range of conflicts within itself. "Tradition" is no monolith, but
rather a certain kind of sustained critical conversation, a point that is
not admitted readily enough by Nietzsche or most modernists. To speak
of *the* Christian tradition — as MacIntyre, Lindbeck, and Nietzsche all
do, although they all know better — is already a falsification. As I have
stressed *throughout* this book, some of the most significant aesthetic
moments are achieved when the tradition and its values are held up to
close scrutiny, challenged, and even rejected in large part.[130] I will attempt to demonstrate in the next chapter that Mark's gospel is also the
product of such a conflict — that his artistic and theological genius derives from the intensity of his criticisms. Mark's literary and theological
achievement gives the lie to many of Nietzsche's most trenchant remarks.
Finally, it is beginning to be clear why I feel that MacIntyre keeps returning to Nietzsche without ever quite taking him on: his own root
metaphor, of "traditions in conflict," is itself Nietzschean to the core.

In any case, when two traditions attempt to enter into a conversation, they need first to make sense to one another. This task *requires*
translation. At the outset, we get what we should expect from Alasdair
MacIntyre, namely, a scathing indictment of the Enlightenment confidence in universalizability, in the *idea* of translation. We would do well,
he seems to want to say, to consider the parable of Esperanto — a "language" that wanted to be universal but that failed precisely because it
was not anchored in any tradition whatsoever.[131] Languages cannot be
created out of whole cloth for the same reason that it is nonsensical to

---

130. And the theater was often one crucial social space in which that cultural inter-
rogation took place. See Jean-Christophe Agnew, *Worlds Apart: The Market and the
Theater in Anglo-American Thought, 1550–1750* (Cambridge: Cambridge Univ. Press,
1986).

131. MacIntyre, *Whose Justice? Which Rationality?* 17, 327–328.

speak of "language in general." We need to remember the lesson of the "tragedy" of Babel; if there ever was a time of universal communicability, of one common language, it resides in our distant past, in a past, moreover, that is a myth. It is no longer possible; such tragedies end badly.

MacIntyre presses this point in a penultimate chapter, entitled fittingly "Tradition and Translation." He makes his case — and again this cannot surprise us — by radically particularizing the notion of language. Not only is it an illusion to speak of "language as such"; we should not even deceive ourselves with superficial talk about "*the* English language." The phenomenon of language, it would seem, is far more particular even than that:

> It will be obvious that on this view of language there can be no such language as English-as-such or Hebrew-as-such or Latin-as-such. There are not even, it must seem, such languages as classical Latin or early modern Irish. There is only Latin-as-written-and-spoken-in-the-Rome-of-Cicero and Irish-as-written-and-spoken-in-sixteenth-century-Ulster. The boundaries of a language are the boundaries of some linguistic community which is also a social community.[132]

Two questions immediately present themselves. The first concerns this problematic notion of "community." Who is drawing these boundaries? And on what basis? The quest for the kind of "community" MacIntyre longs for is the real chimera, as illusory and problematic as the Nietzschean quest for "unity of style." One searches in vain for some illumination as to how and why MacIntyre chooses to draw the lines as he does. In the name of the radical particularity for which he is best known, I see no reason why we should not move further in the direction he has sketched out for us until we conclude that there is no "English-as-such," but only "English-as-spoken-(or written)-*by-my-friends-and-I-on-this-particular-day*." We are all strangers to one another, foreign to one another's inaccessible realms of private meanings, lost in our private prisons.[133] This is naturally a caricature, yet it is one to which Lindbeck, MacIntyre, and probably Nietzsche have no rational answer.

And now something very strange happens. Not only does MacIntyre *not* say this, he very nearly says the opposite. Traditions, it would seem, as well as the languages in which they are at home, *do* translate. MacIntyre quite suddenly introduces the fascinating idea of learning "a new and second first language,"[134] much as anthropologists do when-

132. Ibid., 373.
133. *Daybreak*, §§116–117.
134. MacIntyre, *Whose Justice? Which Rationality?* 364, 373.

ever they put themselves in the field. Not only are traditions potentially translatable, they are also potentially friendly, accessible to us in the syntheses that are part and parcel of any dialogue. There exists a broader perspective in which both "we" and "they" may be integrated. It was Aquinas' novelty, and his particular philosophical genius, to conceive of such a synthesis — a very rare thing in cultural world history. Historically speaking, in Aquinas' day Aristotle's *Ethics* and *Politics* were still being used to ground a theory of the ultimate *telos* of human life, precisely at a time when natural teleology was being rejected in the realm of physics and metaphysics. Moreover, Aristotelian virtues were still being taught at the very time when Christian theology was nailing the lid on the coffin of any works-righteousness.[135] Pagan and Christian traditions are "designed to be discrepant."[136] The medieval period quite suddenly looks like a surprisingly "modern" moment, with its

> gradual discovery...that no appeal to any agreed conception of *the* good for human beings, either at the level of practice or of theory, was now possible.[137]

There was a clear fork in the philosophical road — between Aristotle and Augustine — and it was Aquinas' *singular* genius to cut a middle path less traveled-by, which has made all the difference since then. He negotiated between what were believed to be incompatible ways of thinking, "traditions in conflict" — the Christian and the Greek, Dionysus and the Crucified.

I rehearse all of this in some detail simply to highlight the apparent tension. Translations *are* possible; we *all* use them, *all* the time. Cultural syntheses are possible; the periods of greatest cultural florescence, as both Nietzsche and MacIntyre are gratefully aware, are invariably their firstfruits. It is this thought that makes Nietzsche's scathing criticisms of Christianity so one-sided.[138] It also makes MacIntyre's recent talk about Aquinas rather strange. It represents a far sharper break with his own intellectual odyssey — and his own ambivalent place within the *Nietzschean* tradition — than he seems prepared, thus far, to admit.

VIII

The relevance to Nietzsche studies in all of this is not far to find. Nietzsche's fascination with the dynamics of mastery and slavery, of power, renders him incapable of exploring the cooperative experiment that is

---

135. Ibid., 209–210.
136. MacIntyre, *After Virtue*, 55.
137. MacIntyre, *Whose Justice? Which Rationality?* 209–210.
138. Again, see John Casey, *Pagan Virtue*, 211–226.

culture. "If a temple is to be erected *a temple must be destroyed.*" This "law" denies the archaeological *fact* that temples are very rarely destroyed; they are merely put to new uses, over and again.[139] Culture, while it *is* caught in the dynamics of power, is never completely mastered by them. Culture knows a language other than sheer force.

But Nietzsche was a polar thinker; his genius lay in the crafting of dramatic, if none-too-careful, dichotomies. The first and most dramatic of these appears already in *The Birth of Tragedy,* where Nietzsche sets out the antithesis of Apollonian and Dionysian principles and translates them "into the realm of metaphysics."[140] Nietzsche would later admit that these contrasts were too sharp; in fact, what endures from this early work is his "discovery of the Dionysian" — not as one principle among others, but as the *only* one, the essential will to life (and power) that alone makes sense of Greek drama, philosophy, and culture.[141] Not a duality, but a unity[142] — and a unity that, like culture itself, is ever-changing: "new or not at all."[143]

Nietzsche is memorable for his studied contrasts, far more than for his later retractions. As with Hegel before him, most modern discourse assumes the worst aspects of the thought and ignores the best, *their tragic vision.* The contrasts, the phenomenal gift Nietzsche had for painting images that burn themselves into the mind — these are his chief legacy. And yet they are of a piece with many of his most troubling and uncritical assertions. Sometimes he treats Judaism and Christianity as a single phenomenon; other times they themselves are traditions at war.[144] Both are symptoms of a more general religious *ressentiment,* the decadence of despair, of a fatigue that he calls "nihilism." He even refers to Christianity as the ultimate revenge of Jews upon a hostile and oppressive Roman world.[145] The sticking point is also one of Nietzsche's chief legacies: namely, this problematic notion of the "stylistic unity"

---

139. Even the biblical book of *Joshua,* which on the whole presents such a gruesome picture of complete cultural annihilation, admits as much. After the conquest, when the people have a covenant renewal ceremony at Shechem, their God reminds them: "I gave you a land on which you had not labored, *and cities which you had not built,* and you dwell therein, you eat the fruits of the vineyards and oliveyards which you did not plant" (*Joshua* 24:13).

140. *Ecce Homo,* "The Birth of Tragedy," §1; *Sämtliche Werke,* VI, 310.

141. See his later 1886 preface to *The Birth of Tragedy,* as well as *The Will to Power,* §§1050–1051. This insight lies at the heart of Kaufmann's reading of Nietzsche's development in his *Nietzsche,* 129, 155–156, 178, 281–283.

142. See Kaufmann, *Nietzsche,* 236–246.

143. Norman O. Brown, *Love's Body* (New York: Random House, 1966) 234. See also *The Antichrist,* §53.

144. MacIntyre, *Whose Justice? Which Rationality?* 10–11.

145. *On the Genealogy of Morals* I, §8, but see also III, §22; *The Gay Science,* §§137, 140; *The Antichrist,* §§24, 31, 44; and *The Will to Power,* §§158–216.

of a culture and of the *necessary* conflict between one "genuine" culture and another.[146] If a culture is genuine, which is to say healthy, then it is by definition *strong* — strong enough to fight and resist. There is no growth, no fluidity here; flux and change, while appropriate for a Zarathustra or a Heraclitus, are anathema to "a people."

Now perhaps we are prepared to appreciate both the insight and the narrowness of his definition of one particular culture: *Christian* culture, the only one he seems interested in discussing by condemning:

> The task for the years that followed now was drawn out quite clearly. After the Yes-saying part of my task had been solved, the time had come for the No-saying, *No-doing* half: the revaluation of contemporary values themselves, the great war — conjuring up a day of decision.[147]

Nietzsche's reading of this tradition is, again not surprisingly, strictly negative. It accords fully with his overall framework:

> "If a temple is to be created then a temple must be destroyed";
> "Dionysus against the Crucified."

If Dionysus is defined as Antichrist, then the symmetry is complete. *For Christ is also anti-Dionysus.* From the pagan point of view, and inverting the Johannine formula, "We *hate* the Christians because they first *hated* us." Building upon his root metaphor of *ressentiment*, Nietzsche insists that Christianity, whatever else it may be, is a strictly *antipagan* phenomenon:

> Even in the midst of Graeco-Roman splendor [*Herrlichkeit*], which was also a splendor of books, in the face of an ancient literary world that had not yet eroded and been ruined, at a time when one could still read some books for whose possession one would nowadays exchange half of some national literatures, the simplicity and vanity of Christian agitators — they are called Church Fathers — had the temerity to declare: "we, too, have our classical literature, *we have no need of the Greeks*"; and saying this they pointed proudly to books of legends, letters of apostles, and apologetic tracts, much as the English "Salvation Army" today employs similar literature in its struggle against Shakespeare and other "pagans."[148]

It must be confessed that there is much to commend this insight to us, and Nietzsche is nothing quite so well as he is a critic of hypocrisy, particularly the hypocrisies of the academy and the church. And, since we are speaking of confessing, it should be noted how very Augustinian is

---

146. See *Human, All-Too-Human*, §§24, 170, 444, 470; *Daybreak*, §27; *The Gay Science*, §§362, 377; *Twilight of the Idols*, preface and "Morality as Anti-Nature," §3; and *The Will to Power*, §56.

147. *Ecce Homo*, III, §1; *Sämtliche Werke*, VI, 350.

148. *On the Genealogy of Morals*, III, §22; *Sämtliche Werke*, V, 393.

his understanding of the church,[149] and how odd it would have sounded to the roughly contemporary Cappadocian thinkers in the Christian East.

What is needed is a liberal dose of genuine history, if for no other reason than to demonstrate the *multi*valence of the early Christian experiment in culture. Here is no cultural monolith, still less a destructive cultural nihilism waging war on countless enemies, such as Nietzsche would have us believe. That the charges he levels against the Christian community *are* founded is beyond dispute; that they are *universally* founded is absurd. The case that Nietzsche is so desperate to make might best be made with the figure of Augustine,[150] and even here a psychological sensitivity — such as Nietzsche displays so well elsewhere — could illumine the degree to which Augustine's mature antipaganism derived from his own abundant classical training[151] and his later rejection of a past he considered perverse. In any case, it is a shortsight of epic proportions that Augustine is known, if he is read at all today, solely for his *City of God* and, perhaps, for his *Confessions*. For *The City of God* is an extended polemic against the very pagan culture in which Augustine had himself been raised; the radical either/or is disingenuous, given his own history, and hardly representative of his best thought. It is, moreover, precisely the kind of *ressentimental* iconoclasm for which Nietzsche justly censures the church. Here is Augustine's view:

> And the whole of this discussion may be summed up in the following syllogism: The Greeks give us the major premiss: If such gods are to be worshipped, then certainly such men may be honored. The Romans add the minor: But such men must by no means be honoured. The Christians draw the conclusion: Therefore such gods must by no means be worshipped....
>
> Must we not here award the palm to a Greek, Plato, who, in framing his ideal republic, conceived that poets should be banished from the city as enemies of the state? He could not brook that the gods be brought into

---

149. It would be interesting to reflect upon how Augustinian the *confessio* in Nietzsche's own autobiography was intended to be. He has given us, in a sense, an atheistic manifesto, at times mimicking the very style and tone of Augustine: "On this perfect day, when everything is ripening and not only the grape turns brown, the eye of the sun just fell upon my life: I looked back, I looked forward, and never saw so many and such good things at once. It was not for nothing that I buried my forty-fourth year today; I had the *right* to bury it; whatever was life in it has been saved, is immortal.... *How could I fail to be grateful to my whole life?* — and so I tell my life to myself" (*Ecce Homo*, preface; *Sämtliche Werke*, VI, 263). He speaks to himself, not God; *that* is the revaluation.

150. Augustine appears very rarely in Nietzsche's work, but see the telling remarks in *The Antichrist*, §59, and *The Will to Power*, §§214, 578, 862.

151. Peter Brown's biography, *Augustine of Hippo* (Berkeley: Univ. of California Press, 1967), makes this case extremely well.

disrepute, nor that the minds of the citizens be depraved and besotted, by the fictions of the poets.[152]

Small wonder that Nietzsche should feel compelled to reject the Christian tradition, if it really does counsel cultural warfare against the tragic legacy of Greece.[153] But Augustine is not synonymous with Christianity. He is Latin-speaking, Western (as, ironically enough, was most of North Africa in this period). Even his own attitudes to classical culture are not any more consistent than Hegel's and Nietzsche's. The Christian tradition, like any genuine culture, does not possess a "unity of style"; it is, like most world religions, a many-splendored (our word is 'multicultural') thing.

Perhaps more than any other cultural historian, Werner Jaeger sought to document the manifold ways in which the Greek ideal of *paideia* (a word that denotes both "education" and "culture," similar to the German *Bildung*) lives on in its newer, Christian context. While Augustine's writings, particularly *The City of God*, reflect an undeniably rigorist Western–North African extreme of the early Christian experience, the "Christian neoclassicism" of the Cappadocian East[154] represents another:

> Little attention has been paid to the fact that we have in the fourth century AD, the age of the great fathers of the church, a true renaissance that has given Greco-Roman literature some of its greatest personalities, figures who have exercised a lasting influence on the history and culture of later centuries down to the present day. It is characteristic of the differences between the Greek and Roman spirits that the Latin West had its Augustine while the Greek East through the Cappadocian fathers produced a new culture.[155]

With enormous sensitivity to the richness and plurality of the phenomenon of culture, Jaeger paints a marvelous portrait of the intellectual and artistic excitement, the real cultural fluorescence of the emergent Christian East. Two of the three Cappadocians — Basil of Caesarea and Gregory of Nazianzus — had been educated in Athens. All had profited from the linguistic scholarship of Jerome, as well as from the

---

152. *The City of God*, II, §13, trans. Marcus Dods, D.D. (New York: Modern Library, 1950). One might also look at Tertullian's *De Spectaculis* (*Ante-Nicene Fathers*, vol. III, trans. A. Cleveland Coxe, D.D. [New York: Charles Scribners Sons, 1926] 79–93), for an even more extreme rejection of the classical pagan tradition.

153. See Hans-Georg Gadamer, *Hegel's Dialectic*, trans. P. Christopher Smith (New Haven: Yale Univ. Press, 1971) 108–109.

154. See Jaroslav Pelikan, *Christianity and Classical Culture: The Metamorphosis of Natural Theology in the Christian Encounter with Hellenism* (New Haven: Yale Univ. Press, 1993).

155. Werner Jaeger, *Early Christianity and Greek Paideia* (Cambridge, Mass.: Belknap Press of Harvard Univ., 1961) 75–85.

lofty theological speculations of Origen.[156] The syntheses at the heart of their thinking provided an enduring vision of a new culture and a new world for many generations of Christian thinkers, particularly within the Eastern Orthodox tradition.

Most emphatically, their vision provided a lofty spiritual impetus for the Italian Renaissance, a cultural renaissance, again, grounded in the same synthetic embrace of Christian *and* Greek:

> The question of how this Christian form of the Greek paideia affected the Latin world concerns us immediately. The details of this great process are to a large extent still unexplored, but they can be pursued through the Middle Ages; and from the Renaissance the line leads straight back to the Christian humanism of the fathers of the fourth century AD and to their idea of man's dignity and of his reformation and rebirth through the Spirit.... Their influence on the thought of the Renaissance, both in Italy and throughout Europe, is still largely an unsolved problem, but the number of manuscripts of their works in the library collections of that period surpasses by far those of the classical authors....
>
> In the last analysis [Erasmus'] Christian humanism goes back to the Greek fathers who had created it in the fourth century....
>
> [T]his study is not only the last chapter in the history of the ideal of paideia in the late ancient Greek world but also the prologue to the history of its medieval Latin transformations.[157]

In order to understand how monumental was this root assumption of cultural warfare in Nietzsche's work, and how misguided, we need do no more than go to Italy — perhaps Florence first of all. There, to our infinite delight, we find something that Nietzsche tells us we cannot ever see: a harmonious cultural coalescence of Christian, Greek, and Jew.[158] In the Uffizi Museum, in the Palazzo Pitti, as also in the central piazza, one sees here a David, there a Poseidon, here a Pietá, there a Perseus and a Homer. That Dionysus must stand emphatically *against* the Crucified would have been news to *this* culture. Nietzsche, an ardent and lifelong lover of Italy, knew this and explained it away in short — much too short — order: the effulgent promise of the Renaissance was hamstrung and decapitated by the Reformation. *"If a temple is to be erected a temple must be destroyed."* "Rome against Judea; Judea against Rome":

---

156. It must be admitted that Origen's teaching was later declared to be heretical at the fifth ecumenical council in 553 C.E., but it needs to be said that similar ideas, expressed by the Cappadocians themselves, became *credal* instead.

157. Jaeger, *Early Christianity and Greek Paideia*, 100–101.

158. See Wayne Meeks and Robert Wilken, *Jews and Christians in Antioch: In the First Four Centuries of the Common Era* (Missoula, Mont.: Scholars Press, 1978), for the description of another fascinating urban center in which these same groups creatively commerced in the same public and intellectual spaces.

There was, to be sure, in the Renaissance an uncanny and glittering reawakening of the classical ideal, of the noble mode of evaluating all things; Rome itself, oppressed by the new superimposed Judaized Rome that presented the aspect of an ecumenical synagogue and was called the "church," stirred like one awakened from seeming death [*Scheintodter*]. But Judea immediately triumphed again, thanks to that thoroughly plebeian (German and English) *ressentiment* movement called the Reformation, and to that which was bound to arise from it, the restoration of the church — the restoration too of the ancient sepulchral repose [*Grabesruhe*] of classical Rome.[159]

We find in this analysis much that is typical of Nietzsche: the white-hot intensity of a critical insight couched in the rhetoric of his own too-sharp contrasts. In obedience to his own first principle — stylistic unity — as well as his growing interest in contests of *power,* Nietzsche stands firm in his conviction that, where a temple is to be created, a temple must be destroyed first.

IX

Throughout this chapter, I have attempted to draw out what I take to be the murky theories of "culture" that lie behind such a view. In so doing, I have made the point more than once that temples — like cultures — are seldom destroyed; rather, they are simply put to new uses. The archaeological record, particularly in places like Israel or Greece, bears this out, yet it bears out aspects of Nietzsche's philosophy, too. For, in the new uses to which old monuments are put, there is seldom, if ever, something gained without a commensurate loss — tragedy's inescapable lesson. If one wants to add a new tower or buttress, some ancient stones and statuary will have to be removed. This tragedy teaches, first of all: "You never gain something but that you lose something" — as Hegel and Nietzsche both knew well. It was Nietzsche's genius to apply this formula consistently and emphatically to the phenomenon of human culture.[160] His excess lay in the fact that he emphasized the losses, not the gains (for a more detailed analysis of this point, with an histor-

---

159. *On the Genealogy of Morals* I, §16; *Sämtliche Werke,* V, 286–287. Essential other texts are *Human, All-Too-Human,* §237; *The Gay Science,* §§35, 148, 149, 358; *The Antichrist,* §§4, 10, 58, 61; and *The Will to Power,* §§87–89, 93, 381, 419, 842, 957, 1017. It should at least be noticed how far Nietzsche stands from Hegel here. In his later political writings, Hegel viewed the Reformation as a triumphant discovery of the principle of freedom and private conscience. Luther was thus the first truly "modern" man. Nietzsche does not see it this way. If Hegel is too quick to synthesize Christian and Greek, too quick to unqualified praise of Luther, then Nietzsche is too slow.

160. See *Daybreak,* §27.

ical and archaeological illustration from the Athenian Parthenon, see appendix 1).

Beyond all of this, Nietzsche is a prophet — and that in two directions. He reads the Greeks extremely well. He also anticipates much of the modernist posture. His *Birth of Tragedy* represents one of the most sophisticated analyses of the tragic genre and its development "out of the spirit of music," which is to say, out of the Chorus. His sensitivity to the richness and vitality of classical Mediterranean culture was unsurpassed. At a time when most classical philologists still read as canonical Winckelmann's statements about the Greeks' "noble simplicity and quiet grandeur," Nietzsche gave us a glimpse of a previously unsuspected presence — the Dionysian, the volcanic life-force:

> Winckelmann's and Goethe's Greeks, Victor Hugo's Orientals, Wagner's Edda-heroes, Walter Scott's 13th Century British — some day or other the whole comedy will be exposed. It was historically false in every way — but modern, to be sure![161]

Winckelmann's popularity stemmed largely from his first pamphlet, "Reflections on the Imitation of Greek Works in Painting and Sculpture," written in 1755. It is one of those peculiar ironies of art history that Winckelmann's most famous and best-remembered phrase — "noble simplicity and quiet grandeur" — should have appeared in a discussion of the Laocöon group.[162] One can scarcely imagine a less simple, a less quiet, piece of Hellenistic sculpture. "Why he should have chosen this particular group as an example of the very qualities it lacks, is no easy question to answer."[163] I would like to include his comments in their entirety, to underscore the undeniable insights he *does* possess, as well as to take careful note of his tone, which was a philological marvel in Nietzsche's day, and as such, the very thing Nietzsche meant to reject:

> The universal, exquisite characteristic of the Greek masterpieces is, finally, *a noble simplicity* and *a quiet grandeur* [*eine edle Einhalt und eine stille Grosse*], as much in the pose as in the expression. Just as the depths of the sea remain calm always, no matter how wildly the sea's surface may rage, even so the expression in Greek figures demonstrates in the midst of any passions soever a great and quiet soul. This principle reveals itself in the face of Laocöon (and not only in the face) in the midst of violent suffering. The agony, which reveals itself in all the muscles and fibers of

---

161. *Sämtliche Werke*, XIII, 140.

162. For more on this, see Simon Richter, *Laocöon's Body and the Aesthetics of Pain* (Detroit: Wayne State Univ. Press, 1992) 38–61. In subsequent chapters, Richter deals with Lessing's, Herder's, Moritz's, and Goethe's reading of the same sculptural group.

163. E. M. Butler, *The Tyranny of Greece over Germany* (New York: Macmillan, 1935) 47.

his body even prior to a close inspection of the face and other parts, one comes to feel oneself, with one's whole being, solely from the painful contraction of his abdomen — this agony, I say, nevertheless transforms itself in the face and in the whole pose. It elevates his dreadful cry, which Virgil immortalizes in *his* Laocöon. The opening of the mouth here does not allow it; it is much more an anxious and resigned groan, as Gadolet described it. The agony of the body and the grandeur of the soul have been distributed with equal strength throughout the whole composition, and so have canceled one another. Laocöon suffers, but he suffers as Sophocles' Philoctetes does: his agony pierces us to the soul; yet we should wish to be able to endure agony even as does this great man.[164]

Over against this, we have the chthonic, eruptive force of Nietzsche's prose, *his* "tragic" sensitivity, his revelation in

> Dionysian experiences: here is the great depth, the great silence, in all matters Greek — *one does not know the Greeks* as long as this hidden subterranean entrance lies blocked. Importunate scholars' eyes will never see anything in these things, however much scholarship still has to be employed in this excavation. Even the noble zeal of such friends of antiquity as Goethe and Winckelmann here has something unpermitted, even immodest about it.[165]

Each of these positions has a real claim upon our aesthetic sympathy, and each appeals to something that is really in the sculptural group. How, then, do we negotiate between them?

It is poetically fitting that Hegel should be the mediating figure here. In fact, his reading of the Laocöon, and of Greek art more generally, has a foot in each world — Winckelmann's and Nietzsche's. Hegel points to the same elegance that had moved Winckelmann so, yet he also has a feeling for the disruptive energies that bring it into such stark relief:

> There has been much discussion to determine whether Virgil's description is modelled on the work of sculpture, or vice versa; and further, whether Laocöon is actually crying out, and whether it is appropriate for sculpture to attempt to express a cry, and other questions of this kind. But the essential thing about this group is that, despite the profound agony and the spasmodic tension and contraction of all the muscles of the body, the nobility of its beauty is preserved without lapse into grimaces, distortion and deformation.[166]

---

164. The text of *Gedänken Über die Nachahmung der griechischen Werke in der Malerei und Bildhauerkunst* may be found in Winckelmann's *Werke* (Stuttgart: Hoffmannische Verlags Buchhandlung, 1847), vol. 2. This section, §79, appears at p. 12. The translation is mine.

165. *The Will to Power,* §1051; *Sämtliche Werke,* XI, 681–682; see also §§830, 849, and *Twilight of the Idols,* X, §§3–4.

166. Paolucci, *Hegel: On the Arts,* 95.

Hegel seems to have an inkling of something else in the piece, something that is neither quiet nor still. Hegel says what Winckelmann does not — namely, that this sculpture is late Hellenistic, not classical at all. Yet there is something that keeps the Laocöon from being symptomatic of a broader cultural decline, "decadent" in Nietzsche's sense. The Laocöon, and other sculptures like it, are *necessarily* what they are. As art develops, historically, from classical to Romantic, it outgrows its various media. What the Laocöon longs to express — Nietzsche calls it the "great depth" — will require *other* artistic forms: painting and poetry and (shades of Nietzsche again) music:

> [The Greek gods] have no higher spiritual mode of being. They are blessed where they are and as they are. Yet, as all who have most deeply experienced the power of Greek art have felt, those blessed gods, even in their unmatched loveliness, seem to be saddened by their blessedness in bodily form. In their very faces we can read the Fate that awaits them — a Fate which, by making manifest the inherent contradiction between loftiness and particularity, between spirituality and sensuous existence, must bring classical art as such to its downfall.[167]

In short, there is a bittersweetness about such a sculpture that derives its spiritual force from both Nietzsche's "great depth" and Winckelmann's "quiet grandeur." There are abundant insights in each of these accounts, and that is the point to conclude with here. Nietzsche is not entirely right; however, he is saying something that had not been said so well before. It really *was* very untimely philology.

Even the archaeological record is amenable to some of Nietzsche's insights. During the second invasion of Attica, when the Persians actually did destroy the Archaic temple compound on the Akropolis, before they were repulsed at Salamis and Plataea in 480/79 B.C.E., the Athenians had no way of being sure that the Persians were not coming back. They threw up a new fortification wall as quickly as possible, mortaring in whatever lay ready to hand upon the Akropolis. Bits and pieces of marble, as well as the abundant statuary from the Archaic temple, served as the anomalous foundation for new fortifications. Other sculptures, undamaged but polluted by the Persians, were ritually buried there. When these were brought to light in this century, we learned something else remarkable about the Greeks — they *painted* their statues and buildings. Just as one may envision the Greek Chorus in a musical frenzy, one must imagine their Parthenon — *painted*. Only Nietzsche would not have been surprised.

Yet his most prophetic words were trained upon the future, not the past. Nietzsche saw, more clearly I think than anyone, the subtle temp-

167. Ibid., 30.

tation that nihilism would represent both culturally and philosophically in the twentieth century.[168] His emphatic Yes to life, as well as his open hostility to every Christian thing, will be misunderstood if they are not read in this light.[169] Nihilism — what he calls the pessimistic foundation of all modern culture — is perhaps best illustrated by our rather pathetic and uncritical preference for stories that end unhappily. Anything else is considered naïve. Nietzsche did not castigate Christianity for its optimism; just the opposite. He hates it for its hostility to a more affirmative, pagan past. He both is and is not a tragic posturer.

More to the point, and ultimately less favorably, he laid his sensitive fingers upon one of the chief concerns of our century: how "tragedy and culture" — or in his own terms, "Hellenism and Pessimism" — are connected. Must a temple really be destroyed every time we wish to build one? Probably not, although such things have happened, quite recently in fact. This conflictual model of cultural growth and decay is an attractive one, but it is ultimately unfounded. Just as telling the story of history is made easier — deceptively easier — by the dramatic turning points of decisive battles and imperial conquests, so too in the realm of cultural history, we want something that is neatly stratified. We want concrete places and times when one culture ends and another begins, little apocalypses in every case. Greeks... and then Christians... and then "something else." We are all archaeologists of culture:[170] when we sink our analytic trenches into the past, we long to find destruction-layers, where our task will be easiest, and cleanest... but least true to life.

Nietzsche helps us frame what has been one of the most important questions in the past two decades, both in philosophical and theological discussion. Can we have our Greeks and our Christians, too? Nietzsche says No. Here alone, he negates in emphatic terms. Dionysus is against the Crucified, as surely as Christ is against Dionysus. If all Christians do not yet realize this, then their dishonesty will be their undoing.[171] If a temple is to be created (or re-created, like the Parthenon), then one

---

168. See Martin Heidegger's essay "The Word of Nietzsche: God Is Dead," in *The Question concerning Technology and Other Essays,* trans. William Lovitt (New York: Harper and Row, 1977) 66–70, 109–110.

169. Compare Matthew Arnold, *Culture and Anarchy,* ed. J. Dover Wilson (Cambridge: Cambridge Univ. Press, 1932, 1990), to Stanley Rosen, "Nietzsche's Revolution," in *The Ancients and the Moderns,* 189–208.

170. This metaphor, so essential to Foucault, derives primarily from the 1886 preface to *Daybreak,* §§1–2.

171. Jürgen Habermas, in his *The Philosophical Discourse of Modernity,* trans. Frederick Lawrence (Cambridge, Mass.: MIT Press, 1987) 92–93, elucidates very well the manner in which Nietzsche's hostility to German Romanticism grows out of this same soil. Where the Romantics wanted to have Dionysus *and* the Crucified, and even went so far as to equate them ("Dionysus *is* the Crucified"), Nietzsche insists on the antithesis. Dionysus stands *against* the Crucified, and only there.

must be destroyed (the church). In this fundamentally agonistic model of human culture, there can be no syncretism, no "cultural borrowing." Or if it has a place, it is simply as a sign of disease and *décadence*. Stichomythia, not dialectics:

> The Christian church is an encyclopedia of prehistoric cults and conceptions of the most diverse origin, and that is why it is so capable of proselytizing.... It is not what is Christian in it, but the universally heathen character of its *usages,* which has favored the spread of this world-religion.... One may admire this *power* [*Kraft*] of causing the most various elements to coalesce, but one must not forget the contemptible quality that adheres to this power: the astonishing crudeness and self-satisfaction of the church's intellect during the time it was in process of formation, which permitted it to accept *any food* and to digest opposites [*Gegensätze*] like pebbles.[172]

As though it could have been otherwise! As if Christianity could have erupted into the world as some sort of cultural *a priori,* defined by some elusive, God-given "unity of style."[173] This is George Lindbeck's assumption, and I have pointed briefly to what are, I think, its fatal assumptions — it violates the very history of the tradition it wants to illumine. Cultures simply do not develop, or change, in this scheme.

Nietzsche's criticisms — the place, I am suggesting, where he went most wrong — help us to reassess what is the true essence of the Christian tradition, and more particularly, how very *Greek* it is. I want now to read the gospels, particularly the Passion narratives, as Christian *tragedy* — and to read Christianity as a tradition where the Yes and No are inextricably bound up, just as they were for the Greeks in the tragic age. With this insight, we leave Nietzsche behind — Nietzsche, whose attempt to say only Yes, "not to negate any more," boils down to the very crude *ressentiment* he had criticized so prophetically and so well. Who, finally, are these characters: Dionysus? Zarathustra? and "The Crucified"? To answer this question, we need to read a gospel. And in so doing, we need to recognize — for better *and* for worse — that we are doing what Nietzsche is no longer willing to do. Before we begin with that task, let Nietzsche warn us one last time — to be honest:

> I do not like the "New Testament," that should be plain; I find it almost disturbing that my taste [*Geschmack*] in regard to this most highly esteemed and overestimated work should be so singular (I have the taste

---

172. *Daybreak,* §70; *Sämtliche Werke,* III, 68–69.
173. Burton L. Mack, in his *A Myth of Innocence: Mark and Christian Origins* (Philadelphia: Fortress Press, 1988) 1–9, shows how pervasive this assumption really is. But there is one point at which we *strongly* disagree. Mack (pp. 370–372) would agree with me that the tragic posture is necessarily grounded in a myth of origins, what he calls "a myth of innocence." But he charges Mark with the *creation* of this myth. I think Mark is precisely out to *undo* it.

of two millennia *against* me): but there it is! "Here I stand, I cannot
do otherwise" — I have the courage [*Muth*] of my bad taste.... In [it]
I find nothing but petty sectarianism, mere rococo of the soul, involu-
tions, nooks, queer things, the air of the conventicle, not to forget an
occasional whiff of bucolic mawkishness that belongs to the epoch (*and*
to the Roman province) and is not so much Jewish as Hellenistic. Humility [*Demuth*] and self-importance slapped together; a garrulousness
of feeling that almost stupefies; impassioned vehemence, without passion;
embarrassing gesticulation; it is plain that there is no trace of good breed-
ing. How can one make such a fuss about one's little lapses as these pious
little men do! Who gives a damn? Certainly not God. Finally, they even
want "the crown of eternal life," these little provincial people; but for
what? to what purpose? Presumption can go no further. An "immortal"
Peter: who could stand him? Their ambition is laughable: people of *that*
sort regurgitating their most private affairs, their stupidities, sorrows, and
petty worries, as if the Heart of Being [*An-sich-der-Dinge*] were obliged
to concern itself with them; they never grow tired of involving God himself in even the pettiest troubles they have got themselves into. And the
appalling taste of this perpetual familiarity [*Auf-du-und-du*] with God!
This Jewish and not merely Jewish obtrusiveness of pawing and nuzzling
God![174]

I *do* like the New Testament. I do not like all of it, and in fact the majority of Paul's letters have singularly failed to move me.[175] But that is
precisely the point of Nietzsche's stimulating categories — at first glance
so attractive, but on further reflection too simple and abrupt. If one dis-
likes any part of the New Testament, he seems to suggest, then one is
obliged to reject all of it. If one likes it, then one is compelled to accept
it all — in the name of some alleged stylistic "unity." That is the chief
implication of his overemphasis on cultural attitudes and the unity of
style. The New Testament possesses a tremendous plurality of styles and
of theological perspectives. Among them, I have always been drawn to
the gospels and to Mark's tragic vision preeminently. It is time now to
say why.

---

174. *On the Genealogy of Morals* III, §22; *Sämtliche Werke*, V, 393–394.

175. Nietzsche's critique of the Pauline psychology seems to me one of the most penetrating, in *The Antichrist*, §§41–42, 47, 58. "At bottom there was only one Christian,
and he died on the Cross," says Nietzsche. "The 'gospels' died on the Cross" (§39).

Chapter 4

MARK'S TRAGIC VISION
Gethsemane

God, whose law it is
that those who learn must suffer.
And even in our sleep
pain that cannot forget
falls drop by drop upon the heart;
and in our own despite,
against our will,
comes wisdom to us
by the awful grace of God.

— Aeschylus, *Agamemnon*

This book began with a close reading of a single tragedy — Sophocles' *Antigone* — although other plays, particularly Sophocles' *Ajax* and *Oedipus* as well as Aeschylus' *Seven against Thebes,* all left their tragic mark. The book ends, now, with a close reading of a single gospel (Mark's) and a key moment in that gospel — the prayer in Gethsemane, which is the pivot around which the rest of the tragedy revolves.[1] In this reading, comparative analyses of the other three gospels play an essential role.

There is a certain deliberateness, if not actually a necessity of sorts, about this narrative structure. The canonical texts — tragedies and gospels — sandwich a long philosophical discussion of two philosophers

---

1. "At Gethsemane the arrow changes its course," says George Steiner, "and the morality play of history alters from tragedy to *commedia*" (Steiner, *The Death of Tragedy* [New York: Hill and Wang, 1961] 13). While I worry about his distinction between tragedy and comedy, and will explain that in some detail at the end of the chapter, it is interesting that Steiner mentions *Gethsemane.* Not Golgotha, where the atoning death takes place, and not an empty tomb, where resurrection is realized. It is in Gethsemane, where Jesus begs off of this tragedy, that the message of the gospel is best encapsulated.

who encourage us to think rather differently about Greek tragedy than the modern posture will allow. Tragedy, giving way to philosophy, giving way to the gospels in turn.

Historically speaking, gospels grow out of tragedies. Simply by participating in the Hellenistic literary world, and indeed by being written in Greek, the gospels *are* Greek in fascinating ways. They are, generically speaking, Greek *tragedies*. Yet the connections run deeper than this. The gospels also participate in this tragic world of thought. They portray a tragic universe.

These claims become acute in the Passion narrative and also help to explain why we have gone on so long in exploring Hegel's and Nietzsche's tragic vision. Tragedy, an inescapable *fact* of human life, emerges out of the fact that *there is more than one will in the world*. So says Hegel. As we shall see, that is precisely what is at stake in Gethsemane, particularly in Mark's performance. Tragedy, as an emphatically *affirmative* genre, refuses to be broken by the fact of human suffering, no matter how egregious. Tragedy, in fact, speaks of the transformative power that certain redemptive moments of suffering possess. As such, it portrays relationships — human and divine — that cannot be sundered *and that can have no end*. This Nietzsche knew. As we shall see, Mark knew these things as well. That Christian churches have failed to teach this more clearly, that the Western, Latin-speaking Christian world has forgotten its Greek roots so long and so well, is one of the things that has made *this* book necessary.

I

The first question that needs asking here is similar to the question with which we concluded the last chapter. In that discussion, I accused Nietzsche of some real ambiguity in many of his central concepts. We still do not know who Zarathustra or Dionysus is, nor, so I am arguing, are we given to see how different Dionysus really is from the Crucified in the end. In order to clarify that issue, we need to read a gospel. But now we discover another, equally fundamental question: *What exactly is a gospel?* This question — the question of a *genre* — has occupied New Testament scholars for fully three decades now, and we are still a world away from anything even vaguely resembling a scholarly consensus. The comparatively recent discovery, translation, and publication of so many *other* "gospels," and particularly the Gnostic "gospels" found at Nag Hammadi along the Nile River Valley, have lent an even greater urgency to this question.[2] How broadly are we to draw the boundaries of the

_____

2. See Ron Cameron's *The Other Gospels: Non-Canonical Gospel Texts* (Philadel-

genre? How inclusive does our definition of a "gospel" need to be? The very idea of the canon is at stake.[3] For all these texts, taken together, share very little in common — stylistically, formally, or theologically. Many, most really, of these documents the church rejected, even went out of its way to destroy some of them. The survival of so many of these texts is something of an archaeological and cultural miracle in its own right, and sets the Christian mind reeling.

I will not have much to say about these extracanonical texts, except peripherally and by inference, both because I am no expert in this material and also, more important, because the question is difficult enough when we deal only with the four gospels we find in the New Testament. What in the world do *these* texts share in common? As anyone who is remotely acquainted with Christian literature knows, the first three gospels are called "Synoptic," a Greek word implying that they "see things the same way" (a view I hope to call into question in this chapter). Over against these three, there is *John*, a document that the church thought long and hard about before including in the canon at all, a document that frankly contradicts many of the statements in the first three gospels, a document that necessitated the writing of countless gospel "harmonies" in the first several centuries of the common era[4] — a document that is, however, far and away the most popular devotional book in the entire New Testament, with the possible exception of certain passages in some of Paul's letters. No less a scholar than Luther insisted that the real essence of the New Testament message — "the true kernel and marrow of all the books" — may be found in John's gospel and these same selections from Paul. Everything else could be read later, at one's leisure, and some of it (like the epistle of James) might be better left unread.[5] The real heart of the message — the "gospel," as it is called — could be found in these select places.

---

phia: Westminster Press, 1982); John Dominic Crossan's *Four Other Gospels: Shadows on the Contours of Canon* (New York: Winston Press, 1985); and Robert J. Miller, *The Complete Gospels* (Sonoma, Calif.: Polebridge Press, 1992). For an eminently readable and sensitive presentation of the theological questions raised by all these "other gospels," see Elaine Pagels' *The Gnostic Gospels* (New York: Random House, 1979).

3. For an interesting, if somewhat conservative, discussion of the implications of a literary "canon" for the church, see Bruce M. Metzger, *The Canon of the New Testament* (Oxford: Oxford Univ. Press, 1987) 271–288.

4. Among the most notable of these are Tatian's *Diatesseron;* Origen's *Contra Celsum;* Augustine's and Eusebius' gospel harmonies. Eusebius' in particular, or at least an excerpted portion of it, is discussed in appendix 2, where I address the problem of the ending of Mark's gospel.

5. See Luther's preface to his translation of the New Testament, which may be found in the American edition of *Luther's Works,* ed. E. Theodore Bachmann, vol. 35 (Philadelphia: Muhlenberg Press, 1960) 361–362. It is here too that Luther dismisses the epistle of James as "an epistle of straw."

What, then, is a "gospel"? As we noted in chapter 1, it is often easier — particularly in theological circles — to say what something is not. We negate before we define ourselves (Sophocles), before we affirm (Nietzsche). Thus, a gospel is pretty clearly *not* a simple collection of the sayings of Jesus — we have a number of these, the *Gospel of Thomas* being the most famous — but they all clearly read, and sound, very different than any of the four gospels in the New Testament. There is a narrative structure, a narrative "frame," that places each of Jesus' many sayings in a context where they will make a certain kind of sense, and not just any sense we choose.[6] "Scene and saying go together."[7] Moreover, these gospels have a real stylistic and narrative unity that, as Aristotle tells us in his discussion of tragedy, comes from clearly marking out their beginning, middle, and end. We will need to think more about this when we discuss the problematic notion of the "end" of a gospel, but a beginning and a narrative middle they very clearly *do* have. The end, particularly in *Mark,* is another story.

By the same token, the gospels are pretty clearly not "Passion narratives with a preface,"[8] as had been the popular assumption of a number of scholars, following Martin Kähler at the turn of the century. The Passion certainly does lie at the very heart of the story that the gospels tell, but to say that everything else is merely prefatory denigrates the rich middle, virtually ignores the beginning, and places far too much weight on a very problematic ending. The gospels tell a story that is meaningful in all its moments, not merely at the end. The early church also was well aware of this dilemma, as it struggled to define for itself what "imitating" Jesus really entailed. If imitating his teachings, then it counsels a certain kind of life.[9] If imitating his death, it counsels a martyr's Fate, however, one "comformable to the gospel."[10]

It may be misleading to speak of "gospels" at all, at least if we insist

---

6. It was one of the chief tenets of the form-critics that these sayings of Jesus circulated independent of any narrative context in the early Christian communities, and one of the things that makes New Testament "literature" so primitive (shades of Nietzsche here) is the fact that the "frames" are so shabbily and briefly constructed. A careful reading of *Mark,* let us say, tells a very different story. See Martin Dibelius, *From Tradition to Gospel,* trans. Bertram Lee Woolf (Greenwood, S.C.: Attic Press, 1971, 1982); Rudolf Bultmann, *A History of the Synoptic Tradition,* trans. John Marsh (New York: Harper and Row, 1963); and William Wrede, *The Messianic Secret,* trans. J. C. G. Grieg (Greenwood, S.C.: Attic Press, 1971).

7. Burton L. Mack and Vernon K. Robbins, *Patterns of Persuasion in the Gospels* (Sonoma, Calif.: Polebridge Press, 1989) 66.

8. Martin Kähler, *The So-Called Historical Jesus and the Historical, Biblical Christ,* trans. Carl E. Braaten (Philadelphia: Fortress Press, 1964) 80 note 11; see also 125–127.

9. Often referred to as "the way," as in the Didache, found in Cyril C. Richardson, *Early Christian Fathers* (New York: Macmillan, 1970) 161–179.

10. See "The Martyrdom of Polycarp, Bishop of Smyrna," in Richardson, *Early Christian Fathers,* 141–158, esp. 149.

on assuming that they represent a distinct genre, *generically un*like other kinds of books and stories. The word that we translate as "gospel," *euangelion,* is a rather ambiguous Greek word. When Mark begins, at his beginning, he says quite explicitly: "The beginning [*archē*] of *the gospel* of Jesus Christ."[11] This might also be translated, "The beginning of *the good news* of Jesus Christ," as it often is. Which is to say that when Mark, and the other gospel authors who follow him, use this ambiguous word — 'gospel' — it is not at all clear that they saw themselves inventing a new kind of literature or writing a generically different kind of book. 'Gospel' is *not* a proper noun. Luke, at the very least, has his feet firmly planted in the Hellenistic literary world — he knows how to recognize history when he sees it, and he knows how to write it, as he intends to do in his own gospel and in *Acts of the Apostles.* Thus, a gospel — and the whole question about how to "define" one — *may* be a scholar's question only, rather far from any question that the writers thought to ask themselves about what they were writing.

I would like to shift the focus of this discussion a bit. In the quest for a genre, for a label, scholars have posed an incredible array of suggestions: the gospels are clear examples of Greco-Roman biography, modeled on the great portraits of Socrates painted by Plato and Xenophon;[12] or they are hagiographies, modeled on the narrative of the *theios anēr,* the "divine man," who comes to earth, like Apollonius of Tyana, working wonders and revealing sacred mysteries;[13] or they are essentially apocalyptic literature, endeavoring to define this problematic notion (discussed at length, especially in the preceding chapter) of the end;[14] or they are, taken as a whole, extended parables, attempting

---

11. *Mark* 1:1; it is a disputed matter in the manuscripts if he goes on to call Jesus a "son of God."

12. See Richard A. Burridge, *What Are the Gospels? A Comparison with Greco-Roman Biography* (Cambridge: Cambridge Univ. Press, 1992); Vernon K. Robbins, *Jesus the Teacher: A Socio-Rhetorical Interpretation of Mark* (Philadelphia: Fortress Press, 1984); Charles Talbert, *What Is a Gospel? The Genre of the Canonical Gospels* (Philadelphia: Fortress Press, 1977); and Clyde W. Votaw, *The Gospels and Contemporary Biographies in the Greco-Roman World* (Philadelphia: Fortress Press, Facet Series, 1970).

13. Paul Achtemeier, *Mark* (Philadelphia: Fortress Press, 1975); but see Theodore H. Weeden, *Mark: Traditions in Conflict* (Philadelphia: Fortress Press, 1971), who argues that Mark wrote his gospel as an extended polemic *against* this very *theios anēr* christology.

14. The classic statement of this view, which claimed moreover to have "discovered" the perspective of "thoroughgoing eschatology," is Albert Schweitzer's *Quest of the Historical Jesus,* trans. W. Montgomery (New York: Macmillan, 1968). See also John J. Collins, *The Apocalyptic Imagination: An Introduction to the Jewish Matrix of Christianity* (New York: Crossroad, 1984), and Dan O. Via, Jr., *The Ethics of Mark: In the Middle of Time* (Philadelphia: Fortress Press, 1985), along with *Kerygma and Comedy in the New Testament* (Philadelphia: Fortress Press, 1975o) 78–90. For a very sensitive reading of the very special kind of apocalypse envisioned by Mark, see Ched Myers, *Binding the Strong Man: A Political Reading of Mark's Story of Jesus* (Maryknoll, N.Y.:

(much like the Gnostic literature) to express the ineffable in words and images;[15] or they are the conscious extension of the Old Testament historical narrative, carefully picking up and playing with the prophecies in order to demonstrate that the Messiah, and the kingdom that he is bringing, have come at last.[16]

It will surprise no one by now to learn that I am interested in using the analogy of Greek drama to think about the gospels. Each gospel might best be thought of as the "performance"[17] of a common *mythos*. This term is obviously a dramatic one.[18] In thinking about the Greek theater, there is a single, absolutely essential, theatrical fact: *these people did not go to the theater to learn what happens (they already knew what happened); they came to learn something new about themselves.*[19] This innocent comment, more of a truism than a "theory" of Greek tragedy, is a far dicier claim in the world of canonical religion. For we

---

Orbis Books, 1988) 413–423. An essential question for Christian theology seems to me to be the careful distinction between fulfillment and ending.

15. William Beardslee, "Parable, Proverb, and Koan," *Semeia* 12 (1978) 151–177; John Dominic Crossan, "A Form for Absence: The Markan Creation of Gospel," *Semeia* 12 (1978) 41–55, and *The Dark Interval: Toward a Theology of Story* (Allen, Tex.: Argus Communications, 1975); Werner H. Kelber, *Mark's Story of Jesus* (Philadelphia: Fortress Press, 1979); and Frank Kermode, *The Genesis of Secrecy: On the Interpretation of Narrative* (Cambridge, Mass.: Harvard Univ. Press, 1979).

16. It is telling that *Mark* 1:2 continues the explanation of what this "gospel" is all about in the following terms: "as it is written in *Isaiah* the prophet..." See Claude Pavur, "As It Is Written: The Nature, Purpose and Meaning of Mark's Gospel," Masters thesis, Jesuit School of Theology, Berkeley, Calif. (1985).

17. I am indebted to Vernon K. Robbins for this term — 'performance' — which seems more and more appropriate the longer I think about it. For a methodological commentary, see Mack and Robbins, *Patterns of Persuasion*, 18–22, *passim*. The chief resonance that this term obviously possesses is dramatic. And it is fascinating to note how readers, in a wide variety of disciplines and with an equally wide range of scholarly interests, have come to some awareness of the dramatic *and tragic* dimension of the gospel — Mark's in particular. See Gilbert Bilezikian, *The Liberated Gospel* (Ann Arbor, Mich.: Baker Book House, 1977); Kelber, *Mark's Story of Jesus*, 9, 79, 85, 88–96; Kermode, *The Genesis of Secrecy*, 69ff.; David Rhoads and Donald Michie, *Mark as Story* (Philadelphia: Fortress Press, 1982); Myers, *Binding the Strong Man*, 3–37, 91–135, 364–367; Robert Tannehill, "The Disciples in Mark: The Function of a Narrative Role," *Journal of Religion* 59 (1977) 386–405; Weeden, *Traditions in Conflict*, 12–19; and Via's *Kerygma and Comedy in the New Testament;* and Christopher Bryan, *A Preface to Mark: Notes on the Gospel in Its Literary and Cultural Settings* (New York: Oxford Univ. Press, 1993) 163–170.

18. Alec McCowen's solo "performance" (that is, his dramatic recitation) of Mark's gospel in America and Britain makes the point I want to make best. See his reflections on Mark's gospel, through the "eyes" of oral performance, in *Personal Mark: An Actor's Proclamation of St. Mark's Gospel* (New York: Continuum, 1985). See also Janet K. Larson, "St. Alec's Gospel," *Christian Century* 96:1 (1979) 17–19; and John Koenig, "St. Mark on the Stage: Laughing All the Way to the Cross," *Theology Today* 36:1 (1979) 84–86.

19. James Redfield, "Drama and Community: Aristophanes and Some of His Rivals," in *Nothing to Do With Dionysus? Athenian Drama in Its Social Context,* ed. John J. Winkler and Froma I. Zeitlin (Princeton, N.J.: Princeton Univ. Press, 1990) 324–325.

moderns tend to assume — much too quickly, I am afraid — that the gospels served an "evangelical" purpose. These texts, we think, were written to introduce people to a story they had *not* heard before. Form precedes function, and our own word — 'evangelical' — has hopelessly muddled the way we think about the *euangelion*. In fact, the gospels may well have been written by people and for people who already *knew* and accepted the Christian *mythos*, the story[20] — people who came to these performances not to learn how the story ends (to the degree that it *does* end, as in *Mark*), but to learn something new about themselves.

Honesty compels me to admit, albeit briefly, that we are on to a critical and controversial conviction of my own. I think that this may well be the crux of the matter concerning the vast differences between the Synoptic gospels and *John*. The Synoptic gospels are the very kind of dramatic literature that the mature Christian community began composing for itself. *John* is written, by contrast, with an eye to evangelism in the "modern" sense — that is, for the "conversion" of people who did *not* know the story and had *not* heard it before.[21] It is far from irrelevant to note that John's gospel is almost invariably the text of choice among contemporary evangelicals, particularly when they are meaning to speak with "outsiders" who do not know the stories. John alone is a preacher;[22] the other gospel writers are something else again.[23] As Luther remarked, John is best read first; the other gospels need to wait for greater spiritual maturity, that is, guidance and the catechism. In short, one needs to know the story *already* to read the Synoptics.

This dramatic, or more properly *tragic,* analogy has one further implication, which is equally unsettling in the world of biblical studies. The *mythos* is a vague and rather malleable thing. The story that is endlessly retold by the poets in a variety of ways is a "story" only in the sparest sense — a few facts loosely linked in the sparest of narrative chains:

> As Aristotle tells us [in *Poetics* 1453b.24–25], the tragic poet may not alter the essential stories, the plot, the *mythous*. All that matters, and all that the audience has come to see, is that the story be told well [*kalōs*].

---

20. For an excellent discussion of why this assumption is so methodologically crucial, see Myers, *Binding the Strong Man,* 40–47, 65–69, 107–109, 413–423.

21. That in itself might easily become an argument for the priority of John's gospel. See J. A. T. Robinson, *The Priority of John,* ed. J. F. Coakley (Oak Park, Ill.: Meyer-Stone Books, 1985) 47ff.

22. *John* 20:31.

23. All this offered *contra* Kähler, *The So-Called Historical Jesus and the Biblical Christ,* 81.

It is a key part of Aristotle's project to demonstrate just what it would mean to tell a story well.[24]

The essential *mythos* of Oedipus, for instance, is that he killed his father and married his mother. The peculiar manner in which Oedipus moves from Point A (defeat of the Sphinx and the redemption of Thebes) to Point B (incestuous disaster) is the product of the poet and the tragedy he or she wants to tell. All that matters is that it be told "well," and the poet is remarkably free "to create the truth" in the name of aesthetic and philosophical and even theological considerations. But an Oedipus without the patricide, the king without his mother for a queen — this would no longer be Oedipus. The *mythos* would be another one entirely.

Thus, the story, for all of its vagueness, *does* nonetheless draw boundary lines outside of which the poet may not move so freely. And we know of at least one case, Euripides' *Hippolytos* (it was called *Phaedra* then), where the poet crafted the character of Phaedra in such a way that he seemed to violate the very texture of the myth.[25] This mythological rewrite was rejected by the larger Athenian audience, and Euripides subsequently rewrote the play, staging it a second time several years later. Euripides' controversial reputation as a dramatic poet derived largely from this, at times, perverse habit of his (perverse at least to most of the Athenians of his day, and perverse even to Nietzsche): his delight in taking the inherited *mythos* and testing it, stretching it as far as it would go. There is a very real poetic gift demanded by this strategy: one needs to be able to stretch a myth without breaking it. Euripides broke his myths, probably more than once, which as much as anything else accounts for his controversial reputation, as I say, even in antiquity. "Nothing too much," says an ancient Attic proverb inscribed on the temple at Delphi.[26]

It could be argued that this essential *mythos,* vague though it is, both provides the intrinsic interest *in* the story and constitutes the intrinsic value *of* the story. A man who has killed his father and taken his mother

---

24. Gerald F. Else, *Aristotle's Poetics: The Argument* (Cambridge, Mass.: Harvard Univ. Press, 1957) 243–234, 251–263, 320–322, 405–406, 412–417, 543, and *The Madness of Antigone* (Heidelberg: Carl Winter Universitätsverlag, 1976) 42–43.

25. For an extremely learned discussion of what we know about this lost play, and the audience's reaction to the portrait of Phaedra that it painted, see the introduction to W. S. Barrett's critical edition, *Euripides: Hippolytos* (Oxford: Clarendon Press, 1964) 6–29.

26. We shall have occasion to wonder if John's performance of the Passion is merely Euripidean, or whether he has rejected an essential portion of the *mythos.* That is, in Gethsemane, the prayer and the temptation — are they evocative details, or essential aspects of the *mythos,* without which the story is no longer the same? This question takes us to the crucial center of the question of canonicity — who or what defines its limits, who or what determines when stretching becomes breaking, who defines what is "too much"? *Must* a canon be eternally open, in theory?

to bed — *this* is a story we want to hear. So much the more do we long to hear it sung, to see it performed:[27]

> In sculpture and painting, the work of art stands out before us as an independently existent *result* of artistic activity. It does not, however, show us the life process of the productive activity itself. The musical work of art, on the contrary, can be completely realized for us — and in this it approaches the character of dramatic poetry — only by living *performance*, by skilled execution in our very presence.[28]

So too with the early Christian *mythoi*. There is an intrinsic interest in the stories they tell, even in their sparest details. They are stories that we long to hear and to see performed — perhaps, just perhaps, by early Christian poets who would have recited these tales around a fire (or in a synagogue) and even today, still, in the formal liturgical setting of the Orthodox churches. The Gerasene demoniac[29] provides a marvelous example of such a story, how and why it is so memorable: "Tell us the story of when Jesus crossed the sea and exorcised the demon from that terrible [*deinon*] man among the tombs!" Gethsemane provides us with another: "We have heard it said that on the night Jesus was *betrayed* by Judas, he went off alone, was *tempted*, and *prayed* — before he was arrested. Will you tell us the story?" More than this we probably can never say.

II

This idea of a Christian *mythos*, or *mythoi*, also forces another key assumption of biblical scholarship to the surface. What kind of "texts" do we claim to be working with? What exactly *is* a Christian myth, and what function does it serve? Again, the negative definition has priority. A Christian *mythos* is *not* a written text, anymore than a Greek myth is. The various performances of the *mythos* are eventually written down

---

27. It would be well to keep in mind that it seems to have been the *performative* dimension of the Greek theater that ultimately impelled Plato to ban the poets from his ideal republic in book 10. Plato too believes that language has a magic power, and no one plays more eloquently with the spoken word than Socrates. Such playfulness needs to be strictly controlled, however (a characteristic Platonic paradox). Language must always be used in service to the truth. Drama, with its wild, orgiastic music and dance, its flowing poetry, its elaborate costumes and effects, tends to draw attention away from the message, leaving one only with the vacuous spectacle of a play. To qualify our original thesis: the Greeks did not come to the theater *only* to learn something about themselves; they also came to see a good show — and this is what Plato cannot allow. See Eric A. Havelock, *Preface to Plato* (Cambridge, Mass.: Harvard Univ. Press, 1963).

28. Paolucci, *Hegel: On the Arts* (New York: Frederick Ungar, 1979) 140.

29. *Mark* 5:1-20; *Matthew* 8:28-34; *Luke* 8:26-39.

of course, but these writings are themselves intended for oral performance — just like the tragedies. A gospel, like drama, is a primarily oral
event.

The reasons for emphasizing this are twofold. In the first place, while
the gospel writers all obviously *did* write, they did so for people who,
with rare exceptions, *did not*. The primary mode of communication in
late Hellenistic society was oral, not written.[30] The implications of this
fact are profound.[31]

Plutarch tells a charming story — at the conclusion of a far from
charming biography — about the Athenian hoplites sent to work as
slaves in the Syracusean mines, after the disastrous defeat of the Athenian fleet in 416 B.C.E. It seems that the Sicilians were great lovers
of Euripides, among the most devoted fans he had, loving to trade
fragments from the poet back and forth as a sign of culture and con-
temporaneity and wit. Many Athenians who had been sold off as slaves
earned their freedom by teaching the members of their households "all
that they remembered [*ememnēnto*] from his poems," while the others
who had fled after the battle managed to get food and water from local inhabitants in exchange for a few pirated verses. "In any event,"
Plutarch continues, "it is said that a number of those who were saved in
this way went to visit Euripides, to thank him."[32]

By calling this story charming, I do not mean to say that it is "merely"
a story. Whether such a thing actually happened or not is unimportant.
What *is* remarkable is precisely the thing that Plutarch considers unre-
markable — namely, that so many Athenian hoplites could call so much
of Euripides to mind in the most trying of circumstances and very far
from home. We need to reflect upon what this means, how living "the
word" remains when it is spoken and remembered, not read and tran-
scribed. These soldiers, presumably once part of Euripides' audience,

---

30. The level of literacy in late Hellenistic society is, of course, a very difficult question to broach, but it is at least clear that their levels of literacy were nothing like our
own. We can never assume that a text was intended to be read by everyone. Even Paul's
letters were probably read in the churches to which they were addressed — by someone who could read, for the vast majority who could not. See Walter J. Ong, *Orality
and Literacy: The Technologizing of the Word* (New York: Methuen Press, 1982). For
a very different, and ultimately less successful (because it is so dualistic), application of
these same ideas to Mark's gospel, see Werner Kelber, *The Oral and Written Gospel*
(Philadelphia: Fortress Press, 1982). Better is Myers, *Binding the Strong Man*, 92–99.

31. I am not certain how much of a difference the assumption of "a culture dominated by literary education" in the late Hellenistic world (Mack and Robbins, *Patterns
of Persuasion*, 32) makes for one's view of the gospels — particularly in light of the fact
that I have such sympathy with the rhetorical analyses made there.

32. Plutarch, *The Life of Nikias*, §29. See also Peter Green, *Armada from Athens*
(Garden City, N.Y.: Doubleday, 1970) 347–350. Oddly, this tradition is not reported by
Thucydides where we might well expect him to do so, *The Peloponnesian War*, VII, §87.

heard the songs *one time* and remembered them.[33] An extraordinary feat, by our (or any) standards.

It is clear, too, how scholars — themselves the most bookish, that is *literate,* people of all — have applied their own canons of literacy to a *very* different antique world. The chief problem of both form- and redaction-criticism is that their models presuppose the existence of a "first gospel text," which was then reworked by subsequent writers, most notably by our four evangelists. That there *is* insight to be gained from all of this is beyond dispute.[34] "These men," however, "are like the old Homeric scholars who see small resemblances, but fail to see the significant ones."[35] The *method* is flawless; its *presuppositions* are wrong.

Where the presuppositions are wrong, certain *conclusions* will be as well — the old circularity of beginning and ending, again. Once we grant that the evangelists were slapping together a whole range of preexistent material — material that, as written, could not be altered, despite the fact that it did not all fit together very well — then we are already a long way toward another conclusion that characterized the form- and redaction-critical methods: that these people were, in the end, rather poor writers. Such a conclusion plays right into the hands of the most polemical anti-Christians, Nietzsche chief among them. "It is subtle [*Feinheit*]," he quips, "that when God wished to become a storyteller, he learned Greek — *and* that he did not learn it better."[36] One of the things that I sincerely hope this book can accomplish is the redemption of these people's reputations as storytellers.[37]

Here, as in so many other ways, the most critical biblical scholars want to be good philologists yet have failed to learn from the checkered

---

33. John J. Winkler offers a contrasting thesis that is so fascinating that I cannot resist mentioning it here. Winkler suggests that the Athenian choruses were handpicked members of that year's class of *epheboi,* or young men "graduating" from their military training. Those who were not posted were taken to play in choruses. On this view, the reason so many of these soldiers in Sicily knew the latest songs of Euripides is that a number of them had just been playing him, earlier in the year. See Winkler, "The Ephebe's Song: *Tragōidia* and *Polis,*" in *Nothing to Do with Dionysus?* 20–62.

34. See, for example, Sydney Temple, "The Two Traditions of the Last Supper, Betrayal and Arrest," *New Testament Studies* 7 (1960) 77–85, which is building on the prior work of Vincent Taylor's groundbreaking *The Gospel according to St. Mark* (London: Macmillan, 1963) 653–658.

35. Aristotle, *The Metaphysics,* 1093a.27.

36. *Beyond Good and Evil,* IV, §121; *Sämtliche Werke,* V, 94. "As a matter of fact, no man can be a philologist," he continues, "without also being *Antichrist*" (*The Antichrist,* §47; *Sämtliche Werke,* VI, 225–226).

37. Martin Dibelius, who was himself one of the founders of this modern method of picking a gospel apart, could never really find a place for Christian storytellers, although he knew they must have existed. See *From Tradition to Gospel,* 70, 156–158, as well as the discussion in Mack and Robbins, *Patterns of Persuasion in the Gospels,* 2–10, 16–17; and Via, *The Ethics of Mark's Gospel,* 48.

history of this most classical discipline. Nearly a century ago, German philologists were intent upon compiling the *Urtext* of Homer: stripped of all its later redactional accretions, what we would have is the very poem the poet sang:

> You cannot extract something, even with great commitment, if your mind is small. Until now, small-minded philologists have believed that the true Homer was there for the extracting.
> Antiquity speaks with us when it wants to, not when we do.[38]

The real point is, Homer *sang* — not wrote, but sang, and surely did not sing his poem only once. Philology has come a long way from such hybristic pretensions — by letting antiquity speak, by recognizing how fluid, and how long, is the period of transition from a primarily oral culture to a literary one.[39] By the time a poet writes a poem down, it has been circulating orally for a very long time. And our written versions are simply one performance, frozen in time, among countless others. What is a constant is the *mythos* — the conflict with the Gerasene demoniac, the agony and prayer in the Garden. The *performance* of this story is a many-splendored thing.

If everything is as fluid as I am claiming it is, then what sense does it make to speak about the *mythos* at all? All we have are four major performances (many more if you are inclined to read the extracanonical gospels), and nothing else. Our situation is again very close to the classical philologist's. We are lucky enough to have preserved for us the same *mythos* as performed by the three major Attic tragedians: Aeschylus' *Libation Bearers;* Sophocles' and Euripides' *Elektra*. All three tell the story of two children, Elektra and Orestes, who conspire to kill their mother and her lover (Clytemnaestra and Aegisthus) in order to avenge the murder of their father (Agamemnon). That is the story, the myth.

---

38. Nietzsche, *Wir Philologen*, 3[56]; *Sämtliche Werke*, VIII, 29. Here Nietzsche has F. A. Wolf's *Prolegomena to Homer* (1795) chiefly in mind, trans. and ed. Anthony Grafton, G. W. Most, and J. E. G. Zetzel (Princeton, N.J.: Princeton Univ. Press, 1985) 67–70. Wolf's chief contributions to Homeric scholarship were fourfold: his insistence on the importance of (1) the ancient, Alexandrian philological commentaries and (2) the Venetian family of manuscripts; (3) the belief in a preliterate Homer; and (4) the faith that the true Homer can be "extracted."

39. The pioneering work in this field was done by Milman Parry, who studied the living tradition of Serbo-Croatian oral poetry and applied what he discovered to the transmission of the Homeric poems. His two articles, "Studies in the Technique of Oral Verse-Making," *Harvard Society of Classical Philology* 41 (1930) 73–147 and 43 (1932) 1–50, were not further refined due to Parry's untimely death. That task was left to his student, Albert Lord, in *The Singer of Tales* (Cambridge, Mass.: Harvard Univ. Press, 1960). For a good discussion of Yugoslavian oral poetry, to be appreciated in its own right, and not merely as a prelude to these Homeric studies, see Svetozar Koljevic, *The Epic in the Making* (Oxford: Clarendon Press, 1980). Finally, see Alasdair MacIntyre's *After Virtue* 2d ed. (Notre Dame, Ind.: Univ. of Notre Dame Press, 1984) 37, 121, 216.

And beyond that, the three performances share very little in common. The story is secure, undeniably a *single* story; but it is performed according to the tastes, and the interests (we might even say, the *theology*), of the poets.

I would like to propose a thought-experiment[40] in order to begin to talk about the Christian *mythos* of Gethsemane. In order to do that, we need to begin by being ironically more "textual" than the text-critics. It is a commonplace in New Testament scholarship that the Synoptic evangelists, in addition to "seeing things the same way," shared a written source in common. Many, in fact, claim that Mark's gospel as a whole *is* that source, used by both Matthew and Luke when they decided to flesh out his account a bit, with the use of other sayings — the proposed Q Source — not available to the first evangelist. Much is then made of the tremendous verbal agreement between the three gospels, taken as a whole. In order to test this assumption, I have compiled a "text" of all the words that really are common to all three Synoptic performances of the Gethsemane story (we will need to look at *John* separately). When we do this, we end up with a papyrus-like document[41] which runs roughly as follows:

"GETHSEMANE"

[ ] [form of ἔρχομαι] ...
[3 sg. of λέγω] ([ ] τοῖς ... μαθηται[ ]) ...

(προσευ[ ]) ...

καὶ ... προσ[ ]υχ[sg.] ...

[ ]λεγ[ ]ν
Πατ[ ]ρ ...
παρ[ ] τὸ ποτήριον (τοῦτο) (ἀπ᾽ εμοῦ) ...
οὐ[ ]/μὴ θελ[ ] ἀλλ ... σ[2 sg.] ...

_____

40. I am indebted to Vernon K. Robbins for the outlines of the "method" of reading that follows here.

41. A few notes on how this "text" was compiled. Any words that appear here appear in *all three* Synoptic performances of the story. Square brackets indicate portions of a word that are different from one performance to another, although the root is the same; since the Greek language is far more sensitive to case-endings and quantity than English, the same word will very often have a different ending in different syntactic constructions. I have kept only those portions of the word that are identical. Parentheses indicate that the same word appears in a different part of the narrative, although almost invariably in the same sentence. All that is different is word-order. Beyond that, the only thing that needs to be emphasized is that this "papyrus-like" scroll is *not* a text in any real sense of that word, and I certainly do *not* assume that any of the evangelists had such a worm-eaten manuscript sitting on the writing table. Jesus has a great deal to say about putting our faith in things of this world that can be so easily consumed by rust and worms. The value of this "text" — like the values of the heart — lies elsewhere.

καὶ [form of ἔρχομαι]...
εὑρ[3 sg.]...αὐτοὺς...καθεύδ[pl.]...

καὶ [sg. form of λέγω]...[ ]τ[dat.]...
προσεύχεσθε, ἵνα μὴ [ ]έλθητε εἰς πειρασμὸν...

ἔτι αὐτοῦ λαλοῦντος...

Ἰούδας εἰς τῶν δώδεκα...αὐτο[ ]...(ὄχλος)...

καὶ...[ ]τῷ...[ ]φίλησ[ ] αὐτόν...δὲ...

εἰς...[ ]τῶν...(μάχαιρι[ ])...τὸν δοῦλον (τοῦ ἀρχιερέως)...
ἀφεῖλεν αὐτοῦ (τὶ [ ]ο[acc. sg.])...

Ἰησοῦς (εἶπεν) [ ]το[ ]ς...

ὡς ἐπὶ λῃστὴν ἐξήλθατε μετὰ μαχαιρῶν καὶ ξύλων...;
καθ' ἡμέραν...ἐν τῷ ἱερῷ...οὐκ ἐ[ ]ατε [ ]με.

When "translated," this document reads roughly as follows:

went...

he said (to his disciples),...

("pray")...

and...prayed...

saying,
"Father...
(this) cup (from me);...
not [my] will, but...y[ours]."

And...he came...
found them (sleeping)...

and he said to them...
"pray that you may not enter into temptation";

while he was still speaking...
Judas, one of the Twelve,...(crowd with him)...

and...to him...
kiss[ed] him...then...

one of them...(sword)...
the slave of the high priest...cut off his (ear)...

Jesus said to them,...
"Have you come out against me like a criminal,
with swords and clubs...?
Every day...in the temple...
you did not...me."

On the basis of this sketchy "manuscript," what can we say about the Christian story of Gethsemane? We find much that we should expect, given the dramatic and tragic analogies I have been pursuing. We find a story only in the sparest sense of the word, but a story nonetheless. It could never be mistaken for any other, anymore than the myth of Oedipus could be. Something decisive and unmistakable has happened here. Jesus goes off somewhere with his disciples. He discusses prayer with them. Following on the heels of this discussion, he himself goes off alone to pray that "this cup" be taken from him — but then he steels himself to "the will" of his Father. That "will" is couched in terms of blind Fate or tragic Destiny, depending upon whose performance one is reading. Jesus returns to find his disciples sleeping. Again he calls their attention to prayer, this time as a way of avoiding "temptation." At that point, and *immediately* ("while he was still speaking... "), Judas arrives on the scene and betrays his teacher with a kiss. After a brief, violent encounter between the followers of Jesus and the mob, Jesus is taken. He makes a parting, ironic comment about the way he is being taken — late at night, in secret, like a criminal. He has, after all, been highly visible by day, *every* day, in the temple. And then he is taken away.

Clearly, we *do* have all the elements of a complete story here. We even have a remarkable verbatim agreement in places, although nothing that is beyond the capabilities of an oral, preliterate culture. Form-critics often use the analogy of a joke, where, no matter how different the story may be on each retelling, the punchline is always the same.[42] So, too, with the decisive words of Jesus. I prefer to take our analogy from Plutarch: important words, and especially poetry,[43] are always remembered in their essentials, whether the words are Euripides' or Jesus'. Let us comment finally on a few of the concrete elements of this particular Christian myth.

Jesus has gone away to a new place where he speaks privately, and for the last time, with his student-disciples.[44] His first words to them

---

42. John C. Meagher, *Clumsy Construction in Mark's Gospel: A Critique of Form- and Redaktionsgeschichte* (New York: Edwin Mellen Press, 1979) 3–15.

43. By "poetry," I mean rhythmic speech. It is interesting that both of the "speeches" of Jesus that are common to the three Synoptic performances appear in simple, easily memorizable, iambic lines. An iambic line is composed of six "feet," each of which consists of two or three syllables, short and long. This was the basic tragic meter, at least in the stichomythia, throughout the tragic period. Jesus' words that are recalled here are all vaguely iambic:

1) proseuchesthe, hina mē []elthēte eis peirasmon

2) hōs epi lēistēn exēlthate meta machairōn
   kai xulōn... kath' hēmeran... en tōi hierōi... ouk e[]ate []me

44. I have elected to translate the term *mathētēs* with this rather unwieldy term for

concern prayer (*proseuchomai*); in fact, this verb appears, in some form, *three times* in each of the Synoptic performances. The Gethsemane story is, by all accounts, a decisive discussion of what it means to pray. At several points in this book, I have referred suggestively to the Orthodox tradition as the one that perhaps best exemplifies the vital link between the Christian faith and the spirit of classical antiquity. One of my chief reasons for saying so is the unique perspective in which this tradition places prayer. "Spiritual prayer," says St. Evagrios the Solitary, in the early fourth century, "is food for the intellect, just as bread is food for the body and holiness food for the soul."[45] This seems to be Orthodoxy's answer to the riddle of Gethsemane. A tradition that is perhaps more accessible to most of us is the black church in America — which underscores many of the same spiritual themes of suffering and of prayer.[46]

At any rate, this threefold repetition is preserved in a variety of ways in the different performances. We will be paying particularly close attention to *how* prayer is discussed in each performance. After the first discussion, Jesus separates himself, going off to a lonely spot to pray. There is common agreement upon the precise substance of the prayer — perpetuating the same vaguely eucharistic image. Jesus asks his father to take this cup[47] away from him. He then recants with a terse afterthought: "not my will, but yours." We will need to watch this emphasis upon the will (*thelō*, as a verb; *thelēma*, as a noun). It has a profound range of theological and tragic implications — from Fate to Destiny — as Hegel and Nietzsche saw so clearly.

When Jesus returns from prayer, he finds his student-disciples[48] asleep

---

several reasons. My own inclination is to refer to Jesus' followers simply as "students," since this is what the Greek word means. But to refer to Jesus' followers "merely" as students flies in the face of a long tradition. Thus, I have elected to combine the terms, so that we all know whom we are talking about — the disciples — but do not fail to recognize what their relationship to Jesus really is, at least as the evangelists define it: they are *students*, and Jesus is a *teacher*.

45. The requisite text for any introduction to Orthodoxy is *The Philokalia*, compiled by St. Nikodimos of Mount Athos and St. Makarios of Corinth. The first volume of this eight-volume encyclopedia of spiritual discipline was translated by G. E. H. Palmer, Philip Sherrard, and Timothy Kallistos Ware (London: Faber and Faber, 1979). The text, which is comprised of writings that extend over a thousand-year period, has an astonishing thematic unity, a unity that ultimately derives from the "Jesus Prayer," which is its spiritual essence.

46. The relationship between African Christianities and the Orthodox tradition has become a matter of some interest in recent years. This book will conclude with a cursory reflection on the matter.

47. *Touto to potērion*, the cup of his blood, or the Socratic cup of poison, at *Mark* 14:23? For an excellent discussion of this word's richness, see Gerhard Kittel's *The Theological Dictionary of the New Testament*, trans. and ed. Geoffrey W. Bromiley (Grand Rapids, Mich.: William B. Eerdmans, 1968) s.v. "Poterion," VI, 148–158.

48. As "apostles," *apostolous, Mark* 3:13–19; *Matthew* 10:1–4; *Luke* 6:12–16.

(*katheudō*). His response is startling (and Luke repeats it a second time): "Pray that you may not enter into temptation." The immediacy of the events that follow is emphatic. Whereas only Mark uses his favorite phrase (*kai euthus,* "and immediately"), all are agreed that Judas approaches while Jesus *is still* speaking. Judas, moreover, is identified as "one of the Twelve," an extraordinary detail, evoking the Last Supper narrative that immediately precedes this one. Judas is fully and completely one of the Twelve, from the first commissioning of the student-disciples, right up to the present moment. There is a fascinating chiastic dimension in this story. When the Twelve are first mentioned *as* "the Twelve," Judas is immediately identified as "the one who betrayed him." Now, in the very act of betrayal, Judas has once again become simply "one of the Twelve." For now, in this awful moment, *all* will betray him. Only in this light may the full horror of these events be appreciated — to say nothing of the fact that the Teacher is betrayed with *a kiss.*

In response to the kiss — which was the definitive sign — the crowd makes a move to seize Jesus. Rallying to his defense, some one of Jesus' followers strikes the slave of the high priest, cutting off his ear.[49] This fascinating detail, which has been preserved in each performance, serves a different purpose in every case. These differences are due, in their turn, to the distinctive theological interests of each poet, as we shall see.

Finally, the Synoptic performances all agree, verbatim, on the substance of Jesus' response to this hostile crowd: "Have you come out against me like a criminal [*lēistēs*], with swords and clubs?"[50] Jesus adds, with heavy irony, that he has been teaching in the temple every day, and no one dared touch him there. They come at nighttime not because he is a criminal, but because *they* are. This ironic climax highlights the chief dichotomies of this story: the house of God, over against the world of evil; the crowded city, and the lonely place, now invaded by a crowd; the earlier crowds from Galilee who had "crowded around" Jesus like sheep, now become an armed and hostile crowd that is here to slaughter him; a defenseless, abandoned Messiah, now delivered into their violent hands, betrayed by a kiss. Faith and disbelief; following and fleeing — love is a lie. That is how this story "ends."

---

49. The precise word is distinct in each performance: *ous* in *Luke; ōtion* in *Matthew; ōtarion* in *Mark.*

50. There is a wide-ranging scholarly debate about exactly what this word, *lēistēs,* means. Most view it — as I do here — as a common word, denoting a simple "criminal." Others insist that it bore a very specific meaning in this context, referring to a Jewish "freedom fighter," or Zealot — thereby implying that Jesus definitively rejects that role here. Barabbas was called a *lēistēs,* at *John* 18:40, and he *was* a Zealot. Moreover, Jesus is later crucified between two of them, *duo lēistēs,* at *Mark* 15:28.

The Christian *mythos* of Gethsemane, as performed by the Synoptists, consists of three essential components: a temptation, a prayer, a betrayal. Without these components, it would not *be* the story of Gethsemane. Let us look now at the particulars of each gospel performance.

III

And he went out, as was his custom, to the Mount of Olives; and the students followed him. And when he came to the place, he said to them, "Pray that you may not enter into temptation." And he himself went off from them about a stone's throw, knelt down, and prayed, saying, "Father, if you will, take this cup away from me. Still, let not my will be done, but yours."

[Then an angel from heaven was seen with him, strengthening him. And his agony intensified as he prayed, and his sweat fell like drops of blood to the earth.]

Then he stood up from prayer, came to his students and found them sleeping, far from sorrow, and he asked them, "Why are you sleeping? Get up and pray that you may not enter into temptation."

While he was still talking — behold, a crowd — and the one called Judas, one of the Twelve, went before them, and he drew near to Jesus to kiss him. But Jesus said to him, "Judas, are you betraying the Son of Man with a kiss?" And when those who were with him saw what would happen, they said, "Lord, should we strike with a sword?" And one of them struck the high priest's slave and cut off his right ear. In response, Jesus said, "Stop it!" And he touched the ear and healed it.

Then Jesus said to those who had surrounded him, the high priest and the officers of the temple and the elders, "Have you come out against me like a criminal, with swords and clubs? Every day I was with you in the temple and you did not lay hands on me. Still, this hour is yours, and the power of darkness."[51]

Luke's is far and away the sparest of the Synoptic performances, although he characteristically maximizes the impact he gets out of fewer words. He also seasons his story with an extraordinary wealth of classical allusions, most of them Homeric. That is significant, since Homer is often taken to be one of the more "fatalistic" of ancient poets. If there are no atheists in foxholes, there are certainly many determinists there. Luke is waging a different kind of war, to be sure, but his fatalism is as profound.

Luke alone tells us that Jesus went out to the Mount of Olives, as it was his custom to do (*kata to ēthos*), and that the student-disciples *followed* him. In the other Synoptic performances the student-disciples are

---

51. *Luke* 22:39–53.

with Jesus, but no mention is made of the fact that they are "following" him anywhere. Obedient following is a prominent idea in all the gospels. Luke, however, galvanizes the term, lending it an additional force in his Passion narrative. The student-disciples have "followed" Jesus, unwittingly involving themselves in grand cosmic events, awful temptation, and great personal danger. We know, as they do not, that they have followed Jesus to the brink of disaster, and when the cost of discipleship is made apparent to them, they will all be found wanting. Peter himself will "follow" Jesus, albeit at a distance (*makrothen*, 22:54), from the Mount of Olives all the way to the home of the high priest. This journey will prove to be a vain one. Peter has come this far only to refuse to go one step further; he has come to the seat of power only to abandon his friend there.

It is a commonplace that Luke's gospel is saturated with prayer, that Luke's Jesus is first and foremost a praying saviour.[52] There is ample support for such a claim here: some form of the word appears four times in five verses (five times in seven verses if we include the controversial vv. 43–45).[53] Upon their arrival at the Mount of Olives, Jesus issues a solemn injunction to his student-disciples: "*Pray*, that you may not enter into temptation." This unexpected warning is not explained: What temptation (*peirasmon*) is Jesus talking about? Exactly what is he anticipating? Why here? and Why now? The term *peira* is widely used in the New Testament,[54] but it is used as ambiguously as its cognates in the Septuagint — one generic term for a whole range of more specific Hebrew words. The term is much like our own 'temptation,' for we may be tempted by many things and into all sorts of behavior. Apart from these many vague referents, "There is a distinctly religious understanding of the concept."[55] The great religious temptation that underwrites all the others is the temptation to disobey, or even to deny, God.[56] "That is

---

52. A glance through a biblical concordance makes this point nicely. One discovers there word-counts such as the following: "pray," 12/4/12/4; "prayed," 3/3/5/0; "prayer," 5/3/5/0; "prayers," 1/1/2/0; "praying," 1/1/6/2; and so on.

53. B. P. Robinson, in "Gethsemane: The Synoptic and the Johannine Viewpoints," *Church Quarterly Review* 167 (1966) 4–11, sees an allusion to *Zechariah* 14:5 in verse 22:44: "Then the LORD your God will come, *and all his holy ones with him*," but this seems to me to make too much of too little evidence. Better is Joseph A. Grassi's analysis of parallels to the story of Abraham's sacrifice of Isaac in "Abba, Father: Another Approach," *Journal of the American Academy of Religion* 50 (1982) 449–458. It should be noted that both articles assume, as I do, that these disputed verses could well be genuine.

54. See the entry on *peira* in *Theological Dictionary of the New Testament*, VI, 23–36.

55. *Theological Dictionary of the New Testament*, VI, 24.

56. R. S. Barbour, "Gethsemane in the Tradition of the Passion," *New Testament Studies* 16 (1970) 231–251, concludes that there are two recognizably distinct forms of temptation in the scriptures — from God, and from Satan. What is fascinating about

to say, the temptation placed the Lord in a situation of open choice between surrender to God's will and revolt against it."[57] The implications of this view in Gethsemane are apparent. The *peirasmon* applies to Jesus and his student-disciples, both. Harsh choices are being demanded of everyone. God's way seems to involve arrest, abandonment, and death. The temptation to disobey God, to deny the will of heaven, is naturally greatest at this point. In Luke's performance, Jesus understands the full implications of what is about to take place, as his closest followers decidedly do not.[58]

In any event, Jesus removes himself "about a stone's throw" (a characteristic insertion of detail) and prays that *he* not be led to the test. This prayer — which is the heart and soul of the whole *mythos* of Gethsemane — is qualified in every performance by the theological interests of each evangelist. We shall need to save discussion of this crucial point until we have examined each performance in its turn. For now, suffice it to say that Luke's Jesus qualifies himself in the following manner: "Father, *if you will,* take this cup away from me."

The oddity of the exchange between Jesus and his student-disciples should not be missed. As this small band of itinerants wander about upon the Mount of Olives — as they have long been in the habit of doing — overlooking the holy city that had been the goal of all their travels, Jesus' warning about some imminent temptation must look like a sailor's warning of an approaching storm when the sky is still blue. The confusion is surely heightened when Jesus immediately sets himself apart from them, offering no explanation at all of what "temptation" he has in mind. Next, we see — what his students do not see, namely, exactly *what* they are supposed to pray. For Jesus prays that he, too, may escape the test, and then, by implication, that he be empowered to accept a will other than his own. The phrase is unique to Luke, in that God's will and Jesus' will are radically offset, appearing in different grammatical cases: *plēn mē to thelēma* mou *alla to* son *ginesthō,* "still, let not my will be done, but yours." And Luke — predestinarian that he is[59] — wants a world in which God's will is all in all. God is subject, grammatically and

---

Luke's performance of Gethsemane is that both moments coalesce in the Passion: Jesus is abandoned, which is to say, tempted, by his Father; and he wrestles with the powers of darkness in this very place, in this very hour, and then later on the Cross.

57. *Theological Dictionary of the New Testament,* VI, 33.

58. It needs only to be added that "John has no express account of any temptations of Jesus" (*Ibid.,* VI, 36). This is a point to which we will need to return, since the Gethsemane story has become, for John, a very simple story about Jesus' triumphant march toward coronation on a Cross. Gethsemane was not a simple story, and I am put to wonder, again, if John's is even the same story, lacking, as it does, a prayer and any real temptation.

59. *Acts* 3:18; 4:28; 13:48.

otherwise; we are object. This prayer, which the student-disciples also ought to be praying, is highlighted by their twofold failure to respond to Jesus' explicit, if ambiguous, warning that they do so.

Jesus has prayed, as his student-disciples have not. He is now equipped to deal with the imminent crisis as they presumably are not. In the anticipation of suffering lies the strength to endure it. As I noted in the last chapter, this is one of the chief tenets of existential thought, what Heidegger called "anticipatory resoluteness."[60] It is also the lesson of Aeschylus' *Prometheus,* and the words that we hear now seem to be Prometheus' as well as Jesus', when he too prays as he does, a long stone's throw from *his* people:

> O holy aether and fleet, wingéd winds;
> O rushing water of the sea's waves, laughing
> endlessly; O Earth, mother of all;
> and you, all-seeing circle of the sun —
> I call upon you all.
> You see me, how I, who am a god myself,
> suffer the gods.
> I have received such blows
> that I am worn to nothing by my endless
> fight with time.
> The new commander of the Blessed Ones
> ordains a pitiless bondage for me.
> Woe and grief! I groan for the present
> sorrow. Will there ever be an end [*termata*]
> to my agonies?
> But what am I asking? Every future I know exactly.
> No sorrow of mine wears a new face.[61]

For Jesus, in opposition to his closest followers, the imminent crisis will not come with a new face, and that seems to be Luke's essential point.

---

60. See Martin Heidegger, *Being and Time,* trans. John MacQuarrie and Edward Robinson (New York: Harper and Row, 1962) 352–358.

61. Aeschylus, *Prometheus Bound,* 88–102. Of further interest is how Prometheus concludes his prayer:

> One must bear Fate [*tēn pepromenēn*] as easily
> as one may, recognizing that
> Necessity's [*anankēs*] strength is absolute. (103–105)

This poem is offered up in the same spirit as R. S. Barbour's analysis of Luke's performance in "Gethsemane in the Tradition of the Passion," 240: "The real struggle is now over and we are witnessing the necessary unrolling of a tragic course of events which we well know will be cancelled on Easter morning. If Luke is here following Mark he has not felt it necessary to reproduce the elaborate three-fold structure of the Marcan Gethsemane-story, for in this understanding of the matter it is, though terrible, fundamentally simple."

Resoluteness comes with anticipation. Our own wills are transformed, if not eliminated, by God's. From this moment, the distance between Jesus and the student-disciples steadily increases. If he was physically a stone's throw from them, he has moved miles beyond them spiritually, and his character will be continually on the rise even as events conspire against him.

There is a variant reading in the manuscripts at this point (22:43–45), which suggest that Jesus went through the fullest agony of his despair in this moment, alone, and that "his sweat fell like drops of blood to the ground." This same image appears in the *Iliad*, book 16, where Zeus weeps *tears of blood* in mourning over the imminent death of *his* beloved son, Sarpedon. After this most intense of all Jesus' many moments, he returns to the student-disciples, only to find them asleep, *apo tēs lupēs*. How to translate this? It is commonly rendered "sleeping for sorrow." This makes little sense — who, after all sleeps when most upset? — and it makes nonsense of the passage. Far better to render this "sleeping far from sorrow," an image that is, again, right out of the *Iliad*[62] and that more effectively demonstrates the obliviousness of the student-disciples to the true nature of the drama in which they are participating. When Jesus rises from prayer and sees them, he is nonplussed: "Why are you sleeping?" He then repeats the injunction to pray for deliverance from a temptation that still has not been clearly defined.

Thus, the first half of this performance is strongly seasoned with prayer. Upon his entrance into "the place" (*topos*), Jesus tells his student-disciples to *pray* (*proseuchesthe*, 22:40). Next, Jesus goes off about a stone's throw and *prays* (*prosēucheto*, 22:41) himself. In the company of an angel from heaven, his agony intensifies *in prayer* (*prosēucheto*, 22:44). After sweating drops of blood in this agony, Jesus rises from *prayer* (*proseuchēs*, 22:45) and returns to his student-disciples, only to find them still asleep. In response, Jesus repeats his warning as a command: *Pray* (*proseuchesthe*, 22:46).

Events move quickly from here. While Jesus is still speaking — behold, the crowd approaches with Judas at its head. Judas draws near to kiss him but is prevented from so doing. It should be observed that only Matthew and Mark provide the background information necessary to make this scene intelligible — Judas has told the chief priests and elders

---

62. The reader might examine, for instance, *Iliad*, 8:553–9:8; 10:1–4, 25–28, 299–301. When I say that this image is "right out of the *Iliad*," I am not suggesting that there is any sort of literary dependence at work. The whole idea of something being "right out of the *Iliad*" means something far different to us than it does in a semi-literate society among whom these stock cultural images clearly circulated. I cannot deny the very real possibility that the four evangelists, and especially Luke, "knew Homer," however we understand this type of "knowledge."

that the man he kisses will be the one they seek. In *Luke,* we have none of this; Jesus once again knows what we do not. It is Jesus who equates the kiss with betrayal, asking and explaining in a single breath, "Judas, are you betraying (*paradidōs*) the Son of Man with a kiss?" (22:48).

The second, smaller crowd rallies to Jesus' defense and asks, "Lord, should we strike with a sword?" (22:49). Before Jesus can answer, someone from the crowd answers his own question, cutting off the *right* ear (*to dexion,* again, a characteristic Lukan detail) of the chief priest's slave. Jesus responds curtly, *Eāte heōs toutou,* "Stop it!" (22:51),[63] and he immediately heals the ear. As always in Luke, it is left to Jesus to undo the damage others do. Jesus then ironically interrogates the crowd and concludes with a fascinating observation: "Still, this hour [*hōra*] is yours, and the power [*exousia*] of darkness." This notion of the power of darkness and the wisdom of yielding to it is again thoroughly Homeric,[64] and it is at this point that Jesus is spirited away.

Such are the tragic necessities of Luke's "Gethsemane." For reasons unknown or unstated, God does not wish to take this suffering cup away. The reasons are *pre*destinate because there is no Destiny where there is no (personal) will. As Christopher Durang tells us in an alternately witty, and caustic, play, all of our prayers *are* answered. "What people don't realize is that sometimes the answer to a prayer is no."[65] Jesus, too, gets No for an answer, but the way he has framed the question allows him to deal with the painful consequences of that fact: God's will (*thelēma*) is otherwise. And when God wills, our will tends to disappear — a conclusion that Mark, for his part, refuses to draw.

So it is that Jesus remains the commanding presence even in the course of being betrayed: he prevents Judas from kissing him; he alone understands the signs; he undoes the wrongheaded violence of the crowd; and he voluntarily submits to the exigencies of the hour and its power. Jesus is the protagonist, the primary, really the *only,* actor, before

---

63. The verb *eaō* and the imperative, *eāte,* which appears here, are ambiguous. Scholars have usually assumed that it means something like "Enough!" Kenneth J. Dover, in his *Greek Homosexuality* (Cambridge, Mass.: Harvard Univ. Press, 1978) 6, 95, 116 (R 463), refers to an obscure vase-painting that is kept in the Boston Museum of Fine Art (#63.873, *par.* 360 [id. no. 74 *quater*]). This piece depicts a young male rejecting the erotic advances of an older male, the boy exclaiming *Eāson:* "Stop it!" or "Leave me alone!" Since this vase surely represents colloquial speech, it is fair to translate Jesus' words colloquially: "Stop it!"

64. The clearest example here is *Iliad,* 7:282, 293, where the single-combat between Hektor and Aias is concluded with an injunction that is repeated twice — once by the elders and once by Hektor himself: "Night is already upon us; it is good [*agathon*] to give way to the night." This concern for the authority and power of Night is a very ancient idea and appears throughout the Homeric poems.

65. Christopher Durang, *Sister Mary Ignatius Explains It All for You,* in *Christopher Durang: Five Plays* (New York: Avon Books, 1983) 132.

whom all other characters — even the follower who betrays him and the crowd that condemns him — serve merely as a dramatic backdrop to the essential story.

IV

Then Jesus went with them into the region called Gethsemane, and he told his students, "Sit here, while I go over there to pray." Then taking aside Peter and the two sons of Zebedee, he became sorrowful and distressed. And he told them, "My soul is very sorrowful until death. Stay here and watch with me." And when he went ahead a little further, he fell upon his face, praying, "My Father, if it is possible, then let this cup pass me by. Still, not how I want it, but how you do." Then he went back to his students and found them sleeping, and he said to Peter, "Are you not strong enough to watch for one hour with me? Watch and pray that you may not enter into temptation. The spirit is willing, but the flesh is weak." Then again, a second time, he went away and prayed, saying, "My Father, if it is not possible that this pass me by unless I drink it, then let your will be done." And when he came again he found them sleeping, for their eyes were heavy. So he left them and he went away again and he prayed a third time, saying the same thing again. Then he returned to the students and said to them, "Are you still sleeping and resting? Behold, the hour has come and the Son of Man is betrayed into the hands of sinners. Get up; let's go. Behold, the betrayer has come for me."

And while he was still speaking, behold, Judas, one of the Twelve, came, and with him a great crowd with swords and clubs from the high priests and elders of the people. Now the betrayer had given them a sign, saying, "He whom I kiss will be the man; seize him." And immediately he went up to Jesus and said, "Hello, Rabbi," and he kissed him. But Jesus said to him, "My friend, has it come to this?"

Then those who came up laid hands upon Jesus and seized him. And behold, one of those with Jesus raised his hand, drew a sword, and struck the slave of the high priest and cut off his ear. Then Jesus said to him, "Return your sword to its place, for all who take up the sword will die by the sword. Do you suppose it is impossible for me to call upon my Father, who would immediately send me more than twelve legions of angels? But then how could the scriptures be fulfilled, that it must happen this way?" In that same hour Jesus said to the crowds, "Have you come out to seize me like a criminal with swords and clubs? Every day I sat in the temple teaching and you did not seize me. This all has happened in order that the writings of the prophets might be fulfilled." Then all the students left him and fled.[66]

Matthew sets his performance, the longest of the four, in a place (chōrion) with a name — Gethsemane — a detail that Mark alone

---

66. *Matthew* 26:36–56.

shares with him. Matthew's performance shares a pathos and intensity with Mark's as well. Upon entering the place, Jesus instructs his student-disciples to sit down while he goes off to pray. Having said this, presumably to all of the student-disciples, Jesus takes aside his inner circle of three ("Peter and the two sons of Zebedee," v. 37), and with them alone, he begins to agonize — presumably much as he did in the Lukan performance. Jesus rather uncharacteristically *tells* them about his inner state of mind, rather than merely *showing* them (as Luke showed us): "My soul is very sorrowful until death," he says. "Stay here and watch with me [*met' emou*]" (v. 38). This sorrow (*lupēs*) is the very thing to which Luke had said the student-disciples were oblivious. There they slept, far from it. Here, Jesus himself tells them of it, twice. Jesus now leaves even the three behind and goes on a little farther, alone — at which point he falls upon his face and prays: "My Father, *if it is possible,* then let this cup pass me by. Still, not how I want it, but how you do" (v. 39). Concluding this prayer, Jesus returns to the student-disciples only to find them not watching, but sleeping. Jesus responds specifically to Peter, but his accusation is addressed in the plural, to the whole group. "Are you not strong enough to watch for one hour with me [*met' emou*]?" (v. 40).

This repeated emphasis — "with me" — is a powerful stylistic turn, directing attention to Jesus' awful abandonment and loneliness. Matthew's performance highlights the pathos of the whole scene. Jesus' loneliness is ironically heightened by his student-disciples' presence. He would probably feel less alone, and surely less abandoned, without them. Their presence is a presence in name only; they are with him, yet not with him. Because they have failed to watch with him, Jesus now intensifies his warning: "Watch and pray that you may not enter into temptation. The spirit is willing, but the flesh is weak" (v. 41). If they cannot watch with Jesus, at the very least they can pray with him.

The concluding sneer about willing spirit and weak flesh sticks to Jesus, too ("My soul is very sorrowful until death"). It is a self-referential sneer. We are put to wonder why Jesus has counseled and criticized his student-disciples in this way. In Matthew's judgment, prayer seems to serve the intensely personal purpose of reconciling the individual to the painful and, at times, unfathomable will of God. This idea is akin to what we found in Luke, and it serves a similar dramatic purpose. But here, Jesus' "anticipation" seems somehow far less "resolute." It is in this sense that the student-disciples *need* prayer much as Jesus does, although as future events make clear, they fail to pray "with him" just as surely as they have failed to "watch."

This point is made when Matthew's Jesus prays not once, but twice —

as no truly "resolute" soul would pray, but as a human soul well might in its hour of distress. When Jesus goes off a second time to pray, Matthew includes the prayer a second time. In general outline, the prayers match up, but they are *not* the same. In fact, the subtle differences in this second prayer clearly demonstrate Jesus' gradual reconciliation to the will of his Father, a resoluteness that is earned, not just anticipated: "My Father, *if it is not possible* that this pass me by *unless I drink it,* then let your will be done" (v. 42). The progression in Jesus' spiritual reasoning is now quite clear:

(v. 39)	(v. 42)
My Father	My Father,
[*Pater mou*],	
if it is possible	if it is *not* possible
[*ei dynaton estin*],	[*ei ou dynatai*]
then let this cup pass	that this pass me by [*parer-*
[*parerchomai*] me by.	*chomai*], *unless* I drink it,
Still, not how I want	then let your will [*thelēma*]
[*thelō*] it, but how you do.	be done.

Both prayers are similarly addressed: "My Father" (*Pater mou*). But whereas Jesus' first prayer wonders what is possible, his second prayer *concludes* that it is not possible for the cup to pass "*unless* [he] drink it.*" In the conclusion to the second prayer, all mention of Jesus' will has disappeared.[67] Only God's will exists now that Jesus' has been extinguished. Jesus' singular role is that of the obedient servant who drinks the cup that has been prepared for him. Yet the language here is less eucharistic than Luke's. This cup is Socrates' — a cup of poison, not yet one of redemptive blood.

At the conclusion of this second prayer, Jesus returns to his student-disciples and again finds them asleep. Without a word, he returns to a lonely place and a repeated prayer. The prayer is not given a third time; we must assume that it is the same again.[68] Jesus returns to his own people, incredulous that they are sleeping still, and wakes them with a curt command — "Get up; let's go!" Equally curt is his statement that the hour (*hōra*) and the betrayer (*paradidous*) are at hand (*ēngiken*, repeated twice).

---

67. This same phrase — "your will be done" — also appears in the Lord's Prayer (only in Matthew; it is absent in Luke), thereby highlighting the sense in which Jesus' prayers are presented as models by Matthew — prayers that student-disciples, and other oral recipients of the story, ought also to pray.

68. The repetitive sequence of events is emphasized by the fourfold appearance of the word, *palin*, "again."

It is in Jesus' response to the eruption of violence in the crowd that Matthew's performance is most distinctive, and actually strangest. Jesus tells an anonymous follower to sheathe his sword, "for all who take up the sword will die by the sword" (v. 53). He then adds, ironically, "Do you suppose it is impossible for me [*ou dunamai*] to call upon my Father [*ton patera mou*], who would immediately send me more than twelve legions of angels? But then how could the scriptures be fulfilled, that it must happen [*dei genesthai*] this way?" (vv. 53–54). Three points bear notice here. First, Jesus does not explicitly reject the use of violence here; his reply presupposes the existence of "legions" in the divine economy. Second, the comment makes nonsense of the very prayer Jesus has just now made in Gethsemane. After all, Jesus has *just* been praying for deliverance and concluded that it was impossible (*ou dunatai*). Third, and by far the most important, Jesus here at last explains *the reason* it is not possible for God to take this cup away, far more clearly than he did in prayer. The scriptures *must* (*dei*) be fulfilled (v. 54) and can be fulfilled in no other way. This point is reiterated, lest we miss it, two verses later when Jesus again affirms, "This all has happened in order that the writings of the prophets [*tōn prophetōn*] might be fulfilled" (v. 56). Matthew never tires of making this continuity explicit — his performance of the Christian *mythos* always seeks to bring the Hebrew scriptures to a close. That story is now fulfilled.

Tension and ambiguity typify Matthew's performance. The pathos of Jesus' abandonment is agonizing. But the ambiguity is more profound than this. Two kinds of reasoning are at work in the performance — one at verses 39–42 and another at verses 53–54 — that invite entirely different conclusions about what is taking place. These conclusions, if not actually contradictory, are at best maintained in a tenuous logical relationship. Jesus is at one and the same time the man who begs God for deliverance ("My Father, if it is possible...," v. 39), but also the mighty prophet at whose command stand all the legions of heaven ("Do you suppose it is impossible...?" v. 53). He is a man who vaguely senses that it is somehow impossible for him to escape death ("My Father, if it is *not* possible...," v. 42), and yet at the same time he is a seer who discerns quite clearly the greater necessity of the will of heaven ("Then how could the scriptures be fulfilled?" v. 54). The inviolability of this divine script he accepts in the end, even at the cost of his life. Two ways always: Matthew's is the most explicitly *incarnational* of the four performances of this *mythos*. It would not be too much to say that this same tension, which Matthew has mapped out so elegantly in Gethsemane, is the very thing that later became credal at Nicaea and Chalcedon. Jesus is *two* things, at once.

V

When Jesus said these things, he went out with his students across the Kedron Valley where there was a garden; then he and his students entered it.
Now Judas, the one who betrayed him, also knew the place, since Jesus
often gathered there with his students. Therefore Judas took a body of
soldiers from among the chief priests and Pharisees, and they went there
with torches and lanterns and weapons. Since Jesus already knew everything that was to happen to him, he went out and said to them, "Whom
are you seeking?" And they answered him, "Jesus the Nazarene." He said
to them, "I am he." Judas, the one who betrayed him, was also standing
among them. But when he said to them, "I am he," they all fell back and
fell upon the ground. Therefore, he asked them again, "Whom are you
seeking?" And they said, "Jesus the Nazarene." Jesus responded, "I told
you that I am he. If then you are looking for me, let these others go."
This was in order to fulfill what the *logos* said: "I lost none of all those
you have given me." Now Simon Peter had a sword, and he drew it and
struck the high priest's slave and cut off his right ear. The slave's name
was Malchus. Then Jesus said to Peter, "Put the sword in its sheath. The
cup which the Father has given me — shall I not drink it?"[69]

The performance of the *mythos* we call "Gethsemane" appears in two
different places in *John* (12:27; 18:1–11). John thus makes explicit what
was already implicit in Matthew's performance — namely, that there is
no really *logical* or consistent connection between the agony Jesus experiences in Gethsemane and Jesus' clarity of purpose when he is suddenly,
subsequently betrayed. The prayer and the temptation have nothing to
do with the betrayal itself — and in *John* they actually have precious
little to do with Jesus at all. As is well known, there is no absence of
clarity *anywhere* in the Johannine portrait of Christ. He is ever the man
from above who is in the world, but not of it. His will, as we shall see,
is his Father's. Even when abandoned, Jesus is "not alone, for the Father is with [him]" (16:31–32). Such a faith makes the performance of
Gethsemane deeply problematic.

At the conclusion of his public ministry, Jesus' words vaguely recall
Gethsemane, but rhetorically. Synoptic words are used by John to make
the opposite point. Jesus says, in all transparency, "Now is my soul troubled. And what shall I say? 'Father, save [*sōson*] me from this hour'? No,
for this purpose [*dia touto*] I have come to this hour" (12:27). The tension that is, to varying degrees, internalized in the Synoptic accounts of
an inner anguish and private debate (a prayer, a temptation) is now ex-
ternalized, made visible for all to see — as a fairly simple christological
monologue, demonstrating that there is no distance between the vision

---

69. *John* 18:1–11, translation mine.

and the virtue of the Johannine Christ. The spirit is willing, and the flesh, to the degree that he has it at all, is strong.

Jesus' betrayal and arrest do not take place immediately, but must wait until six chapters later (18:1–11). In the interim, we are privy to some of the loveliest statements of faith in who Jesus is — clearly "evangelical" in that they are designed for people who do not "know" Jesus, they are also triumphant to the last. And they form an eloquent transition to John's performance of Gethsemane that will be — ironically enough, and in contrast to all three Synoptics — simply another triumph.

When we finally *do* get to Gethsemane, we find a curious agreement with Luke.[70] Jesus goes across the Kedron Valley to a garden,[71] a garden that Judas also knows, "since Jesus often gathered there with his students" (v. 2). Luke has already informed us that Jesus went to the Mount of Olives "as he was in the habit of doing." The two will later agree on the curious detail that the slave of the high priest lost his right (*dexion*) ear. Beyond these surface details, however, the performance as a whole is unique to John. Jesus "already knew everything that was to happen" (v. 4),[72] and so he takes command even of a situation in which he is to be the sacrificial victim. The lamb is here leading the priests to the sacrifice. He approaches the heavily armed crowd (v. 3) and demands of them: "Whom are you seeking?" (*tina zēteite*, v. 4). When the crowd learns that he is the man, *ecce homo*, they fall back away from him and onto the ground. Jesus forces the issue a second time, and forces the crowd to seize him in order, it would seem, that what the *logos* has said (the scriptures, or his own words? v. 9) may be fulfilled.

The structure of this performance is so different, and so carefully crafted, that we ought perhaps to dwell on it a bit longer. In focusing upon John's omissions, we get a clearer sense of what "Gethsemane" is meant to mean, Synoptically. The first point to be noticed is the prominent place Judas occupies in the scene. Whereas the Synoptic performances customarily define him solely *by his activity* (*ho paradidous*, the betrayer), John gives prominence to his name. He is in fact, just like

---

70. See Pierson Parker, "Luke and the Fourth Evangelist," *New Testament Studies* 9 (1963) 317–336; and Michael Goulder, "From Ministry to Passion in John and Luke," *New Testament Studies* 29 (1983) 561–568.

71. B. P. Robinson suggests, in his "Gethsemane: The Synoptic and the Johannine Viewpoints," 5–7, that John often inverts Jewish symbolism in his performance. Only John tells us that "Gethsemane" was a garden (*kēpos*) — presumably the place where humanity will begin the laborious task of reentering a paradise once lost.

72. It should be added that this foreknowledge — or tragic "reconciliation with reality," as Hegel would have it — is precisely what *prayer* vouchsafes to Jesus in the Lukan and Matthean performances, much as it did for Prometheus. The point to notice here is that John's Jesus does not *need* to pray; *his* foreknowledge derives from the fact that he has always been with the Father: "Truly, truly I say to you, before Abraham was, I am" (8:58); "I and the Father are one" (10:30).

Antigone, being defined *by his name*. It is his character, his Destiny. The name Judas (*Ioudas*) sounds virtually identical to the Greek word for "Jew" (*Ioudaios*). This might be clearer were we to spell the betrayer's name phonetically, "Jewdas." Now, we cannot know how such a proper name would have been heard in antiquity (probably something akin to Judah), any more than we can determine how much we today think of cabinet-making when introduced to a person named Carpenter. What *is* clear is that John very carefully links the name (Jewdas) to the action (betrayal) — a not so very surprising fact in this gospel, which goes to such extraordinary lengths to intensify the polemic against a Jewish community that has seen, but refused to believe.[73]

In fact, John's performance of this scene may be neatly divided in half by carefully noticing the placement of the phrase "Judas, the one who betrayed him" (*Ioudas ho paradidous auton*, vv. 2, 5). At the outset, in the Garden, we are told that "Judas, the one who betrayed him, also knew [*ēidei*] the place" (v. 2). The form of the verb here is an unusual pluperfect, "he knew." The second half of the story is again introduced in the pluperfect: "Judas, the one who betrayed him, was also standing [*heistēkei*] among them" (v. 5).[74] As was the case in Matthew's performance, so too here: in the first half of the drama, the essential elements of the second already appear:

Whom are you seeking? (v. 4)	Whom are you seeking? (v. 7)
[*Tina zēteite?*]	
Jesus the Nazarene. (v. 5)	Jesus the Nazarene. (v. 7)
[*Iēsoun ton Nazōraion.*]	
I am he. [*Egō eimi*, v. 5.]	I told you that I am he. (v. 8)

---

73. For a helpful analysis of this anti-Jewish polemic in John, see J. Louis Martyn, *History and Theology in the Fourth Gospel* (Nashville: Parthenon Press, 1968). In a different vein, see Richard L. Rubenstein, "Religion and the Origin of the Death Camps," in *After Auschwitz* (Indianapolis: Bobbs-Merrill, 1966) 30ff. While it would take us too far afield to explore this further, it seems to me that the word *Ioudaios*, in John's gospel, simply means someone who is from Judea. John carefully divides his gospel-world into three regions: *Judea*, from whence the Messiah must come (7:40–43); *Samaria*, a region of impure faith, with its own temples and holy places (4:20–26); and *Galilee*, where Jesus is ironically most successful (4:43–44; 7:1). So it is that John's astonishing claim: "Salvation is from the Jews" (4:22) means, quite simply, that the Messiah must be from Judea. John's anti-Judah-ism is a very peculiar thing, indeed.

74. Vernon Robbins' careful eye for such rhetorical details first convinced me of how important they are. The pluperfect tense *intrudes* into the rhetorical flow of the performance (a story that otherwise is told in the simple past) and clearly indicates points of transition. Why this is important is obvious: at points where the author chooses "to start all over," underlying themes become suddenly sharper than they were before. Commentators have often wondered why John introduces Judas into the text again at v. 5 — we already know he is there — and many form-critics have detected "a seam" in the text here. But the rhetoric of the construction is seamless and consistent with John's larger theological purposes.

Unlike Matthew's performance, this recapitulation changes nothing. Jesus is a hero of truly astonishing, and very nearly Sophoclean, resolve. Always resolute, he has anticipated this drama since the beginning of time. It is only *the crowd,* like the *Ajax's* Chorus, that wavers. After the first exchange, the crowd falls away from Jesus, presumably in awe before his courage ("I am he") and mystical "otherness" (*Egō eimi*).[75] After the second exchange, it is Jesus' persistence alone that ensures that God's will be done. Jesus, the shepherd of his people and very clearly the director of this scene, draws the conclusion for the crowd, his "captors": "It is me that you seek" (*Eme zēteite,* v. 8). And this conclusion is couched in terms of the shepherd's steadfast concern for his sheep: "If then you are looking for me, let these others go!" (v. 8).

At this point, Simon Peter draws a sword and cuts off the right ear of a slave named Malchus (v. 10). It is interesting that both of these characters — Peter and Malchus — are named only in *John.* Names are characters that are destinies — a formula we have seen before and will see again. Jesus' response is equally telling and unique to this performance. He commands Peter to sheathe the sword: "The cup [*to potērion*] which my Father has given me — shall I not drink it?" (v. 11).[76] If "Gethsemane" is a story about *praying* in the face of *temptation,* then this is no longer the same story at all. Of the three elements that I said were indispensable to this *mythos,* John retains only the betrayal — and even *that* is different. There is no prayer, and there is most assuredly no temptation. The very phrases that had lent such pathos and humanity to the Synoptic Passion narrative — "Father, take this cup away from me ... " — are uttered now in a voice dripping with irony. These are sentiments for lesser mortals, not for Jesus. And it is precisely here that the essence of the tragedy that is Gethsemane has been lost.

While certain Synoptic words and phrasings repeat themselves in the Johannine performance of the *mythos,* the *sense* of the scene is wholly

---

75. This phrase is the essence of John's christology. It implies two different, yet complementary, things when spoken by the God-man, Jesus Christ. In its reference to Jesus as a man, the phrase serves to identify him much as Judas' kiss did in the Synoptic performances. In its reference to him as God, the phrase recalls the divine name (*YHWH*) that was vouchsafed first to Moses (*Exodus* 3:14) and through Moses to the entire covenant community. For a useful discussion of the variety of Hebrew phrases rendered in the Septuagint as *egō eimi,* see Raymond E. Brown, *The Gospel according to John,* "The Anchor Bible," (New York: Doubleday, 1966), vol. 29, appendix IV, 533–538. For a more concrete discussion of the function of the phrase in this particular setting, see vol. 29A, 817–818.

76. The irony of this question is highlighted by an intensive double-negative (*ou mē piō auto*). In a related passage, 18:36, Jesus offers an additional rationale for putting up the sword: "My kingship is not of this world; if my kingship were of this world, my servants would fight, that I might not be handed over *to the Jews;* but my kingship is not from there."

other. There is no ambiguity in the course of events, still less in the will
of the Christ. The betrayal comes, as it must come. In fact, it comes
only because he himself *forces* it to come. Jesus, the heroic champion
of the divine will — which is also his own — seizes the cup that his Father has given him and drinks it to the dregs. Nothing less, it would
seem, could be expected of this man who "has overcome [*nenikēka*] the
world" (16:33).

VI

And they came to a region, the name of which is Gethsemane, and he said
to his students, "Sit here while I pray." And he took Peter and James and
John along with him, and he began to be agitated and greatly distressed,
and he said to them, "My soul is in agony until death. Stay here and
watch." And he went on a little farther and fell upon the ground, and he
prayed that, if possible, the hour might pass him by; and he said, "Abba,
the Father, all things are possible for you. Take this cup away from me.
Still, not what I want, but what you do."
    And he came and found them sleeping, and he said to Peter, "Simon,
are you sleeping? Were you not strong enough to watch one hour? Watch
and pray that you may not enter into temptation. The spirit is willing,
but the flesh is weak." And again he went away and prayed saying the
same thing. And when he returned again he found them sleeping, for
their eyes were heavy, and they did not know how to respond to him.
And he came a third time and said to them, "You are still sleeping and
resting? Get up. The hour has come. Behold, the Son of Man is betrayed
into the hands of sinners. Get up; let's go. Behold, my betrayer draws
near."
    And immediately, while he was still speaking, Judas came along, one
of the Twelve, and with him a crowd armed with swords and clubs, along
with the chief priests and the scribes and the elders. The betrayer had
given them a common sign, saying, "The one I kiss will be the man. Seize
him and lead him away under close guard." And going immediately to
him, he said, "Rabbi!" and he kissed him. Then they threw hands upon
him and seized him. Someone standing there drew his sword and struck
the slave of the high priest and cut off his ear. And Jesus, responding, said
to them, "Have you come out against me like a criminal, with swords
and clubs? Every day I was with you in the temple teaching and you did
not seize me. But the scriptures shall be fulfilled." And all left him alone,
and fled.
    Now a young man followed behind him, with a robe cast over his
naked body, and they seized him. But, leaving the robe behind, he too
fled, naked.[77]

---

77. *Mark* 14:32–52.

In his lectures on tragic poetry, Hegel noted that there are two distinct tragic dimensions, two axes or tragic trajectories.[78] I touched upon them briefly in the second chapter and want to return to them now. Building upon his own starting point — namely, that tragedy is defined, not by happy or unhappy endings, but by a certain kind of *Kollision* — Hegel adds that these collisions take place in different dimensions and along different axes. *Horizontally* — and here Sophocles' *Antigone* is the model — there are collisions between law and justice, disparate definitions of what is right. Such collisions, "moral" in the traditional sense, are animated by the inescapable distance between human laws and the equally binding yet "unwritten laws" of heaven, between *nomos* and *themis*. The Christian movement emerged out of one such prophetic debate about the Law — its letter and its spirit.

There is, however, another kind of tragedy, a *vertical* tragedy. Sophocles' *Oedipus Tyrranos* is the model here, and Hegel's interpretation points to the view — a *tragic* vision, which is at least as old as the *Iliad* — that there is more than one will in the world. The gods will, Oedipus wills, and out of their conflict — a *constitutive* collision — Oedipus' Destiny emerges for the first time. Fate is what the gods will. Destiny is what we make of it. This is also an essential movement in Mark's gospel.

It is important to keep these issues distinct, Hegel goes on to say, for a tragedy that tries to do two things at once very rarely succeeds — although I think it does succeed in the gospels (Hegel himself seems to suggest as much). More often than not, what results is a loss of focus and a morass of insoluble moral conflict. And that, as we saw in chapter 2, makes for the kind of tragedy Hegel does not like, if it is tragedy at all. I mention this because it so well illustrates what I take to be the first question we need to ask about the *mythos* of Gethsemane and about *Mark*. If I am right in wanting to read it as a tragedy, then *what kind* of tragedy is it? Is this the story of one man's *necessary* collision with the religious and political authorities, a collision whose impulse derives from Jesus' extraordinary insight into the essence of what is right (unwritten laws, again) and the necessity of speaking to the entire human family? Is Mark's gospel a moral tragedy, and does Mark mean to provide us with an ethical agenda?

Or is this story — particularly here, in this lonely place — the story of one man's encounter with a world he did not make, a will not his own, and his anguished attempts to convert these things into a Destiny? In emphasizing this, the *vertical* dimension of Jesus' tragedy, I naturally gravitate toward the figure of Jesus himself — particularly when

---

78. Paolucci, *Hegel: On the Arts*, 186–187.

he is alone, wrestling with his Fate, in Gethsemane. By contrast, those
who read Mark's performance as a horizontal tragedy[79] tend to highlight the confrontations, temptations, and failures that take place in a
strictly political arena: Jesus' *execution* by the principalities and powers,
not merely his abandonment, mortality, and death. Is tragedy political,
metaphysical, or both? In pursuing a political, a horizontal, reading, one
naturally gravitates toward the student-disciples, who are called upon to
"follow" Jesus, who "has gone before" them (16:7) — to Galilee. I do
not think these are antithetical readings, but they *are* distinct. And in
any case, I will not be developing Mark's ethical vision at the conclusion of this chapter. I would like to read this gospel vertically, in the
quiet conviction that this performance, perhaps Mark's most of all, is a
tragedy in which Christ's Destiny is of the essence.

Let us now look more closely at Mark's performance. It agrees with
Matthew's in that we are given a name for this "place" — it is Gethsemane (*Gethsēmani*). Luke referred simply to the Mount of Olives, and
John to "a garden" across from the Kedron Valley. The name seems
to derive from the Hebrew *gat-she-ma-nim,* or "oil-presses," an appropriate name for a spot traditionally held to be on or close to the
Mount of Olives.[80] Jesus immediately instructs his student-disciples to
"sit here while [*heōs*] I pray,"[81] yet as we already saw in the Matthean
performance, there is a certain inconsistency regarding just how alone
Jesus really is. Mark's Jesus characteristically takes his inner circle (Peter,
James, and John) with him, apart from the others. This image recalls the
first parable (4:1–9) in Mark's gospel that Jesus tells about God's kingdom: a great quantity of seed is sown, the vast majority of which fails
to take root, withers, and dies. The whole progress of Mark's performance might be viewed as the dramatic enactment of this parable.[82] As

---

79. I am thinking here chiefly of Ched Myers' *Binding the Strong Man,* a book
that, for all its insights, seems at times close to the tragic posture itself. Myers is radically disenchanted with the modern world, although he is ambivalent about whether
contemporary problems and hypocrisies are unique. He also lapses at times into a romanticization of the early Christian past. And he has never quite made up his mind as
to whether or not "tragedies" end unhappily.

80. Vincent Taylor, *The Gospel according to Saint Mark,* 551.

81. The preposition *heōs* is normally translated "while," but it really only bears this
meaning when followed by a verb in the present indicative tense. That is not the tense
used here. The word is problematic since it will be repeated in the very next verse (34),
where Jesus complains that his soul is in agony "*until* death," or perhaps "*while* dying."

82. Frank Kermode, in his *The Genesis of Secrecy* (Cambridge, Mass.: Harvard Univ.
Press, 1979), reads it this way. He mentions vv. 1–9 only in passing, to establish the
categories of "insiders" and "outsiders" that are crucial to his analysis. He dedicates the
book "to those outside." Far more interesting to Kermode is Mark's reference to *Isaiah*
in 4:10–11. On its basis, Kermode pursues a reading of *Mark* that draws out its essential
paradoxes (pp. 141–145). Those on the inside remain outside, in an important sense;
the more clearly things are revealed, the more problematically they are concealed. This

Jesus moves decisively south, the crowd gradually falls away from him. By sundown on the evening of what will be the Last Supper, only the Twelve are left, and we know that one of them is a betrayer. Now, Judas gone, other disciples are pared away, and only the inner circle, the three, remain. Jesus will shortly leave them behind as well and "go on a little farther" (v. 35) to pray. The communion with God he seeks will result only in another abandonment. No answer is forthcoming, save that his plea is denied. And then the Christ, abandoned, agonized, and alone, is swallowed up one last time into the crowd — when it kills him.

There is a critical question of translation here as well. At the end of this first parable, Jesus concludes with words that will become a haunting refrain: "He that has ears to hear [akouein], let him hear [akouetō]" (4:9). Translated this way, Jesus' words are not only paradoxical; they are actually unfair. Those with ears *have to* hear — they are passive recipients to the words God has sown. Translate this phrase afresh — "Let those with ears to *listen, listen*" — and suddenly the image changes.[83] The difficulties of looking, of listening, and of understanding do not, properly speaking, disappear. But we have now been invited inside by Jesus' words, and if we remain "outside," it is because we choose to do so. Our Destiny, not Fate.

We need also to pay careful attention to Mark's frequent use of the passive voice.[84] Mark is interested not only in the inner world of his main characters, but also in the fact that Jesus now is more acted upon than acting — he has taken on an uncharacteristically passive role. Jesus has continually insisted that his student-disciples learn to act and think for themselves. Now, in what is probably the first instance of independent action, Judas acts, decisively — and betrays the entire mission. And Jesus, who has been the only one in full control of himself — in the midst of a violent and violating world — is now in control of these same powers. Now he "began to be greatly distressed and troubled" (v. 33). "And he said to them, 'My soul is in agony [perilupos] until death'" (v. 34). Violently disturbed (ekthambeisthai is an extremely intensive verb) and

---

reading makes Jesus' teaching more like Zen Buddhism, and Martin Heidegger, it seems to me, than Mark's performance finally allows. For all of these apparent paradoxes are subsumed into the single essential paradox of the faith: it is only by losing life that one may find it. This central Markan insight comes to its fullest, and definitive, expression in Gethsemane. Here is no paradox for paradox' sake. Rather, it points to the fundamental tenet of the Christian proclamation: love and obedience to God, a God who is more than an abstract principle in the last analysis, but a very real, and very troubling presence. "Verily, you are a God who hides yourself" (*Isaiah* 45:15).

83. The same thing is naturally true for the passage from the Greek text of *Isaiah*: "Looking, they will look, but not see, and listening [akouontes], they will listen [akouōsin] but not hear" (4:12). See also Myers, *Binding the Strong Man,* 174.

84. While this is not a commonly recognized aspect of the Markan text, I think that a close reading of Mark's Greek bears out this characteristic of Mark's performance.

radically alone, Mark's Jesus seeks his solace in God — solace that, as we have seen, he will not find. His prayer fully reflects this inescapable paradox: "Abba, the Father, *all things are possible for you*. Take this cup away from me. Still, not what I want, but what you do" (v. 36).

The details of this prayer should not be missed. Whereas Matthew and Luke both have Jesus address God personally in the vocative (*Pater*), and whereas in John's performance the union between Jesus and God is virtually complete, here in *Mark*, Jesus addresses a God who is suddenly, mysteriously distant: "Abba, *the* Father" (*Abba ho Patēr*).[85] His prayer asks that "this cup" be taken away, a request that we have seen in every performance. Now we are finally ready to compare the qualification the request receives in each performance. In so doing, we will see careful attention paid to the will, *Jesus' will*, without which there can be no tragedy.[86]

In *Luke*, Jesus prays, "Father, *if you will*, take this cup away from me. Still, let not my will be done, but yours." This condition stands out markedly from that which qualifies Jesus' prayer in the other Synoptic performances. In *Matthew*, Jesus prays, "My Father, *if it is possible...*" and again, "*if it is not possible...*" In *Mark*, the conditions are just as we have seen: "Abba, the Father, *all things are possible to you....*" The meaning that each of these three conditions lays upon the action that follows is radically different and — at least in Mark's case — truly astonishing.

For Luke, the conclusion is clearly that Jesus' Father did not wish (or "will") to take this suffering cup away. If we were to construct a syllogism out of the Passion narrative, we would find something like the following:

1. "Father, *if you will*, take this cup away from me."

2. The cup is not taken away.

3. God did not wish to remove it.

For Luke, God's will is otherwise, and Jesus' will disappears. For Matthew, the implication is rather that the cup cannot be avoided. It represents a sort of scriptural Fate:

1. "My Father, *if it is possible*, take this cup from me."

---

85. See Joseph A. Grassi, "*Abba*, Father: Another Approach," *Journal of the American Academy of Religion* 50:3 (1982) 449–458, for a fine discussion of this invocation.

86. It would not be too much to say that the church spent nearly four centuries hammering out the full implications of the claim that Jesus had a real human body, on the one hand, and a will of his own, on the other. Gethsemane is precisely the story that forces that issue.

2. The cup is not taken away.

3. It is not possible for God to remove it.

We are subsequently told *why* this is not possible. The answer is Fate. The script of this passion-play was written long ago: "It is necessary [*dei*] that the writings of the prophets be fulfilled." Mark, by contrast, leaves the theodicy in its starkest form, and entirely unanswerable.[87] As he has it, no answer is possible, and no reprieve is forthcoming:

1. "Abba, the Father, *all things are possible for you.*"

2. The cup is not taken away, as Jesus asks.

3. We are left to wonder why.... [88]

The agony of this prayer cannot be missed. The extraordinary communion that Jesus enjoys with God, while seldom explicitly mentioned by Mark, has been graphically apparent in word and deed. John tells; Mark shows. Jesus' Father, while a God of few words, has been a God of decisive deeds. Quite suddenly, his silence speaks louder than his words or deeds have ever done.

In proper Aristotelian fashion, Mark has introduced definitive statements of God at the beginning, the middle, and now at the end of his performance.[89] At the outset of the ministry, when Jesus is first baptized into the Spirit and his mission, God's voice came from heaven, proclaiming personally, "*You [Su]* are my beloved Son; *in you [en soi]* I am well pleased" (1:11). Again in the middle of the ministry, immediately prior to the decisive southern turn, Jesus was elevated upon a mountaintop into the very presence of God's servants, Moses and Elijah, when God's

---

87. "The 'danger' of the Markan approach to prayer is not that it will be taken too seriously, but that the formative document of the community that experienced both divine power and devastating persecution will be trivialized by a church that experiences neither" (Sharon E. Dowd, " 'Whatever You Ask in Prayer Believe' [*Mark* 11:22–25]: The Theological Problem of Prayer and the Problem of Theodicy in *Mark*," Ph.D. diss., Emory University [1986]; that work is now available as *Prayer, Power and the Problem of Suffering: Mark 11:22–25 in the Context of Markan Theology*, SBL Dissertation Series, [Atlanta: Scholars Press, 1991]).

88. See Robbins and Mack, *Patterns of Persuasion in the Gospels*, 141, for the general lack of closure in Mark's syllogisms.

89. See Kelber, *Mark's Story of Jesus*, 71–72: "Mark's passion narrative is shrouded in darkness, gloom, and tragedy. More than Matthew, Luke and John, his is the story of an execution, of the victim's Godforsakenness, and of the demise of the victim's closest followers. There is an oppressive air hovering over the final days, and almost no relief from the horror of death. Divine intervention is not forthcoming during Jesus' hour of suffering. The heavenly voice which sounded at baptism (1:11) and on the mount of transfiguration (9:7) is silent during the agony on the cross. There is, as we shall see, no resurrection appearance to lighten up and overcome the anguish. Death has cast its long shadow almost to the very end of the Marcan story." See also Vernon Robbins, *Jesus the Teacher*, 135, and Ched Myers, *Binding the Strong Man*, 365.

voice again descended from heaven, proclaiming to the three student-disciples who were present, "*This* [*Houtos*] is my beloved Son; listen to *him* [*akouete autou*]" (9:7). Given all that we have seen, and heard, it will not be too much to expect a final, definitive proclamation from heaven now in Jesus' great moment of crisis, precisely when he needs it most and has explicitly asked for it. If we are not exactly waiting on Matthew's twelve legions of angels, we could at least have a word. These dramatic expectations have been very carefully cultivated. Immediately prior to his entry into Jerusalem, Jesus unambiguously proclaimed the power of faithful prayer: "Have faith [*pistin*] in God. Truly I say to you that if someone were to say to this mountain, 'Be lifted up and cast into the sea!' and if he is not divided [*diakritēi*] in his heart, but believes [*pisteuēi*] that what he says will come to pass, then he shall have it" (11:22–23).

As so often in Mark, a difficulty has been presented, not to be re-solved, *not yet,* but rather to be left in its most jarring form. God has spoken to Jesus, and to his student-disciples, decisively, twice. Now God is silent, perhaps gone for good. Faithful prayer is said to be a certainty. Are we to suppose that Jesus' heart is now divided? Has *his* faith fal-tered? All things are possible with God. Jesus asks that the cup be taken away. It is not taken away.

And Jesus' last agonized prayer meets only with the awful loneliness of some dark corner of a broken world, the dreadful silence of heaven. "What is impossible in logic becomes true in life, and the contradiction lodged within the soul tears it to pieces."[90] The time is out of joint, and in this seeming end-less-ness, Jesus' will is tempered and his soul is rent. That is the essence of Mark's gospel, the tragic in this tragedy.

After this prayer and its irresolution, Jesus returns to his student-disciples and finds them asleep (a strange word for Mark — Jairus' daughter was said to be merely asleep, when she actually had died). Jesus addresses Peter alone: "Simon, are you sleeping? Were you not strong enough to watch one hour? Watch and pray that you may not enter into temptation. The spirit is willing, but the flesh is weak" (vv. 37–38). A number of points crystallize around these comments. First, Jesus refers to Peter by his old name — Simon — an appellation that has been absent from the performance so long as Peter's behav-ior conforms at least roughly to the expectations of student-discipleship. Hence a note of failure, even rejection, enters into the Garden. The rep-etition of the word 'watch' (*grēgoreō*) bears resonances to the earlier insistence upon "looking" (*blepō*) and "listening" (*akouō*), especially in

90. Simone Weil, "L'Iliade, ou, le Poème de la Force," in *La Source Grèque* (Paris: Editions Gallimard, 1953) 16.

Jesus' parabolic discourse. Those who have ears must listen; those with eyes must look (4:12). This invitation is now intensified, commanded: "Watch." Jesus concluded his discussion of the coming tribulations, the so-called miniapocalypse, with the clear commandment: "What I say to you, I say to all: Watch" (*blepete* and *grēgoreite*, 13:33, 34, 35, 36). That command is repeated here, in the very moment of penultimate failure.

It is interesting that Mark should introduce the notion of tempta-tion (*peirasmon*) only now. His account of the events following Jesus' baptism lacks any explicit "temptation" narrative, something that was dramatized by both Matthew and Luke. If he knows such stories, Mark chooses not to tell them. In the wilderness, Jesus is not threatened; he is ministered to by angels (as he always seems to be, until now, in "lonely places").[91] And yet now, alone for the first time in a *truly* lonely place, Jesus is threatened, in agony, tempted. The flesh *is* weak, no matter how willing the spirit may be. To be the Christ makes this, if anything, more true. It is an awful burden for a person to bear:

> Human suffering is laid bare, and we see it in a being who is at once divine and human. The accounts of the Passion show that a divine spirit, incarnate, is changed by misfortune, trembles before suffering and death, feels itself, in the depths of its agony, to be cut off from man and God.[92]

Now, upon this third repetition of Jesus' praying and the student-disciples' sleeping, Jesus asks in near astonishment how they can still be asleep. It is enough, and the hour (*hōra*) has come (v. 41). Simon had been told to watch (v. 37) for one hour. That hour is now ended. No one is watching. Now, they are sleeping; soon, they will flee. And the Son of Man is betrayed (*paradidōmi*) into the hands of sinners. A powerless Jesus now asks his disciples to arise (*egeireō*). In happier times, he had healed the sick and raised the dead with such a word; now he can only summon them to their temptation — and their failure to meet it.

Immediately (*euthus,* repeated twice, vv. 43, 45), Judas arrives on the scene accompanied by a crowd (*ochlos*). Mark describes the crowd in all of its imposing, violent reality (Matthew does this too, John intensi-fies it, while Luke excises all of it). The crowd is armed with "swords and clubs" and is composed of "chief priests and scribes and elders" (an unholy trinity for Mark, who clearly does not see himself as a scribe).

---

91. Admittedly, Mark does tell us that Jesus was in the wilderness "being tested by Satan" (*peirazomenos hupo tou Satana,* 1:13), but the point is that this is *all* he says. There is no concrete, threefold temptation narrative as we find in *Matthew* and in *Luke*. Is it impossible that "Gethsemane," with its threefold repetition of the prayer, represents Mark's singular understanding of what it means to be tempted?

92. Simone Weil, "L'Iliade, ou, le Poème de la Force," 27.

Note the characteristic flashback inserted at this point (v. 44). The be-trayer (*ho paradidous*) has already arranged with the crowd to single Jesus out by kissing him. He now approaches the Teacher ("Rabbi!" v. 45). He kisses him. The crowd seizes him. The spare phrasing here — clauses piled on top of clauses, words on top of words — set off against the far richer narrative hypotaxis of the preceding scenes, sets the tone perfectly.

And now something altogether remarkable happens. One of Jesus' anonymous followers strikes the slave of the high priest and cuts off his ear (*to ōtarion*). Only Mark tells us this without elaboration. Mark char-acteristically leaves things unelaborated *and* unresolved. The reasons for this are not far to find. Jesus has continually insisted, throughout this performance, in an almost hymnic refrain, that those with ears must lis-ten (4:9). That is what God wants. It would not be too much to call looking and listening the very essence of student-discipleship in Mark. In this violent assault at Gethsemane, listening itself has become sud-denly impossible. An ear has been intentionally severed. If those with ears must listen, what are those who have been deprived of ears sup-posed to do? Jesus is no longer up to undoing the damage, as he did in *Luke.* The failure of Jesus' followers, either to understand their mission or to act with even the vaguest sensitivity to what he is saying, could not be more dramatically rendered. And it is at precisely this moment that Jesus is spirited away.

Mark's performance emphasizes the sheer totality of the failure. All (*pantes*) forsook him. All fled. And yet — here is another story that only Mark will tell us — a mysterious young man (*neaniskos*) followed be-hind Jesus (*sunēkolouthei*) as the student-disciples were unable to do, with only a linen cloth (*sindōn*) to cover his naked body (*gymnou*).[93]

---

93. Most commentators on Mark's performance do not deal with this scene. It is often related to the final scene in the gospel (16:5), if only because the term *neaniskos* appears only in these two places. So Robin Scroggs and Kent I. Groff, "Baptism in Mark: Dying and Rising with Christ," *Journal of Biblical Literature* 92 (1973) 542: "But the parallelism involves more than the repetition of the word *neaniskos*. There is similarity also in that pointed attention is given to the clothing." This article is one of the finest recent attempts to deal with this troublesome story, and it seems to confirm where we have left it — namely, focused upon an abandoned robe. I agree that this mysterious *neaniskos,* by his very anonymity, invites the reader into the story, that is, into identification with his vulnerability and subsequent flight. The controversy concerns what we are invited into. Scroggs and Groff are convinced that this mysterious *neaniskos* is some sort of archetypical Christian initiate — replete with the necessary baptismal markers of nakedness and a white robe. The reader, through the *neaniskos,* is invited to "die" with Jesus at 14:51–52, and thereby to be resurrected with him at 16:5. Such an interpretation hinges on a rather more positive view of Mark's final scene, 16:1–8, than I am willing to allow: "Mark 16:1–8 is in fact seriously misnamed when it is called an 'empty tomb' story. It is rather a resurrection-announcement story pointing to heavenly exaltation, not earthly manifestation as Matthew and Luke chose to understand it"

When the crowd attempts to seize (*kratousin*) him, just as they seized Jesus, he drops his robe to the ground and flees, naked (*gymnos*). The young boy here anticipates the young boy at the empty grave (16:5–6),[94] hovering over Jesus' abandoned burial cloth. So many important words are repeated here in such short order — *the robe* covers his *nakedness, the robe* dropped to the ground, leaving him *naked*. Mark is carefully playing with a repetitive vocabulary as he is so often wont to do — but with one glaring exception, the two verbs that refer to this anonymous young man: he *follows*...he *flees*. Like everyone else in Mark's performance, in the fateful moment, he cannot, and does not, stand where he means to stand.

Perhaps it is best to cast the scene dramatically, and to leave it precisely as Mark does. Mark, after all, has a lovely dramatic touch.[95] As the lights fade from the torches of the crowd, and the curtain draws down over this scene, neither Jesus nor his student-disciples are visible. The former has been swallowed up in the crowd; the latter have abandoned him. The last anonymous companion who attempted to follow in Jesus' way also fails to do so. He, too, finally flees. The spotlight slowly fades on an empty linen robe, soiled and imperfectly folded, trampled by the crowd (see appendix 2 for more on the complex debate concerning the ending of Mark's gospel).[96]

(p. 536). I prefer to take Mark at his word: we are left at an *empty* tomb and the Lord "is *not* here." This reading is crucial to my understanding of Gethsemane and of Mark's performance as a whole. For some recent work on this topic, see Crossan, *Four Other Gospels: Shadows On the Contours of the Canon,* 91–124, and Kermode, *The Genesis of Secrecy,* 55–65, esp. 62–63, which support my conclusions here.

94. J. D. Crossan has argued in several places that this empty tomb really lies at the heart of Mark's concern for the experience of God's *absence*. Neither God nor Jesus is "here" in any "place" to which the first-century Christian, or we, can point. Crossan goes on to argue that this was a pointed message to the naïvely optimistic Christians of Mark's own day, with their simple assumption that Jesus is present, whether at table with them in the Eucharist, or in the trials and tribulations of martyrdom. See Crossan, "Empty Tomb and Absent Lord," in *The Passion in Mark,* ed. Kelber, 135–152, and his follow-up article "A Form of Absence: The Marcan Creation of Gospel," *Semeia* 12 (1978) 41–55. See also Vernon K. Robbins, "Last Meal: Preparation, Betrayal, and Absence," in *The Passion in Mark,* 35, 38.

95. "In the nineteenth century critics decided that Mark's was the first of the four Gospels to be written, and it was given much greater attention in the hope that it would yield really secure historical information about Jesus and his teaching. These hopes were not fulfilled. But it may be no accident that Mark has received serious attention *as a writer* only in the age of cinema. For he begins and ends his book abruptly; he gives us sudden changes of scene; he has flashbacks, stories inserted within stories,...that fast pace with all its 'and's' and 'immediately's'" (Christopher Burdon, *Stumbling on God: Faith and Vision through Mark's Gospel* [Grand Rapids, Mich.: William B. Eerdmans, 1990] 79).

96. See Raymond E. Brown, "The Passion according to Mark," *Worship* 59 (1985) 118, 124.

VII

The first word of Mark's gospel is 'beginning' (*archē*). The last word is not 'end,' but a form of 'fear.' It might be interesting to point out how precisely these prayers in Gethsemane coincide with Jesus' final words in each gospel performance — words that come to us from the cross. As we will recall, Luke's version of the prayer leads inescapably to the conclusion that God *does not wish* to take the suffering cup away from Jesus. Jesus finally accepts God's will and dies with these very words of radical acceptance on his lips: "Father, into your hands I commit my spirit."[97]

For John, as we have seen, there really can be no prayer for deliverance — because there was no temptation in the first place. John's gospel as a whole may be read as the enactment of the very thing that Mark and the others place in prayer — that is, a way to show that God's will and Jesus' are completely one. Jesus is himself the parable. He has come to this world, and to this hour, for no other purpose. His death on the cross represents the ultimate fulfillment of the divine mission, and Jesus departs the scene with a single word, *Tetelestai,* "It is finished."[98]

In Matthew's performance, Jesus concludes that *it is impossible* for God to take the cup away. This naturally leads to the next question — Why? — a question that is then intensified by the way Mark tells his story. In *Mark,* Jesus affirms that all things *are* possible for God, and yet the cup *still* is not taken away from him. Are we to assume that God simply does not wish to do so and that Jesus is unwilling to accept what he has already accepted in Luke? The natural question for Jesus, and for the listener, is inescapable: Why? The full agony of this question is expressed only on Golgotha and only by Mark and Matthew: "My God, my God, why have you abandoned me?"[99]

St. Paul himself wrote: "If Jesus Christ be not risen, then is our faith vain." And yet the death on the cross is something more divine than the Resurrection; it is the point where Christ's divinity is concentrated. Today the glorious Christ veils from us the Christ who was made a malediction; and thus we are in danger of adoring in his name the appearance, and not the reality, of justice....

Plato, in going so far as to suppose that the perfectly just man is not recognized as just, even by the gods, had a premonition of the most pierc-

---

97. *Luke* 23:46.
98. *John* 19:30.
99. *Mark* 15:34 and *Matthew* 27:46. It would not be too much to say that this prayer is really the only question that Jesus ever asks, the answer to which even he does not know.

ing words of the Gospel: "My God, my God, why have you forsaken me?"[100]

There is a straight line that moves inexorably from Gethsemane to Golgotha. And one can scarcely imagine a more powerful, or more fitting, conclusion to Mark's performance of this story than the underscoring of such a question.

Recall the distinction between Fate and Destiny, which we have made many times in this book. I introduced it in the first chapter and discussed Hegel's views in some detail in the second. Nietzsche talks about little else than Fate, and will, as we saw in the third chapter. Tragedy, from the time of Homer on, attempts to wrestle with the uncommon notion that there are *two* wills at war in the world — that which we want and that which God, or the gods, want. Certain things are *necessary,* bound to happen, yet the tragic hero is left to make sense of necessity, to convert these brutal and blind facts into something vital and personal and visibly real. Tragedy cannot have anything to do with the blind fatalism of *Njal's Saga.* If all we were given in the *Oedipus* was the story of a doom (*atē*) coming to fulfillment, it would not be much of a play. What is thrilling to see is suffering *enacted,* the process whereby Fate is gradually accepted and embraced, if never *fully* understood. The acceptance of *another* will takes place *without* the sacrifice of our own. In the end, there is still something left for Oedipus to do. Tragic "reconciliation" is a very heady and difficult business. Luke's performance of the Passion seems to me to lose much of the tragedy implicit in this *mythos,* for the simple reason that Jesus' future is all Fate and no Destiny. His is not to question why — when he does, he dies. God does not wish to deliver him from the hour of Gethsemane. We do not know why — the implication seems to be that we do not *need* to know why — and yet we *are* asked to accept it and even to participate in it.

On my view, John tells a story that is so fundamentally different that it has violated the very texture of the tragedy. The whole power of Gethsemane — a story about prayer and temptation, as much as it is about betrayal — derives from the fact that we here witness the collision between wills, a tragic struggle for self-definition in which we are invited to participate and which we recognize as our own: that is, simply put, the struggle to accept the will of heaven. Here, if anywhere, Fate becomes Destiny. John misses all of this because his theology cannot allow for two wills in the world, nor for a divided picture of Christ. John's Jesus is so heroically self-present, so transparent to the divine will, that

---

100. Simone Weil, *Intimations of Christianity among the Ancient Greeks,* translated variously (London: Routledge and Kegan Paul, 1957, 1987) 142–143.

there is no tragedy and no real suffering — only triumph. We are as close to the Gnosticism of Njal as we will ever come in the New Testament.

It is in Matthew, and then again more intensively in Mark, that the tragic dimension of this story is underscored. By refusing to let go of the essential question — *Why?* — they have done even more than construct a dramatic world that each of us will recognize. They have pointed the way toward a tragic understanding of Destiny: two wills, not one.[101]

Yet there remains a sense of failure that dominates the literary horizon of Mark's world. It remains now only to say why the penultimacy of failure is emphasized so. The student-disciples' failure to understand Jesus' teaching, to recognize suffering, rejection, and death — the *vide tragoediam* — as the natural consequence of sowing God's word has been a dominant theme in Mark's performance at least since Peter's confession of Christ at Caesarea Philippi[102] and almost certainly before then. There is much more at stake here than the culmination of a narrative idea. Jesus is truly alone for the first time in Gethsemane, *his* will suddenly ignored, even by God. This, the same God who had addressed him as a "beloved Son" at the baptism and who had identified him as such to the inner circle of student-disciples at the Transfiguration — Gethsemane is the *necessary* prelude to the desperate cry from the cross.

Mark's gospel, more than the others, might easily be seen as a dramatic illustration of the true nature of being schooled in the way of Jesus. No cheap optimism disrupts the tragic tones in which Mark paints such schooling. "I believe...but help my unbelief" (9:24) is the best that one can ever say.[103] This performance is about tragic education as well as it is about Jesus — a horizontal and a vertical tragedy at once. The teaching means one thing in Mark's story that it does not mean so emphatically in the other gospels. It leads *necessarily* to Gethsemane, abandonment, and the cross. To find life, you must lose it first. There is a terrifying identity between Jesus and his student-disciples. His road will be their road, completely — even if they do not yet understand this (10:38). "The readers in Mark's time," in fact, "who understand the nature of the crisis, are invited to complete the journey left incomplete by the disciples."[104] Throughout the ministry, Jesus has been sympathetically present to his disciples, helping their unbelief, encouraging them and sustaining them: "Don't be afraid; simply believe" (5:36). Gethsemane represents the first — and really the only — moment when Jesus' faith falters. It is *his* moment of Destiny. An essential part of the tragedy

---

101. See Via, *The Ethics of Mark's Gospel*, 182.
102. *Mark* 8:27–30; *Matthew* 16:13–20; and *Luke* 9:18–21.
103. Via, *The Ethics of Mark's Gospel*, 186–192.
104. Kelber, *Mark's Story of Jesus*, 94. This is also the essential thesis of Myers' *Binding the Strong Man*.

is that his followers are unable to minister to him, even for this one hour. They abandon him instead. And this sober warning — about our inability to do what we long to do and our inability to believe what we know and long for — lies at the very heart of Mark's performance.

Failure, nonetheless, may be of many types, like pessimism itself. Tragedy may involve suffering, yet it is as far from any sort of passive resignationism or pessimism as it could possibly be. There is, as we have seen, a sense in which tragedy is a far more elevating genre than comedy, being what it is and treating the topics it does.[105] Satire, insisted Hegel, is a sign of decadence and decline; tragedy is for spiritual and cultural powers that are still ripe and in full flower. "Human life," says Sartre, "begins on the far side of despair."[106] So, too, Hegel — Hegel, who insists, as we have seen before, that the true task of philosophy is "to stare the negative in the face and to dwell with it."[107] The notion is hardly novel; it derives from the classical tradition of Athenian theater, a heritage that, if we understood it better, might provide important clues for a proper understanding of the gospels. *For the gospel, too, is a tragedy.*[108]

The Greek theater was a complex undertaking, the dramatic festivals intricately and painstakingly orchestrated. On each day of the festival, one poet presented three tragedies, at the conclusion of which, in the late afternoon and on toward evening, the moment was "right" for comedy of a sort. It is almost as though tragedy — a day *full* of tragedy — set the stage and created the tone in which comedy might be properly viewed.[109] Only a tragic perspective makes genuine comedy possible. Genuine laughter emerges only on the far side of tears. Socrates insists that the same poet who writes comedy must write tragedy, too.[110] And

---

105. That is the essential thesis of Walter Kerr's *Tragedy and Comedy* (New York: Simon and Schuster, 1967).

106. Jean-Paul Sartre, *The Flies*, act III.

107. Hegel, *The Phenomenology of Spirit*, §32; Baillie, 93. One will find the connection to Hegel, and specifically Hegel's dramatic theory, made explicit by Sartre almost everywhere in his discussion of the theater, both in critical essays and in interviews. See *Sartre: On Theatre*, ed. Frank Jellinek (New York: Random House, 1976).

108. See Myers, *Binding the Strong Man*, 100–106, 120, 134, 357, 399–401, 420, 457, for a variety of statements that suggest many different things: that "tragedy" is about disaster, failure, unhappy endings,... or — at his best — about a story *that can have no end.*

109. See Dana F. Sutton, *The Greek Satyr Play* (Meisenheim am Glan: Verlag Anton Hain, 1980) 164–166; see also 1–13, 134–157. Her comments become particularly suggestive at pp. 158–179, where Sutton argues that satyr-play is the real mediating link between comedy and tragedy. "The comic technique here is to create momentarily a serious mood, evocative of tragedy, and then deliberately destroy it" (p. 162). Not so scatological or sexually outrageous as Old Comedy, the satyr-play invites one to laugh at intrinsically serious matters.

110. *Symposium*, 223c–d.

so it was in the classical moment. Tragicomedy is no solution. 'Tragi-comic' is a word that would have made no sense to the Greeks in the tragic age,[111] for the two ideas are always already linked.[112]

Heard in this light, Mark's gospel, especially now in its Passion, takes on a new luster and brilliance. It is suddenly clear why Mark's performance of Gethsemane is so uniquely troubling, why his gospel, alone among the four, ends with an empty tomb, panicked flight, and the lingering uncertainty of everyone who ever took to this road. It is not that Mark does not believe in the resurrection. All of his Passion-predictions make it clear that he does.[113] Nor is it the case that Mark is so "contemporary" a thinker as to invite comparison with "modern," and "posttheistic," playwrights. Mark is *un*modern, not antimodern, like Nietzsche at his best. There is nothing more wrongheaded than try-ing to make Mark postmodern. Mark's heroes await the Parousia, not Godot. Mark's world is not a stage with "No Exit," but rather a cosmic theater, enclosed in dark glass, through which faint images of the divine may still be glimpsed, however fleetingly. His is a tragedy that paves the way for that happier ending which is to come — possibly, at day's end — *but not yet.*

For this vision is vouchsafed only on the cross. You must lose your life to find it. Mark's Jesus comes bearing *two* things: good news and hard sayings. Only by dwelling with the negative — the suffering and hardness of life — may the good news be appreciated for what it is. It could almost be said that a sincere faith in the resurrection makes dwelling with the Crucified practically impossible. If you know how a story ends, you can never hear its beginning or middle quite the same way again. Once accepted as a reality, how can the "fact" of the resur-rection fail to qualify *all* of our ideas about death, even such a death on a cross? For an answer to this question we do not have far to look in early Christian history. It cannot fail to do so.

The earliest patristic texts provide ample evidence of the fact that death not only lost its power to oppress the first generation of Christian

---

111. James Redfield, "Drama and Community: Aristophanes and Some of His Rivals," in *Nothing to Do with Dionysus?* 317–321.

112. This is what makes Dan O. Via's conclusion to *Kerygma and Comedy in the New Testament* unsatisfying. He concludes that Mark's gospel as well as Paul's kerygma were comedy or "tragicomedy." His reasons for saying so are that the image of death-and-resurrection lies at the heart of comedy (xi, 49, 56–57, 77, 93, 124; see also *The Ethics of Mark's Gospel*, 10, 13, 34–37, 53). The image derives much more profoundly from *tragedy*, it seems to me, and in any case Dionysus presided over *both* festivals, comic *and* tragic alike. I suspect that the real issue here is that both stories — gospel and kerygma — *end well*. But that does not make a tragedy (or a tragicomedy) comic, as I have said countless times. For an excellent discussion of the implications for Mark's gospel, see Myers, *Binding the Strong Man*, 358, 365–367, 397–401.

113. Via, *The Ethics of Mark's Gospel*, 56.

martyrs; they actually sought it out. The early history of the church is littered with the bleached bones of the martyrs, men and women who actually sought out the arenas of Rome, the holy contest of faithful dying.[114] Here is a contest (agōn) oddly and surreally without conflict (agonia). Fate, not Destiny — with a single will in the world.

Or so such Christians, in their spiritual myopia, had hoped. But we also learn of countless would-be "martyrs" whose faith faltered, who found in the depths of their private Gethsemanes neither Destiny nor the grace to accept all things. Rather, they are confronted by the sheer terror of the unknown, the overwhelming blindness of Fate. And in this terror, they apostatize, or — like all of Jesus' followers in Mark's gospel performance — they flee.

If this is the case in the first and second "Christian" centuries, it is not true of these times alone. Every age abounds with these same tensions. The times in which Mark was writing were, if anything, more confusing and fanatical. Rome was still the great oppressor, the Beast, whether she was crushing Jewish insurrection in Palestine or martyring Christians in the arena. What we have in Mark's gospel is an authentically timeless piece that is a period-piece at the same time. It speaks of what it means to live, and to die, in a violent and brutal world. The names of the oppressor may change — Pilate, Caligula, Ananias, Nero, Titus — but it is always really Rome. The names of the oppressed may change — Theudas, John the Baptist, Zealots, Jews, Christians — but the dynamic of oppression and injustice remains what it always was. That is the timeless dimension to the drama Mark has crafted.[115]

In this milieu, Mark's gospel makes a tragic kind of sense. His warning reverberates through the corridors of time and speaks to us still, if we have the ears and the eyes and the stomach for it. Dwell with the negative, and face the horror of the crucifixion, the awful sense of abandonment in the Garden and on the cross. "The Lord is not here" (16:6).

This fact does not make faith impossible. Hope is not disqualified. Such is, in fact, the very marrow of the only hope worthy of this story; a hope, that is, that can stand the test of temptation and the test of time. The way to new life takes us through death — there is no gain without a loss — and it is only through the loneliness of Gethsemane

---

114. For me, the letters of Ignatius, Bishop of Smyrna, are paradigmatic in this regard. He wants his bones crushed, "to be ground into bread for Christ." See *Early Christian Fathers,* ed. Cyril C. Richardson (Philadelphia: Westminster Press, 1953) 74–120. The more balanced view, as the church seems to have realized when it sought to define "a martyrdom conformable to *the* gospel," was Polycarp's. See note 10.

115. See Myers, *Binding the Strong Man,* 39–86, for an insightful exposition of the sociohistorical atmosphere in Palestine from the time of Jesus, and before, to the time of Mark, and after.

and the coronation on a cross that Christ came into *his* kingdom. Our expectations are all turned upside down. This turnabout is *never* easy — *not* for Jesus, *not* for his student-disciples, and certainly *not* for us, who are still attempting to listen to the story. Mark's vision is an unsettling one. But it is true, and those who would seek a simpler answer to the riddles of existence, who would like to trade in their Destiny for a mess of fated pottage, want to live in a world other than the one we have been born to. This Mark's Jesus refuses to do; and perhaps in telling his story, Mark equips later generations to undertake the same labor.

One word more, and we really *are* at the end. There may seem to be a contradiction here, but in fact there is not. In what, precisely, does the "tragedy" of the gospels consist? I have already accused John (if not Luke as well) of attempting to go "beyond tragedy" — almost as if tragedy were about unbearable suffering after all, pure and simple. Yet Lucien Goldmann accused Sophocles himself of trying to move "beyond tragedy,"[116] for much the same reason, and I sharply criticized that thesis in the second chapter. What, then, is the difference?

Tragedies can be resolved, although they do not really *end*. The principle of resolution, of redemption, does not a teleology make. The early Christian movement made a reformation out of this distinction: between "fulfillment" and "ending." The Law, they insisted, was fulfilled, but not ended. It was Paul, arguably, who tried to end it all. The postmodern agenda, it seems to me, is out to subvert this whole distinction — between resolution and ending — and that is what makes Mark's gospel such a rich site for their deconstructive experiments.[117] Mark, I have said several times now, is not postmodern (or antimodern, for that matter) — precisely because he wants to tell a story that *will be resolved,* although it *is not finished* (the opposition to John's gospel is again clear). In the absence of an end, so the modern argument runs, no resolution is possible. We are no longer willing to "wager on transcendence,"[118] on the principles of resolution, the possibility of redemption.

Mark, as an authentic Christian tragedy, like most all Greek tragedies, sees things very differently. For reconciliation — even resurrection — *does* have a place in the tragic universe. The fact that Christians (even Mark, as troubled as he is) believe in a resolution at the end does not make religious thought *un*tragic — as Nietzsche, MacIntyre, and

---

116. Lucien Goldmann, *The Hidden God: The Tragic Vision in Pascal's Pensées and the Tragedies of Racine,* trans. Philip Thody (Atlantic Highlands, N.J.: Humanities Press, 1964, 1977) 44 note 1.

117. This is what Burton Mack intends when, building upon Foucault, he views apocalypticism as necessarily antiworldly rather than other-worldly. See his *A Myth of Innocence,* 353–376.

118. Goldmann, *The Hidden God,* 46–48.

countless others have argued that it does. Resurrection *is* the paradigmatic happy ending, and yet Mark manages, for his part, to be far from happy about it. The Christian *mythos* is a tempting invitation *to become* tragically insensitive and degenerately comic — if one fails to take the suffering seriously, like John, or hands over the will, like Luke. The Christian goes "beyond tragedy" *not* when he or she believes in resurrection, *but only* when he or she claims that this faith will take your pain away. Tragedies *can* end well — and still be "tragic." But if genuine suffering is ignored, or simply painted away in colors that distract the eye, if the agony of the struggle to believe and to understand is not faced in all earnestness, *then* it is no tragedy. *Salvation is through suffering, not from it.*[119] Suffering is not necessarily tragedy's last word, but it is decidedly the first; if it is not "the end," it is definitely "the beginning" of a tragedy. And here is precisely where tragedies and gospels are speaking the same language: in the performance of human suffering, in the refusal to accept it blindly, in the will to understand something through it, and in the understanding, to see it transformed.

There were three men on crosses, Mark tells us. But the cross was a Destiny to one only.

---

119. See *Hegel: The Letters,* trans. Clark Butler (Bloomington: Indiana Univ. Press, 1984) 57.

Afterword

The Tragic Vision

✥

Let's say that now we are first facing the light of the world,
    That our ships never set sail for Troy
    And the Mycenaean kings didn't go hunting lions,
    For the artisans to engrave their golden memories on the metal of
       immortality.
Let's say that the Persians haven't come yet
    To ask for our land
    And the buzzards at Marathon haven't counted their bodies
    And the shells in the sea of Salamis
    Haven't clung to the sunken triremes;
    That Pheidias' hands
    Are the tiny hands of this newborn baby
    Awaited by the unwrought marbles of our country.
Let's say that the masterpieces of Aeschylus and Sophocles
    Are still these bright sparks
    In the eyes of the youth who passes us by;
    That the golden age is that fair wheat
    We sow in sweat with the vision of Threshing;
    That the leaves of this wild olive tree we are now grafting
    Will some day shine like silver
    At the flowering of Platonic thought.
Let's say that now we are first facing the light of the world
And let's say only that the others call us: Greeks.

—Yiannis K. Papadopoulos

I

We have come a long and circuitous way, traversing that ambiguous and ill-defined middle-ground that Plato called the erotic *metaxu*[1] — that which separates the beginning from the end. We, all of us, think and write and live in this "in-between," between what Frank Kermode has

---

1. *Symposium*, 202a–b.

aptly called "the *tick* of birth and the *tock* of death."[2] This book began as a rather narrow conversation and disagreement with a modern
posture so well represented by Alasdair MacIntyre and George Steiner,
among others. That may seem a liability, a sign of decadence even, in
Nietzsche's terms. "One should observe our scholars closely," he warns
us, "they have reached the point where they think only *reactively*, i.e.,
they need to read before they can think."[3] Lucien Goldmann looks at
this same phenomenon in a somewhat more favorable light. Every classic viewpoint, he observes, tends to emerge out of fruitful engagement
and sustained conflict with some one other point of view.[4] Even the
"classic" needs a starting point. Achilleus had his Agamemnon; Antigone had her Creon; Kant had his Hume; and Hegel, in turn, had Kant.
While I am far from claiming any sort of "classic" status for this book,
I have had MacIntyre and Steiner — and the tragic posture they represent so elegantly — always in the front of my mind. I have learned
enormously from them — primarily as, like Nietzsche, diagnosticians of
modern culture. It is the medicines that MacIntyre, for his part, prescribes that seem more poison than preventative, more condemnation
than corrective. Even in objecting in such strong terms — 'posture' *is*
a rather strong word — I am not rejecting his point of view outright.
Rather, much as Hegel tried to do with Kant, I have wanted to draw
out of this philosophy things that are, I think, implicit there. That has
been my hope — by focusing on the concept of *tragedy*, as we meet it in
Sophocles and in Homer, first of all.

What began, then, as a rather local conversation with a single
thinker has necessarily become something else again. I began with a certain disquiet, a certain suspicion of the mannered apocalypticism that
constitutes the dominant tone in contemporary moral and theological
reflection, so well embodied in MacIntyre's views. "Fanatics are pic-
turesque," Nietzsche warns us, "and people like looking at *postures*
[*Gebärden*] more than listening to *reasons*."[5] It is this posture, the *tragic*
posture, that has been my chief preoccupation.

Still, we cast our net a good deal more broadly, and we may seem to
have brought in a confusing variety of fish. What narrative thread ties
together thinkers as apparently diverse as Hegel and Nietzsche, texts as

2. Frank Kermode, *The Sense of an Ending* (New York: Oxford Univ. Press, 1971)
58.

3. Nietzsche, *The Will to Power*, trans. Walter Kaufmann and R. J. Hollingdale
(New York: Random House, 1967) §916; *Sämtliche Werke*, XII, 553.

4. Lucien Goldmann, *The Hidden God: The Tragic Vision in Pascal's Pensées and
the Tragedies of Racine*, trans. Philip Thody (Atlantic Highlands, N.J.: Humanities Press,
1964, 1977) 20–25.

5. Nietzsche, *The Antichrist*, trans. H. L. Mencken (Torrence, Calif.: Noontide
Press, 1980) §54; *Sämtliche Werke*, VI, 237.

diverse as the *Antigone* and Mark's gospel? The first, the shorter, answer to this question has been the *leitmotif* of this essay: these thinkers, and these texts, are not nearly so different as is customarily supposed. In fact, they share a really rather remarkable thematic interest. They are not mere period pieces from a bygone era, but remarkably relevant books for our own perplexities and problems. This is a part of what makes them "classic."

There is a second answer to this question, however — a bit more involved, and if no less satisfying, then certainly far less clear. It is an Hegelian idea, at heart, one I mentioned at the beginning of the first chapter. The beginning is never merely arbitrary, but it *is* always empty, hollow. Only at *the end,* after we have traversed the long and tortuous path of the negative — whether it be the thinking through of an involved philosophical idea or the concrete experience of social life and social death — does the beginning take on a depth and a thickness that it simply could not have possessed at the start. Things, Hegel reminds us, take *time.* His is a sobering counsel to grand philosophical patience. On his view, this essay can justify itself only in conclusion, to the degree that it is justifiable at all.

Nietzsche qualifies this in an important way. It is a way that ought to have been open to Hegel himself, had he kept his own tragic counsel more consistently. Tragedies simply are not as interested as we moderns seem to be in the end.[6] Consider, for example, the rich flesh tones of Homer's "ending." Here we are confronted with the marvelous reconciliation of two men, Priam and Achilleus, whose entire lives and social roles counsel them to hate one another. Achilleus, his fury now spent, is reconciled to giving away the body of his sworn enemy, the man who had killed his dearest friend. Priam, who had witnessed the murder of his own son, and who now bends his knee to kiss "the terrible man-slaughtering hands" of Achilleus that had slaughtered so many of his sons, is unable to contain his grudging respect for the physical excellence and abundant virtues of the man before him. This reconciliation takes place, however, under a cloud of doom. Those who knew the story knew all too well what happened next: how Achilleus shortly met his death on the plains before Troy, killed by an arrow from Paris' quiver — Paris, *who is Priam's son;* and how Priam met *his* end at the point of Neoptolemus' sword — Neoptolemus, *who was Achilleus' son.* These men's lives are intertwined in an agony of Fate and Destiny. This ending, whatever else it may be, is neither optimistic nor pessimistic. Such

---

6. This criticism is directly related to what I have called the "bad teleology" of MacIntyre's account in *After Virtue,* 2d ed. (Notre Dame, Ind.: Univ. of Notre Dame Press, 1984) 52–55, 148, 185, 215–219, 243.

words do not really apply to the poem at all. It is something else entirely; our language longs for another word. Perhaps the best, and most appropriate, thing to do is simply to do as the Greeks did and to call it "tragic."

If that is the case with Homer, it is even more true of the tragedy Mark tells. There, at the end, we are left at an empty tomb, where two women draw tentatively to its open entrance, only to meet a mysterious young man with an ambiguous message — and who then flee in terror, telling no one anything at all. Neither text "ends," at least not in a manner that would be appreciated by most moderns, who like their tragedy neat. "Perhaps humanity comes closer to its goal [*Ziel*] in the middle of the journey," Nietzsche concluded, "rather than at some end."[7] There is never merely one end; but always there is the journey. This is the tragic counsel I mean to defend here, and it seems to me to imply that if my essay is really to defend itself, it has surely already done so. The proof, in any case, remains in the reading.

If this essay *has* justified itself, then it will have done so largely by making clear how far, and specifically in what measure, the postures of the modern age miss the real force of classical and Christian tragedy.

The tragic posture counsels a pessimistic regard for the "modern" present, an apocalyptic belief that we are, somehow, "ending" now. Tragedy counsels a more sober and balanced assessment of the situation — a setting ripe with unique, but by no means overwhelming or irredeemable, problems and conflicts.

The tragic posture is romantically optimistic about the spiritual condition of the past and in fact *uses* the past, *needs* it, to make its own desperate analyses stick. Here again, tragedy prescribes a dose of sober realism. The philologist's task, Nietzsche insisted over a century ago, is to be skeptical about the past, not to feed the myth-machine of modernity.

The tragic posture insists that tragedies end badly, that *we* are, even now, "ending" in the worst way imaginable. Whether we are waiting for St. Benedict, the Parousia, or Godot, we are in every case stagnant, *waiting*. That is the source of modernity's, and now postmodernity's, failure of nerve. By now it should be clear to the point of redundancy what I mean when I say that tragedy — both classical and Christian — does not necessarily end. It is not concerned with ending.

In the course of this book, I have used Alasdair MacIntyre — and to a lesser degree George Steiner — as a representative of this tragic posture. But it is my chief conviction that the list of such representative thinkers is infinitely expandable. This posture characterizes the very

---

7. Nietzsche, *Wir Philologen*, 5[185]; *Sämtliche Werke*, VIII, 92.

age in which the great majority of modern thinkers claim to be living. I have attempted to trace out a set of loosely organized beliefs in which we will all recognize ourselves. "Modernity" is itself an apocalyptic and highly academic idea, fed by a romantic rhetoric and an idealization of the past. By contrast, Hegel and Nietzsche represent what is, to my mind, the most sophisticated challenge to this tragic posture — Sophocles and Mark being two eloquent exemplars of the "unmodern" view. Neither Hegel nor Nietzsche makes the case alone, but taken together, their contributions to an undoing of the modernist morass is inestimable. I hope now that the narrative links of the book are clearer: why, for instance, it is that MacIntyre's work, and his telling failure to discuss tragedy himself, requires that we read a tragedy ourselves; why it is that the *Antigone,* and the questions that Sophocles raises about civil disobedience and some premier social virtues, are so pertinent; why the *Antigone* invites, in turn, most of Hegel's questions, both interpretive questions concerning the play as well as more general questions of moral philosophy; why it is that Hegel sets the stage for Nietzsche by tracing out the main trajectories of "tragic" philosophy as somehow "beyond optimism and pessimism"; and why Nietzsche's strident insistence that we must choose between Dionysus and the Crucified requires us to read a gospel — in order to determine if he was right. We began with a tragedy, and we ended with a gospel — twin sides of a common coin, a fitting circularity worthy of my main thesis. It has been my further hope that this book will ideally provide a deeper understanding of *both* types of religious drama, Greek and Christian. If nothing else, it is my earnest hope that anyone who has read this essay will never hear the words 'tragedy' (or 'gospel') or 'modern' quite the same way again. These words need to be underscored in the lexicon of our philosophies.

II

The vast majority of "modern" writing seems obsessed with this matter of the end. There is a curious brand of "after-ness," or "posteriority," that characterizes most modern thought, a remarkable number of "afterwords" that are emblematic of modernist rhetoric. Without the apocalypse, the ideas would not be very interesting, and in fact most of the arguments would not hold up at all. It is precisely the tempering of this apocalypticism in his latest work that has convinced me that Alasdair MacIntyre is no longer engaged in the same project at all. Like Nietzsche, his instinct for postures and polemics often leads him to overstate the case. His central thesis was that we are living somehow "after" virtue.[8] George Lindbeck essays the future of religion and theology in a "*post*liberal" age.[9] George Steiner wonders if we are not in fact living in a "*post*culture."[10] In every case, the theories hold only if we are living at the end. If there is no end, then there is no apocalypse; and absent the apocalypse, *their* conceptual centers cannot hold.

In each of these cases, there is also subtle agreement about another crucial, if unstated, thesis: religion is a crucial, perhaps *the* crucial, component to any healthy society. Religious ideas are what bring us, and bind us, together. Modernity is thus primarily a moral and *spiritual* crisis. "Modernity," in fact, is a spiritual event.[11] The question concerning technology can be, at best, a secondary issue, a mirror reflecting upon a far deeper crisis of thought and belief. Articulating that crisis has been the self-appointed task for a full century of social theory, beginning with Max Weber and, to a somewhat lesser degree, Emile Durkheim. There is a myth of religion as "the sacred canopy" that lies behind most of it.[12] This myth represents what is probably the high-water mark in modern apocalyptic, the theory of "secularization." There is, so we are told, a sacred canopy of shared meanings, values, and beliefs that helps each of us to order our world. Outside of this protective umbrella, the world is blustery and cold — the inevitable threat of chaos and entropy, death and decay. We seek to hold these things at bay, to warm ourselves with sacred fire. But the inherently chaotic universe gradually chips away at the canopy, and when it tears — as it eventually must — a spiritual crisis is the inevitable result. We are very close, it seems to me, to the root-imagery and the cold cosmology of *Njal's Saga;* we are light years away from Homer. There are no final answers to the problems of *theodicy,* says the tragic posture. There are only the stopgap measures of sacred canopies, the noble (and not so noble) lies that are as ultimately doomed

---

8. This is, of course, the chief apocalyptic tenet of MacIntyre's groundbreaking *After Virtue.* If we were living "after" virtue then, MacIntyre now speaks — much more appropriately — as if we are still "in" the age of virtue, whatever it is. Some of the implications of this ambivalence I have traced out in "After Virtue? On Distorted Philosophical Narratives," *Continuum* (1994).

9. George Lindbeck, *The Nature of Doctrine: Religion and Theology in a Post-Liberal Age* (Philadelphia: Westminster Press, 1984).

10. George Steiner, *In Bluebeard's Castle: Some Notes toward a Redefinition of Culture* (New Haven: Yale Univ. Press, 1971) 33, 59–93. It is fascinating that Steiner also argues that this "post-culture" is best characterized by a "new stoic or ironic pessimism" (pp. 80–81). While I think he is largely right in this characterization, it should be clear by now that I consider the pessimism itself dismaying and quite wrong.

11. See MacIntyre, *After Virtue,* 1–5, 36, 262–263; and Steiner, *In Bluebeard's Castle,* 34, 88–89, 121ff.

12. See Peter Berger, *The Sacred Canopy* (New York: Doubleday, 1967); and Steiner, *In Bluebeard's Castle,* 51–55. An astonishingly similar idea animates MacIntyre's myth of heroic and premodern society, as I have argued at length. See *After Virtue,* 27–28, 33–34, 121–130.

as little boys who play around leaky dykes. In the modern age, we have lost that battle — our sacred canopy has come undone. We all live now in an age "*beyond* belief."

All of the elements of the tragic posture are in place here. There once was a time when the world made more perfect sense, an age of seamless social meanings, an age when religious faith was "easier," when it was "good for you"[13] — an elaborate, romantic mythology of the religious past. That world is ours no longer, and faith is, if we are to be honest about it, impossible in the modern world — a grand, sweeping pessimism for the present. "Modernity" has taken on the sudden, subtle stature of a Fate. The canopy *had to* come undone — secularization is an inevitable erosive force — and the battle that we all fought to weave a warm, meaningful tapestry against the cold winter night of truth was a battle we were fated to lose from the start. This Njal knows in a way that Achilleus never could.

This elaborate theory, and the postured myth that lies behind it, sounds compelling enough until we pause to recall that a "tradition" is more about good questions than it is about simple answers. Climbing "outside" of the sacred canopy — as Achilleus and Antigone and Jesus did, as (in a very different way) Hegel and Nietzsche did — might just as easily be viewed as an ascent upward into the sunlight. Nietzsche certainly saw it that way: as daybreak, not twilight, at least until the twilight of his own career. The dynamic of so doing is, in any case, as old as the oldest Homeric poem. Whatever the "modern" world is, we cannot claim that it differs from the ancient world, that which we call "premodern societies," because they once had a coherent and seamless worldview of which we are no longer capable. Tragedy teaches the *permanence,* not the *modernity,* of social conflict and civil disobedience.

This point also takes us back to Humpty-Dumpty, whom we left shattered in the introduction, after "a great fall." Modern social theory views the sacred canopy much like an egg — just as fragile and just as certain of eventual toppling and collapse. Humpty-Dumpty *must* fall; the sacred canopy *must* tear in pieces. The forces of gravity, like the law of entropy itself, is simply too strong. The universe tends toward disorder. The gods are abusive, pitiless, and cruel. We will *never* succeed in putting these shattered things back together again.

Humpty-Dumpty speaks rather differently in a tragic idiom. He can be put back together again, but he will always have the cracks. Not only

---

13. I am building here on Mary Douglas' trenchant criticisms in her "The Effects of Modernization on Religious Change," in *Religion in America: Spirituality in a Secular Age,* ed. Stephen Tipton and Mary Douglas (Boston: Beacon Press, 1982) 25–43. She concludes: "Here I stop. Everything is wrong because the stereotype of premoderns is wrong. It has been constructed to flatter prejudged ideas" (p. 42).

will the cracks always show; they always *did* show. Humpty-Dumpty was broken from the very beginning; an egg is an intrinsically fragile thing. As is the creation. Being human involves the desire to put broken things together again. Archaeologists and philologists do it for a living; to some degree we *all* do it. To claim that the king's horses and men could not do so is simply to buy into modern postures and prejudices. The fact that this task of putting together, of restitching and weaving, gluing and pasting, is never completed is no argument against the process. Of course there is no end to it. Tragedy *tells us* that there is no end. Only the tragic posture counsels us not to try.

III

There is another component of the whole "sacred canopy" argument, to which I alluded briefly in the introduction. It concerns the fear that tragedy itself has "died" in our own day,[14] that we are no longer capable of it, no longer able to bear its bitter truths. Why I consider this more of a posture than an argument should be clear by now: as Kant said, one ought not to confuse the difficulty of a task with its impossibility. Tragedy *is* difficult, now as it ever was. Steiner himself speaks of the atmosphere of "miraculous occasion" that surrounds the tragic experience and describes the emergence of a national theater as a "splendid accident."[15] But then, so is Antigone's way, so is Mark's gospel. So, I am arguing, is faith.

Steiner's reasons for arguing in this manner seem to me to be twofold. In the first place, tragedy *needs* the gods, needs what Nietzsche called "faith in a metaphysical world." But modernity is "secular." Now, with the gods all dead, tragedy, too, has died. The only theatrical options still available to us are comedy, political satire, and the absurd. Yet there is a deeper point. As I emphasized in the last chapter, the Greek audience that filled the theater of Dionysus knew the stories before it attended. This was a crucial aspect of what took place there. This kind of cultural literacy is no longer available to us, say the doomsayers.[16] And the reasons for that are, again, clear enough. We do not know whether

---

14. This is the admittedly ambiguous thesis of George Steiner's *The Death of Tragedy* (New York: Hill and Wang, 1961).

15. Ibid., 106–107.

16. Precisely this worry has animated Allan Bloom in his *The Closing of the American Mind* (New York: Simon and Schuster, 1987), but his polemics tend to overdraw the extent of the "crisis." A good corrective to this posture may be found in Eric D. Hirsch's *Cultural Literacy* (Boston: Houghton Mifflin, 1987), where the argument is, very plainly, that such literacy is as available to us now as it ever was — and our failure to take advantage of the cultural resources available to us is our Destiny, not our Fate.

to be pagan or Judeo-Christian. The eyes of our souls wander aimlessly between Athens and Jerusalem, never quite at rest, never quite at home.

Now up to a point, there is something compelling about these images. Broadway *is* a disappointment, an incredible resource that has been left largely untapped. Its very priciness puts it out of reach of the vast majority of Americans, and it caters more to the cult of Hollywood personality and the "sure thing" of sequelizing than it does to the sustenance of great contemporary art. America has *never* had a national theater, and creative local theater is "miraculously occasional." Hence the importance of contemporary debates about federal funding for the arts. All of these arguments are equally true of poetry in general. Americans have never had a poet laureate either; most American poetry today is an elite enterprise written *by* poets, *for* poets, and for virtually no one else. All of this looks pretty desperate, particularly when we compare the state of American art to, say, the Balkan countries, where poetry and theater still comprise an essential part of daily life.[17] As I say, there is something compelling, and even vaguely attractive, about the image.

Yet it is attractive only in the way that a car accident or other spectacle is attractive — we are gazing at something forbidden, something attractive primarily for its anomaly and horror. A few years ago, I was fortunate enough to see a play that changed all of this. I was deeply moved, and my understanding of our theatrical "situation" has never been quite the same. That work is *The Gospel at Colonus,* a stunning recapitulation of the Oedipus myth — the *whole* myth, the redemption as well as the disaster — but played now in the setting of a black American Pentecostal church.[18] The setting is itself already infinitely telling. As I suggested, all too briefly, in the last chapter, there is no more fascinating brand of American Christianity, nor one closer to the spirit of Orthodoxy, than the celebratory tradition of African-American spirituality. Moreover, the staging of this *Greek* trilogy in an African/American church vividly displays some of the continuities — both cultural and theological — that I have been tracing out in this essay. Pagan or Christian? The very question may be misguided — and seems to me to lead to a good many of MacIntyre's, Steiner's, and other modernist errors. Pagan *and* Christian — the attempt to embrace, and to understand, the unsettling presence of God in an inescapably cracked creation.

17. See Czeslaw Milosz, *The Witness of Poetry* (Cambridge, Mass.: Harvard Univ. Press, 1982) 6–7, 30–31, 65. So Steiner, *In Bluebeard's Castle,* 110–111, where he claims that "America is the representative and premonitory example. Nowhere has the debilitation of genuine literacy gone further.... Could it be that the United States is destined to be the 'museum culture'?"

18. We are fortunate now to have this screenplay available as *The Gospel at Colonus,* an adaptation by Lee Breuer (New York: Theatre Communications Group, 1989).

Lee Breuer's stage directions make this all very clear. "The ceremony, while pagan, should recall contemporary religious rituals," he notes.[19] "The robes [of the congregation] are a mélange of motifs: church Sunday, African, Greek."[20] When the Preacher descends to the podium and begins to speak in the sudden hush that has fallen over his flock, we are all immediately called upon to inhabit *two* worlds — Christian and Greek — simultaneously:

> Welcome, brothers and sisters.
> I take as my text this evening the Book of Oedipus.
> Oedipus! Damned in his birth, in his marriage damned,
> Damned in the blood he shed with *his own* hand.
> Oedipus! So pitifully ensnared in the net of *his own destiny*...[21]

Very soon thereafter, the Preacher himself takes on the role of Oedipus *and acts him out,* as do most other members of the congregation at various stages of the performance. Antigone, Polyneices, Ismene, Creon — all come to life out of the bosom of this Christian congregation.[22] Moreover, the words they speak are, as often as not, Sophocles' own. Among the Sophoclean passages that are quoted, or sung, are the choral "Ode on Man," the "Ode to Eros," and the stunning last words of Oedipus to his daughters.[23] Equally significant is a theme we met briefly in Herodotus: "Call no man happy until death."[24] Everything is in place here for a crucial cultural synthesis of Christian and Greek, in a word, for *tragedy.* I think that we come to a better, and certainly more vital, understanding of the function and the potential *power* of a Greek Chorus in this play than in any other "modern" play known to me — that great spring from which, according to Nietzsche, tragedy first came to life. Building, again, upon the rich musical tradition of the black church in the United States, each and every scene is punctuated with song and dance — lending a vital contemporary cadence to words that (we must constantly remind ourselves) are twenty-five hundred years old. It was, and is, a stunning cultural accomplishment. And any theory that wants to claim that theater, or at least tragedy, is "dead" in our own day will need to come to terms with plays like this one. Masterpieces, admittedly, do not happen every day. But they do happen — even in a world as allegedly "modern," and fragmented, as our own.

---

19. Ibid., 17.
20. Ibid., 4.
21. Ibid., 4–5.
22. Ibid., 8, 14, 17, 23–7, 35–9, 44, 46.
23. In each case, they are based on the verse translations of Robert Fitzgerald; see ibid., 30–31, 42, 54.
24. Ibid., 7, 43.

The play, finally, makes some important claims about tragedy, as a conceptual idea. The way the myth is staged, and the whole dramatic movement, confirms most of what I have been trying to say in this book. It displays all of Hegel's and Nietzsche's best points — in verse. For all of the Fate that lies behind the myth, Oedipus stands alone. The net in which he is ensnared is that of *"his own* Destiny." The dramatic movement of the whole is arguably the play's most important point. It begins, as any tragedy *must* begin, with radical anguish — with suffering:

> Let every man in mankind's frailty
> Consider his last day; and let none
> Presume on his good fortune until he find
> Life, at his death, a memory without pain. Amen...

> Majestic Oedipus!
> I who saw your days call no man blest —
> Your great days — like ghosts gone.
> Of all men ever known
> Most pitiful is this man's story...
> For I weep the world's outcast.[25]

But the tragedy ends, as Sophocles and Mark alike envisioned it, with *redemption.* Not optimistic, and certainly not naïve, nonetheless it *is* a story that is *resolved.* In triumph:

> For he was taken without lamentation
> Suffering or pain. Indeed his end
> Was wonderful if mortal's ever was.

> Now let the weeping cease.
> Let no one mourn again.
> The love of God will bring you peace.
> There is no end.[26]

---

25. Ibid., 7–8.
26. Ibid., 55.

Appendix 1

The Athenian Parthenon:
On Building and Destroying Temples

The image of Nietzsche's well-loved Parthenon, which ironically he him-self never saw,[1] perhaps best makes the point I am after in chapter 3.[2] One can read, as it were, the history of pre- and postclassical Greece in the complex history of this temple. One finds, in the Parthenon's history, both a confirmation of and a substantial contradiction to the central tenet of Nietzsche's cultural archaeology — the maxim that you must destroy a temple if you will create one.[3]

After its foundation was laid on the much larger scale of the Periclean Akropolis project, the Parthenon became the cultic, cultural, and finan-cial center of the Delian League (which was, practically speaking, the

---

1. In the nineteenth century, it was the British and French philhellenes who actually made a fad of traveling east to Greece. One thinks of Lord Byron, or even Napoleon. Most of the German classicists in that same generation — Winckelmann, Goethe, and Nietzsche — never made it further than Italy, if they traveled outside of Germany at all. Heinrich Schliemann, the archaeologist who uncovered Mycenae and Troy, was one of the first Germans actually to travel to the sites.

2. The Parthenon has, of course, generated an unbelievable bibliography, and new things continue to be learned every year. For a helpful presentation of the main outlines of the brief history I am sketching out, one might consult any of the following: John Boardman and David Finn, *The Parthenon and Its Sculptures* (London: Thames and Hudson, 1985) 1–46, 212–216; Brian F. Cook, *The Elgin Marbles* (London: Trustees of the British Museum, 1984) 1–17; R. J. Hopper, *The Acropolis* (London: Weidenfeld and Nicolson, 1971) 115–126; John Travlos, *A Pictorial Dictionary of Ancient Athens* (New York: Praegar, 1971) 52–71, 444–457; and R. E. Wycherly, *The Stones of Athens* (Princeton, N.J.: Princeton Univ. Press, 1978) 105–126.

3. The best case for Nietzsche's views might be made by appealing to the history of *the* temple, in Jerusalem, rather than to the Parthenon. That temple was indeed destroyed, twice, and has never yet been rebuilt. Doing so now would require the de-struction of the Muslim temple, the Dome of the Rock, which stands on its foundations. An exhaustive comparative study of the Parthenon and the Jerusalem-temple remains to be written, but one senses that Nietzsche was himself intrigued by the idea. As he notes in the same essay where he generates his formula for temple-creation: " 'Rome against Judea; Judea against Rome' — there has hitherto been no greater event than *this* struggle, *this* question, *this* deadly contradiction" (*On the Genealogy of Morals*, I, §16).

Athenian Empire). An earlier, Archaic Parthenon had been demolished and burned by Persian invaders.[4] It should be noted that they left *no* temple in its place—since they came *only* to destroy, not to create. Had they intended to leave a temple behind, doubtless the Archaic Parthenon would still be standing. One seldom *levels* an edifice that one can otherwise use again.

When the Athenians decided to rebuild, after their own empire was more secure, they generously expanded the original plans. The Parthenon was destined to dominate not only the local landscape, but also the brainscape of the postclassical Mediterranean world. It became a symbol—long after the Athenian hegemony had collapsed in the aftermath of the Peloponnesian War and Alexander's empire had dissolved in its turn—of everything, culturally speaking, that had survived. The *idea* of some temples, as Judaism teaches us, can *never* be destroyed. It was as much for the Parthenon as anything else that Athens continued to be the cultural *sine qua non* throughout late antiquity, as is evidenced by the endless spate of patronage and new building in Athens, funded by one Roman emperor after another attempting to curry the favor of the gods and the peoples residing upon this timeless spot. Nietzsche's aphorism applies far better to armies, and to empires, than it does to temples— only with the former does novelty *necessitate* destruction.

Yet cultural developments are never so neat as archaeologists might wish, and here Nietzsche demands a careful hearing. For not all empires have been as benevolently disposed toward classical antiquity, nor so broad-minded in their cultural attitudes. The history of the Christian empire marks the first act of the tragedy that plays itself out upon the Akropolis. When the Parthenon was converted into the Orthodox basilica of Agia Sophia, or "Holy Wisdom," the Christian architects took great pains to scale three sides of the building in order to chisel off the faces of the metope figures. They were pagan and thus fit only for destruction. Only the southern metopes were left intact, since they were not visible from the Greater Propylea, the entrance to the Akropolis compound, and it was considered unnecessary to undertake the enormous labor of defacing them. Luckily or unluckily, the tremendous cryselephantine statue of Athena Parthenaios had already been removed to the Byzantine capital of Constantinople in the fifth century; no one knows what became of it thereafter. It may have been destroyed with other Greek antiquities in the Fourth Crusade by the Venetians and other so-called Crusaders in the sack of 1204 C.E. More likely it was melted down long before then. Finally, the eastern entrance to the Par-

---

4. See William B. Dinsmoor's "The Date of the Older Parthenon," *American Journal of Archaeology* 38 (1934) 408–448.

thenon was closed off; an apse was added — at the expense of the central pedimental sculptures that were destroyed to make room for it; and a new door was cut into the western face of the building.

When the building changed hands again, and the Franks supplanted the Byzantines — the Latins for the Greeks, the Catholics for the Orthodox — little changed in the Parthenon. The Franks, characteristically, added new fortifications all around the Akropolis and an enormous tower over the Propylea that was not dismantled until 1874 — at Heinrich Schliemann's personal expense. Still, and on the whole, Frankish occupation meant surprisingly little to the Parthenon.

After the Ottoman conquests in the East and the expulsion of the Franks in 1456 C.E., the Parthenon became a mosque. A minaret now appeared at the forward-facing western end of the building, the general architecture was braced, but the sculptures and such were still intact. As for the minaret, Nietzsche would certainly have seen in it more of the will to power than the will to prayer. Yet, even still, *after nearly two millennia,* this temple had not been "destroyed."

Few today realize how well-preserved was the Parthenon — which had been in virtually constant use since its original foundation — until 26 September 1687. On that fateful day, Venetian troops stormed the Akropolis and bombarded it from a neighboring hilltop. Fully aware of the fact that the Turks were using the Parthenon as an enormous powder magazine at the time (the Propylea, which had served a similar purpose, had been struck by lightning some years previously and badly damaged), the Venetians shelled it anyway, and a direct hit on the south side literally tore the building apart:

> In this way, that famous temple of Minerva which so many centuries and so many wars had not been able to destroy, was ruined.[5]

The irony of this all is compounded by the fact that both Athenians and Venetians were forced to abandon the city in the very next year (1688),[6] and the Turks held it continuously thereafter until their final expulsion in the Greek War for Independence, which ended in 1831.[7] Our loss is impossible to calculate, but some sense of its magnitude comes from

5. This comes from an eyewitness account of the shelling and destruction of the Parthenon, written by Cristoforo Ivanovich, an aide to the Venetian Count Morosoni. See *The Parthenon,* ed. Vincent J. Bruno (New York: W. W. Norton, 1974) 124–128.

6. Moreover, the Venetian plan *to level completely the entire Akropolis compound,* so that the Turks would have no fortifications left to use, was not carried out solely because they lacked the manpower and the time. See Cornelia Hadjiaslani, *Morosoni, the Venetians, and the Akropolis,* trans. George Huxley (Athens: Gennadius Library, 1987).

7. Dating "the end" of the Greek War for Independence is difficult because it was accomplished in stages. Greek independence was formally recognized by the Turks already in September 1829. But it was not until 9 October 1831 that John Capodistrias

a collection of fortuitous sketches that had been made about ten years earlier by an amateur French architect, probably Jacques Carrey.[8] They give us some sense of what we, the "modern" barbarians, have undone. I use this term deliberately, to make the equation between Europeans and Persians explicit. The Parthenon was destroyed only twice — by the Persians, and by the Venetians — and in both cases they had no interest in leaving *anything* of substance behind. It was a strictly technical, military undertaking, with nothing "cultural" about it. Nietzsche is eloquently, and precisely, wrong: "If a temple is to be *created,* an older temple must be *preserved.*"

The history of the Parthenon since that fateful day pushes us further along the trajectories Nietzsche traced out so prophetically. The best of the surviving Parthenon sculptures do not reside in the Akropolis Museum — as they certainly should — but rather in London. The Elgin Marbles, as well as a host of other classical treasures, were carted away by the British (*and* the French under Napoleon, *and* the Germans under Hitler) at the height of their own colonial and imperial strength.[9] While there has been much talk of righting an ancient wrong — the late Greek cultural minister Melina Merkouri was its most eloquent and passionate spokesperson — it is doubtful that the marbles will be in Athens any time soon. There is a parable in these stones, in the fact that empires have been more willing to part with conquered territory than they have been to return stolen cultural artifacts.

The spectacle of technology, too, takes its turn upon the Akropolis, and this fact directly recalls my brief comments in the introduction.[10] Technology is by far the most brutal of the Akropolis's many conquerors, and its damage is not to be undone. We have rebuilt portions of what the Ottomans and Venetians tore apart; we have excavated much of what the Persians ravaged. Against technology, we do not yet have the tools. When the Greek archaeological service sought to put the Parthenon back together again at the turn of this century, it failed to learn from the technical sophistication of its classical forebears. Every block

---

was named president of the provisional government, and it was not until 7 May 1832 that Prince Otto of Bavaria was elected as the first king of modern Greece.

8. See *The Carrey Drawings of the Parthenon Sculptures,* ed. Theodore Bowie and Diether Thimme (Bloomington: Indiana Univ. Press, 1971).

9. Elgin's notoriety has been assured by a new coinage in the French language, a new word for plunder, *elginisme.* For a nicely balanced portrait of Lord Elgin — less as a crude plunderer and more as a victim of the cupidity of the British government — see Russell Chamberlin, *Loot! The Heritage of Plunder* (London: Thames and Hudson, 1983) 7–38.

10. For an excellent summary of these latter developments, see *The Akropolis at Athens: Conservation, Restoration and Research, 1975–1983,* trans. Judith Binder (Athens: Ministry of Culture Committee for the Preservation of the Akropolis Monuments, 1985).

of every major Greek building is jointed and braced with iron brackets, invisible from the exterior. These brackets were sheathed in soft lead by the ancients; when the modern architects sought to repair as much of the Venetian damage as they could, they omitted the lead casings at the joints. As the iron oxidizes now, it expands. The joints of the new/old Parthenon are literally tearing the temple-blocks to pieces.

If one were to travel to the Parthenon today, one would find an enormous crane inside, scaffolding and train tracks all around, and a virtual army of stonecutters chiseling away: the building is being disassembled, a block at a time, so that the iron may now be replaced with titanium fittings. As for the damage that the smog and acid rains are doing each year to *all* of the Akropolis monuments, it may well be too late to do anything. The only truly apocalyptic moment in the tortured history of this temple is "modern" — by which I mean technological, contemporary, and nothing more.

Appendix 2

The Problematic Ending
of Mark's Gospel

As we have seen, we do not know precisely how Mark's performance "ends." Scholarly opinion is divided on this question and has in fact been so divisive that the debate has prompted at least one book-length monograph.[1] Many of the oldest surviving manuscripts that we possess have Mark's gospel ending at verse 16:8 — that is, with an empty tomb and a very palpable state of agonized confusion.[2] No one knows what has happened; everyone is too afraid to believe, to hope against hope, too afraid to speak. There is no explicit appearance of the risen Christ, no comforting words to the faithful followers he has redeemed and left behind, no privileged glance ahead into the future. We are all left in our personal Gethsemanes — staring into an absence, an abyss, listening but failing to hear, to a God grown suddenly, maddeningly silent.

The issue is further complicated by the fact that many other antique manuscripts testify to two different versions of a later epigraph, what is essentially a later, added ending, an explicit and unambiguous resurrection appearance.[3] In the shorter version, which consists of a single verse

---

1. William R. Farmer, *The Last Twelve Verses of Mark* (Cambridge: Cambridge Univ. Press, 1974). While Farmer claims to be presenting a completely neutral survey of this problem, he very clearly believes, and defends the view, that the longer ending of Mark is genuine and belonged to the Markan autograph (pp. 107–109).

2. For a concise and eloquent exposition of this argument, see R. H. Lightfoot's *The Gospel Message of St. Mark* (Oxford: Oxford Univ. Press, 1962) 80–97. In fact, to speak of the "oldest" manuscript may be misleading. It became a truism for the form-critics in the early 1970s that we face a fundamental paradox here, since "Mark is the earliest Gospel yet the latest, a source for other evangelists, but betraying latinisms, revisions and poetic compression of other Synoptic material" (G. W. Trompf, "The First Resurrection Appearance and the Ending of Mark's Gospel," *New Testament Studies* 18 [1972] 328). See also O. Linton, "Evidences of a Second Century Revised Edition of St. Mark's Gospel," *New Testament Studies* 14 (1968) 321.

3. In actual fact, our papyrological options are fivefold: some manuscripts preserve the longer ending 16:9–20; others preserve it but set it off with asterisks; others insert the much-maligned shorter ending in between 16:8 and the longer epigraph; some Latin

and is surely *not* authentic, Jesus appears to Peter and commissions all his followers to preach "the imperishable good news of eternal salvation." In the longer alternate ending to Mark's gospel (16:9–20), which seems to me to consist of a rather random sampling of the other gospel performances as well as Luke's *Acts of the Apostles,* Jesus appears first to Mary Magdalene and then to two anonymous student-disciples, all of whom pass the news along — *but are not believed.* Jesus himself appears next, commissions and singles out his true followers according to the miraculous powers they shall enjoy, then ascends triumphantly into heaven.

From a strictly practical point of view, it is far easier to imagine a later scribe, rather put off by the way he or she sees Mark "ending" — a little outrageously, and without a resurrection appearance — who chose to write one him- or herself, or rather, to include a sampling of stories he or she knew from the other gospel performances. It is far more difficult to imagine how the final leaf of an antique manuscript — and that arguably the most important one — should have dropped off in antiquity, leaving us with a gospel that breaks off in midstory and, according to some scholars, even in midsentence.[4] If Mark's gospel does indeed end at 16:8, then it ends with a rather curious two-word clause, which is especially clipped writing, even by Mark's curt standards. The two Mary's have met this mysterious young boy (*neaniskos*) at the empty tomb. They are told rather obtusely that Jesus "is not here." In terror, they flee the tomb and say nothing to anyone, "for they were afraid" (*ephobounto gar*).[5]

There are a number of good reasons to assume that Mark's gospel ends deliberately, and quite appropriately, at an empty tomb, without an explicit resurrection appearance. It is indeed a challenging and problematic ending, if it is genuine, but that should not really alarm us in a performance that is so unsettling on the whole. There are four ways of

---

versions possess only the shorter ending; and then, of course, many gospel manuscripts end at 16:8. See James K. Elliott, "The Text and Language of the Endings to Mark's Gospel," *Theologische Zeitschrift* 27 (1971) 255–256.

4. Dan O. Via, Jr., *The Ethics of Mark: In the Middle of Time* (Philadelphia: Fortress Press, 1985) 50–57; and Trompf, "The First Resurrection Appearance and the Ending of Mark's Gospel," 315.

5. Two things are worth noting about this last sentence in Mark's gospel. First is the heavy emphasis on negation, an idea that is as old as the beginning of the *Antigone:* "They told *nothing* to *no* one" (*Oudeni ouden eipan*). And second, this same allegedly problematic phrase, "For they were afraid," had *already* appeared in Mark's gospel: *Ephobounto gar auton,* "For they were afraid of him" (11:18). For another possibility, see Frederick Danker, "Postscript to the Markan Secrecy Motif," *Concordia Theological Monthly* 38 (1967) 24–27, where he argues that a single phrase has been lost from the manuscript: *Ephobounto phobon megan,* "They feared a great fear" — when a scribe's eye strayed too quickly to the end, reading *gar* for *-gan.*

getting at this problem — two of them rather specific, two of them much broader in range and significance. I would like to confront them in an ascending order of difficulty.

The first issue is a grammatical one, and it is rather easily dispensed with. As I have already mentioned, if Mark's gospel performance does draw down the curtain at 16:8, then it brings up the footlights at a particularly inauspicious moment — for the disciples and for Jesus, to say nothing of us. Mark's Greek also trails off, in a sense, with a postpositive particle, *gar*. The question is whether such a conclusion is grammatically possible. P. W. van der Horst has argued, convincingly I think, that it is grammatically acceptable for a book to end with this Greek particle, as Mark does if it ends at 16:8.[6] His reasoning is really very simple: if a sentence contains only two words, then the postpositive particle (which, by definition, must have a word that precedes it) will indeed be the last; if a sentence can end with such a particle, then so, too, can a chapter; and if a chapter can end this way, then so can a book.[7] He then goes on to cite Plotinus' *32nd Treatise,* which is indeed a book that "ends" with a *gar: teleioteron gar.* This makes it far less likely that the curious ending of Mark's gospel — with the self-same particle — is a sign that the final page(s) of an original manuscript was lost. Here, too, Mark's text is "seamless."

Having made his case rather strongly, van der Horst backs off a bit, refusing to commit himself absolutely on the question of whether *Mark* actually does end at 16:8. His only concern was to establish the *grammatical* possibility of a book's ending this way. "The problem is more complicated than that. A gospel without the appearance of the risen Lord is strange indeed."[8] We will be returning to this issue.

A second point is equally simple and concerns the internal evidence of the longer endings themselves. While Nietzsche cautions us to be duly skeptical of bad Christian philology, this is not to say that meaningful assessments of difficult texts can never be made. This is a case where things are relatively clear. One cannot escape the feeling, even on a first reading, that something has happened after 16:8, that "Mark" is no longer speaking the same way, if in fact *he* is speaking at all. While this is all strictly subjective, one *feels* that Mark's text has ended, and something else has been added on. Such subjective judgments begin to take on additional force when one considers certain statistical facts.[9] It

---

6. P. W. van der Horst, "Can a Book End with a *GAR?* A Note on *Mark* 16:8," *Journal of Theological Studies* 23 (1972) 121–124.

7. This phrase also appears much less strange, as I say, when we reflect that a similar phrase, *Ephobounto gar auton,* has already appeared at *Mark* 11:18.

8. Van der Horst, "Can a Book End with a *GAR?*" 123.

9. Farmer, *The Last Twelve Verses of Mark,* 103, is justly skeptical of making too

is surely astounding that, in an appendix consisting of only ninety-two different words, no fewer than twenty-four appear nowhere else in the entire gospel, or else appear in ways that do not square with Mark's normal understanding of the words.[10] And if this is not enough, it is surely telling that many of the words reflect direct borrowing from the other gospels — all of it accomplished with a lack of real sophistication and subtlety, when compared to Mark's performance as a whole.

So much, then, for the concrete, practical questions that seem to point toward a genuine Markan ending at 16:8. We need now to leave the somewhat firmer ground of philology for the slippier slopes of history and human error. We are entering upon the very difficult history of manuscripts themselves — how they were copied, edited, and handed on in antiquity. The task is further complicated by the fact that there are two kinds of evidence to consider: the oldest gospel manuscripts and "families" that derive from them, on the one hand; the discussions of the early church fathers, on the other, particularly in their gospel "harmonies" to which I have already referred in chapter 4. In most cases, we can argue only weakly from exclusion: if a particular writer does not refer to the text in a place where we should expect that he would, then we can often assume that he does not know the text, that the gospel known to him ends without one of these dubious appendices. This is not a particularly strong argument, but it is strengthened when we find specific mention — as we do in the gospel harmony composed by Eusebius in the fourth century — of "these words" (*ephobounto gar*) with which

> almost all copies of the gospel according to Mark ... [come] to an end. What follows — *which is met with seldom, and only in some copies, certainly not in all* — might be dispensed with; especially if it should prove to contradict the record of the other Evangelists.[11]

An apparently stunning proof of the point that the crude additions to the gospel were grafted later onto the original Markan text.

William Farmer has an interesting way of dealing with these matters. He argues that the ending of Mark *was deleted* from the manuscripts at a relatively early date (the second century) by some overzealous Alexandrian scribes who, once again, were philologists applying what they had learned from Homeric criticism to the gospels. There were two overriding principles that animated their decision to excise a text: (1) the most ancient readings are to be preferred (which counts as evidence to *support* an original ending at 16:8); and (2) passages should be deleted that

---

much of statistics. No author writes with a calculator *and* a pen in hand. Still, his own opinions lead him to ignore what is surely some very strong evidence.

10. Elliott, "The Text and Language of the Endings to Mark's Gospel," 258–262.

11. See Farmer, *The Last Twelve Verses of Mark*, 4–21.

would be offensive to the gods. It is due to this latter point, Farmer argues, that the Alexandrians would have deleted *Mark* 16:9–20: it does not harmonize with the other resurrection accounts regarding time and setting.

This is a fairly flimsy point on which to base so much of the argument — especially when there are far more pressing matters of chronological divergence in the various gospel performances that were retained. Farmer's conclusion makes too much of Alexandria's ability to alter single-handedly the entire manuscript tradition of Mark's gospel. B. H. Streeter — who himself argued for the inauthenticity of *Mark* 16:9–20 and believed the gospel originally ended in much the same manner that John does — provided a much fuller and more suggestive account of what has happened here.[12]

Streeter divides the manuscript tradition up into five "families" of texts and then traces the subsequent histories of each family through two related levels of testimonia: the subsequent documents that were presumably copied from the original; and the citations of the early patristic writers who were presumably quoting from "their" family of manuscripts. This evidence is suggestive, and I will simply list it here. The five "families"[13] that Streeter identifies are as follows:

Alexandria: The first manuscripts (B, ℵ) both *omit* the longer ending of Mark's gospel. The subsequent documents are *divided evenly* on the question of inclusion.[14] *No early patristic writers* from the area — Origin, Athanasius, or Cyril — quote from it, although all had ample opportunity to do so if they knew it.

Antioch: The parent manuscript (Syr[s]) *omits* the ending. But all subsequent documents *include* it. No real relevant patristic evidence exists.

Caesarea: The first manuscripts (Θ and 565[mk]) *include* the longer ending. Subsequently, the Greek texts *include* it but a compelling number of Armenian manuscripts (and the Georgian manuscripts that were translated from them) *exclude* it.[15] Moreover, the patristic authors, while

---

12. B. H. Streeter, *The Four Gospels* (New York: Macmillan, 1925) 333–360.

13. For Streeter's own extremely cautious definition of what constitutes a "family" or a "text," see his "Caesarean Text of the Gospels," *Journal of Theological Studies* (1924/5) 373–378.

14. See Bruce M. Metzger, "The Ending of the Gospel according to Mark in the Ethiopic Manuscripts," in *Understanding the Sacred Text: Essays in Honor of Morton S. Enslin on the Hebrew Bible and Christian Beginnings,* ed. John Reumann (Valley Forge, Pa.: Judson Press, 1972) 167–180, for an interesting discussion of the complex of traditions (Syriac, Greek, Coptic) that together constitute the phenomenon that is North African Christianity.

15. See Ernest C. Colwell, "*Mark* 16:9–20 in the Armenian Version," *Journal of Biblical Literature* 56 (1937) 369–386; but also Bruce M. Metzger, "The Caesarean Text of the Gospels," *Journal of Biblical Literature* 64 (1945) 457–489, which calls the legitimacy of this whole textual "family" into question.

ambivalent, *all tend toward exclusion*—most notably Origen (who spent time there); Eusebius, as we have seen; and the Cappadocian Fathers.

Italy/Gaul: All authorities *unanimously include* the longer ending.

Carthage: The first manuscript (k[mk, mt]) *omits* the longer ending, while most later texts *include* it. But here again, the patristic authors—as early as Tertullian and as late as Cyprian—*do not know the longer ending* of Mark's gospel.

This manuscript history certainly *is* complicated and ambiguous. But two facts are suggestive. First, it is interesting that the longer ending of Mark is consistently defended *only* in Italy, which is to say, in Rome—which might have had a very clear need of it, lending, as it does, a greater authority to the fallen figure of Peter, their bishop. Evidence points in the direction of exclusion in both North Africa and the Near East—a region much closer to where the Markan autograph would presumably have been deposited. What I find interesting is the same split we observed in the last chapter: between the Latin West and the Greek, the Orthodox East. It is a split that is here embedded in the manuscript tradition itself. And it leads naturally to our next question.

Most of the arguments that worry about a gospel ending as *Mark* does at 16:8 (if it does) all circle around the same question: What in the world is such an ending about? We need first to turn this question around: What in the world is *Mark* 16:9–20 about? In a word, it is a naïve "ending" that violates all the rich nuance and theological subtlety that has characterized Mark's performance up to this point:

> *Mark* 16:9–20 contains promises of Jesus to which the church has never succeeded in accommodating itself, except by unconscious repression. Most Christians do not know what these verses teach. They are seldom if ever expounded from the pulpit and almost never appealed to in didactic circumstances. Christians have long since learned to live with the promises by paying them no serious attention and to regard all efforts to take them seriously as bizarre acts of unfaith on the part of ignorant or misguided sectarians.[16]

Let us be clear. The claims that are ventured in 16:9–20 are nothing short of bizarre, particularly as an appendix to Mark's performance. Suddenly, all of the ambiguity has disappeared. The time of secrecy and mystery is over. Henceforth, the true Christians will be known by powerful signs and magic: they will handle serpents and not be stung; they will drink poison and not die. Anti-Christians long before Nietzsche censured the church for this stupendous claim, which is surely hybristic

---

16. Farmer, *The Last Twelve Verses of Mark,* 65–66.

and, at least in the world Mark has created, borders on the insane. Already in Porphyry, we hear the challenge: if one really wants to test the faithful, give them poison to drink! Let them prove their alleged superiority to Socrates! If they accept, do so, and die, so much the worse for them. If they do not take up the challenge, then their own "faith" is disproved.[17] On my view, this is *precisely* the kind of criticism that *Mark himself* was leveling at the churches of his own day. He crafted his "gospel" performance precisely to counter the cheap optimism and pretentious piety of the Christian community in his own day. On such a view, it would have been positively *perverse* for him to have ended his story this way.

Only one question remains, then, a *theological* question. What in the world *is* Mark's "ending" (at 16:8, now) all about? From a literary perspective, it might seem far less strange. Norman R. Petersen has argued,[18] with great sensitivity to this performance, that Mark's conclusion is far less ambiguous than is often alleged. Those who want to make Mark postmodern try to read the end of his gospel as if it were the end of the matter, almost as if Mark were an existentialist — a completely decentered, perhaps even an atheistic thinker — two thousand years before his time. Mark's gospel tells a different story. While his narrative ends at 16:8, Mark's narrative world extends far beyond it, providing the text with a poetic closure that it appears, on its surface, to lack. Through a series of narrative premonitions, both in the form of Jesus' Passion-predictions (8:31; 9:31; 10:33) and the more extended apocalyptic discourse (chap. 13), Mark has carefully nurtured an expectation in the reader that will not be destroyed by the way this gospel "ends":

> The effect of [chapter] 13 is to minimize the significance of the disciples' abandonment of Jesus and to emphasize the expectation that they will soon abandon their mistaken point of view and return to Jesus....In the final analysis it is the literary fact that the implied reader knows that most of the events of *Mark* 13 *have* come to pass which accounts for the literary and hermeneutical force of the chapter.[19]

The end of this performance is not the end of the story. And one thing more. Given the fact that this document was written, as I have said, by people and for people who already knew the story, its listeners already knew — and believed in — what happened next. Despite the fact that the women run away from the empty tomb terrified and tell no

---

17. See Farmer's discussion in ibid., 68–69.
18. Norman R. Petersen, "When Is the End Not the End?" *Interpretation* 34:2 (1980) 151–166.
19. Ibid., 166.

one what they have seen, God's word still gets out. That is the mystery Mark teaches.

Why, then, does Mark choose to "end" things this way? What were his listeners supposed to learn? Beyond a strictly literary concern for "closure," what is the point of a story that ends, quite literally, at an empty tomb, on a note of abject fear and failed expectations? Perhaps this fear and failure are themselves the point. Hans Conzelmann rejects the traditional view that the Passion narrative is an apologetic attempt on the part of the early Christian community to portray its saviour as a man who was not overwhelmed by catastrophe but rather willingly and in full control embraced his Fate. That is much more the Johannine view — Fate, not Destiny. The Synoptists — and Mark most dramatically — tell another story:

> This explanation is insufficient. It does not do the text justice. The intention is not to explain that the offense of the cross is removed by the resurrection. The intention of the text is precisely the opposite. It wishes to show that the *passion* is the necessary condition for glory, and therewith for the continuing qualification of faith even after Easter. For that reason, the story of suffering is an indispensable ingredient of the gospel. Through it the scandal is *retained*.... The passion narrative is a bolt which bars every opening to a *christologia gloriae*.[20]

The point, for Mark, is that the Passion is a significant and "closed" moment in and of itself. The resurrection is another such moment. The Passion itself, if not exactly glorious, is the necessary prelude to glory, the very stuff of which the tragedy is made. "Life is to be understood out of *suffering* — that is the tragic in tragedy."[21] It is the *failed understanding* of those closest to Jesus that seems to animate a narrative that ends so oddly, yet so decisively, in this fashion.

Thus it is grammatically, literarily, and theologically possible that Mark's gospel was conceived with this end in mind. Which is to say, he tells us a story that — like all the best tragedies — has a clear beginning, but no end.

---

20. Hans Conzelmann, "History and Theology in the Passion Narratives of the Synoptic Gospels," *Interpretation* 24:2 (1970) 185.
21. Nietzsche, *Wir Philologen*, 6[20]; *Sämtliche Werke*, VIII, 106.

Acknowledgments

It might seem a bit odd to be thanking others for their assistance in helping expose me to tragedy. Odder still it must seem to be thanking others for their tragic sense of life, that vision of which this book has hopefully been one expression. It is one of my primary contentions that such thanks are most in order, that there is little else to be quite so profoundly thankful for. But I have been working on many of these thoughts for the better part of a decade now, and will not be able to thank everyone I should be thanking.

Some of these ideas, particularly the ones equating gospels and tragedies, were addressed for the first time in a masters thesis composed at Duke University under the gentle direction of Stuart C. Henry, Emeritus Professor of American Christianity. In addition to being the best read and most reflective person I knew in those years, Stuart became a dear personal friend. I recall as a sort of watershed moment the first time he reminded me of a Platonic thought my soul surely had known once — namely, that the Greeks did not go to the theater to learn the stories, which they already knew, but rather to see them performed, and thus, to learn something about *themselves*. It is Stuart's deep sensitivity to the lived, performative reality of tragic drama — the lovely necessities of human life on the stage — that is, I hope, with me still in this book.

In the first year of my transition from a masters program at Duke to a doctoral program at Emory University, I was delighted to make the acquaintance of William Arrowsmith and Herbert Golder, both then in the Classics Department. They generously invited me in to their Greek translation seminars. I had already spent a propitious year translating Euripides with Peter Burian at Duke — another watershed event. I continued to read Euripides with William Arrowsmith, then spent a second year reading Sophocles and Plato with Herbert Golder. I customarily provide my own translations of the classical material in this book, unless otherwise noted, and while my own translations are scholarly and wooden, falling far short of their much easier grace, I owe virtually everything I know or do not know about translating to these men. I learned an aesthetic sensitivity, a passion for the fullest turn of phrase

(Bill once called translation "breaking the spine of the original"), from them.

William Arrowsmith passed away rather suddenly in 1992. A true Coriolanus of the mind, Bill helped me to realize — through Sophocles and Euripides, of course, but also through Shakespeare and Eliot, Nietzsche and Jerome, Aristophanes and Petronius, and Antonioni, and even John Jay Chapman — that there is indeed "a world elsewhere." His educational vision was, quite simply, his own passionate version of the tragic vision I am after here. As such, his vision was the purest extension of him-self. He is sorely and profoundly missed.

When my thoughts returned to the gospels, particularly to Mark's gospel, I was blessed to find in Vernon K. Robbins a fellow-traveler along that complex path which leads us, through them, back into the mysteries of the Greco-Roman world. My dissertation would not have been completed without Vernon's constant support and gracious friendship, nor would this book have been written.

The same holds true for a group of fellow students in the Department of Ethics and Society who were unusual, by any standards, for their deep commitment both to one another and to the betterment of our thinking and of our world. Among them Robert Carle, Barbara Elwell, Arthur E. Farnsley II, Peter Gathje, Fred Glennon, Gary Hauk, Christine Pohl, Adele Resmer, Karen Root, Jim Thobaben, Scott Thumma, and Darryl Trimiew all listened to more of my tragic ruminations than anyone should be forced to do. That they did so with such unflagging good cheer and enthusiasm is a testament to their scholarly, and other, virtues.

So also for the members of my doctoral committee at Emory, who saw this project through to that most tentative of scholarly conclusions we call a "dissertation." Nancy Ammermann, Clinton Gardner, Stephen Tipton, and Theodore Weber all provided moments of insight and support when needed most. A special word of thanks is due to Jon P. Gunnemann, who directed the dissertation, but who even more generously reviewed the manuscript in its present form. In that analysis, it was clear that Jon understood aspects of what I had been attempting to say better than I did, and so has done what teachers ideally do best — *educate*. Jon is one of the purest teachers and educators it has been my good fortune to know.

I completed my dissertation during a two-year tenure as a Visiting Scholar at the American School of Classical Studies in Athens, Greece. Blessed as I had been in Atlanta, I was even more so in Athens. The school was an uncannily generous intellectual environment and a most congenial place in which to work. Special thanks are due to William Coulson, the president of the school, who so kindly sponsored my visit;

to Nancy Winter, custodian of the Blegen Library, a really remarkable collection of classical and postclassical resources; and especially to Robert Bridges, then Secretary of the school, who became both a good personal friend and an eager conversation partner on all matters philosophical, cultural, and humane.

A related word of thanks is due to the Charlotte W. Newcombe Dissertation Fellowship Committee, whose financial and institutional support allowed me to stay on for a second year in Athens, and so to finish both the dissertation and the degree. Luck, as the Greeks knew well, does play a role in a human life.

Returning to one's alma mater can be a trying experience. In my case it was not, doubtless in part because my academic homes have all been so friendly. I returned to Atlanta and to Emory University in the spring of 1991, where I began teaching in the undergraduate Department of Religion. Year by year, I am happily there still. Given the impossibly complex relationships between graduate seminaries and undergraduate departments in the major American universities, my new/old colleagues were mostly unknown to me. So, as Eliot would have it, I was coming home to a place that I was also seeing for the first time. My colleagues here have been almost embarrassingly congenial and welcoming. It is largely through the gentle prodding and quiet enthusiasm of our chairman, Paul Courtright, that my own work has begun to see its way into print. Paul's contagious enthusiasm for everything intellectual and departmental has helped to create an environment of real nurture and care, so necessary to work that otherwise can seem damningly lonely at times.

That is equally true of my editor at Continuum, Justus George Lawler, whose enthusiasm for a short piece I published on Mark's gospel led to further discussions out of which this book has finally emerged. I have found in George that marvelous balance between patient forbearance and firm prodding; he has stood firmly by suggestions that have made the book infinitely better, all the while reminding me that the book is mine and needs to say what I would have it say. Yet the book, of course, is not simply mine, thanks to his careful and loving assistance.

A family relationship to a scholarly book is always a little hard to place. The sad fact is that a family can only look on in a kind of muddled awe as the thinker goes off, book in one hand and coffee cup in the other, to think, *alone*. When the book deals with tragedy, the muddling is doubled, perhaps even trebled. My parents made the generous gift of a computer to me one Christmas shortly before I jetted off to Greece. Since I have composed this *entire* book on that machine, my mother and father have been present in this project, quite literally, every day.

So too has my brother Tom, an aspiring young comedian who has — through the force of his humor and shining personal example — helped to remind me of that deep connection between that which delights us and that which we dread. He is my sore conscience, a chuckling reminder of the book that this might have become, and did not become. There is no gain without a loss.

In my first year of graduate study, I visited my other brother Clifford, who was then a religion major at Williams College. I recall, as another sort of watershed moment, a dinner party in which he and his friends welcomed me to an autumn in the Berkshires. Cliff and his roommate, Miguel Vatter, made passing and repeated reference to something they laughingly called "the tragic posture" over several bottles of good red wine. They may have forgotten this. I have not. I have spent the past eight years trying to figure out what the joke was all about. This book is my first tentative answer, addressed in part to them. It emerges at the same time that Cliff has engaged to marry — in fact, by the time this book *is* a book, he will be a husband. Here again, a human life mirrors a text: tragic postures giving way to real, and profound, and magic-making joy. The fact that there is more than one will in the world is a blessing to be treasured, as my soon-sister-to-be, Patty Carlson, is.

This book is, quite naturally, devoted to others as well. My graduate career was blessed by two friendships that far exceed my ability to say or repay. Jeffery Wilson, who is currently roughing out a dissertation on Kant's *Critique of Judgment* is, simply put, the most careful reader, and thinker, it has ever been my good fortune to know. His quiet insistence, his passion really, for the well-chosen word and the well-worked idea has inspired me and daunted me throughout the preparation of this manuscript. It is my hope that the book is worthy of his further musings.

James J. Winchester was one of the first graduate students I ever met in Atlanta. He is teaching now at Spelman College and has recently completed an important book entitled *Nietzsche's Aesthetic Turn* (State Univ. of New York Press, 1994) which is a familiar title in my footnotes. His gifts are too numerous to list. Suffice it to say that it was he who first gave me a taste of Nietzsche's more *human* face, the credibility and real passion of a philosopher I had not been inclined to personally or professionally before then. I now like both the man and the thought, very much, and deeply love the friend who introduced us. Jim and his wife, Eve, recently received (if that is the proper image) their first child, Sophia, on the first of April; with the passing of time, the birthing of new thoughts and new lives, a sense of life's overabundant mystery grows apace.

Life's mystery *and* life's richness. These last words of thanks are also the most difficult, aware as I am of the word's inadequacies. Barney L. Jones was a mentor to me throughout my college career; he and his wife, Marjorie, have been even more precious friends since then. Barney has graciously and quietly and devotedly read *every* word I have ever written since our first meeting in 1981. He has pushed me to write, even and especially when I did not wish to do so. He helped me understand, first, that this really *is* what I love to do, and second, *why* it is so. Apart from long walks on the Bridgehampton beaches, and endless hours in his garden and study, I would never have thought this book through at all. Barney's gentle and worldly wisdom, *his* faith and love, stand behind *every* word here. And it is to him that this book is dedicated, with my profoundest gratitude and love.

Working Bibliography

General: Introduction and Afterword

Agnew, Jean-Christophe. *Worlds Apart: The Market and the Theatre in Anglo-American Thought, 1550–1750.* New York: Cambridge Univ. Press, 1986.

Arrowsmith, William. "The Criticism of Greek Tragedy." *Tulane Drama Review* 3:3 (1959) 31–57.

———. Editor's and translator's introduction to *Alcestis,* vii–xi, 3–29. New York: Oxford Univ. Press, 1974.

———. "The Future of Teaching." *ARION* 6:1 (1967) 5–22.

———. "A Greek Theater of Ideas." *ARION,* o.s., 2:3 (1963) 32–56.

———. "St. Jerome on Translation: A Breviary." *ARION,* n.s., 2:3 (1976) 358–367.

Barbour, John D. *Tragedy as a Critique of Virtue: The Novel and Ethical Reflection.* Chico, Calif.: Scholars Press, 1984.

Bellah, Robert, et al. *Habits of the Heart: Individualism and Commitment in American Life.* Berkeley: Univ. of California Press, 1985.

Benjamin, Walter. *Illuminations: Essays and Reflections.* Edited by Hannah Arendt and translated by Harry Zohn. New York: Schocken Books, 1968.

———. *The Origin of German Tragic Drama.* Translated by John Osborne. New York: New Left Books, 1977.

Bentley, Eric, ed. *The Classic Theatre.* New York: Doubleday:
   Six Italian Plays. Vol. 1 (1958);
   Five German Plays. Vol. 2 (1959);
   Six Spanish Plays. Vol. 3 (1959);
   Six French Plays. Vol. 4 (1961).

———. *The Dramatic Event: An American Chronicle.* Boston: Beacon Press, 1954.

Berger, Peter. *The Sacred Canopy: Elements of a Sociological Theory of Religion.* Garden City, N.Y.: Doubleday, 1967.

Bevington, David M. *From Mankind to Marlowe: Growth of Structure in the Popular Drama of Tudor England.* Cambridge, Mass.: Harvard Univ. Press, 1962.

Bloom, Allan. *The Closing of the American Mind.* New York: Simon and Schuster, 1987.

Blumenberg, Hans. *The Legitimacy of the Modern Age.* Translated by Robert M. Wallace. Cambridge, Mass.: MIT Press, 1983.

Browne, E. Martin. *Religious Drama II: Mystery and Morality Plays*. New York: Meridian Books, 1959.

Butler, Eliza Marian. *The Tyranny of Greece over Germany*. New York: Macmillan, 1935.

Corrigan, Robert W. *Tragedy: Vision and Form*. San Francisco: Chandler, 1965.

Cross, R. C. "Logos and Form in Plato." *MIND* 63:252 (1954) 433–450.

Cumming, Robert Denoon. *Starting Point: An Introduction to the Dialectics of Existence*. Chicago: Univ. of Chicago Press, 1979.

Davidson, H. R. Ellis. *Gods and Myths of Northern Europe*. New York: Penguin Books, 1964.

Derrida, Jacques. *Dissemination*. Translated by Barbara Johnson. Chicago: Univ. of Chicago Press, 1981.

——. *Of Grammatology*. Translated by Gayatri Chakravorty Spivak. Baltimore: Johns Hopkins Univ. Press, 1974, 1976.

——. *Positions*. Translated and annotated by Alan Bass. Chicago: Univ. of Chicago Press, 1981.

Devereux, Daniel T. "Particular and Universal in Aristotle's Conception of Practical Knowledge." *Review of Metaphysics* 39 (1986) 483–504.

Dinsmoor, William Bell. "The Athenian Theatre in the Fifth Century." In *Studies Presented to David M. Robinson*. Vol. 1 (1951) 309–330.

——. "Debunking Greece." *Art Digest* (July 1936) 13–33.

——. "Intellectual Relations between Greece and the United States." *Columbia University Quarterly* 30 (1938) 111–120.

Donegan, Alan. *The Theory of Morality*. Chicago: Univ. of Chicago Press, 1977.

Douglas, Mary, and Steven Tipton, eds. *Religion and America: Spiritual Life in a Secular Age*. Boston: Beacon Press, 1982.

Dover, Kenneth. *Aristophanic Comedy*. Berkeley: Univ. of California Press, 1972.

——. *Greek Homosexuality*. Cambridge, Mass.: Harvard Univ. Press, 1977.

——. *Greek Popular Morality in the Time of Plato and Aristotle*. Berkeley: Univ. of California Press, 1974.

Eliot, T. S. *Essays on Elizabethan Drama*. New York: Harcourt, Brace and World, 1960.

Else, Gerald F. "The Origin of *TRAGODIA*." *Hermes* 85 (1957) 17–46.

——. *Aristotle's Poetics: The Argument*. Cambridge, Mass.: Harvard Univ. Press, 1957.

Farley, Wendy. *Tragic Vision and Divine Compassion: A Contemporary Theodicy*. Louisville: Westminster/John Knox Press, 1990.

Fergusson, Francis. *The Idea of a Theater: A Study of Ten Plays*. Princeton, N.J.: Princeton Univ. Press, 1949.

——. *Shakespeare: The Pattern in His Carpet*. New York: Delacorte Press, 1958, 1970.

Flanagan, Hallie. *Arena*. New York: Duell, Sloan and Pearce, 1940.

Flynn, Thomas R. *Sartre and Marxist Existentialism: The Test Case of Collective Responsibility*. Chicago: Univ. of Chicago Press, 1984.

Giddens, Anthony. *The Nation-State and Violence*. Berkeley: Univ. of California Press, 1985.
———. *The Consequences of Modernity*. Stanford, Calif.: Stanford Univ. Press, 1990.
Girard, René. *Violence and the Sacred*. Translated by Patrick Gregory. Baltimore: Johns Hopkins Univ. Press, 1972, 1977.
Golden, Leon. "Toward a Definition of Tragedy." *Classical Journal* 72:1 (1976) 21–33.
Goldhill, Simon. "The Great Dionysia and Civic Ideology." In *Nothing to Do with Dionysus? Athenian Drama in Its Social Context*, edited by John J. Winkler and Froma I. Zeitlin, 97–129. Princeton, N.J.: Princeton Univ. Press, 1990.
Goldmann, Lucien. *The Philosophy of the Enlightenment*. Translated by Henry Maas. Cambridge, Mass.: MIT Press, 1968, 1973.
Gomme, A. H. *Jacobean Tragedies*. New York: Oxford Univ. Press, 1969.
Green, Peter. *The Shadow of the Parthenon*. Berkeley: Univ. of California Press, 1972.
Gunnemann, Jon P. "Human Rights and Modernity: The Truth of the Fiction of Individual Rights." *Journal of Religious Ethics* 161 (1988) 160–189.
Habermas, Jürgen. *Communication and the Evolution of Society*. Translated by Thomas McCarthy. Boston: Beacon Press, 1976, 1979.
———. *The Philosophical Discourse of Modernity*. Translated by Frederick Lawrence. Cambridge, Mass.: MIT Press, 1985, 1987.
———. *The Theory of Communicative Action*. Translated by Thomas McCarthy. 2 vols. Boston: Beacon Press, 1981, 1984, 1989.
———. *Toward a Rational Society*. Translated by Jeremy J. Shapiro. Boston: Beacon Press, 1968, 1970.
Halverson, Marvin. *Religious Drama*. Vols. 1 and 3. New York: Meridian Books, 1957, 1959.
Hamilton, Edith. *Echo of Greece*. New York: W. W. Norton, 1957.
———. *The Greek Way*. New York: W. W. Norton, 1930.
———. *The Roman Way*. New York: W. W. Norton, 1932.
———. *Three Greek Plays*. New York: W. W. Norton, 1937.
Harrison, Jane Ellen. *Themis: A Study of the Social Origins of Greek Religion*. Cambridge: Cambridge Univ. Press, 1912.
Hauerwas, Stanley. *After Christendom? How the Church Is to Behave If Freedom, Justice and a Christian Nation Are Bad Ideas*. Nashville: Abingdon, 1990.
———. "Can Aristotle Be a Liberal? Or, Nussbaum on Luck." *Soundings* 72:4 (1989) 675–691.
———. *A Community of Character*. Notre Dame, Ind.: Univ. of Notre Dame Press, 1981.
———. *The Peaceable Kingdom*. Notre Dame, Ind.: Univ. of Notre Dame Press, 1983.
———. *Truthfulness and Tragedy*. Notre Dame, Ind.: Univ. of Notre Dame Press, 1977.

————. *Vision and Virtue*. Notre Dame, Ind.: Univ. of Notre Dame Press, 1974.

Havelock, Eric A. *The Greek Concept of Justice*. Cambridge, Mass.: Harvard Univ. Press, 1978.

Henderson, Jeffrey. "The *Dēmos* and the Comic Competition." In *Nothing to Do with Dionysus? Athenian Drama in Its Social Context*, edited by John J. Winkler and Froma I. Zeitlin, 271–313. Princeton, N.J.: Princeton Univ. Press, 1990.

Hirsch, E. D. *Cultural Literacy: What Every American Needs to Know*. Boston: Houghton Mifflin, 1987.

Hirzel, Rudolf. *Themis, Dike, und Verwandtes: Ein Beitrag zur Geschichte des Rechtsidees bei den Griechen*. Hildesheim: Georg Olms Verlagsbuchhandlung, 1966.

Hollander, Lee M., trans. *The Saga of the Jómsvíkings*. Austin: Univ. of Texas Press, 1955.

Jaeger, Werner. *Aristotle: Fundamentals of His Development*. London: Oxford Univ. Press, 1934, 1967.

————. *Paideia: The Ideals of Greek Culture*. Translated by Gilbert Highet. 3 vols. New York: Oxford Univ. Press, 1939, 1945.

————. *The Theology of the Early Greek Philosophers*. Translated by Edward S. Robinson. Westport, Conn.: Greenwood Press, 1947, 1960, 1980.

Janko, Richard. *Aristotle on Comedy: Towards a Reconstruction of Poetics II*. Berkeley: Univ. of California Press, 1984.

Kagan, Donald. "The Speeches in Thucydides and the Mytilene Debate." *Yale Classical Studies* 24 (1979) 71–94.

Kallen, Horace M. *The Book of Job as a Greek Tragedy*. New York: Hill and Wang, Dramabooks, 1918, 1959.

Kant, Immanuel. *The Critique of Judgment*. Translated by Werner S. Pluhar. Indianapolis, Ind.: Hackett, 1987.

————. *The Critique of Practical Reason*. Translated by Lewis White Beck. New York: Macmillan, 1956, 1985.

————. *Foundations of the Metaphysics of Morals*. Translated by Lewis White Beck. Indianapolis: Bobbs-Merrill, 1959.

————. *Lectures on Ethics*. Translated by Louis Infield. New York: Harper and Row, 1934, 1960.

————. *Religion within the Limits of Reason Alone*. Translated by Theodore M. Greene and Hoyt H. Hudson. New York: Harper and Row, 1934, 1960.

Kaufmann, Walter. *Existentialism: From Dostoevsky to Sartre*. New York: World, 1956.

————. *Tragedy and Philosophy*. Princeton, N.J.: Princeton Univ. Press, 1968, 1979.

Kelsen, H. "Aristotle and Hellenic Macedonian Policy." *Journal of International Ethics* 48:8 (1937) 1–64.

Kerr, Walter. *The Decline of Pleasure*. New York: Simon and Schuster, 1962.

————. *Tragedy and Comedy*. New York: Simon and Schuster, 1967.

Kokolakis, Minos. "Homeric Poetry and Tragedy." Athens: Univ. of Athens Offprints Series, 1975.

Krieger, Murray. *The Tragic Vision.* Baltimore: Johns Hopkins Univ. Press, 1960.

Lindbeck, George. *The Nature of Doctrine: Religion and Theology in a Postliberal Age.* Philadelphia: Westminster Press, 1984.

Longo, Oddone. "The Theater of the *Polis.*" Translated by John J. Winkler. In *Nothing to Do with Dionysus? Athenian Drama in Its Social Setting,* edited by John J. Winkler and Froma I. Zeitlin, 12–19. Princeton, N.J.: Princeton Univ. Press, 1990.

Lukács, Georg. *Soul and Form.* Translated by Anna Bostock. Cambridge, Mass.: MIT Press, 1974.

MacIntyre, Alasdair. *After Virtue,* 2d ed. Notre Dame, Ind.: Univ. of Notre Dame Press, 1984.

———. *Against the Self-Images of the Age: Essays on Ideology and Philosophy.* Notre Dame, Ind.: Univ. of Notre Dame Press, 1978.

———. "Ancient Politics and Modern Issues." *ARION,* n.s., 1:2 (1974) 425–430.

———. "How Virtues Become Vices: Values, Medicine and Social Context." In *Evaluation and Explanation in the Biomedical Sciences,* edited by H. T. Engelhardt and S. Spicher, 97–121. Dordrecht: D. Reidel, 1975.

———. *Marxism and Christianity.* Notre Dame, Ind.: Univ. of Notre Dame Press, 1968, 1984.

———. "Relativism, Power, and Philosophy." In *After Philosophy,* edited by Kenneth Baynes, James Bohman, and Thomas McCarthy, 385–411. Cambridge, Mass.: MIT Press, 1987.

———. *A Short History of Ethics.* New York: Macmillan, Collier Books, 1966.

———. *Three Rival Versions of Moral Enquiry: Encyclopedia, Genealogy and Tradition.* Notre Dame, Ind.: Univ. of Notre Dame Press, 1990.

———. *The Unconscious.* London: Routledge and Kegan Paul, 1958.

———. *Whose Justice? Which Rationality?* Notre Dame, Ind.: Univ. of Notre Dame Press, 1988.

Magnusson, Magnus, and Herman Pálsson, trans. *King Harald's Saga.* New York: Penguin Books, 1966.

———. *Njal's Saga.* New York: Penguin Books, 1960.

Mead, George Herbert. *Mind, Self and Society.* Edited by Charles W. Morris. Chicago: Univ. of Chicago Press, 1934.

———. *Movements of Thought in the Nineteenth Century.* Edited by Merritt H. Moore. Chicago: Univ. of Chicago Press, 1936.

Miller, Fred D. "Aristotle on Rationality in Action." *Review of Metaphysics* 37 (1984) 499–520.

Nelson, Robert J. "Tragedy and the Tragic." *ARION* 2:4 (1963) 86–95.

Newman, John Kevin. *The Classical Epic Tradition.* Madison: Univ. of Wisconsin Press, 1986.

Nussbaum, Martha Craven. *Aristotle's "De Motu Animalum."* Princeton, N.J.: Princeton Univ. Press, 1978.

————. *The Fragility of Goodness: Luck and Ethics in Greek Tragedy and Philosophy.* Cambridge: Cambridge Univ. Press, 1986.

————. *Love's Knowledge: Essays On Philosophy and Literature.* New York: Oxford Univ. Press, 1990.

————. "Non-relative Virtues: An Aristotelian Approach." *Midwest Studies in Philosophy* 13 (1988) 32–53.

————. "Shame, Separateness, and Political Unity: Aristotle's Criticism of Plato." In *Essays on Aristotle's Ethics,* edited by Amelie O. Rorty, 395–435. Berkeley: Univ. of California Press, 1980.

Nussbaum, Martha Craven, with Amelie O. Rorty. *Essays on Aristotle's "De Anima."* Oxford: Clarendon Press, 1992.

Ong, Walter J. "Agonistic Structures in Academia: Past to Present." *Daedalus* 103:4 (1974) 229–238.

Pálsson, Hermann, and Paul Edwards, trans. *Egil's Saga.* New York: Penguin Books, 1976.

————. *Eurbyggja Saga.* New York: Penguin Books, 1972.

Pickard-Cambridge, Sir Arthur. *Dithyramb, Tragedy and Comedy.* Oxford: Clarendon Press, 1927.

————. *The Dramatic Festivals of Athens.* London: Oxford Univ. Press, 1968.

Redfield, James M. *Nature and Culture in the Iliad: The Tragedy of Hector.* Chicago: Univ. of Chicago Press, 1975.

Rorty, Amelie O., ed. *Essays on Aristotle's Ethics.* Berkeley: Univ. of California Press, 1980.

Rose, Martial. *The Wakefield Mystery Plays.* New York: Doubleday, 1963.

Ross, W. D. *Aristotle.* London: Methuen, 1923, 1956.

Ruprecht, Louis A., Jr. "After Virtue? On Distorted Philosophical Narratives." *Continuum* (1994).

————. "His House, Her Home: Heidegger on the Ancient Greeks and Germans." *ARION* (forthcoming).

————. "In the Aftermath of Modernism: On the Postures of the Present and Their Portrait of the Past." *Soundings* 75:2/3 (1992) 255–285.

————. "Martha Nussbaum: On Tragedy and the Modern Ethos." *Soundings* 72:4 (1989) 589–605.

Sartre, Jean-Paul. *The Age of Reason.* Translated by Eric Sutton. New York: Bantam Books, 1947, 1959.

————. *Being and Nothingness.* Translated by Hazel Barnes. New York: Philosophical Library, 1943, 1956.

————. *L'Etre et le Néant.* Paris: Editions Gallimard, 1943.

————. *Nausea.* Translated by Lloyd Alexander. New York: New Directions Paperbacks, 1949, 1959.

————. *No Exit and Three Other Plays.* Translated by Stuart Gilbert and Lionel Abel. New York: Random House, 1955.

————. *Sartre: On Theater.* Interviews translated by Frank Jellinek. New York: Random House, 1976.

————. *The Words.* Translated by Bernard Frechtman. New York: George Braziller, 1964.

Steiner, George. *After Babel: Aspects of Language and Translation*. New York: Oxford Univ. Press, 1974.

———. *In Bluebeard's Castle: Some Notes toward a Redefinition of Culture*. New Haven: Yale Univ. Press, 1971.

———. *The Death of Tragedy*. New York: Hill and Wang, Dramabooks, 1961.

———. *George Steiner: A Reader*. London: Penguin Books, 1984.

———. "Real Presences." The Leslie Stephen Memorial Lecture. Cambridge: Cambridge Univ. Press, 1986.

———. *Real Presences*. Chicago: Univ. of Chicago Press, 1989.

———. "Why English?" The English Association Presidential Address (July, 1975).

———, ed., with Robert Fagles. *Homer: A Collection of Critical Essays*. Englewood Cliffs, N.J.: Prentice-Hall, 1962.

Stout, Jeffrey. *Ethics after Babel: The Languages of Morals and Their Discontents*. Boston: Beacon Press, 1988.

Taylor, Mark C. *ERRING: A Postmodern A/Theology*. Chicago: Univ. of Chicago Press, 1984.

Turner, Victor. *From Ritual to Theater: The Human Seriousness of Play*. New York: Performing Arts Journal Publications, 1982.

———. *The Ritual Process: Structure and Anti-structure*. Chicago: Univ. of Chicago Press, 1969.

Unamuno, Miguel de. *The Tragic Sense of Life*. Translated by J. E. Crawford Flitch. New York: Dover, 1921, 1954.

Velacott, Philip. *The Logic of Tragedy*. Durham, N.C.: Duke Univ. Press, 1984.

Vilar, Jean. "Secrets." *Tulane Drama Review* 3:3 (1959) 24–30.

Vlastos, Gregory, ed. *The Philosophy of Socrates: A Collection of Critical Essays*. Garden City, N.Y.: Doubleday, 1971.

Vos, Hermann. *Themis*. Bibliotheca Classica Vangorcumiana, 7, 1956.

Walzer, Michael. *Spheres of Justice: A Defense of Pluralism and Equality*. New York: Basic Books, 1983.

Weil, Simone. *Gravity and Grace*. Translated by Arthur Mills, with an introduction by Gustave Thibon. New York: G. P. Putnam's Sons, 1952.

———. "L'Iliade, ou, La Poème de la Force." From *La Source Greque*, 11–43. Paris: Editions Gallimard, 1953.

———. *Intimations of Christianity among the Ancient Greeks*. Translated variously. London: Routledge and Kegan Paul, 1957, 1987.

———. *The Need for Roots*. Translated by Arthur Wills, with a preface by T. S. Eliot. New York: Octagon Books, 1984.

Whitman, Cedric. *Homer and the Homeric Tradition*. Cambridge, Mass.: Harvard Univ. Press, 1958.

Williams, Bernard A. O. *Ethics and the Limits of Philosophy*. Cambridge, Mass.: Harvard Univ. Press, 1985.

———. *Moral Luck*. New York: Cambridge Univ. Press, 1981.

Winkler, John J., and Froma I. Zeitlin. *Nothing to Do with Dionysus? Athenian Drama in Its Social Context*. Princeton, N.J.: Princeton Univ. Press, 1990.

Wolff, Robert Paul, Barrington Moore, and Herbert Marcuse. *A Critique of Pure Tolerance*. Boston: Beacon Press, 1965.

Woolf, Virginia. "On Not Knowing Greek." In *The Common Reader,* 23–38. New York: Harcourt Brace Jovanovich, 1925, 1984.

Young, Jean I., trans. *The Prose Edda of Snorri Sturlusson*. Berkeley: Univ. of California Press, 1954.

Sophocles' Tragic Vision: Chapter 1

Sophoclis: Fabulae. New York: Oxford Univ. Press, 1961.

•

Aristotle. *Metaphysics*. Translated by Richard Hope. Ann Arbor: Univ. of Michigan Press, 1952.

———. *Nicomachean Ethics*. Translated by Martin Ostwald. Indianapolis: Library of the Liberal Arts, 1962.

———. *Poetics*. Translated by Gerald F. Else. Ann Arbor: Univ. of Michigan Press, 1965.

———. *Politics*. Translated by Ernest Barker. Oxford: Clarendon Press, 1946, 1958.

———. *Rhetoric*. Translated by George A. Kennedy. New York: Oxford Univ. Press, 1991.

Benardete, Seth. "A Reading of Antigone." *Interpretation* 4:3 (1975) 148–196, 5:1 (1975) 1–55, and 5:2 (1975) 148–184.

Blundell, Mary Whitlock. *Helping Friends and Harming Enemies*. Cambridge: Cambridge Univ. Press, 1989.

Bremmer, Jan. *The Early Greek Concept of the Soul*. Princeton, N.J.: Princeton Univ. Press, 1983.

Brown, Richard Emil. Translator's introduction to the *Antigone*, 3–18. New York: Oxford Univ. Press, 1973.

Burton, R. W. B. *The Chorus in Sophocles' Tragedies*. Oxford: Clarendon Press, 1980.

Campbell, D. A. *Sappho and Alcaeus*. Cambridge, Mass.: Harvard Univ. Press, 1982.

Coleman, Robert. "The Role of the Chorus in the *Antigone*." *Proceedings of the Cambridge Philological Society* 198 (1972) 4–27.

Else, Gerald F. *The Madness of Antigone*. Heidelberg: Carl Winter Universitätsverlag, 1976.

Ferry, Luc, and Alain Renaut. *Heidegger and Modernity*. Translated by Franklin Philip. Chicago: Univ. of Chicago Press, 1990.

Garland, Robert. *The Greek Way of Death*. Ithaca, N.Y.: Cornell Univ. Press, 1985.

Geertz, Clifford. *The Interpretation of Cultures*. New York: Basic Books, 1973.

———. *Local Knowledge: Further Essays in Comparative Anthropology*. New York: Basic Books, 1983.

Goheen, Frank. *The Imagery of Sophocles' Antigone*. Princeton, N.J.: Princeton Univ. Press, 1951.

Golder, Herbert. "Sophocles' *Ajax:* Beyond the Shadow of Time." *ARION,* 3d ser., 1:1 (1990) 9–34.

Heidegger, Martin. *Being and Time.* Translated by John MacQuarrie and Eduard Robinson. New York: Harper and Row, 1962.

———. *An Introduction to Metaphysics.* Translated by Ralph Manheim. New Haven: Yale Univ. Press, 1959.

Hester, D. A. " 'Either . . . Or' versus 'Both . . . And': A Dramatic Device in Sophocles." *Antichthon* 13 (1979) 12–18.

———. "Law and Piety in *Antigone.*" *Wiener Studien,* n.s., 14 (1980) 5–11.

Hogan, James C. "The Protagonists of the *Antigone.*" *Arethusa* 5 (1972) 93–100.

Hölderlin, Friedrich. "Antigonae." In *Werke und Briefe,* vol. 2, 737–790. Frankfurt: Insel Verlag, 1969.

Kahn, Charles H., ed. *The Art and Thought of Heraclitus: Fragments with Translation and Commentary.* Cambridge: Cambridge Univ. Press, 1979.

Kells, J. H. "Problems of Interpretation in the *Antigone.*" *Bulletin of the Institute of Classical Studies at the University of London* 10 (1963) 47–64.

Loraux, Nicole. *Tragic Ways of Killing a Woman.* Translated by Anthony Forster. Cambridge, Mass.: Harvard Univ. Press, 1987.

Morgan, J. "The First Burial of Polyneices." *Classical Journal* 64 (1969) 289–295.

Murdoch, Iris. *The Sovereignty of Good.* London: Routledge and Kegan Paul, 1970.

Ober, Josiah, and Barry Strauss. "Drama, Political Rhetoric and the Discourse of Athenian Democracy." In *Nothing to Do with Dionysus? Athenian Drama in Its Social Context,* edited by John J. Winkler and Froma I. Zeitlin, 237–270. Princeton, N.J.: Princeton Univ. Press, 1990.

O'Brien, Jean. "Sophocles' Ode on Man and Paul's Hymn on Love: A Comparative Study." *Classical Journal* 71 (1976) 138–151.

Oudemans, C. W., and A. P. M. H. Lardinois. *Tragic Ambiguity: Anthropology, Philosophy and Sophocles' Antigone.* Leiden: E. J. Brill, 1987.

Plato. *Symposium.* Translated by Suzy Q. Groden. Amherst: Univ. of Massachusetts Press, 1970.

Redfield, James. "Drama and Community: Aristophanes and Some of His Rivals." In *Nothing to Do with Dionysus? Athenian Drama in Its Social Context,* edited by John J. Winkler and Froma I. Zeitlin, 314–335. Princeton, N.J.: Princeton Univ. Press, 1990.

Rohde, Erwin. *Psyche: The Cult of Souls and Belief in Immortality among the Greeks.* Translated by W. B. Hillis. 8th ed. London: Kegan Paul, 1925.

Rosavitch, Vincent J. "The Two Worlds of the Antigone." *Illinois Classical Studies* 7 (1979) 16–26.

Segal, Charles. *Interpreting Greek Tragedy: Myth, Poetry, Text.* Ithaca, N.Y.: Cornell Univ. Press, 1986.

———. *The Theme of the Mutilation of the Corpse in the Iliad.* MNEMOSYNE: Bibliotheca Classica Batava, supp. 10. Leiden: E. J. Brill, 1971.

————. *Tragedy and Civilization*. Cambridge, Mass.: Harvard Univ. Press, 1981.

Steiner, George. *Antigones*. New York: Oxford Univ. Press, 1986.

————. "Antigones." The Twelfth Jackson Knight Memorial Lecture, delivered at the University of Exeter, 2 March 1979.

Taylor, Mark C. *Nots*. Chicago: Univ. of Chicago Press, 1993.

Versenyi, Laszlo. *Man's Measure*. Albany, N.Y.: State Univ. of New York Press, 1974.

Vickers, Brian. *Towards Greek Tragedy: Drama, Myth, Society*, 495–552. London: Longman, 1973.

Viketos, Emanuel. "A Note on Creon's Edict in Sophocles' *Antigone*." *Hermes* 116:4 (1988) 485–486.

————. "A Study of *Deinos* (Sophocles' *Antigone* 332–3) in Its Dramatic Context." *Platon* 40 (1988) 79–81.

Winnington-Ingram, R. P. *Sophocles: An Interpretation*. Cambridge: Cambridge Univ. Press, 1980.

Zeitlin, Froma I. "Thebes: Theater of Self and Society in Athenian Drama." In *Nothing to Do with Dionysus? Athenian Drama in Its Social Context*, edited by John J. Winkler and Froma I. Zeitlin, 130–167. Princeton, N.J.: Princeton Univ. Press, 1990.

Hegel's Tragic Vision: Chapter 2

Hegel's Werke in 20 Bänden. Frankfurt am Main: Suhrkamp Verlag, 1969–1971.

Early Theological Writings [1796–1809]. Translated by T. M. Knox. Philadelphia: Univ. of Pennsylvania Press, 1971.

Lectures on the Philosophy of Religion. Translated by E. B. Spiers and J. B. Sanderson. 3 vols. New York: Humanities Press, 1968.

The Logic of Hegel [1817]. Translated by W. Wallace and J. N. Findlay. New York: Oxford Univ. Press, 1968.

Natural Law [1802, 1803]. Translated by T. M. Knox. Philadelphia: Univ. of Pennsylvania Press, 1975.

The Phenomenology of Mind [1807]. Translated by J. B. Baillie. New York: Humanities Press, 1910, 1966.

The Phenomenology of Spirit [1807]. Translated by A. V. Miller. New York: Oxford Univ. Press, 1977.

The Philosophy of History [1828]. Translated by C. J. Friedrich. New York: Dover Publications, 1956.

The Philosophy of Right [1821]. Translated by T. M. Knox. New York: Oxford Univ. Press, 1967.

The Science of Logic [1812]. Translated by A. V. Miller. Atlantic Highlands, N.J.: Humanities Press, 1969.

Three Essays, 1793–1795. Translated and edited by Peter Fuss and John Dobbins. Notre Dame, Ind.: Univ. of Notre Dame Press, 1984.

"Who Thinks Abstractly?" [1806?]. Translated by Walter Kaufmann and appearing in his *Hegel: A Re-interpretation, Texts and Commentary*, 113–118. Garden City, N.Y.: Doubleday, 1965.

•

Altizer, Thomas J. J. "Hegel and the Christian God." *Journal of the American Academy of Religion* 59:1 (1991) 71–91.

Avineri, Schlomo. "Hegel Revisited." In *Hegel: A Collection of Critical Essays*, edited by Alasdair MacIntyre, 329–348. Notre Dame, Ind.: Univ. of Notre Dame Press, 1972.

Bernstein, Richard J. *Praxis and Action*. Philadelphia: Univ. of Pennsylvania Press, 1971.

Bradiey, A. C. "Hegel's Theory of Tragedy." In *Hegel: On Tragedy*, edited by Anne and Henry Paolucci. New York: Harper and Row, 1962.

———. *Shakespearean Tragedy*. London: Macmillan, 1904, 1950.

Clay, Diskin. "The Tragic and Comic Poet of the Symposium." *ARION*, n.s., 2:2 (1975) 238–261.

Dove, Kenley Royce. "Hegel's Phenomenological Method." In *New Studies in Hegel's Philosophy*, edited by W. E. Steinkraus, 34–56. New York: Holt, Rinehart and Winston, 1971.

Elder, Crawford. *Appropriating Hegel*. Scots Philosophical Manuscripts, no. 3. Aberdeen: Aberdeen Univ. Press, 1980.

Fackenheim, Emil. *The Religious Dimension of Hegel's Thought*. Bloomington: Indiana Univ. Press, 1967.

Findlay, J. N. *Hegel: A Re-examination*. New York: Collier Books, 1962.

———. "Hegel's Use of Teleology." In *New Studies in Hegel's Philosophy*, edited by W. E. Steinkraus, 92–107. New York: Holt, Rinehart and Winston, 1971.   o

Gadamer, H. G. *Hegel's Dialectic: Five Hermeneutical Studies*. Translated by C. Smith. New Haven: Yale Univ. Press, 1976.

Goldmann, Lucien. *The Hidden God: The Tragic Vision in Pascal's Pensées and the Tragedies of Racine*. Translated by Philip Thody. Atlantic Highlands, N.J.: Humanities Press, 1964, 1977.

Habermas, Jürgen. *Knowledge and Human Interests*. Translated by Jeremy L. Shapiro. Boston: Beacon Press, 1968, 1971.

———. *Legitimation Crisis*. Translated by Thomas McCarthy. Boston: Beacon Press, 1973, 1975.

———. *The Philosophical Discourse of Modernity*. Translated by Frederick Lawrence. Cambridge, Mass.: MIT Press, 1985, 1987.

Hippolyte, Jean. "L'Etat du Droit (La Condition Juridique)." *Hegel-Studien*, Beiheft 4 (Bonn, 1966) 181–185.

———. *Genesis and Structure of Hegel's Phenomenology of Spirit*. Translated by S. Chaniak and J. Heckman. Evanston, Ill.: Northwestern Univ. Press, 1974.

Irigaray, Luce. *This Sex Which Is Not One*. Translated by Catherine Porter. Ithaca, N.Y.: Cornell Univ. Press, 1985.

Kaufmann, Walter. *From Shakespeare to Existentialism*. New York: Doubleday, 1960.

———. *Hegel: A Re-interpretation, Texts and Commentary.* New York: Doubleday, 1965.

———. "The Hegel Myth and His Method," and "The Young Hegel and Religion." In *Hegel: A Collection of Critical Essays,* edited by Alasdair MacIntyre, 21–99. New York: Doubleday, 1972.

Kelly, George A. *Hegel's Retreat from Eleusis: Studies in Political Thought.* Princeton, N.J.: Princeton Univ. Press, 1978.

———. "Notes on Hegel's Lordship and Bondage." *Review of Metaphysics* 19 (1966) 780–802.

Knox, T. M. "Hegel's Attitude to Kant's Ethics." *Kant-Studien* 49 (1957–1958) 70–81.

Kojève, Alexandre. *Introduction to the Reading of Hegel.* Translated by J. M. Nicholas, edited by A. Bloom. New York: Basic Books, 1969.

Kosok, Michael. "The Dialectical Matrix: Towards Phenomenology as a Science." *Telos* 5 (1970) 115–159.

———. "The Formalization of Hegel's Dialectical Logic." In *Hegel: A Collection of Critical Essays,* edited by Alasdair MacIntyre, 237–288. Notre Dame, Ind.: Univ. of Notre Dame Press, 1972.

Löwith, Karl. *From Hegel to Nietzsche: The Revolution in Nineteenth Century Thought.* Translated by D. E. Green. New York: Doubleday, 1967.

Lukács, Georg. *The Young Hegel: Studies in the Relations between Dialectics and Economics.* Translated by Rodney Livingstone. Cambridge, Mass.: MIT Press, 1976.

MacCary, W. Thomas. *Childlike Achilles: Ontogeny and Phylogeny in the Iliad.* New York: Columbia Univ. Press, 1982.

MacIntyre, Alasdair. *Hegel: A Collection of Critical Essays.* New York: Doubleday, 1972.

———. "Pascal and Marx: On Lucien Goldmann's *Hidden God.*" In *Against the Self-Images of the Age: Essays on Ideology and Philosophy,* 76–87. Notre Dame, Ind.: Univ. of Notre Dame Press, 1978.

Malamud, René. "Amazons." Translated by Murray Stein. In *Facing the Gods,* edited by James Hillman. Dallas: Spring Publications, 1991.

Marcuse, Herbert. *Reason and Revolution: Hegel and the Rise of Social Theory.* Boston: Beacon Press, 1960.

Merleau-Ponty, Maurice. "Hegel's Existentialism." In *Sense and Non-Sense.* Translated by H. L. Dreyfus and P. A. Dreyfus, 63–70. Evanston, Ill.: Northwestern Univ. Press, 1964.

Paolucci, Anne, and Henry Paolucci, eds. *Hegel: on Tragedy.* New York: Harper and Row, 1962.

Paolucci, Henry, ed. *Hegel: On the Arts, Selections from the Philosophy of Fine Art.* New York: Frederick Ungar, 1979.

Popper, Karl. *The Open Society and Its Enemies.* Vol. 2, *The High Tide of Prophecy: Hegel, Marx, and the Aftermath.* London: George Routledge and Sons, 1945.

Rosen, Stanley. *The Ancients and the Moderns: Rethinking Modernity.* New Haven: Yale Univ. Press, 1989.

Schopenhauer, Arthur. *The World as Will and Representation.* Translated by E. F. J. Payne. New York: Dover, 1969.

Sieburth, Richard. *Hölderlin: Hymns and Fragments.* Princeton, N.J.: Princeton Univ. Press, 1984.

Slater, Niall. "The Idea of the Actor." In *Nothing to Do with Dionysus? Athenian Drama in Its Social Context,* 385–395. Princeton, N.J.: Princeton Univ. Press, 1990.

Solomon, R. C. "Hegel's Concept of *Geist.*" *Review of Metaphysics* 23 (1970) 642–666.

Taylor, Charles. *Hegel.* New York: Cambridge Univ. Press, 1975.

———. "The Opening Arguments of the Phenomenology." In *Hegel: A Collection of Critical Essays,* edited by Alasdair MacIntyre, 151–188. New York: Doubleday, 1972.

Taylor, Mark C. "*Itinerium Mentis in Deum:* Hegel's Proof of God's Existence." *Journal of Religion* 57 (1977) 211–231.

———. *Journeys to Selfhood: Hegel and Kierkegaard.* Berkeley: Univ. of California Press, 1980.

———. "Towards an Ontology of Relativism." *Journal of the American Academy of Religion* 46 (1978) 41–61.

Verene, David Philip. *Hegel's Recollection: A Study of Images in the Phenomenology of Spirit.* Albany: State Univ. of New York Press, 1985.

———, ed. *Hegel's Social and Political Thought.* Atlantic Highlands, N.J.: Humanities Press, 1980.

Winfield, Richard Dien. "The Route to Foundation-Free Systematic Philosophy." *The Philosophical Forum* 15:3 (1984) 323–343.

Nietzsche's Tragic Vision: Chapter 3

Nietzsche: Sämtliche Werke, Kritische Studienausgabe in 15 Bänden. Berlin: Walter de Gruyter, 1967–1977.

The Antichrist [1888]. Translated by H. L. Mencken. Torrance, Calif.: Noontide Press, 1980.

Beyond Good and Evil: Prelude to a Philosophy of the Future [1886]. Translated by Walter Kaufmann. New York: Random House, Vintage Books, 1966.

Beyond Good and Evil: Prelude to a Philosophy of the Future [1886]. Translated by Helen Zimmern. New York: Modern Library, n.d.

The Birth of Tragedy and *The Case of Wagner* [1872, 1888]. Translated by Walter Kaufmann. New York: Random House, Vintage Books, 1967.

The Birth of Tragedy and *The Genealogy of Morals* [1872, 1887]. Translated by Francis Golffing. New York: Doubleday, Anchor Books, 1956.

Daybreak [1881]. Translated by R. J. Hollingdale. Cambridge: Cambridge Univ. Press, 1982.

Ecce Homo [1888]. Translated by R. J. Hollingdale. New York: Penguin Books, 1979, 1982.

The Future of Our Educational Institutions and *Homer and Classical Philology* [1871]. Translated by J. M. Kennedy in *The Complete Works of Friedrich Nietzsche*, edited by Oscar Levy. New York: Russell and Russell, 1964.

The Gay Science [1882]. Translated by Walter Kaufmann. New York: Random House, Vintage Books, 1974.

Human, All-Too-Human [1878, 1879]. Translated by Marion Faber. Lincoln: Univ. of Nebraska Press, 1984.

On the Genealogy of Morals and *Ecce Homo* [1887, 1888]. Translated by Walter Kaufmann. New York: Random House, Vintage Books, 1969.

Philosophy in the Tragic Age of the Greeks [1873]. Translated by Marianne Cowan. Chicago: Henry Regnery, 1962.

Thus Spoke Zarathustra [1883, 1885]. Translated by Walter Kaufmann. New York: Viking Press, 1966.

Twilight of the Idols [1887]. Translated by Walter Kaufmann in his *The Portable Nietzsche*, 463–563. New York: Viking Press, Penguin Books, 1954, 1982.

Untimely Meditations [1873–1876]. Translated by R. J. Hollingdale. Cambridge: Cambridge Univ. Press, 1983.

"We Classicists." Translated and edited by William Arrowsmith. In *Unmodern Observations*, 305–387. New Haven: Yale Univ. Press, 1990.

The Will to Power. Translated by Walter Kaufmann and R. J. Hollingdale. New York: Random House, Vintage Books, 1967.

Wir Philologen [1875]. Translated by William Arrowsmith in *ARION*, n.s., 1:2 (1974) 279–380.

•

Arnold, Matthew. *Culture and Anarchy.* Edited by J. Dover Wilson. Cambridge: Cambridge Univ. Press, 1932, 1990.

Augustine. *The City of God.* Translated by Marcus Dods. New York: Modern Library, 1950.

Binder, Judith, trans. *The Akropolis at Athens: Conservation, Restoration and Research.* Athens: Ministry for the Preservation of the Akropolis Monuments, 1985.

Boardman, John, and David Finn. *The Parthenon and Its Sculptures.* London: Thames and Hudson, 1985.

Bowie, Theodore, and Diether Thimme. *The Carrey Drawings of the Parthenon Sculptures.* Bloomington: Indiana Univ. Press, 1971.

Brown, Norman O. *Love's Body.* New York: Random House, 1966.

Brown, Peter. *Augustine of Hippo.* Berkeley: Univ. of California Press, 1967.

Bruno, Vincent J. *The Parthenon.* New York: W. W. Norton, 1974.

Casey, John. *Pagan Virtue: An Essay in Ethics.* Oxford: Clarendon Press, 1990.

Chamberlin, Russell. *Loot! The Heritage of Plunder.* London: Thames and Hudson, 1983.

Cook, Brian F. *The Elgin Marbles.* London: Trustees of the British Museum, 1984.

Danto, Arthur C. *Nietzsche as Philosopher.* New York: Macmillan, 1965, 1967.

Deleuze, Gilles. *Nietzsche and Philosophy.* Translated by Hugh Tomlinson. New York: Columbia Univ. Press, 1983.

————. *Nietzsche et la philosophie.* Paris: Presses Universitaires de France, 1962.

————. "Nomad Thought." Translated by R. Cohen. In *The New Nietzsche,* edited by David B. Allison, 142–149. New York: Delta, 1979.

Derrida, Jacques. "The Ends of Man." Translated by Sir Eduard Morot. *Phenomenological Research* 30 (1969).

————. *Éperons/Spurs: The Styles of Nietzsche.* Translated by Barbara Harlow. Chicago: Univ. of Chicago Press, 1978.

Dinsmoor, William Bell. "The Correlation of Greek Archaeology with History." In *Studies in the History of Culture,* 185–216. Manasha, Wis.: George Banta, 1942.

————. "The Date of the Older Parthenon." *American Journal of Archaeology* 38 (1934) 408–448.

————. "The Repair of Athena Parthenos: The Story of Five Dowels." *American Journal of Archaeology* 38 (1934) 93–106.

Fernik, Bernard. *Homer and the Nibelungenlied.* Cambridge, Mass.: Harvard Univ. Press, 1986.

Geffre, Claude, ed. *Nietzsche and Christianity.* New York: Seabury Press, 1981.

Gunton, Colin E. *The One, the Three and the Many: God, Creation and the Culture of Modernity.* Cambridge: Cambridge Univ. Press, 1993.

Hadjiaslani, Cornelia. *Morosoni, the Venetians, and the Akropolis.* Translated by George Huxley. Athens: Gennadius Library, 1987.

Hatfield, Henry Caraway. *Winckelmann and His German Critics, 1755–1781: A Prelude to the Classical Age.* New York: King's Crown Press, 1943.

Heidegger, Martin. *Nietzsche: The Will to Power as Art* (I); *The Eternal Recurrence of the Same* (II); *The Will to Power as Knowledge and as Metaphysics* (III); *Nihilism* (IV). Translated by David F. Krell. New York: Harper and Row, 1981, 1984, 1987.

Higgins, Kathleen Marie. *Nietzsche's Zarathustra.* Philadelphia: Temple Univ. Press, 1987.

Hopper, R. J. *The Acropolis.* London: Weidenfeld and Nicolson, 1971.

Jaeger, Werner. *Early Christianity and Greek Paideia.* Cambridge, Mass.: Harvard Univ. Press, 1961.

Kaufmann, Walter. *Nietzsche: Philosopher, Psychologist, Antichrist.* 4th ed. Princeton, N.J.: Princeton Univ. Press, 1974.

Meeks, Wayne, and Robert Wilkins. *Jews and Christians in Antioch: In the First Four Centuries of the Common Era.* Missoula, Mont.: Scholars Press, 1978.

Nehemas, Alexander. *Nietzsche: Life as Literature.* Cambridge, Mass.: Harvard Univ. Press, 1985.

Nietzsche, E. Förster. *The Life of Nietzsche.* Translated by Paul V. Cohn. 2 vols. New York: Sturgis and Walton, 1915.

Pavur, Claude. "In Search of Cultural History." Unpublished essay in partial fulfillment of the requirements for the Ph.D. degree at Emory University, 1988.

Pelikan, Jaroslav. *Christianity and Classical Culture: The Metamorphosis of Natural Theology in the Christian Encounter with Hellenism.* New Haven: Yale Univ. Press, 1993.

Richter, Simon. *Laocöon's Body and the Aesthetics of Pain.* Detroit: Wayne State Univ. Press, 1992.

Ruprecht, Louis A., Jr. "Nietzsche's Vision, Nietzsche's Greece." *Soundings* 73:1 (1990) 61–84.

Sass, Louis A. *Madness and Modernism: Insanity in the Light of Modern Art, Literature, and Thought.* San Francisco: HarperCollins, 1992.

Silk, M. S., and J. P. Stern. *Nietzsche on Tragedy.* Cambridge: Cambridge Univ. Press, 1981.

Travlos, John. *A Pictorial Dictionary of Ancient Athens.* New York: Praeger, 1971.

Winchester, James J. *Nietzsche's Aesthetic Turn: Reading Nietzsche after Heidegger, Deleuze and Derrida.* Albany: State Univ. of New York Press, 1994.

Wycherly, R. E. *The Stones of Athens.* Princeton, N.J.: Princeton Univ. Press, 1978.

Mark's Tragic Vision: Chapter 4

The Greek New Testament. Edited by Kurt Aland, Matthew Black, Carlo M. Martini, Bruce M. Metzger, and Allen Wikgren. 3d ed. New York: United Bible Societies 1966, 1968, 1975.

Synopsis of the Four Gospels. Edited by Kurt Aland. Stuttgart: German Bible Society, 1984.

•

Achtemeier, Paul. *Mark.* Philadelphia: Fortress Press, 1975.

Alter, Robert. *The Art of Biblical Narrative.* New York: Basic Books, 1981.

Auerbach, Erich. *Mimesis: The Representation of Reality in Western Literature.* Translated by Willard R. Trask. Princeton, N.J.: Princeton Univ. Press, 1953.

Barbour, R. S. "Gethsemane in the Tradition of the Passion." *New Testament Studies* 16 (1970) 231–251.

Beardslee, William. "Narrative and History in the Post-modern World: The Case of the Gospel of Mark." In *The Crisis in the Humanities: Interdisciplinary Responses,* edited by Sara Putzell-Korab and Robert Detweiler. Madrid: José Porrua Turanzas, 1983.

———. "Parable, Proverb and Koan." *Semeia* 12 (1978) 151–177.

Bilezikian, Gilbert. *The Liberated Gospel: A Comparison of the Gospel of Mark and Greek Tragedy.* Grand Rapids, Mich.: Baker Biblical Monographs, 1975.

Booth, Wayne C. *The Rhetoric of Fiction.* Chicago: Univ. of Chicago Press, 1961.

Bornkamm, Gunther. *Jesus of Nazareth.* Translated by Irene McLuskey and Fraser McLuskey. New York: Harper and Row, 1960.

———. *Paul.* Translated by D. M. G. Stalker. New York: Harper and Row, 1969.

Bornkamm, Gunther, with Gerhard Barth and Heinz J. Held. *Tradition and Interpretation in Matthew.* Translated by Percy Scott. Philadelphia: Westminster Press, 1963.

Breuer, Lee. *The Gospel at Colonus.* New York: Theatre Communications Group, 1989.

Brown, Raymond E. *The Gospel according to John.* New York: Doubleday, 1966.

———. "The Passion according to Mark." *Worship* 59 (1985).

Bryan, Christopher. *A Preface to Mark: Notes on the Gospel in Its Literary and Cultural Settings.* New York: Oxford Univ. Press, 1992.

Bultmann, Rudolf. *A History of the Synoptic Tradition.* Translated by John Marsh. New York: Harper and Row, 1963.

———. *Jesus Christ and Mythology.* New York: Charles Scribner's Sons, 1958.

———. *Jesus and the Word.* Translated by Louise Smith and Erminie Lantero. New York: Charles Scribner's Sons, 1934, 1958.

———. *Kerygma and Myth.* Translated by H. W. Bartsch. New York: Harper and Row, 1953, 1961.

———. *Primitive Christianity in Its Contemporary Setting.* Translated by R. H. Fuller. New York: Meridian Books, 1956.

Burdon, Christopher. *Stumbling on God: Faith and Vision through Mark's Gospel.* Grand Rapids, Mich.: Eerdmans, 1990.

Burridge, Richard A. *What Are the Gospels? A Comparison with Greco-Roman Biography.* Cambridge: Cambridge Univ. Press, 1992.

Cameron, Ron, ed. *The Other Gospels: Non-canonical Gospel Texts.* Philadelphia: Westminster Press, 1982.

Colwell, Ernest C. "*Mark* 16:9–20 in the Armenian Version." *Journal of Biblical Literature* 56 (1937) 369–386.

Conzelmann, Hans. "History and Theology in the Passion Narratives of the Synoptic Gospels." *Interpretation* 24:2 (1970) 178–197.

Cribbs, F. Lamar. "St. Luke and the Johannine Tradition." *Journal of Biblical Literature* 90 (1971) 422–450.

Crossan, John Dominic. *The Dark Interval: Toward a Theology of Story.* Allen, Tex.: Angus Communications, 1975.

———. "Empty Tomb and Absent Lord." In *The Passion in Mark,* edited by Werner Kelber, 135–152. Philadelphia: Fortress Press, 1976.

———. "A Form for Absence: The Markan Creation of Gospel." *Semeia* 12 (1978) 41–55.

———. *Four Other Gospels: Shadows on the Contours of Canon.* New York: Winston Press, 1985.

Danker, Frederick W. "Postscript to the Markan Secrecy Motif." *Concordia Theological Monthly* 38 (1967) 24–27.

Dibelius, Martin. *From Tradition to Gospel.* Translated by Bertram Lee Woolf. Greenwood, S.C.: Attic Press, 1971, 1982.

Dodd, Charles H. *The Apostolic Teaching and Its Development.* Grand Rapids, Mich.: Baker Book House, 1936, 1980.

————. *Historical Tradition in the Fourth Gospel.* Cambridge: Cambridge Univ. Press, 1963.

Donahue, John R., S.J. "From Passion Traditions to Passion Narrative" and "Temple, Trial, and Royal Christology." In *The Passion in Mark,* edited by Werner Kelber. Philadelphia: Fortress Press, 1976.

Dowd, Sharon E. *Prayer, Power and the Problem of Suffering: Mark 11:22–25 in the Context of Markan Theology.* SBL Dissertation Series. Atlanta: Scholars Press, 1991.

Elliott, James K. "The Text and Language of the Endings to Mark's Gospel." *Theologische Zeitschrift* 27 (1971) 255–262.

Farmer, William R. *The Last Twelve Verses of Mark.* Cambridge: Cambridge Univ. Press, 1974.

Farmer, William R., with D. M. Farkasfalvy. *The Formation of the New Testament Canon.* New York: Paulist Press, 1983.

Frye, Northrop. *The Great Code: The Bible and Literature.* New York: Harcourt Brace Jovanovich, 1982.

Grassi, Joseph A. "*Abba,* Father: Another Approach." *Journal of the American Academy of Religion* 50 (1982) 449–458.

Guelich, Robert A. "The Beginning of the Gospel, *Mark* 1:1–15." *Biblical Research* 27 (1982) 5–15.

Gunn, David M. *The Fate of King Saul.* Sheffield: Journal for the Study of the Old Testament, 1980.

Gustafson, James M. "The Place of Scripture in Christian Ethics: A Methodological Study." *Interpretation* 24:4 (1970) 430–455.

Haenchen, Ernst. "History and Interpretation in the Johannine Passion Narrative." *Interpretation* 24:2 (1970) 198–219.

Havelock, Eric A. *Preface to Plato.* Cambridge, Mass.: Harvard Univ. Press, 1963.

Horst, P. W. van der. "Can a Book End with a *GAR?* A Note on Mark 16:8." *Journal of Theological Studies* 23 (1972) 121–124.

Ice, Jackson Lee. "What Albert Schweitzer Believed about Jesus." *Christian Century,* January 2–9, 1985.

Kähler, Martin. *The So-called Historical Jesus and the Biblical Christ.* Translated by Carl E. Braaten. Philadelphia: Fortress Press, 1964.

Kelber, Werner H. *Mark's Story of Jesus.* Philadelphia: Fortress Press, 1979.

————. *The Oral and Written Gospel.* Philadelphia: Fortress Press, 1984.

————. *The Passion in Mark.* Philadelphia: Fortress Press, 1976.

Kennedy, George A. *New Testament Criticism through Rhetorical Criticism.* Chapel Hill: Univ. of North Carolina Press, 1984.

Kermode, Frank. *The Genesis of Secrecy: On the Interpretation of Narrative.* Cambridge, Mass.: Harvard Univ. Press, 1979.

————. *The Sense of an Ending: Studies in the Theory of Fiction.* New York: Oxford Univ. Press, 1967.

Kingsbury, Jack D. *The Christology of Mark's Gospel.* Philadelphia: Fortress Press, 1983.

Koenig, John. "St. Mark on the Stage: Laughing All the Way to the Cross." *Theology Today* 36:1 (1979) 84–86.

Koester, Helmut, and J. T. Robinson. *Trajectories through Early Christianity.* Philadelphia: Fortress Press, 1971.

Koljevic, Svetozar. *The Making of the Epic.* Oxford: Clarendon Press, 1980.

Larson, Janet K. "St. Alec's Gospel: The Redemption of Joy in the Modern Theater." *Christian Century* 96:1 (1979) 17–19.

Lightfoot, R. H. *The Gospel Message of St. Mark.* New York: Oxford Univ. Press, 1962.

Linton, Olof. "Evidence of a Second Century Revised Edition of Mark's Gospel." *New Testament Studies* 14 (1968) 321–355.

Lord, Albert B. *The Singer of Tales.* Cambridge, Mass.: Harvard Univ. Press, 1960.

McCowen, Alec. *Personal Mark: An Actor's Proclamation of St. Mark's Gospel.* New York: Continuum, 1985.

Mack, Burton L. *A Myth of Innocence: Mark and Christian Origins.* Philadelphia: Fortress Press, 1988.

———, with Vernon K. Robbins. *Patterns of Persuasion in the Gospels.* Sonoma, Calif.: Polebridge Press, 1989.

Martyn, J. Louis. *History and Theology in the Fourth Gospel.* Nashville: Abingdon Press, 1979.

Marxsen, Willi. *Mark the Evangelist.* Translated by R. A. Harrisville. Nashville: Abingdon Press, 1956, 1969.

Meagher, John C. *Clumsy Construction in Mark's Gospel: A Critique of Form- and Redaktionsgeschichte.* New York: Edwin Mellen Press, 1979.

Metzger, Bruce M. "The Caesarean Text of the Gospels." *Journal of Biblical Literature* 64 (1945) 457–489.

———. *The Canon of the New Testament: Its Origin, Development and Significance.* Oxford: Clarendon Press, 1987.

———. "The Ending of the Gospel according to Mark in the Ethiopic Manuscripts." In *Understanding the Sacred Scriptures: Essays in Honor of Morton S. Enslin,* 167–180. Valley Forge, Pa.: Judson Press, 1972.

Moule, C. F. D. "St. Mark 16:8 Once More." *New Testament Studies* 2 (1955/56) 58–59.

Ong, Walter J. *Orality and Literacy: The Technologizing of the Word.* New York: Methuen, 1982.

Pagels, Elaine. *The Gnostic Gospels.* New York: Random House, 1979.

Parker, Pierson. "Luke and the Fourth Evangelist." *New Testament Studies* 9 (1963) 317–336.

Parry, Milman. "Studies in the Epic Technique of Oral Verse-Making," I and II. *Harvard Society of Classical Philology* 41 (1930) 73–147, and 43 (1932) 1–50.

Pavur, Claude. "As It Is Written: The Nature, Purpose and Meaning of Mark's Gospel." Masters thesis, Jesuit School of Theology, Berkeley, Calif., 1985.

Petersen, Norman R. "Myth and Characterization in Mark and John." SBL Literary Aspects Group, 1985.

———. "When Is the End Not the End?" *Interpretation* 34 (1980) 151–166.

Renan, Ernst. *Life of Jesus*. Boston: Roberts Brothers, 1896.

Rhoads, David, and Donald Michie. *Mark as Story: An Introduction to the Narrative of a Gospel*. Philadelphia: Fortress Press, 1982.

Richardson, Cyril C. *Early Christian Fathers*. New York: Macmillan, 1970.

Robbins, Vernon K. *Jesus the Teacher: A Socio-Rhetorical Interpretation of Mark*. Philadelphia: Fortress Press, 1984.

———. "Last Meal: Preparation, Betrayal and Absence." In *The Passion in Mark*, edited by Werner Kelber, 21–40. Philadelphia: Fortress Press, 1976.

———. "*Mark* 1:14–20: An Interpretation at the Intersection of Jewish and Greco-Roman Traditions." *New Testament Studies* 28 (1980) 220–236.

———. "Pronouncement Stories and Jesus' Blessing of the Children: A Rhetorical Approach." *Semeia* 29 (1983) 43–74.

———, ed. *Ancient Quotes and Anecdotes: From Crib to Crypt*. Sonoma, Calif.: Polebridge Press, 1989.

Robinson, B. P. "Gethsemane: The Synoptic and Johannine Viewpoints." *Church Quarterly Review* 167 (1966) 4–11.

Robinson, J. A. T. *The Priority of John*. Edited by J. F. Coakley. Oak Park, Ill.: Meyer-Stone Books, 1985.

Ruprecht, Louis A., Jr. "Mark's Tragic Vision." *Religion and Literature* 24:3 (1992) 1–25.

Schweitzer, Albert. *Out of My Life and Thought*. Translated by C. T. Campion. New York: Henry Holt, 1933, 1949.

———. *The Psychiatric Study of Jesus*. Translated by C. R. Joy. Boston: Beacon Press, 1948.

———. *The Quest of the Historical Jesus*. Translated by W. Montgomery. New York: Macmillan, 1968.

Schweizer, Edward. *The Good News according to Mark*. Translated by Donald H. Madvig. Atlanta: John Knox Press, 1970.

Scroggs, Robin, and Kent I. Groff. "Baptism in Mark: Dying and Rising with Christ." *Journal of Biblical Literature* 92 (1975) 531–548.

Smith, D. Moody. *Johannine Christianity*. Columbia: Univ. of South Carolina Press, 1984.

Streeter, B. H. *The Four Gospels*. New York: Macmillan, 1925.

Sutton, Dana F. *The Greek Satyr Play*. Meisenheim am Glan: Verlag Anton Hain, 1980.

Talbert, Charles. *What Is a Gospel? The Genre of the Canonical Gospels*. Philadelphia: Fortress Press, 1977.

Tannehill, Robert. "Israel in Luke-Acts: A Tragic Story." *Journal of Biblical Literature* 104 (1985) 69–85.

———. *The Sword of His Mouth*. Philadelphia: Fortress Press, 1975.

Taylor, Vincent. *The Gospel according to St. Mark*. London: Macmillan, 1966.

Trompf, G. W. "The First Resurrection Appearance and the Ending of Mark's Gospel." *New Testament Studies* 18 (1972) 308–330.

Via, Dan O. *The Ethics of Mark: In the Middle of Time*. Philadelphia: Fortress Press, 1985.

———. *Kerygma and Comedy in the New Testament*. Philadelphia: Fortress Press, 1975.

Votaw, Clyde Weber. "The Gospels and Contemporary Biographies in the Greco-Roman World." Philadelphia: Fortress Press, 1970.

Weeden, Theodore J. "The Cross as Power in Weakness." In *The Passion in Mark*, edited by Werner Kelber, 115–134. Philadelphia: Fortress Press, 1976.

———. *Mark: Traditions in Conflict*. Philadelphia: Fortress Press, 1971.

Wilder, Amos. *Jesus' Parables and the War of Myths: Essays on Imagination in the Scriptures*. Philadelphia: Fortress Press, 1982.

Wilson, William R. *The Execution of Jesus*. New York: Charles Scribner's Sons, 1970.

Winkler, John J. "The Ephebe's Song: *Tragōidia* and *Polis*." In *Nothing to Do with Dionysus? Athenian Drama in Its Social Context*, edited by John J. Winkler and Froma I. Zeitlin, 20–62. Princeton, N.J.: Princeton Univ. Press, 1990.

Wrede, William. *The Messianic Secret*. Translated by J. C. G. Grieg. Greenwood, S.C.: Attic Press, 1971.

Index